GLENCOE
BUSINESS AND PERSONAL FINANCE

GLENCOE: Your *Real* Business Choice

Teacher Annotated Edition

Jack R. Kapoor
Professor of Business and Economics
Business and Services Division
College of DuPage
Glen Ellyn, Illinois

Les R. Dlabay
Professor of Business
Department of Economics and Business
Lake Forest College
Lake Forest, Illinois

Robert J. Hughes
Professor of Business
Dallas County Community Colleges
Dallas, Texas

Contributing Editor
William B. Hoyt
Wilton High School
Wilton, Connecticut

McGraw Hill Glencoe

New York, New York · Columbus, Ohio · Chicago, Illinois · Peoria, Illinois · Woodland Hills, California

Help your students secure their financial future now...

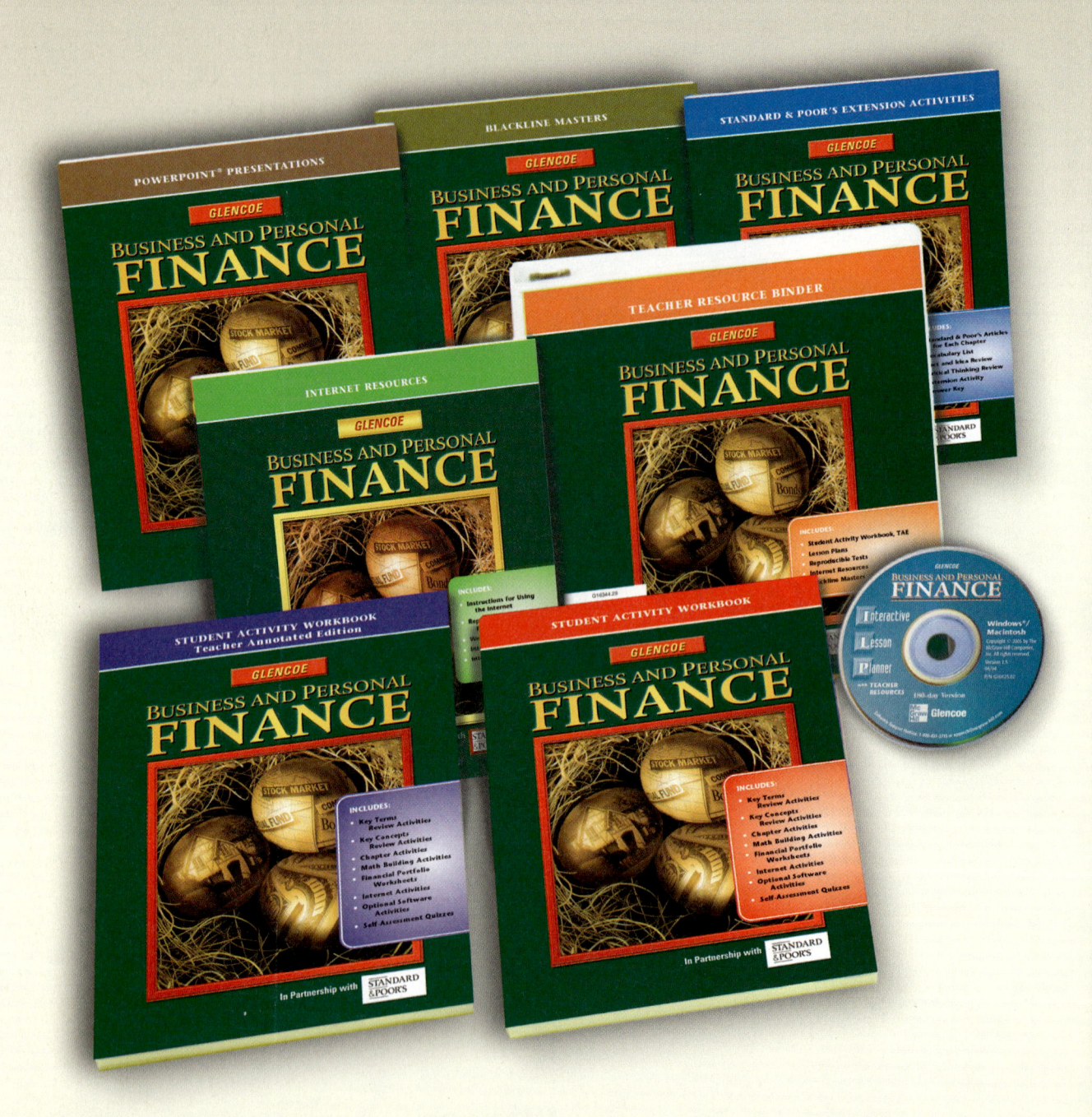

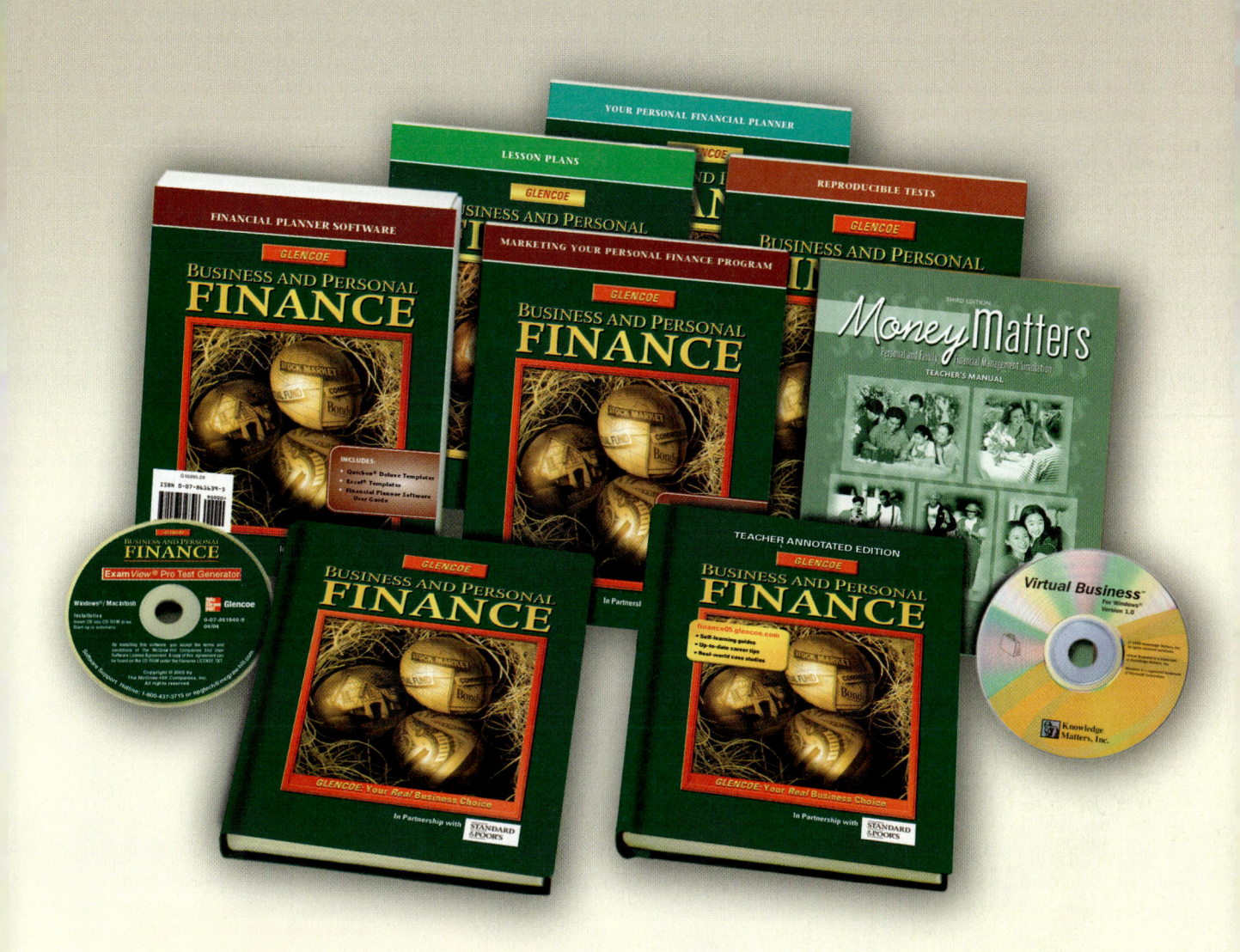

With Glencoe's
BUSINESS AND PERSONAL FINANCE Resources

About the Authors

Jack R. Kapoor
Jack R. Kapoor is professor of business and economics in the Business and Services Division at College of DuPage, where he has taught since 1969. He received his Bachelor of Arts in Business Administration and Master of Science in International Business from San Francisco State College. He received his Doctor of Education from Northern Illinois University. Dr. Kapoor was awarded the Business and Services Division's Outstanding Professor Award for 1999–2000.

Les R. Dlabay
Les R. Dlabay teaches in the Department of Economics and Business at Lake Forest College. He received his Bachelor of Science in Accounting from University of Illinois, his Master of Business Administration in Business Management from DePaul University, and his Doctor of Education in Business and Economic Education from Northern Illinois University. He is a founding member of the Illinois Consumer Education Association.

Robert J. Hughes
Robert J. Hughes teaches business, management, and finance courses at Dallas County Community Colleges. He received his Bachelor of Arts in Business Administration from Southern Nazarene University and his Master of Business Administration and Doctor of Education from the University of North Texas. Dr. Hughes has taught at the high school, community college, and four-year university levels for 34 years. He received the Excellence in Teaching Award at Richland College and has 13 years of experience teaching personal finance courses.

Contributing Editor

William B. Hoyt
William B. Hoyt is an accounting instructor at Wilton High School in Wilton, Connecticut. He has been involved in accounting curriculum development for many years and was a member of the writing task force for the *National Standards for Business Education*. In 1996, Mr. Hoyt was named Connecticut's Outstanding Business Educator of the Year and in 1997 was named National Secondary Teacher of the Year by the National Business Education Association.

NOTICE. Information on featured companies, organizations, and their products and services is included for educational purposes only, and it does not present or imply endorsement of the *Business and Personal Finance* program.

McGraw-Hill Glencoe

The McGraw-Hill Companies

Copyright © 2005 by Glencoe/McGraw-Hill, a division of The McGraw-Hill Companies, Inc. All rights reserved. Except as permitted under the United States Copyright Act, no part of this publication may be reproduced or distributed in any form or by any means, or stored in a database or retrieval system, without prior written permission of the publisher, Glencoe/McGraw-Hill.

Printed in the United States of America.

Send all inquiries to:
Glencoe/McGraw-Hill
21600 Oxnard Street, Suite 500
Woodland Hills, California 91367-4906

ISBN 0-07-861488-0 (Student Text)
ISBN 0-07-861632-8 (Teacher Annotated Edition)

1 2 3 4 5 6 7 8 9   027   09 08 07 06 05 04

Table of Contents

The Importance of Business and Personal Finance — TM6

Inside the Student Edition — TM7
- Welcome to *Business and Personal Finance* — TM7
- Exploring Each Unit — TM7
- Exploring Each Chapter — TM8
- Exploring Each Section — TM9
- Go Figure and Math Skills Builder — TM10
- Chapter Summary and Assessment — TM11
- Focus on Features — TM12

Inside the Teacher Annotated Edition — TM14
- Using the Planning Guides — TM14
- Using the Annotations — TM15
- Using the Lesson Plans — TM16

Teacher Classroom Resources — TM17
- Classroom Resources — TM17
- Money Matters: Personal and Family Financial Management Simulation — TM18
- *Business and Personal Finance* Web Site — TM19
- Technology-Based Resources — TM20
- Standard & Poor's in the Student Edition — TM21

Methodology — TM22
- Developing Reading Strategies — TM22
- Real-World Connections — TM23
- Making *Business and Personal Finance* Real — TM23
- Connecting to Careers — TM23
- Assessment Strategies — TM24
- Developing Thinking Skills — TM26
- Cooperative Learning — TM27
- Addressing Cultural Diversity — TM28
- Cultural Diversity in the Program — TM28
- English Language Learners (ELL) — TM28
- Meeting Individual Needs and Learning Styles — TM29
- Meeting Special Needs — TM30
- Eight Ways of Learning — TM32

Professional Notes — TM34
- No Child Left Behind — TM34
- National Standards for Business Education — TM36
- SCANS Correlation — TM42
- Resources for New Directions: Academies and Exit Exams — TM46
- Block Scheduling — TM47
- Course Planning Guide — TM48

Planning Guides, Lesson Plans, and Answer Keys — TM50

THE IMPORTANCE OF BUSINESS AND PERSONAL FINANCE

According to a national survey by Teenage Research Unlimited, spending among American teens has risen from $141 billion per year to a staggering $170 billion per year over the past five years. In addition the teen population in the United States is growing. Researchers predict that by 2010 there will be 35 million teens—and they will be spending a lot of money.

Unfortunately, research also indicates that teens know very little about managing their money. For example, a recent *Consumer Reports* study of 12-year-olds shows that only seven in ten know that using credit cards is a form of borrowing. Only 40 percent know that banks charge interest on loans. In fact, many students pay for their college education using credit cards with interest rates as high as 22 percent, when the interest on student loan packages has been as low as 3 to 5 percent.

Consider these additional statistics:

- 48 percent of college students have bounced checks.
- Only two out of five college students balance their checkbooks every month.
- 67 percent of college students have credit cards, and 71 percent of those carry a balance.
- An average high school graduate today may earn more than $1 million during his or her adult life.

In her *Washington Post* column, financial writer Jane Bryant Quinn had this to say about teaching young people to manage their finances: "Young people today are plunged into a world of options from the first day they walk out of school. Credit card or debit cards? Buy a car or lease one? Cash value insurance, term insurance, or none at all? Which mutual fund for your 401(k)? What, by the way, *is* a mutual fund? Without even rudimentary knowledge, how can they possibly make intelligent choices?"

Parents, of course, can educate their children about money, but parents may not have complete knowledge themselves. Financial experts like Jane Bryant Quinn think classrooms are excellent forums for teaching financial management. Research shows that in states where financial management courses are required in school, adults tend to save more money and have lower bankruptcy rates.

Business and Personal Finance can help students navigate the financial decisions they face today and tomorrow because the text teaches financial management skills. First, it presents and clearly explains financial concepts, such as consumer purchasing strategies, consumer credit, investing, and insurance. Then, with features and activities, like Common Cents, Savvy Saver, Your Financial Portfolio, and What's Your Financial ID?, students can understand the everyday relevance of newly presented concepts.

Business and Personal Finance will help you teach your students how to use their personal financial resources to enjoy today and be financially secure tomorrow.

Marketing Your Personal Finance Program

Glencoe has provided the following resources in the *Marketing Your Personal Finance Program* booklet:

- *Your Marketing Plan:* ideas about how to get your message to future students and other decision makers
- *Benefits of Personal Finance:* table showing the benefits of a personal finance program for students, parents, teachers, department chairs, superintendents, and the community
- *Back-to-School Night Activities:* creative projects
- *Finance Quiz:* suitable for teenagers and adults
- *Personal Finance Resources:* Web sites for young people and educators

INSIDE THE STUDENT EDITION

WELCOME TO BUSINESS AND PERSONAL FINANCE

Do you remember when you first learned that checks had to be backed by money in the bank, and that you couldn't write a check for just any amount? Do you remember the first time you read a table that explained how many years it would take to pay off a credit card balance including interest if you paid only the minimum balance? Many students today don't fully understand these and many other financial concepts.

Business and Personal Finance introduces students to the world of money management and finance. They will learn what to do with their money by learning about their financial options and responsibilities—and they will learn about the consequences of mismanaged finances.

Business and Personal Finance is a comprehensive text, using the National Standards for Business Education to develop the topics covered in the text. A colorful, sophisticated design, lots of visual interest, and an easy-to-read style invite students of all backgrounds and abilities to explore the content.

Exploring Each Unit

Business and Personal Finance is divided into six units. The first four units cover personal finance, and the last two units focus on business finance. Each unit covers a specific financial topic and consists of three or four chapters.

Unit Introductions prepare students for what's coming up by describing the unit's contents and its relevance to other units.

Reading Strategies explain to students how to get the most from their reading.

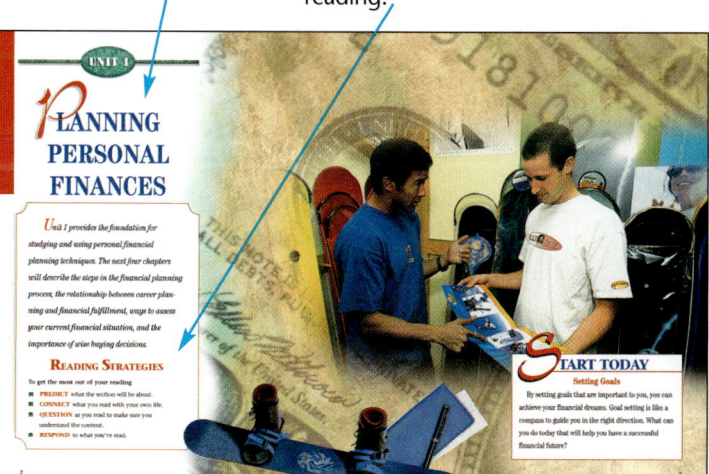

Unit Case Studies are unit simulations that conclude each unit. Entitled *Get a Financial Life!,* each case study provides an opportunity to apply the unit's content to extended activities. The Overview section describes a scenario of a young couple experiencing a variety of real-life, financial situations. The activities require students to critically analyze and synthesize these real-world financial scenarios, and help students develop their business and financial skills. These unit case studies tie several chapters together and help students make sense of the different components of *Business and Personal Finance.*

Start Today is a short feature on why it's important for students to start thinking about managing their finances early in life. Each *Start Today* feature asks a question that will prompt students to apply the feature to their personal lives.

Teacher Manual

TM7

INSIDE THE STUDENT EDITION

Exploring Each Chapter

Each chapter of *Business and Personal Finance* is divided into two, three, four, or five sections in order to facilitate students' ability to manage what they are learning. The chapters are presented in a single-column format to promote readability; sidebar, features, and colorful illustrations maintain student interest. Each chapter begins with an interesting realistic scenario that helps students relate to the chapter's subject.

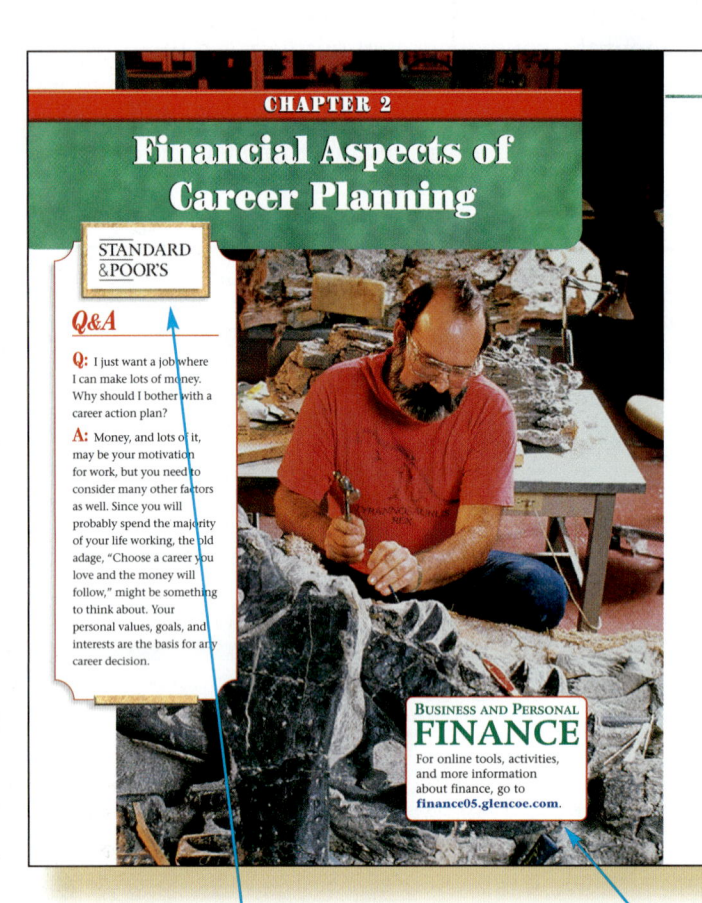

Standard & Poor's Q & A presents financial questions that students might ask. The answers are then provided by experts in Standard & Poor's educational division.

Business and Personal Finance Web site extends the course work with tutorials, case studies, and practical applications. Teachers have access to professional development tools, online answer keys, and finance updates.

INSIDE THE STUDENT EDITION

Exploring Each Section

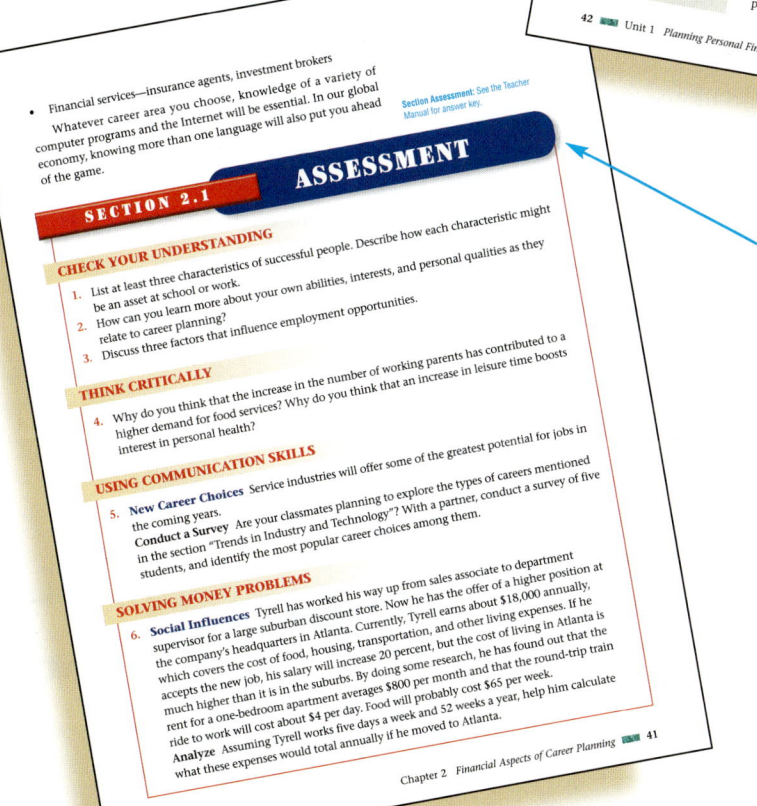

Each section introduces the chapter material in manageable segments.

What You'll Learn and **Why It's Important** at the beginning of each section provide guidance and structure for the student and make the text relevant.

Key Terms at the beginning of each section list major terms presented throughout the section. They are highlighted in red as they are introduced within the sections, and are also accompanied by clear, in-context definitions.

Section Assessments complete each section. Assessments include **Check Your Understanding** questions that relate to the concepts in **What You'll Learn**. Assessments also include critical thinking questions about the material in the section, cross-curricular skill activities, and **Solving Money Problems**, an activity that presents a realistic scenario that requires students to apply a newly presented financial concept.

INSIDE THE STUDENT EDITION

Go Figure

This chapter feature emphasizes relevant math formulas that clearly illustrate a problem. Its purpose is to help students understand the math formulas being presented in the text. The formula is first described in the text and then shown again in the **Go Figure** box. Each formula is broken down into three parts.

SUBTITLE describes the topic covered.

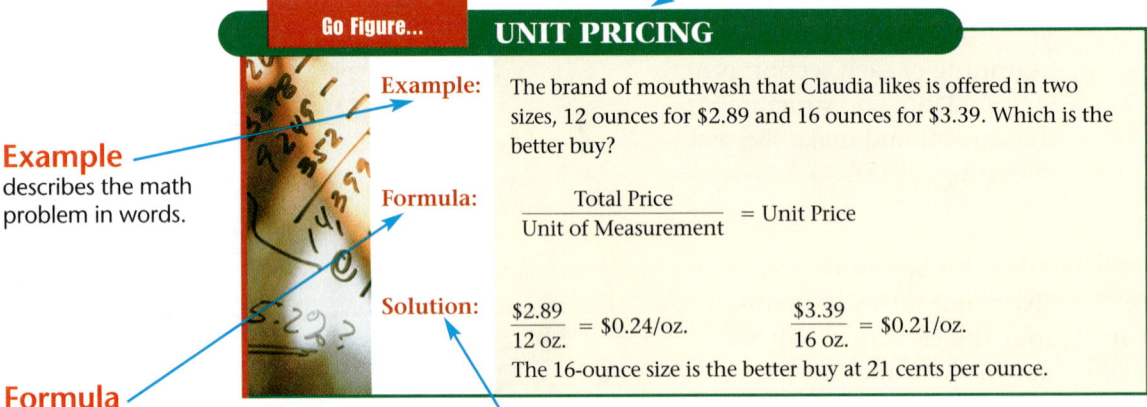

Go Figure... UNIT PRICING

Example describes the math problem in words.

Example: The brand of mouthwash that Claudia likes is offered in two sizes, 12 ounces for $2.89 and 16 ounces for $3.39. Which is the better buy?

Formula explains the calculation in words.

Formula:
$$\frac{\text{Total Price}}{\text{Unit of Measurement}} = \text{Unit Price}$$

Solution:
$$\frac{\$2.89}{12 \text{ oz.}} = \$0.24/\text{oz.} \qquad \frac{\$3.39}{16 \text{ oz.}} = \$0.21/\text{oz.}$$
The 16-ounce size is the better buy at 21 cents per ounce.

Solution shows the numeric calculation.

Math Skills Builder

This appendix feature helps students review and practice certain math fundamentals, such as multiplying or dividing decimals, reading tables and charts, and problem solving using more than one operation.

Each skill-building activity begins with a verbal explanation of the particular math skill.

Example is a numeric example of the problem.

Solution shows step-by-step how to solve the problem.

Problems reinforce the math skill through practice.

Applications show students how to apply the math skill to business and personal financial situations.

TM10

INSIDE THE STUDENT EDITION

Chapter Summary and Assessment

Each chapter ends with a two-page review designed to help students recall, use, and expand on the concepts presented in the chapter.

Chapter Summary is a clearly organized listing of the main points within the chapter.

Review Key Concepts asks questions relating to the key concepts of the chapter.

Problem Solving Today requires students to use problem-solving skills and apply chapter content to a "real-life" situation. Each Problem Solving Today activity includes an optional computer activity.

Real-World Application asks students to use their higher-level thinking skills as they consider the basic concepts of the text. It also helps students connect finance to other fields of academic study.

CHAPTER 5 ASSESSMENT

Chapter Assessment: See the Teacher Manual for answer key.

CHAPTER SUMMARY

- Financial services can be divided into three main categories: savings, payment services, and borrowing.
- Electronic banking services include direct deposit, automatic payments, automatic teller machines (ATMs), and plastic payments.
- You can choose from among deposit-type and nondeposit-type institutions.
- Among the types of savings plans are regular savings accounts, certificates of deposit, money market accounts, and U.S. Savings Bonds. Understanding the costs and benefits of different savings plans will help you make sensible trade-offs.
- Evaluate savings plans on their rates of return, the effect of inflation on interest, tax considerations, liquidity, restrictions, and fees.
- Evaluate checking accounts for their restrictions, fees and charges, interest rates (if any), and special services.
- Using a checking account involves opening an account, writing checks, making deposits, and reconciling your checkbook to the bank's statements.

Understanding and Using Vocabulary

With a partner, practice using these key terms by writing a dialogue between a customer and a bank manager about the bank's services, interest rates, and costs. Use at least eight terms in your dialogue.

automatic teller machine (ATM)	certificate of deposit (CD)
debit card	money market account
point-of-sale transaction	rate of return
commercial bank	compounding
savings and loan association (S&L)	annual percentage yield (APY)
credit union	overdraft protection
	stop-payment order
	endorsement
	bank reconciliation

Review Key Concepts

1. What are the features of an automatic payment service?
2. Name three trade-offs you may have to make when you select financial services.
3. How might you make the most of an investment in a certificate of deposit?
4. What are the main factors to consider when choosing a savings plan?
5. Describe the steps you should follow when writing a check.

Apply Key Concepts

1. Predict some possible drawbacks of using an automatic payment service.

150 Chapter 5 Assessment

CHAPTER 5 ASSESSMENT

2. Explain why people tend to place a greater value on their money than their time when making banking choices.
3. Prepare a profile of a person who would be a good candidate to invest money in certificates of deposit.
4. Using the formula for calculating interest, prepare a table showing how much $100 would grow in one year in a savings account if the annual interest rate is 5 percent, compounded quarterly.
5. Prepare a presentation on the benefits of paying with checks instead of cash.

Problem Solving Today

GETTING THE BEST RATE OF RETURN

After you graduate from high school, you would like to work part-time and enroll in a nearby business school. Your parents have agreed to pay the $20,000 tuition, but they have asked you to pay it back in five years.

Analyze You have $10,000 in a regular savings account and would like to put it in a five-year certificate of deposit. The CD earns 6.5 percent interest, compounded annually. You also plan to give your parents $120 a month from your earnings. Between the certificate of deposit and your earnings, will you have enough money to pay your parents back at the end of five years?

Computer Activity As an alternative activity, use financial software to calculate your interest and devise a plan to repay your parents.

Real-World Application

CONNECT WITH ECONOMICS

You are aware of the benefits of eating lots of fruits and vegetables. Because you want the produce you eat to be fresh, you go to the grocery store at least two times during any given week. Instead of having to remember to carry enough cash, you would like to have a debit card that lets you make online point-of-sale transactions.

Conduct Research Call several financial institutions in your area to find out what you would have to do to obtain the type of card that you want. Be sure to ask what type of savings or checking account is required and whether such a card carries any restrictions or fees.

FINANCE Online

CYBERBANKING SERVICES

You want to learn how to protect yourself from fraud and invasion of privacy when you use financial services.

Connect Using an Internet search engine, look for information about avoiding fraud and maintaining your privacy when banking. Specifically, find answers to the following questions:

1. What are your rights regarding financial privacy?
2. What can you do to keep from becoming a victim of fraud?
3. What can you do if you are the victim of fraud?

Chapter 5 Assessment 151

Understanding and Using Vocabulary presents an interesting activity that helps students review the chapter's key terms.

Apply Key Concepts asks questions that apply the key concepts to the student's personal life.

Finance Online challenges students to use the Internet to answer financial questions and solve financial problems.

Teacher Manual

TM11

INSIDE THE STUDENT EDITION

Focus on Features

High-interest features in each chapter engage students, enhance their understanding, and increase their involvement with real-world situations.

Teacher Manual

What's Your Financial ID?
FIND YOUR PERSONALITY TRAITS

Learning more about your own personality will help you choose a career. Read the characteristics below that describe people's personalities. On a separate piece of paper write down the five traits that best describe you, then answer the question that follows.

Personality Traits

outgoing	ambitious	patient
studious	kind	thoughtful
neat	strong	intelligent
quiet	trustworthy	respectful
playful	warm	happy
energetic	persistent	spontaneous
serious	organized	worried
easygoing	rebellious	sensitive
caring	stubborn	sociable
loyal	responsible	creative
confident	fair	talkative
cheerful	calm	inquisitive
dependable	brave	funny
generous	helpful	athletic
shy	imaginative	competitive

Keeping in mind the five traits that best describe your personality, what kind of work do you think would suit you? For example, if you're persistent, outgoing, and assertive, you might work in sales. If you're inquisitive and creative, you might enjoy a career in writing. List the jobs or careers that you think fit best with your personality.

academic connection
MATH

Ask a local bank for the interest rates, fees, annual percentage yield (APY), and compounding method for the following:
- Regular savings account
- Two types of certificates of deposit (CDs)
- Money market account
- U.S. Savings Bonds

Determine the rate of return if you saved $5,000 for one, two, and three years. Be sure to apply the compounding method that the bank offers on the various savings plans. Based on your figures, which plan would you select?

Common Cents
Money Toss

Empty the change from your pocket or wallet every night and throw it into a jar. At the end of each month, deposit all your "throwaway" money in your savings account. That loose change can really add up.

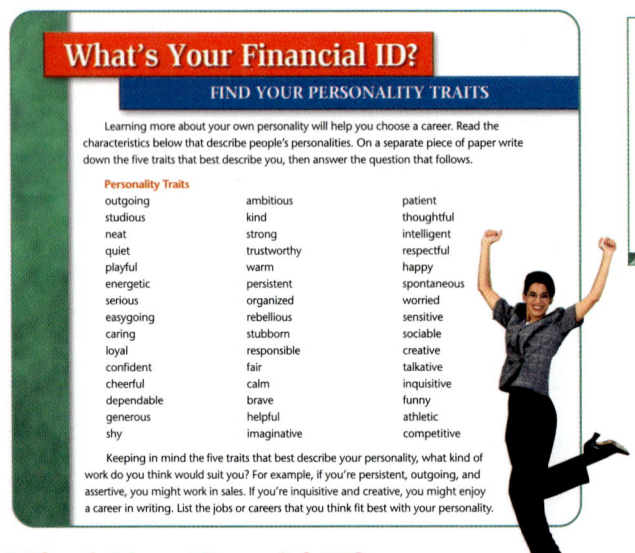

What's Your Financial ID? resembles a quick financial assessment quiz you might find in a magazine. It helps students evaluate and define their own financial sense or personality.

Academic Connection connects finance with another field of study, such as art, language arts, history or social science, law, science, health, or other subjects. This interdisciplinary approach helps students perceive interesting links and observe how business and personal finance apply and relate to a variety of pursuits.

Common Cents offers tips to students regarding managing their money in an everyday context, with the emphasis on saving money.

INTERNATIONAL FINANCE — Switzerland

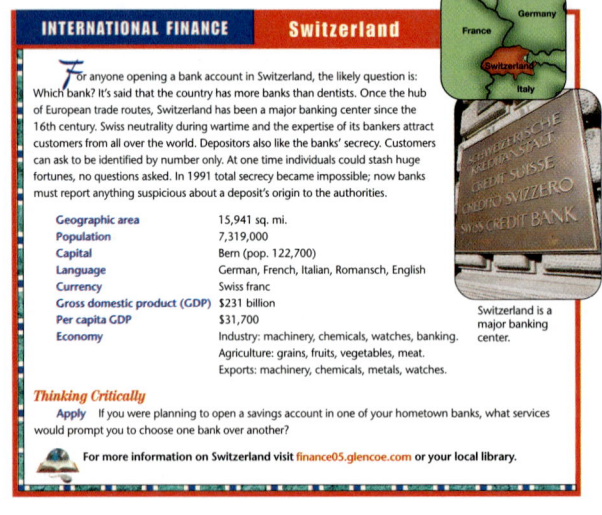

For anyone opening a bank account in Switzerland, the likely question is: Which bank? It's said that the country has more banks than dentists. Once the hub of European trade routes, Switzerland has been a major banking center since the 16th century. Swiss neutrality during wartime and the expertise of its bankers attract customers from all over the world. Depositors also like the banks' secrecy. Customers can ask to be identified by number only. At one time individuals could stash huge fortunes, no questions asked. In 1991 total secrecy became impossible; now banks must report anything suspicious about a deposit's origin to the authorities.

Geographic area	15,941 sq. mi.
Population	7,319,000
Capital	Bern (pop. 122,700)
Language	German, French, Italian, Romansch, English
Currency	Swiss franc
Gross domestic product (GDP)	$231 billion
Per capita GDP	$31,700
Economy	Industry: machinery, chemicals, watches, banking. Agriculture: grains, fruits, vegetables, meat. Exports: machinery, chemicals, metals, watches.

Switzerland is a major banking center.

Thinking Critically
Apply If you were planning to open a savings account in one of your hometown banks, what services would prompt you to choose one bank over another?

For more information on Switzerland visit finance05.glencoe.com or your local library.

$avvy $aver
Bank on It—Finding the Best Savings Account

1. Shop around to find the bank that offers the highest interest rates.
2. Ask if you need to deposit a minimum amount.
3. Find out if the bank pays less on small accounts.
4. Ask the bank how often it credits interest to your account.
5. Ask if you'll receive simple interest or compound interest.

International Finance spotlights an interesting financial or business aspect of another country. Students will learn about the global marketplace and other cultures, as well as be challenged with a critical thinking question.

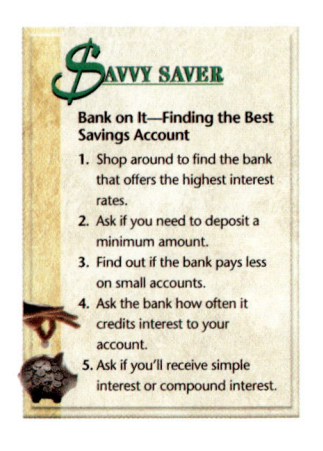

Savvy Saver lists five helpful tips for saving and spending money for a specific financial activity, such as eating out on a budget or finding the best savings account.

TM12

INSIDE THE STUDENT EDITION

Your Financial Portfolio

Comparison Shopping for Banking Services

Enrique is ready to open some bank accounts and is looking for the bank that best suits his needs. He is deciding between the local bank and the credit union where he works.

Enrique's Savings Search

Name of Institution	Kensington Bank	Acme Credit Union
Savings		
Annual interest rate	1.8%	2.5%
Minimum balance required	$100	none
Certificate of Deposit (CD) interest rate 6 months	5.20%	5.40%
Checking		
Monthly service charge	$8.50	$6.00
Minimum balance for "free" checking	$3,000	$1,000
Fees for ATM	Free	no ATMs
Cost of checks	$10.00	$8.75
Overdraft protection	yes	none
Banking hours	Mon.–Sat. 9–6, Closed Sun.	Mon.–Fri. 9–6, Closed Sat. & Sun.

Enrique decided to open a checking account at the bank because he needed the convenience of using the ATM. He opened a savings account at the credit union because it pays higher interest. When he has enough money, he will also purchase a CD at the credit union.

Compare In your workbook or on a separate sheet of paper, list the banking services that are important to you. Then call or visit several banks in your area and compare services, costs, and interest rates that are available to you.

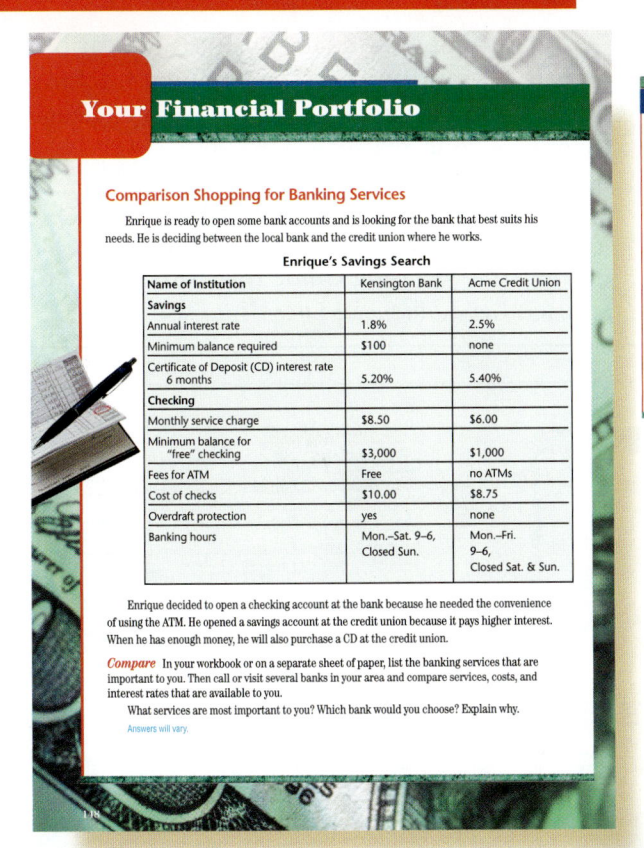

What services are most important to you? Which bank would you choose? Explain why.
Answers will vary.

Careers in Finance
BANK TELLER

Many careers in banking start at the teller's window. Bank tellers cash checks, accept deposits and loan payments, handle withdrawals, and sell traveler's checks. They may do other tasks, depending on the type of banking institution where they work. Because tellers deal with customers' money, they must pay close attention to their work, verifying names, dates, numbers, and identities. Most tellers use calculators and computers as well as other types of electronic equipment.

Skills	Communication, computer, interpersonal, math
Personality	Detail oriented, discreet, honest, likes working with people, tactful
Education	High school diploma and on-the-job training; associate of arts or bachelor's degree; certification from the Institute of Financial Education or the American Institute of Banking may help you advance into management.
Pay range	$13,000 to $25,000 a year, depending on experience, location, and bank
Research	Invite a bank manager to your class to discuss the opportunities available to tellers. Ask questions about the training, experience, and education that a bank teller needs. *Answers will vary.*

For more information on bank tellers visit finance05.glencoe.com or your local library.

Careers in Finance focuses on and describes a specific career that pertains to a topic presented in the chapter. This feature profiles a field, market, or profession, rather than a particular person, and itemizes characteristics of the career, such as skills, personality, education, and pay range. It concludes with a related activity or question.

Your Financial Portfolio presents interesting financial situations and gives students information to evaluate and make wise financial decisions that could affect them now and in the future. Students can calculate real costs and fill out real-life forms, such as a job application and an income tax return. Some other activities include developing a budget, calculating net worth, and comparing banking services. Corresponding worksheets for each chapter are provided in the *Student Activity Workbook*.

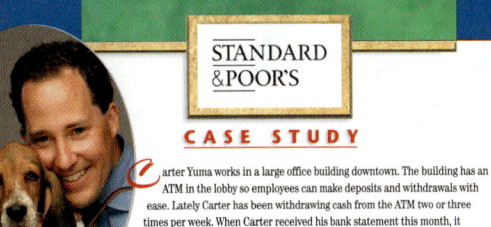

STANDARD & POOR'S
CASE STUDY

Carter Yuma works in a large office building downtown. The building has an ATM in the lobby so employees can make deposits and withdrawals with ease. Lately Carter has been withdrawing cash from the ATM two or three times per week. When Carter received his bank statement this month, it included a few surprises. Withdrawing cash from his checking account caused his balance to fall below the minimum. The bank charges $7.50 when this happens. He was charged fees for the 11 cash withdrawals he made during the month. Carter had one overdraft, which cost him $25. Carter didn't know that banks charged these kinds of fees. Nor did he realize that having easy access to the ATM could lead to overspending. Not knowing what to do next, Carter turned to the experts at Standard & Poor's for advice.

Analysis: Carter is right in wanting to keep an eye on transaction fees, as they can add up to a surprisingly large bill. Using an ATM is not necessarily a bad thing; many people prefer to carry only as much cash as they need. It's important, though, to write down ATM withdrawals and keep track of checking account balances. With a little thought about his spending needs and habits, Carter can find an inexpensive solution that will work for his situation.

Recommendation: Carter can first look for a bank that will base his monthly fees on the total of all the balances in his checking and savings accounts with that bank rather than on individual accounts. Then he can open several accounts, each for a different purpose. The first is Carter's main checking account, used to pay his regular monthly bills. The second should be a savings account that pays interest. Carter can deposit his paycheck into the checking account and then write a check or transfer money to his savings account. To make it easier to limit his cash expenditures, Carter can deposit his weekly spending money in a third account. This is the account from which Carter would make ATM withdrawals, using a machine from his bank in order to avoid extra transaction fees and remembering to record his withdrawals.

Critical Thinking Questions *See the Teacher Manual for answer key.*
1. Why do you think Carter finds it easier to overspend when he withdraws cash from an ATM than when he writes a check for purchases?
2. What factors should Carter consider when selecting a bank with which to do business?
3. What other strategies might Carter use to avoid the temptation of withdrawing more from his account than he'd planned to spend?

Standard & Poor's Case Study presents a realistic scenario applicable to students' lives now or in the future. Experts at the Standard & Poor's educational division provide an analysis of a person's situation and a recommendation for action, as well as three critical thinking questions.

INSIDE THE TEACHER ANNOTATED EDITION

Using the Planning Guides

To help you select activities that will best meet the needs of your students, the **Teacher Annotated Edition** includes a Planning Guide at the beginning of each unit to introduce important concepts. Each chapter also contains a Planning Guide that organizes the chapter's lesson activities into objectives, National Standards for Business Education, features, and resources. Additional teaching activities are provided for in-depth coverage of core concepts.

Unit Planning Guides provide a Unit Overview and Introduction with activities, as well as a Teaching Guide that corresponds to each *Get a Financial Life!* Unit Case Study.

Chapter Planning Guides

provide a chart as well as activities to draw students into the chapter material.

Objectives

column lists specific skills and knowledge students can expect to master as they study each chapter. These measurable objectives guide students to read, discuss, and review the chapter, keeping specific goals in mind.

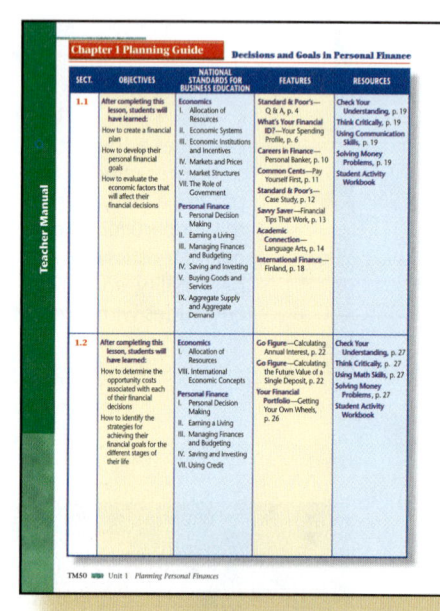

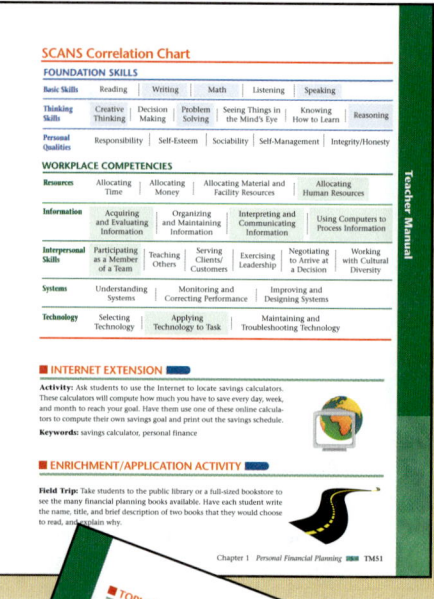

National Standards for Business Education

column lists the correlated standards covered by each section.

Features

in each section are listed in order of their appearance in the text.

Resources

column lists pertinent activities from the text and the ancillaries.

SCANS Correlation Chart

shows you which foundation skills and workplace competencies are covered for the chapter.

Internet Extension

guides your class through an extra Internet activity.

Enrichment/Application Activity

gives ideas for guest speakers and field trips that offer real-life applications for chapter concepts.

Topic Spotlight

provides additional teaching activities combining three of these five topics: ethics, government, marketing, money, and technology.

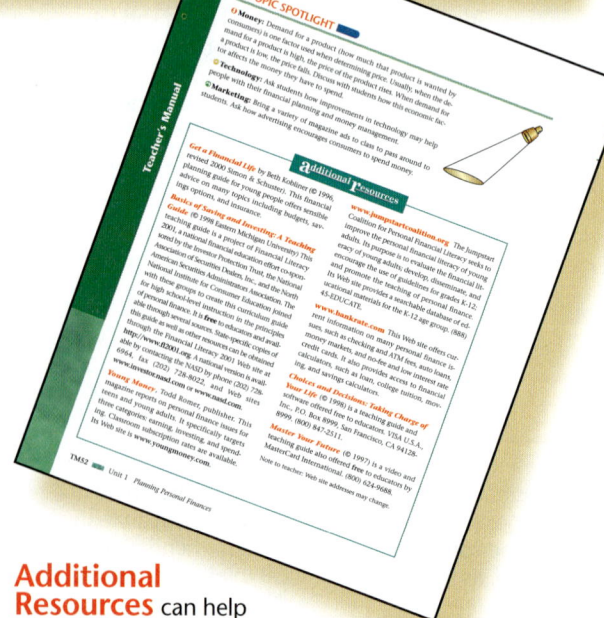

Additional Resources

can help instructors or students explore or extend the chapter material.

INSIDE THE TEACHER ANNOTATED EDITION

Using the Annotations

The annotations provide on-the-spot teaching options and activities. Each chapter features at least one of the following, as well as caption answers:

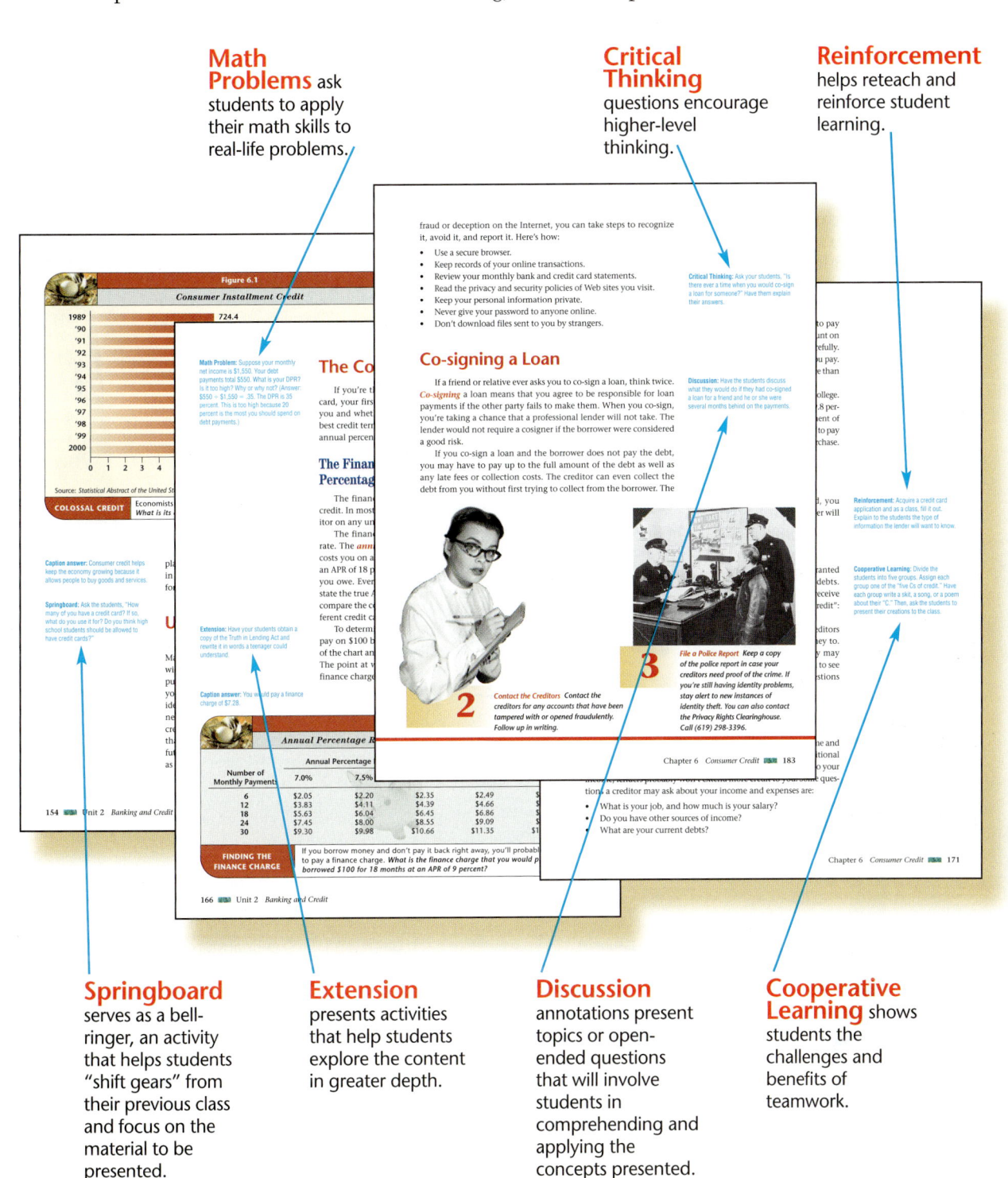

Math Problems ask students to apply their math skills to real-life problems.

Critical Thinking questions encourage higher-level thinking.

Reinforcement helps reteach and reinforce student learning.

Springboard serves as a bell-ringer, an activity that helps students "shift gears" from their previous class and focus on the material to be presented.

Extension presents activities that help students explore the content in greater depth.

Discussion annotations present topics or open-ended questions that will involve students in comprehending and applying the concepts presented.

Cooperative Learning shows students the challenges and benefits of teamwork.

TM15

Inside the Teacher Annotated Edition

Using the Lesson Plans

The Lesson Plans in the *Teacher Annotated Edition* are found in the *Teacher Manual* section and make full and effective use of a mastery approach in four steps: Focus, Teach, Assess, and Close. This widely accepted instructional method develops students' understanding of the subject matter while providing a consistent framework that makes it easy for you to teach the material.

Focus As a teacher, you know that the first step in presenting new material is to capture students' interest. The Lesson Plans suggest a variety of interesting motivational activities to focus students' interest.

Teach The second step in the instructional process encompasses the presentation and exploration of new material. The Lesson Plans present a teaching plan designed to give you maximum flexibility in meeting the needs of your class. The variety of approaches, strategies, and activities provided allow you to help all students assimilate the content of each chapter.

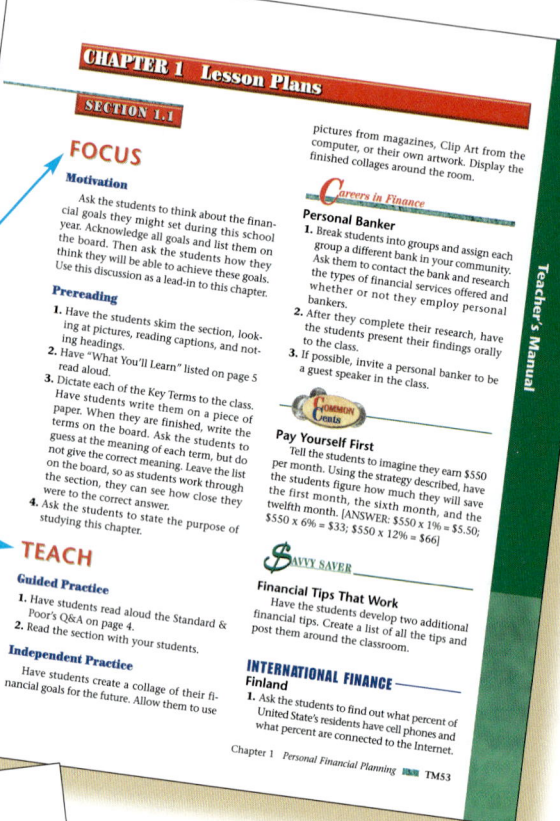

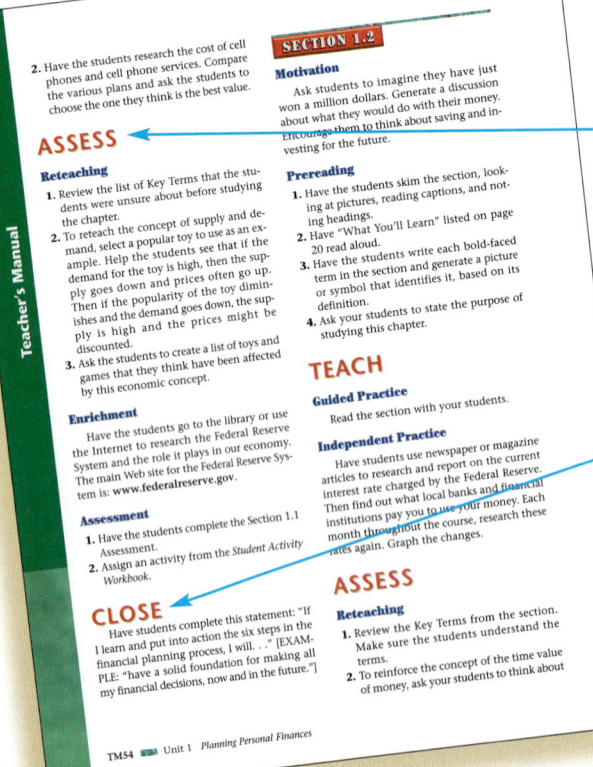

Assess This third step provides a variety of evaluation and reteaching activities designed to accommodate a wide range of learning abilities.

Close The final step of the instructional method allows students to look back over the new material presented in the lesson. Students summarize what they have learned, evaluate their own learning processes, and relate the new material to their own lives.

TM16

TEACHER CLASSROOM RESOURCES

Classroom Resources

The *Business and Personal Finance* program offers a complete selection of teacher support materials. Used in conjunction with the **Teacher Annotated Edition**, these materials will enable you to tailor the program to meet the specific needs of your classes.

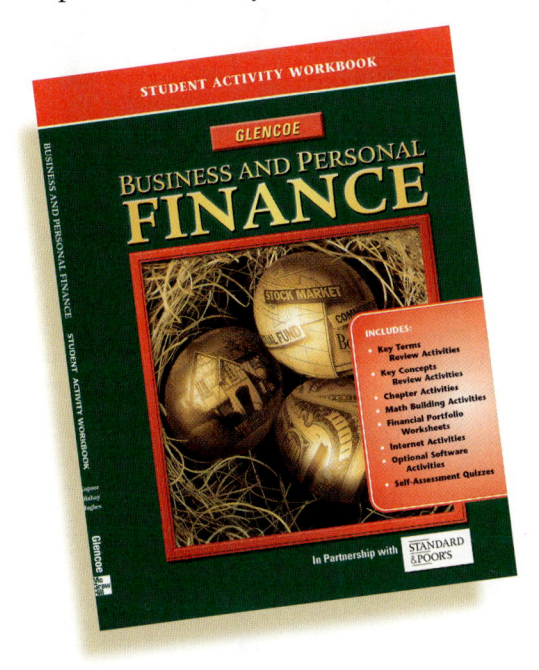

Student Activity Workbook is designed to reinforce student learning with hands-on activities correlated to chapter content.

Your Personal Financial Planner provides real-world forms and worksheets that help prepare students for personal financial situations.

Standard & Poor's Extension Activities present interesting and relevant articles from Standard & Poor's library of publications that relate to chapter content. The activities enable students to expand their knowledge and sharpen their skills. Each chapter includes a vocabulary list that introduces students to the terms used in the articles. Features also include fact and idea review questions, critical thinking activities, and extension activities. Answer keys are provided.

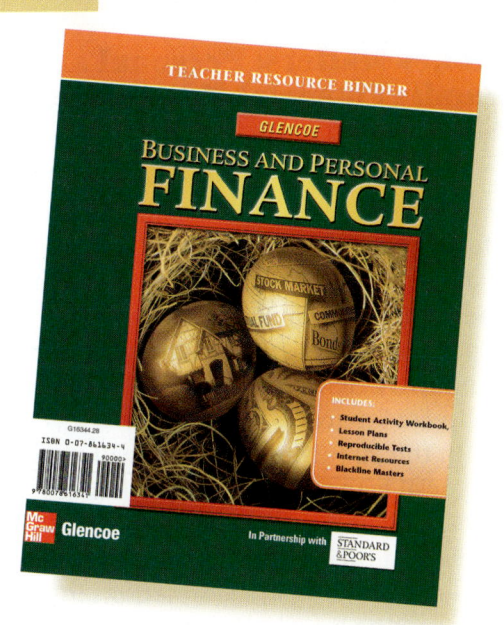

Teacher Resource Binder provides the following resources for your use:
- **Teacher Annotated Edition** of the **Student Activity Workbook** includes answer keys.
- **Lesson Plans** outline lesson objectives and teaching resources for every chapter.
- **Blackline Masters** enable you to visually expand on chapter content.
- **Reproducible Tests** include tests and answer keys for all 22 chapters.
- **Internet Resources** provides activities for using the Internet in your classroom.

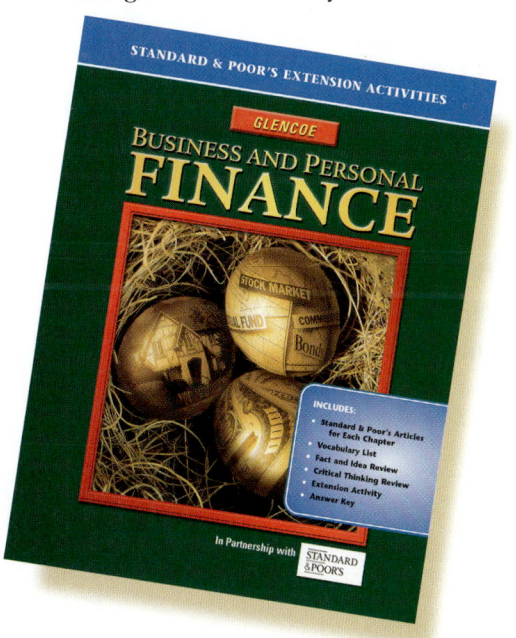

Teacher Classroom Resources

Money Matters: Personal and Family Financial Management Simulation

In the supplement *Money Matters: Personal and Family Financial Management Simulation*, students encounter real-world scenarios and make the same financial decisions made by individuals and families. This simulation combines reality, student creativity, and classroom flexibility, which promotes learning and increases interest.

In this simulation students will learn how financial management is more than just earning an income, paying bills, and saving a few dollars for the future. The five units will help students understand life situations in various stages of the financial life cycle:

- The single person
- The young married couple
- The couple with young children (expanding family)
- The head of household with child
- A couple nearing retirement

Students will see the effects of financial decisions. As they go through the real-life activities, they will have a chance to calculate financial decisions both manually or by using Microsoft® Money, Quicken® Deluxe, or Excel® software.

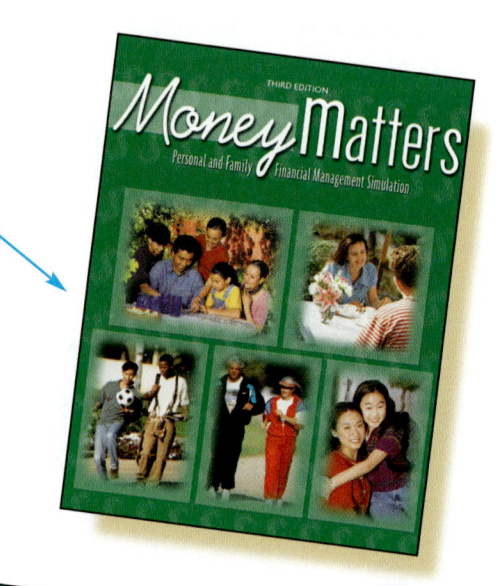

The **Student Edition** focuses on five personal finance stages in life. Each unit contains a friendly narrative, student activities (with software directions), and business documents.

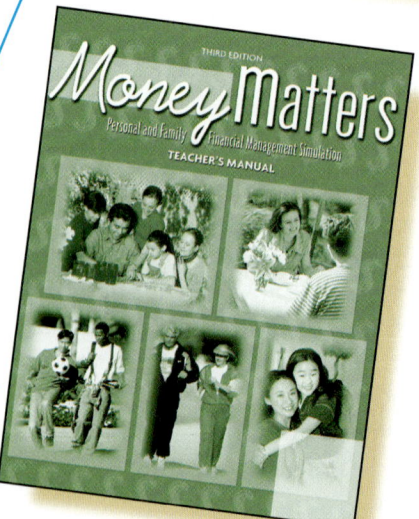

The **Teacher Manual** provides an overview of the simulation, teaching suggestions, evaluations, master copies of the business forms, and the solutions.

TEACHER CLASSROOM RESOURCES

Business and Personal Finance Web Site

The *Business and Personal Finance* Web site includes information, activities, and exercises that are immensely useful to students, teachers, and families:

- Student resources include the Money Smarts activities, which reinforce financial literacy through Web-based exercises.
- Teacher resources include a variety of classroom aids, ranging from teaching tips to content correlations.
- Families will find information on how they can best facilitate student learning and study habits, as well as links to other useful Web sites.

Use this Web site to enhance your students' overall learning experience. The following features are included on the *Business and Personal Finance* Web site:

Students
- NAF Case Studies
- Money Smarts
- Careers in Finance
- International Finance

Teachers
- NAF Case Studies Tips
- Money Smarts Tips
- No Child Left Behind
- Ethics in Finance
- Selected Teacher Links, including Partners and Associations
- Virtual Business
- Sample Classroom Resources
- Content Correlations
- Finance Updates

Family
- Letter to Family
- Web Links

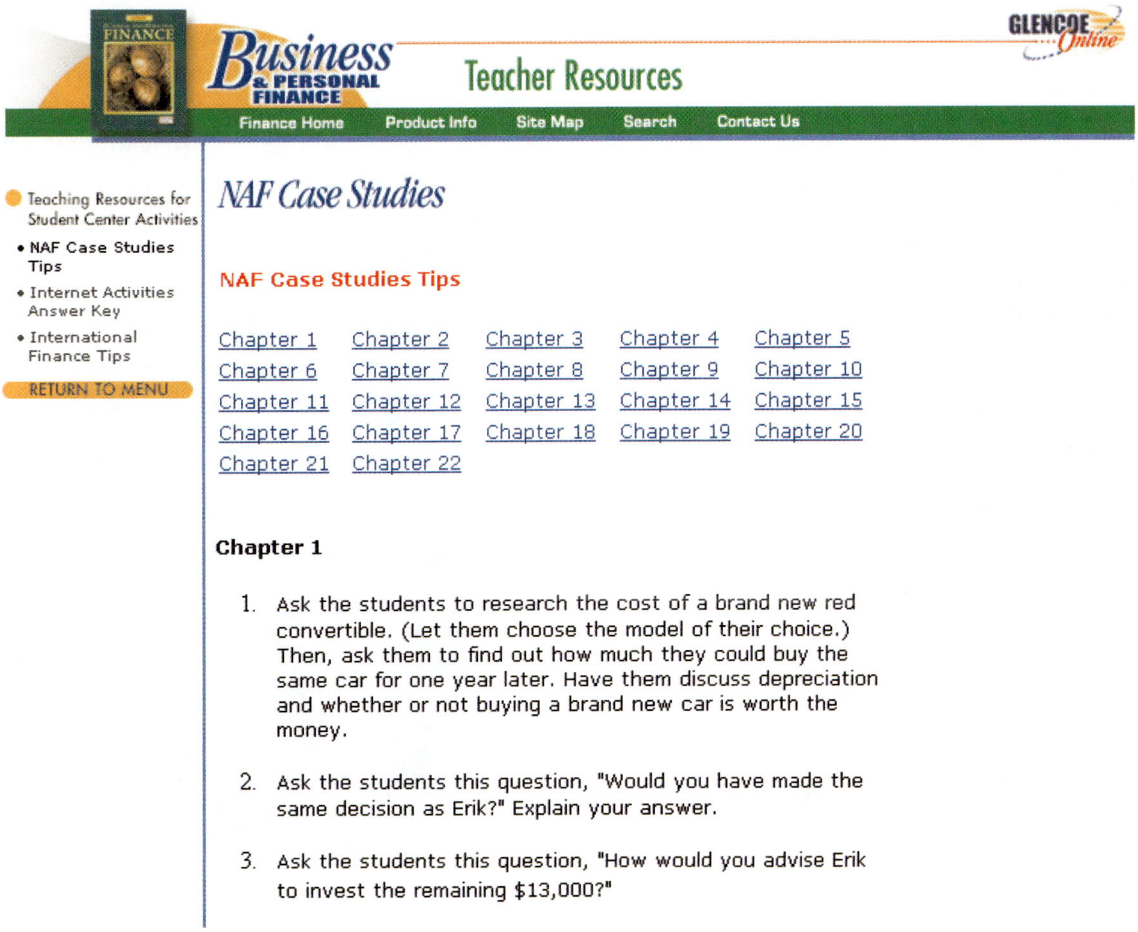

Teaching Resources for Student Center Activities
- NAF Case Studies Tips
- Internet Activities Answer Key
- International Finance Tips

RETURN TO MENU

NAF Case Studies

NAF Case Studies Tips

Chapter 1	Chapter 2	Chapter 3	Chapter 4	Chapter 5
Chapter 6	Chapter 7	Chapter 8	Chapter 9	Chapter 10
Chapter 11	Chapter 12	Chapter 13	Chapter 14	Chapter 15
Chapter 16	Chapter 17	Chapter 18	Chapter 19	Chapter 20
Chapter 21	Chapter 22			

Chapter 1

1. Ask the students to research the cost of a brand new red convertible. (Let them choose the model of their choice.) Then, ask them to find out how much they could buy the same car for one year later. Have them discuss depreciation and whether or not buying a brand new car is worth the money.

2. Ask the students this question, "Would you have made the same decision as Erik?" Explain your answer.

3. Ask the students this question, "How would you advise Erik to invest the remaining $13,000?"

Teacher Classroom Resources

Technology–Based Resources

Interactive Lesson Planner CD-ROM gives you instant access to print resources for *Business and Personal Finance:*

- Teacher Annotated Edition of the Student Activity Workbook
- Lesson Plans
- Reproducible Tests
- Internet Resources
- Blackline Masters

Exam*View*® Pro Testmaker CD-ROM allows you to print out ready-made unit and chapter tests, complete with answer keys. You can also create customized tests. The software can be run by either Macintosh or Windows® platforms.

Virtual Business® is an exciting visual business simulation to integrate into your business and personal finance classroom. By playing *Virtual Business*, your students will find learning how to run a real-world business energizing, motivating, and most importantly, educational. Included in the package are the *Virtual Business* CD-ROM, an Instructor's Manual, a User's Manual, and five QuickCards. The Instructor's Manual includes 22 student assignments and grading sheets covering topics such as Introduction to Business, Accounting and Finance, Entrepreneurship, and Marketing.

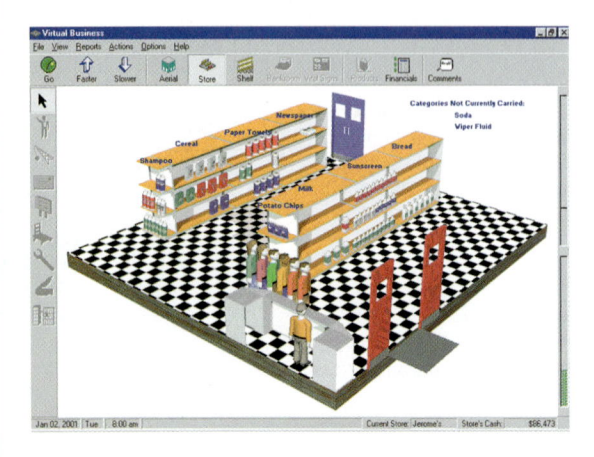

Financial Planner Software allows students to use popular software programs to carry out authentic financial planning activities. The package includes Quicken and Excel spreadsheet templates and solutions, as well as a user guide.

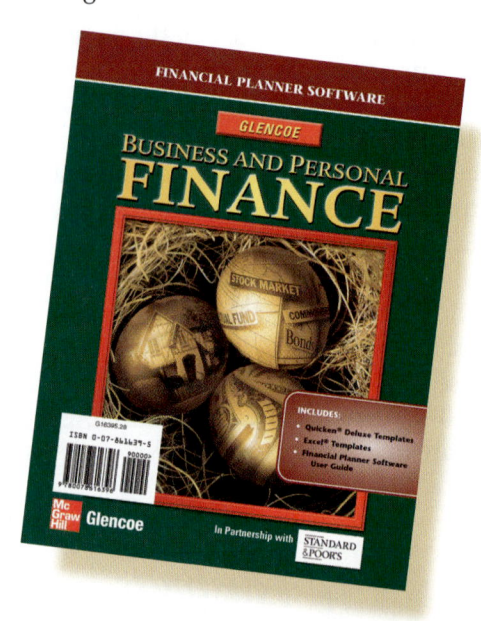

PowerPoint® Presentations provide lecture aids for every unit, chapter, and section of *Business and Personal Finance*. The presentations can be used as bell-ringers or reviews.

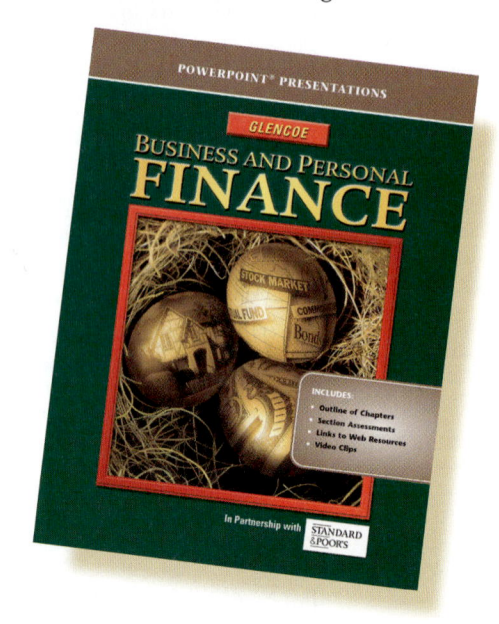

Teacher Classroom Resources

Standard & Poor's in the Student Edition

What comes to mind when you see the name Standard & Poor's? Stock market information? Long-standing reputation? Highly respected investment advice?

Standard & Poor's provides independent financial information, analytical services, advice, and credit ratings to individual investors as well as the world's financial markets. Among the company's many products are the Standard & Poor's 500 Stock Index, the premier U.S. portfolio index; the Standard & Poor's Global 1200 Stock Index, the premier global equity performance benchmark; and credit ratings on more than 290,000 securities and funds worldwide. With more than 5,000 employees located in 19 countries, Standard & Poor's is an integral part of our global infrastructure.

Business and Personal Finance has worked with Standard & Poor's to respond to the kinds of questions and situations faced by today's young people. Both the Standard & Poor's Q & A and Case Study features are prepared by experts in Standard & Poor's education division. These features add to the real-world emphasis of this text and show students that people their own age have legitimate investment questions and issues.

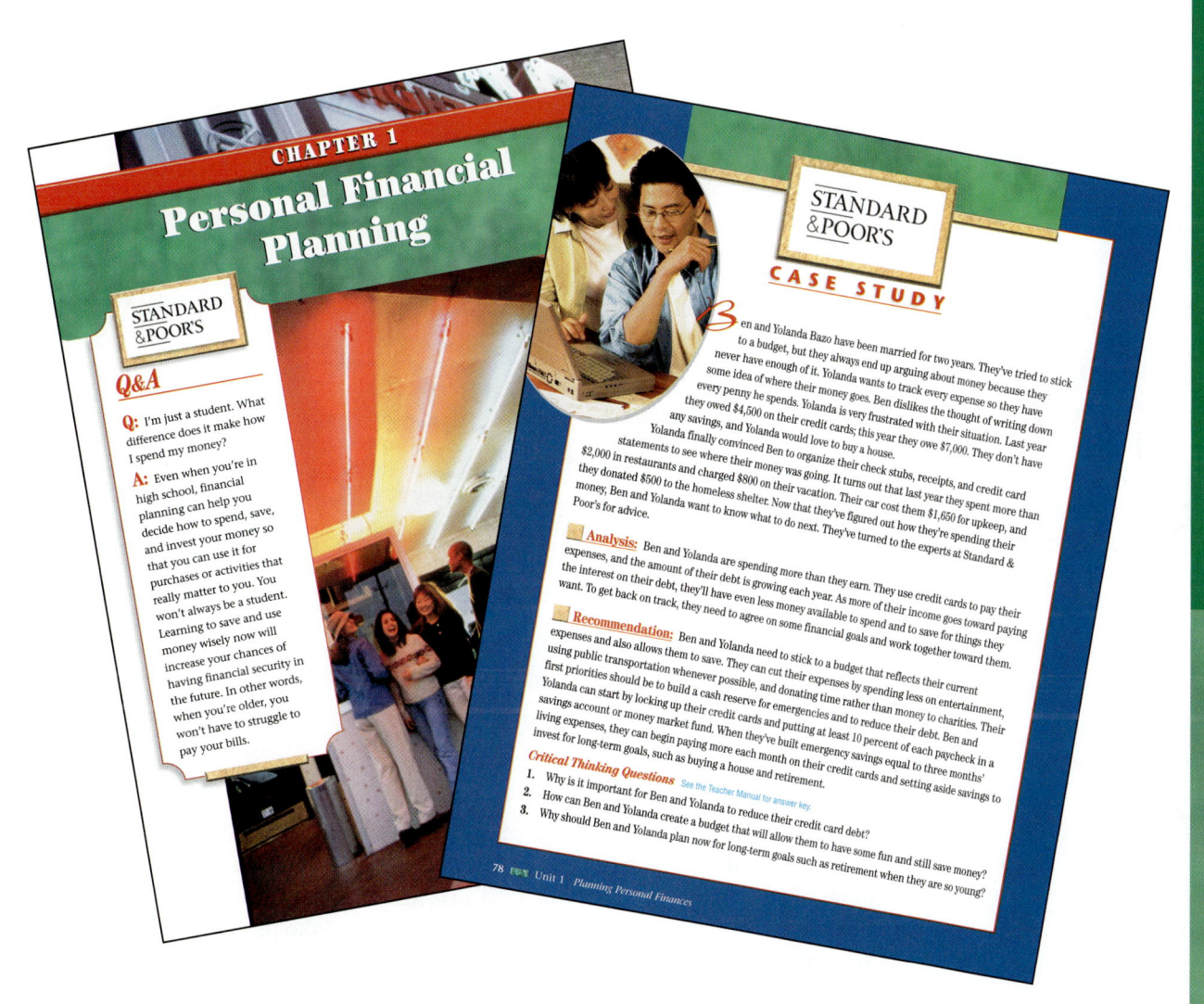

Teacher Manual

TM21

METHODOLOGY

DEVELOPING READING STRATEGIES

How well do your students read? Do they understand what they read? Are they active readers or passive readers? By applying various strategies for reading, you can help your students understand even difficult financial concepts and theories. To begin, have your students analyze their reading skills. Are they good at reading factual material? Is it easy or difficult for them to read and interpret financial data? Do they have a good business and finance vocabulary? Then discuss with your students the different skills needed when reading factual material as opposed to recreational material. In order to get the most from reading, your students need to learn how to become active readers, getting involved with and responding to the material. Active readers are effective readers.

Predict•Connect•Question•Respond

In every Unit Opener, *Business and Personal Finance* includes Reading Strategies for students. Review these strategies with your students. Explain that as people read, they have mental conversations about what they are reading. To help your students read actively and effectively, have them ask themselves questions like these throughout the text.

- **PREDICT** Make educated guesses about what the section is about by combining clues in the text with what you already know. Predicting helps you anticipate questions and stay alert to new information.
- **CONNECT** Draw parallels between what you are reading and the events and circumstances in your own life.
- **QUESTION** Ask yourself questions to help you clarify the reading as you go along.
- **RESPOND** React to what you are reading. Form opinions and make judgments about the section while you are reading—not just after you've finished.

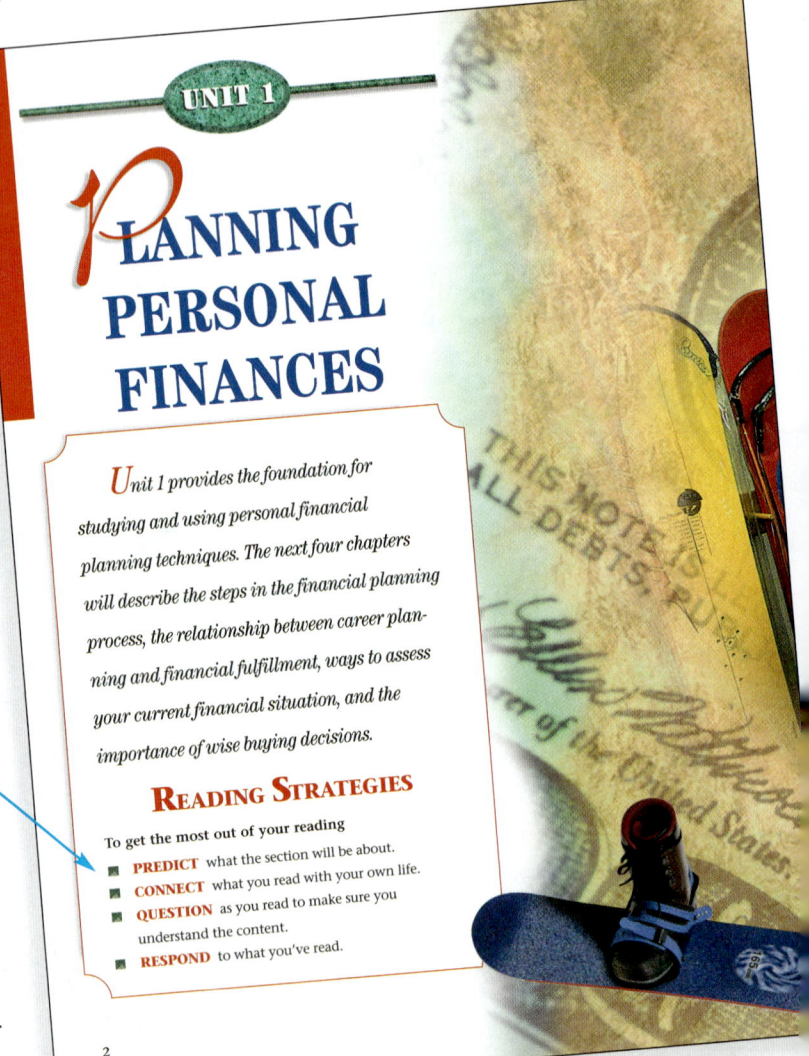

METHODOLOGY

REAL-WORLD CONNECTIONS

Making *Business and Personal Finance* Real

Nothing can bring a classroom topic to life for students like a dose of reality. The *Business and Personal Finance* teacher can easily take advantage of this. Finance is present in every student's life—at home, in the mall, on the news, and around town. Every day brings another chance to give real-life examples of the points you teach in class.

THE INTERNET By visiting the Web sites of financial institutions, financial consultants, and government resources, your students will uncover a wealth of financial information.

NEWSPAPERS AND MAGAZINES You can bring in clippings that you find, or have your students find their own. You can also monitor the media's treatment of finance-related issues. Encourage students to challenge the sources of information and not just rely on them.

TELEVISION Some programs, particularly on Public Broadcast System (PBS) stations, bring up-to-the-minute financial news to viewers. Students can take advantage of the easy access to this information.

GUEST SPEAKERS Small business owners, bankers, personal financial advisors, and tax accountants are just a few of the experts within easy reach of any community.

Connecting to Careers

Students want to see the connections between course work and the real world. Each chapter's **Careers in Finance** feature is an excellent starting point for demonstrating how finance knowledge and skills can apply to a wide array of careers. Expand the discussion by referring to this chart based on the 16 "Career Clusters" defined by the U.S. Department of Education.

CAREER CLUSTER	FINANCE-RELATED POSITIONS
Agriculture, Food & Natural Resources	Loan Officer—Farm Credit Services, Farm Manager, International Development Specialist
Architecture & Construction	General Contractor, Construction Contract Specialist
Arts, A/V Technology & Communication	Film Production Accountant, Editorial Director, Multimedia Producer
Business, Management & Administration	Controller, Chief Financial Officer, Commercial Property Manager
Education & Training	Accounting Teacher, Public School Budget Administrator
Finance	Account Executive (Stockbroker), Credit Counselor, Personal Banker, Certified Financial Planner, Commercial Loan Officer, Tax Preparer
Government & Public Administration	IRS Auditor, Economic Development Advisor, Policy Analyst
Health Science	Insurance Agent, Director of Finance—Hospital Operations
Hospitality & Tourism	Vice President of Hotel Operations, Executive Chef
Human Services	Income Maintenance Program Advisor, Budget Analyst—U.S. Government, Social Services Grant Administrator
Information Technology	Financial Software Designer, E-Commerce Director
Law, Public Safety & Security	Estate Planning Attorney, FBI Agent, Tax Attorney
Manufacturing	Financial Services—Plant Operations, Production Cost Manager
Marketing, Sales & Service	Bank Teller, Real Estate Agent, Personal Property Appraiser
Science, Technology, Engineering & Mathematics	Project Cost Analyst, Industrial Accountant
Transportation, Distribution & Logistics	Purchasing Agent, Transit Authority Contracts Accountant

METHODOLOGY

ASSESSMENT STRATEGIES

As a teacher, you will need a variety of ways to assess what your students have learned. One traditional method of measuring student progress is the written test that evaluates recall of subject content. This program contains an **Exam***View*® **Pro Testmaker CD-ROM** and **Reproducible Tests** as traditional methods of assessment. However, it is also necessary to assess more than students' rote learning skills. Current curriculum objectives focus on the acquisition of knowledge and skills that will help students analyze situations and create plans to address those situations. The acquisition of these skills is not so easily assessed using the traditional paper-and-pencil test.

Performance Assessment

Performance assessment gives you the opportunity to evaluate whether or not a student has learned to analyze and plan under different sets of circumstances. For example, with limited resources, can the student plan to pay for post-high school training? Does the student understand the discipline necessary to spend less than he or she earns? A paper-and-pencil test will not demonstrate your students' skills in these areas.

Business and Personal Finance provides you with many activities, projects, and situations that create opportunities for alternative assessment. At the end of each section and chapter are skill-building activities, many of which are scenario-based. Students must write or respond to these real-life situations. **Problem Solving Today** requires students to analyze a lifelike, contemporary problem, and **Solving Money Problems** and **Real-World Application** require students to debate and advise others about specific financial situations.

Determining Assessment Strategies

The chart shown on the opposite page can help you determine which assessment strategies will work best for you and your students.

Evaluation of student performance is fundamental to the teaching and learning process.

METHODOLOGY

ASSESSMENT STRATEGIES	ADVANTAGES	DISADVANTAGES
Objective measures • Multiple choice • Matching • Item sets • True/False	• Reliable, easy to validate • Objective, if designed effectively • Low cost, efficient • Automated administration • Lends to equating • Measures cognitive knowledge effectively	• Limited on other measures • Not a good measure of overall performance
Written measures • Essays • Restricted response • Written simulations • Case analysis • Problem-solving exercises	• Face validity (real life) • In-depth assessment • Measures writing skills and higher level skills • Reasonable developmental costs and time	• Subjective scoring • Time consuming and expensive to score • Limited breadth • Difficult to equate • Moderate reliability
Oral measures • Oral examinations • Interviews	• Measures communications and interpersonal skills • In-depth assessment with varied stimulus materials • Learner involvement	• Costly and time consuming • Limited reliability • Narrow sampling of content • Scoring difficult, need multiple raters
Simulated activities • In-basket • Computer simulations	• Moderate reliability • Performance-based measure	• Costly and time consuming • Difficult to score, administer, and develop
Portfolio and product analysis • Work samples • Projects • Work diaries and logs • Achievement records	• Provides information not normally available • Learner involvement • Face validity (real life) • Easy to collect information	• Costly to administer • Labor and paper intensive • Difficult to validate or equate • Biased toward best samples or outstanding qualities
Performance measures • Demonstrations • Presentations • Performances • Production work • Observation	• Job-related • Relatively easy to administer • In-depth assessment • Face validity	• Rater training required • Hard to equate • Subjective scoring • Time consuming if breadth is needed
Performance records • References • Performance rating forms • Parental rating	• Efficient • Low cost • Easy to administer	• Low reliability • Subjective • Hard to equate • Rate judgment
Self-evaluation	• Learner involvement and empowerment • Learner responsibility • Measures dimensions not available otherwise	• May be biased or unrealistic

Teacher Manual

METHODOLOGY

DEVELOPING THINKING SKILLS

Introduction

All educational disciplines strive to teach critical thinking skills. Your students will need to apply these skills to make important plans and decisions in their own lives now and in the future. When you teach your students critical thinking, you equip them with skills that are essential to achieve success.

Critical thinking is the process of reasonably or logically deciding what to do or believe and involves the abilities to:

- compare and contrast,
- solve problems,
- make decisions,
- analyze and evaluate,
- synthesize and transfer knowledge, and
- conduct metacognitive exercises.

Critical thinking skills are important for the following reasons:

- Critical thinking skills help students investigate their own ways of solving problems and finding creative resolutions.
- Critical thinking skills lead students to investigations that compare and contrast what they know with unknowns.
- Critical thinking skills allow students to make decisions about their own learning and also make them aware of their own processes.

What Is Thinking?

All learning requires thinking. Benjamin Bloom's taxonomy of the cognitive domain is probably the most widely recognized schema for levels of thinking.

Each of Bloom's cognitive categories includes a list of thinking skills that indicates the kinds of behavior students are expected to demonstrate regarding the objectives or goals of specific learning tasks. Here are some examples:

- *Knowledge:* define, recognize, recall, identify, label, understand, examine, show, collect
- *Comprehension:* translate, interpret, explain, describe, summarize, extrapolate
- *Application:* apply, solve, experiment, show, predict
- *Analysis:* connect, relate, differentiate, classify, arrange, check, group, distinguish, organize, categorize, detect, compare, infer
- *Synthesis:* produce, propose, design, plan, combine, formulate, compose, hypothesize, construct
- *Evaluation:* appraise, judge, criticize, decide

Critical Thinking and Problem Solving in the *Business and Personal Finance* Program

The following are some guidelines for integrating and teaching critical thinking and problem-solving skills.

- Let students know they are engaging in aspects of critical thinking. For example, at the end of each section within the chapter are **Think Critically** questions. Explain to students that when they answer these questions, they are analyzing and evaluating information. Point out that they regularly analyze and evaluate music, conversations with friends, magazine or newspaper articles, and television programs. This will help demonstrate to students that they have had experience in using these skills.
- Use activities that focus on open-ended problems to foster greater growth for creative problem solving. Examples include **Real-World Application**, **Standard & Poor's Case Study**, and **International Finance**.
- Use assessments that measure students' growth and performance. Examples include **Apply Key Concepts**, **Using Communication Skills**, and **Problem Solving Today**.
- Provide feedback and encourage students to feel comfortable experimenting with new ideas and new ways to solve problems.

METHODOLOGY

Cooperative Learning

Introduction

Studies show that students learn faster and retain more information when they are actively involved in the learning process. Studies also show that in a classroom setting, adolescents often learn more from each other about subject matter than from a traditional teacher-led lecture and discussion. Cooperative learning is one method that gets students actively involved in learning and at the same time allows for peer teaching.

The Basic Elements of Cooperative Learning

Cooperative learning involves assigning students to small groups to work together within a classroom setting. This learning structure is especially effective for more difficult learning tasks, such as problem solving, critical thinking, and conceptual learning. The basic elements of a cooperative learning group are as follows:

- Cooperative learning emphasizes working toward group goals as opposed to the traditional emphasis on individual competition and achievement.
- Students discover that not only must they learn the material themselves, but also they are responsible for helping everyone in the group learn the material.
- The successes or failures of the group are shared by all members of the group.

The Benefits of Cooperative Learning Groups

Cooperative learning offers many benefits:

- The use of higher-level thinking skills draws students into learning situations that require them to be directly involved.
- Students discover how to work with people of all types. Schools with racially or ethnically mixed populations often improve relations among students.
- Communication skills are improved.
- Students learn to work through conflicts.
- Students learn valuable social and problem-solving skills that transfer to real-world occupations and work environments.

Cooperative Learning in this Text

In *Business and Personal Finance*, students and teachers have a variety of materials to assist with cooperative learning activities. Many of the features and section and chapter assessment activities can be completed in a cooperative learning environment:

- **Standard & Poor's Case Study** gives students an opportunity to analyze a financial situation and make decisions based on the given information. The *Critical Thinking* questions can be used for a discussion opener, brainstorming session, or classroom presentation.
- **Using Communication Skills** requires students to work together and use their communication skills to solve business and personal finance problems. When students solve these problems cooperatively, they see their peers' logic processes.
- **Solving Money Problems** presents a lifelike scenario that requires students to apply a newly presented financial concept.
- **Finance Online** can be assigned as a classroom cooperative learning activity, group activity in your media center, or interdisciplinary activity with a related course. Students will need access to the Internet.

Cooperative learning activities that are appropriate for the chapter topic are also included as annotations throughout the **Teacher Annotated Edition.**

METHODOLOGY

ADDRESSING CULTURAL DIVERSITY

Introduction

Your students are preparing to enter the "real world," an environment filled with cultural diversity. For students to become productive workers and responsible citizens, they must be open to cultural differences.

Cultural Diversity in the Program

As students learn about skills needed to manage their business and personal finances, they should keep in mind the wide diversity of the people they are likely to encounter in every aspect of their working and personal lives. In the classroom and in one-on-one conferences, you can help your students consider the diversity of the U.S. population, not only in terms of ethnicity, but also in terms of customs, attitudes, religious beliefs, language backgrounds, and physical capabilities.

The **International Finance** feature appears in each chapter. It addresses the global marketplace and gives specific insights about other cultures. You can use this feature as the basis of class discussion on cultural diversity.

During class activities, you may also find it appropriate to integrate questions related to cultural diversity, such as:

- Would your response change if a business associate or coworker were not a native speaker of English? If so, how?

- Would your decision change if a financial advisor were a male or female? From your own ethnic background? From a different background? Why?

English Language Learners (ELL)

According to the National Assessment of Educational Progress, the number of ELL students is growing two-and-a-half times as fast as the general school population. For students who are English language learners, the focus needs to be on overcoming a language barrier. In the business world and in their personal lives, these individuals will be expected to communicate effectively, both in oral and written forms.

As you help these students face the considerable challenges of mastering a new language, it is also important to value the rich cultural diversity that students bring to your classroom. Generally the best way to achieve these dual goals is to provide a variety of ways to learn the concepts of the course.

- **Support the ELL Student's Culture**
  Display photographs, articles, and objects that are familiar to your ELL students. Choose some items that relate to finance in their country.

- **Use Many Visuals and Handouts**
  Handouts and enrichment masters are valuable resources for review and exam preparation at home.

- **Incorporate Cooperative Learning**
  While it is important that each student become proficient in written and spoken English, it is also imperative for successful learning that the ELL student feels like a part of the classroom community. Constructing groups where ELL students are joined with especially helpful class members will facilitate this sense of belonging.

- **Simplify Your Language**
  Speak directly to your students and emphasize important nouns and verbs. Repetition and speaking loudly do not help; rephrasing, accompanied by body language, does. Avoid slang and idiomatic expressions.

- **Outline the Objectives**
  Announce, list, and write the lesson's objectives and activities on the board. Review them orally before the class begins. It is also helpful to place the lesson in the context of its broader theme and preview the upcoming lesson.

METHODOLOGY

MEETING INDIVIDUAL NEEDS AND LEARNING STYLES

Introduction

One of your greatest challenges as a teacher is to provide a positive learning environment for all students in your classroom. Because each student has his or her own unique set of abilities, perceptions, and needs, the learning styles and the physical abilities of your students may vary widely.

In order to help you provide all your students with a positive learning experience, this text provides a variety of activities. This diversity will stimulate student interest, motivate learning, and facilitate understanding.

How Do You Prepare?

Students in your classroom may have orthopaedic impairments. They may have hearing or vision impairments, learning disabilities, or behavior disorders—all of which may interfere with their ability to learn. The learning styles of your students may also vary. Some students may be visual learners; others may learn more effectively through hands-on activities. Some students may work well independently, while others need the interaction of others. Students may come from a variety of cultural backgrounds, and some may be English language learners.

The following process can help you develop strategies for teaching students with special needs:

1. Identify the special needs of your students.
2. Identify areas in the curriculum that may present barriers to some students.
3. Define ways to remove any impediments to their learning.
4. Modify your teaching methods to meet your students' needs.

Teaching Students with Special Needs

Once you determine the special needs of your students, you can identify the areas in the curriculum that may present barriers to them. In order to remove those barriers, you may need to modify your teaching methods.

On the following pages are two charts. The first chart, **Meeting Special Needs**, describes some of the special needs you may encounter with students in your classroom and identifies sources of information. Also provided are tips for modifying your teaching style to accommodate the special needs of your students.

The second chart, **Eight Ways of Learning**, will help you identify your students' learning styles. The chart gives a description of each type of learner; describes the likes of each type, what each type is good at, and how each learns best; and names some famous learners. Once you have identified each student's learning style, you can modify your teaching strategies to best suit his or her needs.

METHODOLOGY

MEETING SPECIAL NEEDS

SUBJECT	DESCRIPTION	SOURCES OF INFORMATION
English Language Learners	Certain students speak English as a second language, or not at all. Customs and behavior of people in the majority culture may be confusing for some of these students. Cultural values may inhibit some of these students from full participation in the classroom.	• *Teaching English as a Second Language* • *Mainstreaming and the Minority Child*
Students with Behavior Disorders	Students with behavior disorders deviate from standards or expectations of behavior and impair the functioning of others and themselves. These students may also be gifted or have learning disabilities.	• *Exceptional Children* • *Journal of Special Education*
Students with Visual Impairments	Students with visual impairments have partial or total loss of sight. Individuals with visual impairments are not significantly different from their sighted peers in ability range or personality. However, a visual impairment may affect cognitive, motor, and social development.	• *Journal of Visual Impairment and Blindness* • *Education of Visually Handicapped* • *American Foundation for the Blind*
Students with Hearing Impairments	Students with hearing impairments have partial or total loss of hearing. Individuals with hearing impairments are not significantly different from their hearing peers in ability, range, or personality. However, a chronic hearing impairment may affect cognitive, motor, social, and speech development.	• *American Annals of the Deaf* • *Journal of Speech and Hearing Research* • *Sign Language Studies*
Students with Physical Impairments	Students with physical impairments fall into two categories—those with orthopaedic impairments (use of one or more limbs severely restricted) and those with other health impairments.	• *The Source Book for the Disabled* • *Teaching Exceptional Children*
Gifted Students	Although no formal definition exists, these students can be described as having above average ability, task commitment, and creativity. They rank in the top five percent of their classes. They usually finish work more quickly than other students and are capable of divergent thinking.	• *Journal for the Education of the Gifted* • *Gifted Child Quarterly* • *Gifted Creative/Talented*
Students with Learning Disabilities	Students with learning disabilities have a problem in one or more areas, such as academic learning, language, perception, social-emotional adjustment, memory, or ability to pay attention.	• *Journal of Learning Disabilities* • *Learning Disability Quarterly*

METHODOLOGY

TIPS FOR INSTRUCTION

- Remember that students' ability to speak English does not reflect their academic ability.
- Try to incorporate students' cultural experiences into your instruction. The help of a bilingual aide may be effective.
- Include information about different cultures in your curriculum to help build students' self-image.
- Avoid cultural stereotypes.
- Encourage students to share their cultures in the classroom.

- Work for long-term improvement; do not expect immediate success.
- Talk with students about their strengths and weaknesses, and clearly outline objectives.
- Structure schedules, rules, room arrangement, and safety for a conducive learning environment.
- Model appropriate behavior for students and reinforce proper behavior.

- Modify assignments as needed to help students become independent.
- Teach classmates how to serve as guides for students with visual impairments.
- Tape lectures and reading assignments for students with visual impairments.
- Encourage students to use their sense of touch; provide tactile models whenever possible.
- Verbally describe people and events as they occur in the classroom.

- Limit unnecessary noise in the classroom.
- Provide a favorable seating arrangement so students with hearing impairments can see speakers and read their lips (or interpreters can assist); avoid visual distractions.
- Write out all instructions on paper or on the board; overhead projectors enable you to maintain eye contact while writing.
- Avoid standing with your back to the window or light source.

- With the student, determine when you should offer aid.
- Help other students and adults understand students with physical impairments.
- Learn about special devices or procedures and if any special safety precautions are needed.
- Allow students to participate in all activities including field trips, special events, and projects.

- Emphasize concepts, theories, relationships, ideas, and generalizations.
- Let students express themselves in a variety of ways including drawing, creative writing, or acting.
- Make arrangements for students to work on independent projects.
- Make arrangements for students to take selected subjects early.

- Provide assistance and direction; clearly define rules, assignments, and duties.
- Allow for pair interaction during class time; utilize peer helpers.
- Practice skills frequently.
- Allow extra time to complete tests and assignments.

METHODOLOGY

EIGHT WAYS OF LEARNING

	DESCRIPTION	LIKES TO…
Verbal/Linguistic Learner	Intelligence is related to words and language, written and spoken.	read, write, tell stories, play word games, and tell jokes and riddles.
Logical/Mathematical Learner	Intelligence deals with inductive and deductive thinking and reasoning, numbers, and abstractions.	perform experiments, solve puzzles, work with numbers, ask questions, and explore patterns and relationships.
Visual/Spatial Learner	Intelligence relies on the sense of sight and being able to visualize an object, including the ability to create mental images.	draw, build, design, and create things; do jigsaw puzzles and mazes; watch videos; look at photos; and draw maps and charts.
Naturalistic Learner	Intelligence has to do with observing, understanding, and organizing patterns in the natural environment.	spend time outdoors and work with plants, animals, and other parts of the natural environment; good at identifying plants and animals and at hearing and seeing connections to nature.
Musical/Rhythmic Learner	Intelligence is based on recognition of tonal patterns, including various environmental sounds, and on a sensitivity to rhythm and beats.	sing and hum, listen to music, play an instrument, move body when music is playing, and make up songs.
Bodily/Kinesthetic Learner	Intelligence is related to physical movement and the brain's motor cortex, which controls bodily motion.	learn by hands-on methods, demonstrate skill in crafts, tinker, perform, display physical endurance, and challenge self physically.
Interpersonal Learner	Intelligence operates primarily through person-to-person relationships and communication.	have lots of friends, talk to people, join groups, play cooperative games, solve problems as part of a group, and volunteer help when others need it.
Intrapersonal Learner	Intelligence is related to inner states of being, self-reflection, metacognition, and awareness of spiritual realities.	work alone, pursue own interests, daydream, keep a personal diary or journal, and think about starting own business.

METHODOLOGY

IS GOOD AT…	LEARNS BEST BY…	FAMOUS LEARNERS
memorizing names, dates, places, and trivia; spelling; using descriptive language; and creating imaginary worlds.	saying, hearing, and seeing words.	Maya Angelou—poet Abraham Lincoln—U.S. President and statesman Jerry Seinfeld—comedian Mary Hatwood Futrell—international teacher, leader, orator
math, reasoning, logic, problem solving, computing numbers, moving from concrete to abstract, thinking conceptually.	categorizing, classifying, and working with abstract patterns and relationships.	Stephen Hawking—physicist Albert Einstein—theoretical physicist Marilyn Burns—math educator Alexa Canady—neurosurgeon
understanding the use of space and how to get around in it, thinking in three-dimensional terms, and imagining things in clear visual images.	visualizing, dreaming, using the mind's eye, and working with colors and pictures.	Pablo Picasso—artist Maria Martinez—Pueblo Indian famous for black pottery Faith Ringgold—painter, quilter, and writer I. M. Pei—architect
measuring, charting, mapping, observing plants and animals, keeping journals, collecting, classifying, participating in outdoor activities.	visualizing, hands-on activities, bringing outdoors into the classroom, relating home/classroom to the natural world.	George Washington Carver—agricultural chemist Rachel Carson—scientific writer Charles Darwin—evolutionist John James Audubon—conservationist
remembering melodies; keeping time; mimicking beat and rhythm; noticing pitches, rhythms, and background and environmental sounds.	rhythm, melody, and music.	Henry Mancini—composer Marian Anderson—contralto Daniel Heifetz—violinist Paul McCartney—singer, song writer, musician
physical activities such as sports, dancing, acting, and crafts.	touching, moving, interacting with space, and processing knowledge through bodily sensations.	Marcel Marceau—mime Jackie Joyner-Kersey—Olympic gold medalist in track and field Katherine Dunham—modern dancer Dr. Christian Bernard—cardiac surgeon
understanding people and their feelings, leading others, organizing, communicating, manipulating, mediating conflicts.	sharing, comparing, relating, cooperating, and interviewing.	Jimmy Carter—U.S. President and statesman Eleanor Roosevelt—former first Lady Lee Iacocca—president of Chrysler Corporation Mother Teresa—winner of Nobel Peace Prize
understanding self, focusing inward on feelings/dreams, following instincts, pursuing interests, and being original.	working alone, doing individualized projects, engaging in self-paced instruction.	Marva Collins—educator Maria Montessori—educator and physician Sigmund Freud—psychotherapist Anne Sexton—poet

PROFESSIONAL NOTES

NO CHILD LEFT BEHIND

The No Child Left Behind Act of 2001, signed into law by President George W. Bush, marks a sweeping reform of the federal government's efforts to improve elementary and secondary education in the United States. Enacted in response to concerns that "too many of our neediest children are being left behind" and described by President Bush as "the cornerstone of my administration," the Act is built upon four fundamental principles:

- Making districts, schools, and teachers more accountable for results
- Emphasizing doing what works based on scientific research
- Expanding parents' options for their children's education
- Increasing local control and flexibility with regard to using federal funds

Crucial to achieving these objectives is an increased emphasis on standardized testing. The following chart illustrates how components in the *Business and Personal Finance* textbook correspond to academic disciplines addressed by standardized tests. Two examples of each component are cited for easy reference. Note that page citations are not exhaustive and are intended to provide only selected instances of each component.

ACADEMIC AREA	COMPONENT	BENEFITS	REFERENCES
English and Language Arts	Reading Strategies	Leads students to become active and effective readers by using a four-step process: Predict, Connect, Question, Respond.	2, 188
	Understanding and Using Vocabulary	Reinforces key terms by giving students opportunities to apply the terms in various contexts.	28, 440
	Using Communication Skills	Requires students to communicate using various methods including essays, letters, speeches, group discussions, and role-plays.	163, 229
	Check Your Understanding	Helps students to relate each section's content to concepts previewed in "What You'll Learn."	193, 326
	Think Critically	Leads students to apply concepts to situations outside the scope of the textbook. Questions require oral or written answers.	113, 515
	Standard & Poor's Case Study	Spotlights a hypothetical scenario relevant to the lives of today's students. Critical thinking questions round out each case study.	103, 392
	Review Key Concepts	Strengthens understanding with questions that require oral or written answers.	56, 408
	Apply Key Concepts	Leads students to relate chapter material to their personal lives.	114, 475
	Real-World Application	Requires students to solve problems using connections to language arts, math, and social studies.	57, 373
	Academic Connection	Helps students to link finance topics to other disciplines. Each feature includes a related student activity.	14, 109

Professional Notes

ACADEMIC AREA	COMPONENT	BENEFITS	REFERENCES
Mathematics	Math Skills Builder	Reviews math concepts in a 32-page appendix. The exercises can be used as practice problems.	722, 753
	Using Math Skills	Reinforces skills by applying mathematical processes to a variety of finance problems.	179, 193
	Go Figure…	Presents students with relevant math formulas that illustrate a step-by-step approach to solving problems.	101, 329
	Your Financial Portfolio	Presents financial situations in which students must use a rational decision-making process. Calculating costs and analyzing financial activities require students to think critically about real-life financial issues.	266, 406
	Real-World Application	Requires students to solve problems using connections to language arts, math, and social studies.	571, 719
	Academic Connection	Helps students to link finance topics to other disciplines. Each feature includes a related student activity.	37, 172
Technology	Finance Online	Strengthens students' Internet research skills with relevant, practical activities.	231, 349
	Problem Solving Today	Requires students to use writing, teamwork, role-playing, and other skills to solve real-world financial problems. Activities include an optional Internet or other technology component.	29, 475
	Business and Personal Finance Web site in chapter opener	Directs students to Web support, activities, and other online resources.	196, 378
Social Studies	International Finance	Showcases a diversity of countries' economies and contributions to the global marketplace. A critical thinking activity accompanies each feature.	34, 243
	Careers in Finance	Highlights a variety of career opportunities in finance. Each feature includes a related research activity.	10, 110
	Get a Financial Life!	Provides in-depth financial research and teamwork projects in which students use a variety of resources and procedures to solve problems.	116, 232
	Real-World Application	Requires students to solve problems using connections to language arts, math, and social studies.	115, 231
	Academic Connection	Helps students to link finance topics to other disciplines. Each feature includes a related student activity.	37, 172

Teacher Manual

PROFESSIONAL NOTES

National Standards for Business Education

The National Business Education Association (NBEA) has developed curriculum standards based on a developmental approach. The high-school-level competencies have been integrated into Glencoe's *Business & Personal Finance* program. They are listed in the Planning Guide for each chapter in the *Teacher Manual* section of the **Teacher Annotated Edition**, as well as in the chart below.

National Standards for Business Education	Chapters/Sections
ECONOMICS STANDARDS	
I. Allocation of Resources *Assess opportunity costs and trade-offs involved in making choices about how to use scarce economic resources.*	1.1, 1.2, 2.1, 3.1, 4.1, 5.1, 5.2, 6.2, 6.4, 7.1, 7.2, 7.3, 8.1, 8.2, 9.2, 10.1, 10.5, 11.1, 11.2, 12.1, 12.3, 13.2, 14.1, 15.4, 19.1
II. Economic Systems *Explain why societies develop economic systems, identify the basic features of different economic systems, and analyze the major features of the U.S. economic system.*	1.1, 2.1, 4.1, 5.2, 9.2, 11.1, 11.2, 12.1, 12.3, 14.1, 17.1, 21.1
III. Economic Institutions and Incentives *Analyze the role of core economic institutions and incentives in the U.S. economy.*	1.1, 2.1, 2.2, 3.1, 4.1, 4.2, 5.1, 5.2, 6.1, 6.2, 6.3, 6.4, 8.1, 9.2, 10.2, 11.1, 11.2, 12.1, 12.3, 13.3, 14.4, 15.1, 15.2, 15.3, 15.4, 16.1, 16.2, 17.1, 17.2, 19.1, 22.2
IV. Markets and Prices *Analyze the role of markets and prices in the U.S. economy.*	1.1, 22.1
V. Market Structures *Analyze the different types of market structures and the effect they have on the price and the quality of the goods and services produced.*	1.1, 2.1, 8.2, 9.2, 11.1, 11.2, 22.1
VI. Productivity *Explain the importance of productivity and analyze how specialization, division of labor, investment in physical and human capital, and technological change affect productivity.*	16.2, 19.2, 21.1, 22.1
VII. The Role of Government *Analyze the role of government in economic systems, especially the role of government in the U.S. economy.*	1.1, 5.1, 6.1, 7.3, 9.3, 10.2, 11.1, 12.1, 12.2, 12.3, 14.2, 14.3, 15.1, 15.2, 15.3, 15.4, 18.1, 20.2
VIII. International Economic Concepts *Examine the role of trade, protectionism, and monetary markets in the global economy.*	1.2, 2.1, 3.3, 4.2, 5.2, 6.4, 7.3, 8.1, 9.2, 10.2, 11.2, 12.3, 13.3, 14.4, 15.3, 16.2, 17.2, 18.2, 19.2, 20.2, 21.2, 22.2
IX. Aggregate Supply and Aggregate Demand *Analyze how the U.S. economy functions as a whole and describe selected macroeconomic measures of economic activity.*	1.1, 2.1, 3.3, 8.1

PROFESSIONAL NOTES

Excerpted from *National Standards for Business Education*, copyright © 2001 by National Business Education Association, 1914 Association Dr., Reston VA 21901-1596

National Standards for Business Education	Chapters/Sections
PERSONAL FINANCE STANDARDS	
I. Personal Decision Making Use a rational decision-making process as it applies to the roles of citizens, workers, and consumers.	1.1, 1.2, 2.1, 2.2, 3.1, 3.2, 3.3, 4.1, 5.1, 5.2, 6.1, 6.2, 6.4, 7.1, 7.2, 7.3, 8.1, 8.2, 8.3, 9.2, 9.3, 10.1, 10.2, 10.3, 10.5, 11.1, 11.2, 12.1, 12.3, 13.1, 13.3, 14.1, 14.2, 14.4, 15.1, 15.2, 15.3, 15.4, 16.1, 16.2, 17.1, 20.1, 20.2, 22.2
II. Earning a Living Identify various forms of income and analyze factors that affect income as a part of the career decision-making process.	1.1, 1.2, 2.1, 2.2, 3.2, 5.1, 5.2, 7.1, 7.3, 8.1, 8.2, 8.3, 9.1, 9.2, 9.3, 10.1, 10.2, 10.3, 10.4, 10.5, 11.1, 11.2, 12.1, 12.2, 12.3, 14.1, 15.2, 15.3, 15.4, 16.1, 16.2, 17.1, 17.2, 18.1, 18.2, 19.2, 20.1, 20.2, 21.2, 22.1, 22.2
III. Managing Finances and Budgeting Develop and evaluate a spending/savings plan.	1.1, 1.2, 2.2, 3.2, 3.3, 4.1, 5.1, 5.2, 6.1, 6.2, 6.3, 6.4, 7.1, 7.2, 7.3, 14.4, 15.1, 15.2, 15.3
IV. Saving and Investing Evaluate savings and investment options to meet short- and long-term goals.	1.1, 1.2, 2.2, 5.1, 5.2, 8.1, 8.2, 8.3, 9.1, 9.2, 9.3, 10.1, 10.2, 10.3, 10.4, 10.5, 11.1, 11.2, 12.3, 14.4, 15.1, 15.2, 16.2, 17.1, 20.2
V. Buying Goods and Services Apply a decision-making model to maximize consumer satisfaction when buying goods and services.	1.1, 4.1, 4.2, 5.1, 6.1, 6.2, 6.3, 7.1, 7.2, 7.3, 11.1, 11.2, 12.2, 12.3, 14.2
VI. Banking Evaluate services provided by financial deposit institutions to transfer funds.	5.1, 5.2, 6.3, 11.2, 19.1, 20.1, 21.1
VII. Using Credit Analyze factors that affect the choice of credit, the cost of credit, and the legal aspects of using credit.	1.2, 5.1, 6.1, 6.2, 6.3, 6.4, 7.3, 16.1, 17.1, 17.2, 21.2
VIII. Protecting Against Risk Analyze choices available to consumers for protection against risk and financial loss.	2.2, 3.1, 5.1, 5.2, 7.1, 7.3, 13.1, 13.2, 13.3, 14.1, 14.2, 14.3, 14.4, 17.1, 18.2, 21.1

PROFESSIONAL NOTES

National Standards for Business Education	Business and Personal Finance Ancillaries	
	Student Activity Workbook	Standard & Poor's Extension Activities
ECONOMICS STANDARDS		
I. Allocation of Resources Assess opportunity costs and trade-offs involved in making choices about how to use scarce economic resources.	1, 2, 4, 5, 6, 7, 8, 9, 10, 11, 12, 13, 14, 15	2, 3, 4, 5, 6, 9, 14, 16, 17, 19, 20
II. Economic Systems Explain why societies develop economic systems, identify the basic features of different economic systems, and analyze the major features of the U.S. economic system.	11, 22	20, 22
III. Economic Institutions and Incentives Analyze the role of core economic institutions and incentives in the U.S. economy.	1, 2, 4, 5, 7, 8, 9, 10, 11, 12, 14, 15, 16, 17, 18, 19, 22	2, 5, 11, 12, 16, 17, 20, 21, 22
IV. Markets and Prices Analyze the role of markets and prices in the U.S. economy.	9, 22	4, 16, 21
V. Market Structures Analyze the different types of market structures and the effect they have on the price and the quality of the goods and services provided.	7, 22	
VI. Productivity Explain the importance of productivity and analyze how specialization, division of labor, investment in physical and human capital, and technological change affect productivity.	21, 22	
VII. The Role of Government Analyze the role of government in economic systems, especially the role of government in the U.S. economy.	6, 10, 11, 12, 13, 14, 15, 18, 19, 20	2, 5, 8, 11, 12, 13, 15, 16, 19, 21, 22
VIII. International Economic Concepts Examine the role of trade, protectionism, and monetary markets in the global economy.	11, 18	
IX. Aggregate Supply and Aggregate Demand Analyze how the U.S. economy functions as a whole and describe selected macroeconomic measures of economic activity.	2, 3, 11	

PROFESSIONAL NOTES

Business and Personal Finance Ancillaries

Your Personal Financial Planner	Teacher Resource Binder		
	Internet Resources	Reproducible Tests	Blackline Masters
	7, 8, 10, 19	1, 2, 3, 4, 5, 6, 8, 9, 10, 14, 16	1, 4, 5, 6, 7, 19
	12, 14, 15		1, 2
1, 5, 7, 8, 12, 13, 14, 15	1, 2, 4, 7, 8, 9, 10, 11, 12, 13, 14, 15, 16, 17, 19, 20, 21	1, 2, 5, 6, 8, 9, 10, 11, 12, 13, 16, 18, 19, 20, 21, 22	1, 4, 6, 16
4		4, 22	
			1, 11, 22
		3, 21, 22	19, 21
	4, 6, 7, 10, 12, 14, 15, 16, 19, 20	1, 2, 4, 6, 7, 8, 10, 11, 12, 13, 14, 15, 17, 19, 20	1, 7, 12
		2	1, 8

Teacher Manual

TM39

Professional Notes

National Standards for Business Education	Business and Personal Finance Ancillaries	
	Student Activity Workbook	Standard & Poor's Extension Activities
PERSONAL FINANCE STANDARDS		
I. Personal Decision Making Use a rational decision-making process as it applies to the roles of citizens, workers, and consumers.	1, 2, 4, 5, 6, 7, 8, 9, 10, 11, 13, 14, 15, 16, 17	2, 7, 9, 11, 14, 15, 16, 17, 18, 19, 20, 22
II. Earning a Living Identify various forms of income and analyze factors that affect income as a part of the career decision-making process.	1, 2, 3, 5, 7, 8, 9, 10, 11, 12, 14, 15, 16, 17, 18, 19, 20, 21, 22	1, 2, 15, 18, 19
III. Managing Finances and Budgeting Develop and evaluate a spending/savings plan.	3, 5, 7, 9, 10, 11, 12, 14, 15, 16	2, 3, 20
IV. Saving and Investing Evaluate savings and investment options to meet short- and long-term goals.	1, 5, 8, 9, 10, 11, 12, 15	1, 5, 8, 9, 10, 11, 15, 18, 19
V. Buying Goods and Services Apply a decision-making model to maximize consumer satisfaction when buying goods and services.	4, 6, 7, 12	5, 9, 12, 14, 15, 16, 17, 22
VI. Banking Evaluate services provided by financial deposit institutions to transfer funds.	5, 6	10
VII. Using Credit Analyze factors that affect the choice of credit, the cost of credit, and the legal aspects of using credit.	1, 4, 5, 6, 7, 11, 16, 17	2, 3, 6, 7, 17
VIII. Protecting Against Risk Analyze choices available to consumers for protection against risk and financial loss.	2, 3, 5, 7, 11, 13, 14, 17, 18, 19, 21	8, 13, 14, 16

Professional Notes

Business and Personal Finance Ancillaries

Your Personal Financial Planner	Teacher Resource Binder		
	Internet Resources	Reproducible Tests	Blackline Masters
1, 4, 7	7, 8, 10, 19	1, 2, 3, 4, 6, 8, 9, 10, 11, 14, 16	1, 2, 4, 6, 7, 11, 14, 15, 16, 17, 20, 22
2, 12	1, 2, 8, 9, 10, 11, 12, 16, 17, 19, 20	2, 5, 9, 14, 20	1, 2, 3, 7, 12, 15, 16, 17, 18, 19, 20, 21
3, 4, 5, 6, 7, 9, 11, 12, 13, 14, 15	1, 2, 3, 8, 9, 10, 11, 16, 17, 19	1, 2, 3, 5, 8, 9, 10, 11, 16, 18, 19, 20	1, 4, 7, 15
1, 3, 5, 8, 9, 10, 15	1, 8, 9, 10, 11, 14	1, 5, 8, 9, 10, 11, 15	1, 8, 9, 12, 15, 17
4, 5, 6, 7, 11, 12, 13, 14, 15	3, 4, 5, 6, 7, 9, 11	4, 6, 7, 14	4, 6, 7, 14
5	5, 6	5	5, 6
1, 4, 6, 7	6	6, 7, 17, 18	1, 6, 17
1, 2, 13, 14	13, 14	5, 7, 13, 14, 15, 19	3, 7, 13, 14

TM41

Professional Notes

SCANS and Business and Personal Finance

In 1991 the U.S. Department of Labor released a report titled "What Work Requires of Schools: A SCANS Report for America 2000," identifying five competencies that lie at the heart of job performance and are needed by all workers in order to prosper in the emerging workplace. Incorporating real-world relevancy, these skills and competencies have been integrated throughout the *Business and Personal Finance* program.

THE FOUNDATION	ACTIVITY CORRELATION	
Basic Skills—reading, writing, math, listening, and speaking. **CHAPTER CORRELATION** Chapters 1–22	**Using Communication Skills** *Writing*—Chapters 6, 9, 10, 11, 13, 15, 16, 18, 22 *Listening*—Chapters 1, 2, 4, 8, 12, 14, 19 *Speaking*—Chapters 1, 2, 4, 7, 8, 12, 13, 14, 15, 19 **Using Math Skills** *Math*—Chapters 1–22 **Think Critically** *Writing*—Chapter 7 **Solving Money Problems** *Reading*—Chapters 5, 7 **Careers in Finance** *Reading*—Chapters 2, 15, 22 *Listening*—Chapters 5, 7 *Speaking*—Chapter 5 **Academic Connection** *Writing*—Chapters 1, 4, 8, 14, 17 *Reading*—Chapters 4, 10, 14 *Math*—Chapters 5, 18 **International Finance** *Reading*—Chapter 18	**Your Financial Portfolio** *Math*—Chapters 1, 3, 4 *Writing*—Chapter 2 *Reading*—Chapters 6, 12 *Speaking*—Chapter 20 *Listening*—Chapter 20 **Understanding and Using Vocabulary** *Writing*—Chapters 3, 4, 5, 7, 10, 12, 20, 21 *Speaking*—Chapters 6, 9, 13, 15, 18 *Listening*—Chapters 6, 9, 13, 15, 18 *Reading*—Chapter 17 **Problem Solving Today** *Reading*—Chapter 11 *Writing*—Chapter 19 **Real-World Application** *Reading*—Chapters 3, 8, 20, 21 *Speaking*—Chapter 11 *Listening*—Chapter 11
THE FOUNDATION	**ACTIVITY CORRELATION**	
Thinking Skills—creative thinking, decision making, problem solving, seeing things in the mind's eye, knowing how to learn, and reasoning. **CHAPTER CORRELATION** Chapters 1–22	**Think Critically** *Reasoning*—Chapters 1–22 *Creative Thinking*—Chapters 4, 9, 14 *Seeing Things in the Mind's Eye*—Chapters 5, 11, 14 *Decision Making*—Chapters 6, 7, 8 **Using Communication Skills** *Creative Thinking*—Chapters 3, 5, 10, 11, 15, 20 *Seeing Things in the Mind's Eye*—Chapters 10, 15 *Decision Making*—Chapter 2	**Solving Money Problems** *Problem Solving*—Chapters 1–22 *Decision Making*—Chapters 3, 4, 5, 7, 10, 14, 17, 19 **What's Your Financial ID?** *Seeing Things in the Mind's Eye*—Chapters 3, 20 **Careers in Finance** *Seeing Things in the Mind's Eye*—Chapters 12, 22 *Creative Thinking*—Chapter 22 (continued on next page)

Professional Notes

THE FOUNDATION	ACTIVITY CORRELATION	
	S & P's Case Study *Decision Making*—Chapters 1, 9, 15 *Creative Thinking*—Chapter 3 **Academic Connection** *Creative Thinking*—Chapters 1, 7, 8, 16, 17 *Seeing Things in the Mind's Eye*—Chapters 1, 7, 16, 17 *Decision Making*—Chapter 5 **International Finance** *Creative Thinking*—Chapters 13, 21 *Seeing Things in the Mind's Eye*—Chapter 13 **Your Financial Portfolio** *Decision Making*—Chapters 5, 13, 16, 18, 20 *Seeing Things in the Mind's Eye*—Chapters 8, 18 *Creative Thinking*—Chapter 18 **Caption Questions** *Decision Making*—Chapter 2 *Seeing Things in the Mind's Eye*—Chapters 19, 21 *Creative Thinking*—Chapter 19	**Reading Strategies** *Creative Thinking*—Chapter 2 *Seeing Things in the Mind's Eye*—Chapter 2 *Decision Making*—Chapter 22 **Understanding and Using Vocabulary** *Seeing Things in the Mind's Eye*—Chapter 6 **Problem Solving Today** *Problem Solving*—Chapters 1–22 *Creative Thinking*—Chapter 7 *Seeing Things in the Mind's Eye*—Chapter 7 *Decision Making*—Chapter 11 **Real-World Application** *Creative Thinking*—Chapter 6

THE FOUNDATION	ACTIVITY CORRELATION	
Personal Qualities—responsibility, self-esteem, sociability, self-management, integrity, and honesty. **CHAPTER CORRELATION** Chapters 1–22	**Using Communication Skills** *Sociability*—Chapters 2, 4, 8, 12, 13, 14, 19 **Solving Money Problems** *Sociability*—Chapters 5, 7, 17 **What's Your Financial ID?** *Self-Management*—Chapters 2, 3, 6, 7, 8, 15, 16, 17, 18, 20, 21, 22 *Responsibility*—Chapters 3, 6 **Savvy Saver** *Self-Management*—Chapters 11, 14 *Responsibility*—Chapters 14, 15, 18 **Careers in Finance** *Integrity and Honesty*—Chapter 9 **S & P's Case Study** *Responsibility*—Chapter 12 *Self-Management*—Chapter 12 *Integrity and Honesty*—Chapter 12	**Academic Connection** *Sociability*—Chapters 9, 16 **Common Cents** *Responsibility*—Chapters 7, 10, 17, 21 *Self-Management*—Chapter 10 **Your Financial Portfolio** *Self-Management*—Chapter 4 *Sociability*—Chapter 20 **Caption Questions** *Self-Management*—Chapters 5, 9, 13 *Responsibility*—Chapters 9, 13 **Understanding and Using Vocabulary** *Sociability*—Chapters 6, 15, 18

Professional Notes

WORKPLACE COMPETENCIES

Resources—allocating time, allocating money, allocating material and facility resources, and allocating human resources.

CHAPTER CORRELATION

Chapters 1–22

ACTIVITY CORRELATION

Thinking Critically
Allocating Money—Chapter 17

Solving Money Problems
Allocating Money—Chapters 19, 20
Allocating Human Resources—Chapter 19

S & P's Case Study
Allocating Money—Chapters 1, 7, 21
Allocating Material and Facility Resources—Chapter 21

Savvy Saver
Allocating Money—Chapter 2

Careers in Finance
Allocating Money—Chapters 6, 22

Common Cents
Allocating Money—Chapters 12, 16
Allocating Time—Chapters 15, 20

Your Financial Portfolio
Allocating Money—Chapters 4, 9, 13, 14, 18
Allocating Human Resources—Chapter 18

Caption Questions
Allocating Time—Chapter 1
Allocating Money—Chapters 3, 5, 8, 10, 15

Reading Strategies
Allocating Human Resources—Chapter 22

Problem Solving Today
Allocating Time—Chapter 3
Allocating Money—Chapter 11
Allocating Human Resources—Chapter 20

WORKPLACE COMPETENCIES

Interpersonal Skills—participating as a member of a team, teaching others, serving clients and customers, exercising leadership, negotiating to arrive at a decision, and working with cultural diversity.

CHAPTER CORRELATION

Chapters 1–22

ACTIVITY CORRELATION

Using Communication Skills
Participating as a Member of a Team—Chapters 2, 4, 8, 12, 13, 14, 19
Teaching Others—Chapters 3, 17, 18, 20
Exercising Leadership—Chapter 13
Negotiating to Arrive at a Decision—Chapter 21

Using Math Skills
Teaching Others—Chapter 10

Think Critically
Teaching Others—Chapters 8, 9

Solving Money Problems
Teaching Others—Chapters 1, 6, 7, 11, 12, 14, 15, 19
Negotiating to Arrive at a Decision—Chapters 1, 5, 17
Participating as a Member of a Team—Chapters 5, 7, 17

Academic Connection
Participating as a Member of a Team—Chapters 9, 16
Teaching Others—Chapter 22

Your Financial Portfolio
Participating as a Member of a Team—Chapter 20
Negotiating to Arrive at a Decision—Chapter 20

Caption Questions
Working with Cultural Diversity—Chapter 10

Understanding and Using Vocabulary
Participating as a Member of a Team—Chapters 6, 15, 18
Exercising Leadership—Chapter 18

Professional Notes

WORKPLACE COMPETENCIES	ACTIVITY CORRELATION	
Information—acquiring and evaluating information, organizing and maintaining information, interpreting and communicating information, and using computers to process information.	**Using Communication Skills** *Interpreting and Communicating Information*—Chapters 7, 14 *Organizing and Maintaining Information*—Chapter 10 **Solving Money Problems** *Interpreting and Communicating Information*—Chapters 4, 9, 18 *Organizing and Maintaining Information*—Chapters 7, 15, 16 **S & P's Case Study** *Organizing and Maintaining Information*—Chapter 18 **Academic Connection** *Organizing and Maintaining Information*—Chapters 8, 9 *Interpreting and Communicating Information*—Chapters 8, 10 **Your Financial Portfolio** *Organizing and Maintaining Information*—Chapters 2, 17 *Interpreting and Communicating Information*—Chapters 6, 12, 13	**Caption Questions** *Organizing and Maintaining Information*—Chapters 4, 13 **Reading Strategies** *Organizing and Maintaining Information*—Chapters 3, 12 **Problem Solving Today** *Interpreting and Communicating Information*—Chapters 15, 16 *Organizing and Maintaining Information*—Chapter 19 **Real-World Application** *Interpreting and Communicating Information*—Chapter 11 **Finance Online** *Using Computers to Process Information*—Chapters 1–22 *Acquiring and Evaluating Information*—Chapters 1–22 *Organizing and Maintaining Information*—Chapter 21
CHAPTER CORRELATION Chapters 1–22		

WORKPLACE COMPETENCIES	ACTIVITY CORRELATION	
Systems—understanding systems, monitoring and correcting performance, and improving and designing systems.	**Using Communication Skills** *Monitoring and Correcting Performance*—Chapter 19 **Solving Money Problems** *Understanding Systems*—Chapter 19	**Problem Solving Today** *Improving and Designing Systems*—Chapter 19
CHAPTER CORRELATION Chapters 19		

WORKPLACE COMPETENCIES	ACTIVITY CORRELATION	
Technology—selecting technology, applying technology to task, maintaining and troubleshooting technology.	**Academic Connection** *Selecting Technology*—Chapters 7, 10 **Your Financial Portfolio** *Selecting Technology*—Chapters 13, 14	**Problem Solving Today** *Selecting Technology*—Chapter 11 **Finance Online** *Applying Technology to Task*—Chapters 1–22
CHAPTER CORRELATION Chapters 1–22		

PROFESSIONAL NOTES

RESOURCES FOR NEW DIRECTIONS

Academies

Business academies are typically "schools within schools." Students learn school-to-work skills through the collaboration of community businesses, local higher education institutions, and motivated teachers. Students admitted to the academy might engage in field trips, job shadowing, mentoring, and internships as part of their course work. They not only take industry-specific courses like travel and tourism, finance, and information technology, but they must also pass the usual state curriculum for graduation.

Academies attract students by offering preparation for higher education, post-high school career themes, professional development, and community partnerships. Students join a cadre of peers with similar interests and excel at their studies. By adopting what is of interest to them—job placement after high school and business technology—they are entering the world of work armed with skills to understand all aspects of the selected industry.

Each business academy may vary in focus and in core competencies. Generally, assessment occurs in the same methods as in English and language arts, mathematics, science, and social studies. The academy faculty might measure students on portfolios, project-based activities, or scores on tests.

The National Academy Foundation (NAF) operates academies in various career themes, including finance. To learn about the Academy of Finance, visit **www.naf.org**.

Exit Exams

Each state approaches the high school exit examination differently. Some states have implemented it, some have delayed it, and some have ignored it. By 2008, at least 24 states will have an exit exam requirement in place. Public concern about students' low performance and failing schools has prompted state policymakers to endorse the high-stakes testing.

The Center on Education Policy (CEP) reports that multiple-choice items are the predominant type of question on state exit exams, followed by short answers and writing prompts. A writing prompt requires the student to write an essay, letter, or other written product. Recent exit exams have included extended response items.

In order for your students to become successful test takers, they need experience in different assessment methods. Glencoe's *Business and Personal Finance* program offers a variety of assessment options.

For more information on exit exams, visit the High School Exit Examination section of the Center on Education Policy Web site at **www.ctredpol.org**.

PROFESSIONAL NOTES

BLOCK SCHEDULING

In most high schools across the United States, the typical school day is made up of six, seven, or eight class periods of 40 to 50 minutes, which meet 180 days a year.

In block scheduling, class sessions are scheduled for longer periods of time over fewer days. For example, a school day of block scheduling might consist of four blocks of 90-minute sessions that run for 90 days, or half a school year.

In the following planning guide for *Business and Personal Finance*, to the right of each unit title is the suggested total number of days for that unit, based on a 90-minute class period. The suggested number is the sum of the days estimated to teach each chapter in that unit.

This schedule provides for the presentation of the following components:

- end-of-chapter activities
- features
- activities from the **Teacher Annotated Edition**
- activities in the **Student Activity Workbook**
- **Unit Tests**
- **Chapter Tests**

Optional activities enhance the chapter but will require more time than given here for each chapter. Typically, optional activities take from one-third to one-half a day each. You may wish to include these optional activities if you find you have some extra time:

- **Standard & Poor's Extension Activities**
- **Your Personal Financial Planner**
- **Internet Resources**
- **Financial Planner Software**
- **Money Matters: Personal and Family Financial Management Simulation**
- *Business and Personal Finance* Web site

UNIT/CHAPTER	DAYS
Unit 1 Planning Personal Finances	**16**
Chapter 1 Personal Financial Planning	4
Chapter 2 Financial Aspects of Career Planning	4
Chapter 3 Money Management Strategy	4
Chapter 4 Consumer Purchasing Strategies and Legal Protection	4
Unit 2 Banking and Credit	**13**
Chapter 5 Banking	4
Chapter 6 Consumer Credit	4
Chapter 7 The Finances of Housing	5
Unit 3 Investing Your Financial Resources	**16**
Chapter 8 The Fundamentals of Investing	4
Chapter 9 Stocks	4
Chapter 10 Bonds and Mutual Funds	4
Chapter 11 Real Estate and Other Investment Alternatives	4

UNIT/CHAPTER	DAYS
Unit 4 Protecting Your Finances	**16**
Chapter 12 Planning Your Tax Strategy	4
Chapter 13 Home and Motor Vehicle Insurance	4
Chapter 14 Health, Disability, and Life Insurance	4
Chapter 15 Retirement and Estate Planning	4
Unit 5 Introduction to Business Finance	**16**
Chapter 16 Introduction to Financial Management for Business	4
Chapter 17 Sources of Funding	4
Chapter 18 Financial Accounting	4
Chapter 19 Managing Payroll and Inventory	4
Unit 6 Organization and Financial Planning	**13**
Chapter 20 Types of Business Ownership	4
Chapter 21 Developing a Financial Plan	4
Chapter 22 Pricing, Costing, and Growth	5

Professional Notes

Course Planning Guide

FULL-YEAR COURSE SCHEDULE SIX-WEEK GRADING SYSTEM

GRADING PERIOD	CHAPTER	CHAPTER TITLE
First	**Unit 1**	**Planning Personal Finances**
	Chapter 1	Personal Financial Planning
	Chapter 2	Financial Aspects of Career Planning
	Chapter 3	Money Management Strategy
	Chapter 4	Consumer Purchasing Strategies and Legal Protection
Second	**Unit 2**	**Banking and Credit**
	Chapter 5	Banking
	Chapter 6	Consumer Credit
	Chapter 7	The Finances of Housing
Third	**Unit 3**	**Investing Your Financial Resources**
	Chapter 8	The Fundamentals of Investing
	Chapter 9	Stocks
	Chapter 10	Bonds and Mutual Funds
	Chapter 11	Real Estate and Other Investment Alternatives
Fourth	**Unit 4**	**Protecting Your Finances**
	Chapter 12	Planning Your Tax Strategy
	Chapter 13	Home and Motor Vehicle Insurance
	Chapter 14	Health, Disability, and Life Insurance
	Chapter 15	Retirement and Estate Planning
Fifth	**Unit 5**	**Introduction to Business Finance**
	Chapter 16	Introduction to Financial Management for Business
	Chapter 17	Sources of Funding
	Chapter 18	Financial Accounting
	Chapter 19	Managing Payroll and Inventory
Sixth	**Unit 6**	**Organization and Financial Planning**
	Chapter 20	Types of Business Ownership
	Chapter 21	Developing a Financial Plan
	Chapter 22	Pricing, Costing, and Growth

FULL-YEAR COURSE SCHEDULE NINE-WEEK GRADING SYSTEM

GRADING PERIOD	CHAPTER	CHAPTER TITLE
First	**Unit 1**	**Planning Personal Finances**
	Chapter 1	Personal Financial Planning
	Chapter 2	Financial Aspects of Career Planning
	Chapter 3	Money Management Strategy
	Chapter 4	Consumer Purchasing Strategies and Legal Protection
	Unit 2	**Banking and Credit**
	Chapter 5	Banking
	Chapter 6	Consumer Credit
Second	Chapter 7	The Finances of Housing
	Unit 3	**Investing Your Financial Resources**
	Chapter 8	The Fundamentals of Investing
	Chapter 9	Stocks
	Chapter 10	Bonds and Mutual Funds
	Chapter 11	Real Estate and Other Investment Alternatives
Third	**Unit 4**	**Protecting Your Finances**
	Chapter 12	Planning Your Tax Strategy
	Chapter 13	Home and Motor Vehicle Insurance
	Chapter 14	Health, Disability, and Life Insurance
	Chapter 15	Retirement and Estate Planning
	Unit 5	**Introduction to Business Finance**
	Chapter 16	Introduction to Financial Management for Business
	Chapter 17	Sources of Funding
Fourth	Chapter 18	Financial Accounting
	Chapter 19	Managing Payroll and Inventory
	Unit 6	**Organization and Financial Planning**
	Chapter 20	Types of Business Ownership
	Chapter 21	Developing a Financial Plan
	Chapter 22	Pricing, Costing, and Growth

PROFESSIONAL NOTES

SEMESTER COURSE SCHEDULE
SIX-WEEK GRADING SYSTEM

GRADING PERIOD	CHAPTER	CHAPTER TITLE
First	Unit 1	**Planning Personal Finances**
	Chapter 1	Personal Financial Planning
	Chapter 2	Financial Aspects of Career Planning
	Chapter 3	Money Management Strategy
	Chapter 4	Consumer Purchasing Strategies and Legal Protection
	Unit 2	**Banking and Credit**
	Chapter 5	Banking
	Chapter 6	Consumer Credit
	Chapter 7	The Finances of Housing
Second	Unit 3	**Investing Your Financial Resources**
	Chapter 8	The Fundamentals of Investing
	Chapter 9	Stocks
	Chapter 10	Bonds and Mutual Funds
	Chapter 11	Real Estate and Other Investment Alternatives
	Unit 4	**Protecting Your Finances**
	Chapter 12	Planning Your Tax Strategy
	Chapter 13	Home and Motor Vehicle Insurance
	Chapter 14	Health, Disability, and Life Insurance
	Chapter 15	Retirement and Estate Planning
Third	Unit 5	**Introduction to Business Finance**
	Chapter 16	Introduction to Financial Management for Business
	Chapter 17	Sources of Funding
	Chapter 18	Financial Accounting
	Chapter 19	Managing Payroll and Inventory
	Unit 6	**Organization and Financial Planning**
	Chapter 20	Types of Business Ownership
	Chapter 21	Developing a Financial Plan
	Chapter 22	Pricing, Costing, and Growth

SEMESTER COURSE SCHEDULE
NINE-WEEK GRADING SYSTEM

GRADING PERIOD	CHAPTER	CHAPTER TITLE
First	Unit 1	**Planning Personal Finances**
	Chapter 1	Personal Financial Planning
	Chapter 2	Financial Aspects of Career Planning
	Chapter 3	Money Management Strategy
	Chapter 4	Consumer Purchasing Strategies and Legal Protection
	Unit 2	**Banking and Credit**
	Chapter 5	Banking
	Chapter 6	Consumer Credit
	Chapter 7	The Finances of Housing
	Unit 3	**Investing Your Financial Resources**
	Chapter 8	The Fundamentals of Investing
	Chapter 9	Stocks
	Chapter 10	Bonds and Mutual Funds
	Chapter 11	Real Estate and Other Investment Alternatives
Second	Unit 4	**Protecting Your Finances**
	Chapter 12	Planning Your Tax Strategy
	Chapter 13	Home and Motor Vehicle Insurance
	Chapter 14	Health, Disability, and Life Insurance
	Chapter 15	Retirement and Estate Planning
	Unit 5	**Introduction to Business Finance**
	Chapter 16	Introduction to Financial Management for Business
	Chapter 17	Sources of Funding
	Chapter 18	Financial Accounting
	Chapter 19	Managing Payroll and Inventory
	Unit 6	**Organization and Financial Planning**
	Chapter 20	Types of Business Ownership
	Chapter 21	Developing a Financial Plan
	Chapter 22	Pricing, Costing, and Growth

Chapter 1 Planning Guide: Decisions and Goals in Personal Finance

Teacher Manual

SECT.	OBJECTIVES	NATIONAL STANDARDS FOR BUSINESS EDUCATION	FEATURES	RESOURCES
1.1	After completing this lesson, students will have learned: How to create a financial plan; How to develop their personal financial goals; How to evaluate the economic factors that will affect their financial decisions	**Economics** I. Allocation of Resources II. Economic Systems III. Economic Institutions and Incentives IV. Markets and Prices V. Market Structures VII. The Role of Government IX. Aggregate Supply and Aggregate Demand **Personal Finance** I. Personal Decision Making II. Earning a Living III. Managing Finances and Budgeting IV. Saving and Investing V. Buying Goods and Services	**Standard & Poor's**—Q & A, p. 4 **What's Your Financial ID?**—Your Spending Profile, p. 6 **Careers in Finance**—Personal Banker, p. 10 **Common Cents**—Pay Yourself First, p. 11 **Standard & Poor's**—Case Study, p. 12 **Savvy Saver**—Financial Tips That Work, p. 13 **Academic Connection**—Language Arts, p. 14 **International Finance**—Finland, p. 18	Check Your Understanding, p. 19 Think Critically, p. 19 Using Communication Skills, p. 19 Solving Money Problems, p. 19 Student Activity Workbook
1.2	After completing this lesson, students will have learned: How to determine the opportunity costs associated with each of their financial decisions; How to identify the strategies for achieving their financial goals for the different stages of their life	**Economics** I. Allocation of Resources VIII. International Economic Concepts **Personal Finance** I. Personal Decision Making II. Earning a Living III. Managing Finances and Budgeting IV. Saving and Investing VII. Using Credit	**Go Figure**—Calculating Annual Interest, p. 22 **Go Figure**—Calculating the Future Value of a Single Deposit, p. 22 **Your Financial Portfolio**—Getting Your Own Wheels, p. 26	Check Your Understanding, p. 27 Think Critically, p. 27 Using Math Skills, p. 27 Solving Money Problems, p. 27 Student Activity Workbook

SCANS Correlation Chart

FOUNDATION SKILLS

Basic Skills	Reading	Writing	Math	Listening	Speaking
Thinking Skills	Creative Thinking	Decision Making	Problem Solving	Seeing Things in the Mind's Eye	Knowing How to Learn	Reasoning
Personal Qualities	Responsibility	Self-Esteem	Sociability	Self-Management	Integrity/Honesty

WORKPLACE COMPETENCIES

Resources	Allocating Time	Allocating Money	Allocating Material and Facility Resources	Allocating Human Resources
Information	Acquiring and Evaluating Information	Organizing and Maintaining Information	Interpreting and Communicating Information	Using Computers to Process Information
Interpersonal Skills	Participating as a Member of a Team	Teaching Others	Serving Clients/ Customers	Exercising Leadership	Negotiating to Arrive at a Decision	Working with Cultural Diversity
Systems	Understanding Systems	Monitoring and Correcting Performance	Improving and Designing Systems
Technology	Selecting Technology	Applying Technology to Task	Maintaining and Troubleshooting Technology

■ INTERNET EXTENSION

Activity: Ask students to use the Internet to locate savings calculators. These calculators will compute how much you have to save every day, week, and month to reach your goal. Have them use one of these online calculators to compute their own savings goal and print out the savings schedule.

Keywords: savings calculator, personal finance

■ ENRICHMENT/APPLICATION ACTIVITY

Field Trip: Take students to the public library or a full-sized bookstore to see the many financial planning books available. Have each student write the name, title, and brief description of two books that they would choose to read, and explain why.

Chapter 1   *Personal Financial Planning*

■ TOPIC SPOTLIGHT

💲Money: Demand for a product (how much that product is wanted by consumers) is one factor used when determining price. Usually, when the demand for a product is high, the price of the product rises. When demand for a product is low, the price falls. Discuss with students how this economic factor affects the money they have to spend.

⊙Technology: Ask students how improvements in technology may help people with their financial planning and money management.

⊙Marketing: Bring a variety of magazine ads to class to pass around to students. Ask how advertising encourages consumers to spend money.

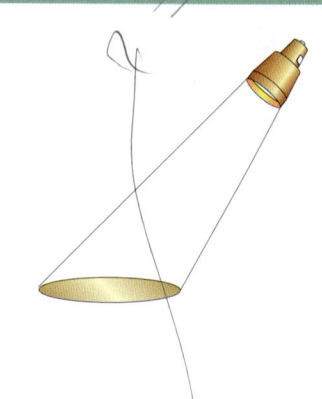

additional resources

Get a Financial Life by Beth Kobliner (© 1996, revised 2000 Simon & Schuster). This financial planning guide for young people offers sensible advice on many topics including budgets, savings options, and insurance.

Basics of Saving and Investing: A Teaching Guide (© 1998 Eastern Michigan University) This teaching guide is a project of Financial Literacy 2001, a national financial education effort co-sponsored by the Investor Protection Trust, the National Association of Securities Dealers, Inc., and the North American Securities Administrators Association. The National Institute for Consumer Education joined with these groups to create this curriculum guide for high school-level instruction in the principles of personal finance. It is **free** to educators and available through several sources. State-specific copies of this guide as well as other resources can be obtained through the Financial Literacy 2001 Web site at **http://www.fl2001.org**. A national version is available by contacting the NASD by phone (202) 728-6964, fax (202) 728-8022, and Web sites **www.investor.nasd.com** or **www.nasd.com**.

Young Money, Todd Romer, publisher. This magazine reports on personal finance issues for teens and young adults. It specifically targets three categories: earning, investing, and spending. Classroom subscription rates are available. Its Web site is **www.youngmoney.com**.

www.jumpstartcoalition.org The Jump$tart Coalition for Personal Financial Literacy seeks to improve the personal financial literacy of young adults. Its purpose is to evaluate the financial literacy of young adults; develop, disseminate, and encourage the use of guidelines for grades K-12; and promote the teaching of personal finance. Its Web site provides a searchable database of educational materials for the K-12 age group. (888) 45-EDUCATE.

www.bankrate.com This Web site offers current information on many personal finance issues, such as checking and ATM fees, auto loans, money markets, and no-fee and low interest rate credit cards. It also provides access to financial calculators, such as loan, college tuition, moving, and savings calculators.

Choices and Decisions: Taking Charge of Your Life (© 1998) is a teaching guide and software offered free to educators. VISA U.S.A., Inc., P.O. Box 8999, San Francisco, CA 94128-8999. (800) 847-2511.

Master Your Future (© 1997) is a video and teaching guide also offered **free** to educators by MasterCard International. (800) 624-9688.

Note to teacher: Web site addresses may change.

Unit 1 *Planning Personal Finances*

CHAPTER 1 Lesson Plans

SECTION 1.1

FOCUS

Motivation
Ask the students to think about the financial goals they might set during this school year. Acknowledge all goals and list them on the board. Then ask the students how they think they will be able to achieve these goals. Use this discussion as a lead-in to this chapter.

Prereading
1. Have the students skim the section, looking at pictures, reading captions, and noting headings.
2. Have "What You'll Learn" listed on page 5 read aloud.
3. Dictate each of the Key Terms to the class. Have students write them on a piece of paper. When they are finished, write the terms on the board. Ask the students to guess at the meaning of each term, but do not give the correct meaning. Leave the list on the board, so as students work through the section, they can see how close they were to the correct answer.
4. Ask the students to state the purpose of studying this chapter.

TEACH

Guided Practice
1. Have students read aloud the Standard & Poor's Q&A on page 4.
2. Read the section with your students.

Independent Practice
Have students create a collage of their financial goals for the future. Allow them to use pictures from magazines, clip art from the computer, or their own artwork. Display the finished collages around the room.

Careers in Finance

Personal Banker
1. Break students into groups and assign each group a different bank in your community. Ask them to contact the bank and research the types of financial services offered and whether or not they employ personal bankers.
2. After they complete their research, have the students present their findings orally to the class.
3. If possible, invite a personal banker to be a guest speaker in the class.

Common Cents

Pay Yourself First
Tell the students to imagine they earn $550 per month. Using the strategy described, have the students figure how much they will save the first month, the sixth month, and the twelfth month. [ANSWER: $550 × 1% = $5.50; $550 × 6% = $33; $550 × 12% = $66]

$avvy Saver

Financial Tips That Work
Have the students develop two additional financial tips. Create a list of all the tips and post them around the classroom.

INTERNATIONAL FINANCE
Finland
1. Ask the students to find out what percent of United State's residents have cell phones and what percent are connected to the Internet.

Chapter 1 *Personal Financial Planning*   TM53

2. Have the students research the cost of cell phones and cell phone services. Compare the various plans and ask the students to choose the one they think is the best value.

ASSESS

Reteaching

1. Review the list of Key Terms that the students were unsure about before studying the chapter.
2. To reteach the concept of supply and demand, select a popular toy to use as an example. Help the students see that if the demand for the toy is high, then the supply goes down and prices often go up. Then if the popularity of the toy diminishes and the demand goes down, the supply is high and the prices might be discounted.
3. Ask the students to create a list of toys and games that they think have been affected by this economic concept.

Enrichment

Have the students go to the library or use the Internet to research the Federal Reserve System and the role it plays in our economy. The main Web site for the Federal Reserve System is: www.federalreserve.gov.

Assessment

1. Have the students complete the Section 1.1 Assessment.
2. Assign an activity from the *Student Activity Workbook*.

CLOSE

Have students complete this statement: "If I learn and put into action the six steps in the financial planning process, I will…." [EXAMPLE: "have a solid foundation for making all my financial decisions, now and in the future."]

SECTION 1.2

FOCUS

Motivation

Ask students to imagine they have just won a million dollars. Generate a discussion about what they would do with their money. Encourage them to think about saving and investing for the future.

Prereading

1. Have the students skim the section, looking at pictures, reading captions, and noting headings.
2. Have "What You'll Learn" listed on page 20 read aloud.
3. Have the students write each bold-faced term in the section and generate a picture or symbol that identifies it, based on its definition.
4. Ask your students to state the purpose of studying this chapter.

TEACH

Guided Practice

Read the section with your students.

Independent Practice

Have students use newspaper or magazine articles to research and report on the current interest rate charged by the Federal Reserve. Then find out what local banks and financial institutions pay you to use your money. Each month throughout the course, research these rates again. Graph the changes.

ASSESS

Reteaching

1. Review the Key Terms from the section. Make sure the students understand the terms.

2. To reinforce the concept of the time value of money, ask your students to think about all the times during the last month that they spent, borrowed, saved, or invested money. Then ask them to reflect on what might have been a better way to use that money. Could they have saved more? Spent less?

Enrichment

1. Have the students write an article for the school newspaper on a topic from this chapter. Some ideas might include financial goal setting, the time value of money, or strategies for achieving financial goals.
2. Have the students use the eight strategies for achieving financial goals, found on page 25, to create a personal journal of how they think they will apply the strategies to their own lives now and in the future.

Assessment

1. Have the students complete the Section 1.2 Assessment.
2. Assign the Chapter Assessment.
3. Administer the test for Chapter 1 from the Reproducible Tests in the *Teacher Resource Binder*.

CLOSE

Ask the students to complete this statement: "By learning to use my money wisely now, I'll be able to… ." [EXAMPLE: "achieve many of my financial goals."]

SECTION 1.1 ASSESSMENT
ANSWERS

CHECK YOUR UNDERSTANDING

1. The six steps used to create a financial plan are: (1) determine your current financial situation, (2) develop your financial goals, (3) identify alternative courses of action (4) evaluate your alternatives, (5) create and use your financial plan of action, and (6) review and revise your plan.

2. Some of your purchases will be consumable goods, which you buy often and use up quickly. Because they will probably cost less than other goods or services, you can set short-term goals to obtain them. Other purchases will be for durable goods, more expensive items that you don't purchase often. You will probably have to set intermediate or long-term goals to obtain these items. Finally, some of your goals may involve intangibles, which will vary in the time required to achieve them.
3. Students should describe two of the following factors: (1) market forces, (2) financial institutions, (3) global influences, (4) economic conditions. Answers will vary.

THINK CRITICALLY

4. You'll be better able to develop financial goals if you understand the difference between what you need and what you want. It's important to recognize that you may be able to satisfy your basic needs with any number of different wants, some of which may cost less than others.

USING COMMUNICATION SKILLS

5. Answers will vary.

SOLVING MONEY PROBLEMS

6. Answers will vary but should reference the six steps of financial planning: (1) Determine your current financial situation; (2) Develop your financial goals; (3) Identify alternative courses of action; (4) Evaluate your alternatives; (5) Create and use your financial plan of action; (6) Review and revise your plan.

SECTION 1.2 ASSESSMENT
ANSWERS

CHECK YOUR UNDERSTANDING

1. Personal opportunity costs and financial opportunity costs.

2. Obtain, plan, spend, save, borrow, invest, manage risk, and retire.
3. It will increase your current income and help your money grow over time.

THINK CRITICALLY

4. The time value of money is the increase in an amount of money as a result of interest earned. If you shop among financial institutions, you might get a higher interest rate. The higher the interest rate, the faster your money will grow.

USING MATH SKILLS

5. Tanya will have $16,578 available in five years. [ANSWER: $3,000 × 5.526 = $16,578] Tanya will need to raise an additional $1,422. [ANSWER: $18,000 − $16,578 = $1,422] (Note to teacher: Students should use the future value table in **Figure 1-4** to answer this question.)

SOLVING MONEY PROBLEMS

6. Debates will vary by group.

CHAPTER 1 ASSESSMENT
ANSWERS

■ **Understanding and Using Vocabulary**
Answers will vary.

■ **Review Key Concepts**
1. What role do your personal values play in your financial decisions? Is it more important to you to spend your money now or to save for the future? Would you rather get a job after high school or continue your education? What are your needs and wants?
2. Short-term goals are those you can reach in one year or less. Intermediate goals are those you plan to reach in two to five years. Long-term goals take more than five years to reach.
3. Your financial goals should be realistic. They should be specific. They should have a clear time frame. They should help you decide what type of action to take.
4. Factors include market forces, financial institutions, and global influences. Conditions include consumer prices, consumer spending, and interest rates.
5. Future value of a single deposit is the amount your original deposit will be worth in the future based on earning a specific interest rate over a specific period of time. Present value of a single deposit is the amount of money you would need to deposit now in order to attain a desired amount in the future.

■ **Apply Key Concepts**
1. Answers will vary.
2. Answers will vary but should reflect the student's understanding that short-term and intermediate goals can lead to achieving long-term goals.
3. Answers will vary.
4. Answers will vary but should show an understanding of supply and demand.
5. $1,504. [ANSWER: $1,000 × 1.504 = $1,504] (Note to teacher: Students should use the future value table in **Figure 1-4** to answer this question.)

Problem Solving Today
Answers will vary. One possible solution is to save an additional $26 per paycheck for the computer. [ANSWER: $26 × 52 = $1,352] By doing this, you will reach your goal in one year. If you decide not to save for one week, then you will have to increase the remaining weeks' savings by that amount. One trade-off you might make to buy your computer is to spend less money on clothes, CDs, movies, and eating out with friends.

■ **Real-World Application**
Answers will vary but should reflect the student's understanding of the six steps in the financial planning process.

FINANCE Online

Answers will vary depending on the student's age, the hourly wage the student earns, and the rate of inflation. Some possible Web sites include:

http://woodrow.mpls.frb.fed.us
   /economy/calc/cpihome.html
www.jsc.nasa.gov/bu2/inflate.html
http://www.bls.gov/cpi

Note to teacher: Web site addresses may change.

READING STRATEGIES
ANSWERS

PREDICT (p. 6): Strategies are:
(1) Obtain financial resources
(2) Plan how to spend your money
(3) Save on a regular basis
(4) Borrow wisely and only when necessary
(5) Spend less than you earn
(6) Manage risk
(7) Invest to increase current income or for long-term growth
(8) Plan for retirement

CONNECT (p. 8): Answers will vary. Some needs may include enough money to purchase food, clothing, shelter, and medical care. Wants may include education, entertainment, travel, automobiles, upscale housing, or leisure activities. The distinction between needs and wants will vary from person to person.

QUESTION (p. 13): Although intangible items don't necessarily cost money, the path to attaining them might cost money. For example, getting a good education may require paying tuition at an expensive college. Happiness sometimes requires at least some sense of financial security. It will be more difficult to be happy if one is always hungry, or worried about paying medical bills.

RESPOND (p. 21): Answers will vary. Most students are likely to admit that they spend at least some money on wants rather than needs. The savings might be used to contribute toward college, toward purchasing a home, or to purchase some other valuable item such as a car.

QUESTION (p. 24): Knowing the future value of a deposit can help you determine the trade-offs, or opportunity costs, of spending now or saving for the future.

STANDARD & POOR'S

CASE STUDY
ANSWERS

1. Dylan will need to begin using some of his savings to pay for college within a few years, so he needs to invest that money in investments that have little risk of losing money in the short term.
2. In general, the higher the return, the greater the risk of loss in the short term due to day-to-day price swings. Holding a number of different types of stocks or stock mutual funds can help reduce short-term losses without sacrificing potential return.
3. The key to selecting investments is to recognize your time frame. The longer you have to invest, the more you can withstand short-term price fluctuations in the pursuit of potentially higher returns.

Chapter 2 Planning Guide
Financial Aspects of Career Planning

Teacher Manual

SECT.	OBJECTIVES	NATIONAL STANDARDS FOR BUSINESS EDUCATION	FEATURES	RESOURCES
2.1	After completing this lesson, students will have learned: How to identify the personal issues to consider when choosing and planning a career How to evaluate the factors that influence employment opportunities	**Economics** I. Allocation of Resources II. Economic Systems III. Economic Institutions and Incentives IV. Markets and Prices VIII. International Economic Concepts IX. Aggregate Supply and Aggregate Demand **Personal Finance** I. Personal Decision Making II. Earning a Living	**Standard & Poor's**—Q & A, p. 30 **What's Your Financial ID?**—Find Your Personality Traits, p. 32 **International Finance**—Belize, p. 34 **Academic Connection**—Health, p. 37 **Common Cents**—Career Center, p. 39 **Standard & Poor's**—Case Study, p. 40	**Check Your Understanding**, p. 41 **Think Critically**, p. 41 **Using Communication Skills**, p. 41 **Solving Money Problems**, p. 41 **Student Activity Workbook**
2.2	After completing this lesson, students will have learned: How to apply effective strategies to obtain employment How to identify the financial and legal issues to consider when looking for employment How to analyze methods that will help them grow and develop in their careers	**Economics** III. Economic Institutions and Incentives **Personal Finance** I. Personal Decision Making II. Earning a Living III. Managing Finances and Budgeting IV. Saving and Investing VIII. Protecting Against Risk	**Careers in Finance**—Cashier, p. 50 **Savvy Saver**—Where to Find Money for College, p. 51 **Your Financial Portfolio**—Applying for a Job, p. 54	**Check Your Understanding**, p. 55 **Think Critically**, p. 55 **Using Math Skills**, p. 55 **Solving Money Problems**, p. 55 **Student Activity Workbook**

Unit 1 Planning Personal Finances

SCANS Correlation Chart

FOUNDATION SKILLS

Basic Skills	Reading	Writing	Math	Listening	Speaking
Thinking Skills	Creative Thinking	Decision Making	Problem Solving	Seeing Things in the Mind's Eye	Knowing How to Learn	Reasoning
Personal Qualities	Responsibility	Self-Esteem	Sociability	Self-Management	Integrity/Honesty

WORKPLACE COMPETENCIES

Resources	Allocating Time	Allocating Money	Allocating Material and Facility Resources	Allocating Human Resources
Information	Acquiring and Evaluating Information	Organizing and Maintaining Information	Interpreting and Communicating Information	Using Computers to Process Information
Interpersonal Skills	Participating as a Member of a Team	Teaching Others	Serving Clients/Customers	Exercising Leadership	Negotiating to Arrive at a Decision	Working with Cultural Diversity
Systems	Understanding Systems	Monitoring and Correcting Performance	Improving and Designing Systems
Technology	Selecting Technology	Applying Technology to Task	Maintaining and Troubleshooting Technology

■ INTERNET EXTENSION

Activity: Ask students to use the Internet to find out what kind of career planning information is available online. They should note the different sources of career information that they find and make note of appropriate Web sites.

Keywords: career planning, help with résumé

■ ENRICHMENT/APPLICATION ACTIVITY

Guest Speaker: Invite the school counselor to speak to the class about the school-to-work program(s) available through your high school, or invite a career counselor from a university, college, or technical school in your area to talk about the career planning and placement office at his or her institution.

■ TOPIC SPOTLIGHT

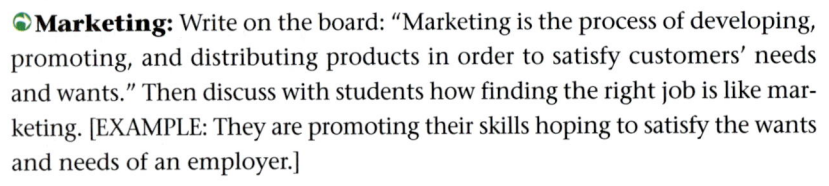

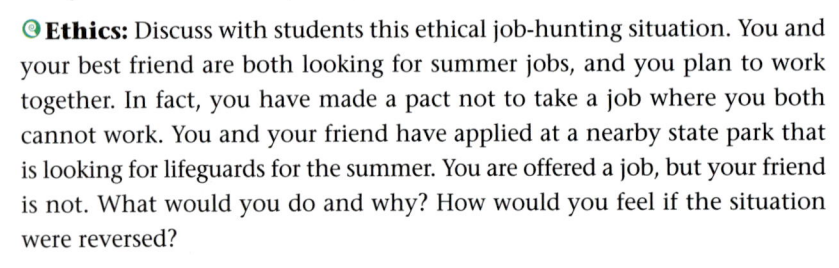

Marketing: Write on the board: "Marketing is the process of developing, promoting, and distributing products in order to satisfy customers' needs and wants." Then discuss with students how finding the right job is like marketing. [EXAMPLE: They are promoting their skills hoping to satisfy the wants and needs of an employer.]

Money: Have each student write a paragraph explaining how important salary is to them and why.

Ethics: Discuss with students this ethical job-hunting situation. You and your best friend are both looking for summer jobs, and you plan to work together. In fact, you have made a pact not to take a job where you both cannot work. You and your friend have applied at a nearby state park that is looking for lifeguards for the summer. You are offered a job, but your friend is not. What would you do and why? How would you feel if the situation were reversed?

additional resources

What Color Is Your Parachute? 2004 by Richard Boles (© 2003, Ten Speed Press). This popular book is a guide for those who are looking for satisfying and fulfilling employment.

Jump Start Your Online Job Search in a Weekend by Pat Kendall (© 2000, Prima Publishing). This book includes online job-search methods, e-résumés, cover letters, and tips for developing a personal marketing strategy.

www.ajb.dni.us America's Job Bank Web site is a listing of many jobs available around the country and is produced as a partnership between the U.S. Department of Labor and the state-operated Public Employment Service.

www.dol.gov/dol/jobs.htm The U.S. Department of Labor offers educational resources at this Web site, such as "Career Exploration and Finding a Job" and "Jobs for Kids Who Like…." Its main Web site is www.dol.gov.

www.princetonreview.com/?popup=no Besides offering a college search that links student preferences to potential colleges and online applications, this Web site provides comprehensive information regarding financing education.

www.fastweb.com This Web site lists more than 3,500 scholarships in its database. The site is updated daily and notifies users by e-mail when matched scholarships are added to its database.

www.mapping-your-future.org This Web site is sponsored by a group of guaranty agencies who participate in the Federal Family Education Loan Program (FFELP) and offers interactive career planning tips.

www.monster.com This Web site offers resources for writing and posting résumés, researching companies, getting career advice, and finding jobs.

www.ja.org This Web site for Junior Achievement gives information about the programs the organization offers students. JA's purpose is to educate and inspire "young people to value free enterprise, business, and economics to improve the quality of their lives."

Note to teacher: Web site addresses may change.

CHAPTER 2 Lesson Plans

SECTION 2.1

FOCUS

Motivation

Write this statement on the board: "Because of the technological changes that are taking place in this digital age, the majority of the jobs available in ten years have not yet been created." How do you plan, research, or train for a career you know nothing about?

Prereading

1. Have your students skim the section, looking at pictures, reading captions, and noting headings.
2. Have "What You'll Learn" listed on page 31 read aloud.
3. Ask the students to read through the list of Key Terms on page 31 and note any that are familiar. Have the students orally define those terms and explain the context in which they were used.
4. Ask the students to state the purpose of studying this chapter.

TEACH

Guided Practice

1. Have students read aloud the Standard & Poor's Q&A on page 30.
2. Read the section with your students.

Independent Practice

Give the students an aptitude test and/or an interest inventory. These tests can be obtained from the guidance department, an occupational specialist, or even from the Internet. Then have the students create a list of ten careers that would match their aptitudes and/or interests.

INTERNATIONAL FINANCE
Belize

1. Have the students research the demographics of Belize, including the type of jobs available and their salary ranges. Ask them if they would like to live and work in Belize.
2. Ask the students to research the Gross Domestic Product (GDP) and the Per Capita GDP for the United States. Then have them compare their findings to the GDP and Per Capita GDP in Belize.
3. Have the students find out what products, if any, the United States imports from Belize.

Career Center

There are hundreds of career Web sites located on the Internet. Have your students research and evaluate Web sites based on how student-friendly and useful they are. Then have them create a handout of the best sites and distribute them through the school career center.

Divide the students into groups. Ask them to prepare a lesson on career planning for middle school/junior high students. Present the lesson to the middle school/junior high students who will be attending your high school.

ASSESS

Reteaching

1. Review the list of Key Terms that the students were unsure about before studying the chapter.
2. Write this quote on the board: "It is unwise to devote one's entire education to learning things that everyone else already knows. One must select a vocation for which there is market demand and for which one has talent, and then pursue expertise and excellence within this niche." (John Bishop, Cornell University)

3. Ask your students how this quote might relate to the decisions they must make when planning their careers.

Enrichment

1. Have your students interview a person in a career field that is of interest to them. Then have the students make a poster that shows the path this person took to his or her career.
2. As a class survey the faculty and staff at your school to find out all the different jobs they have had. Ask how they came to choose a career in education.

Assessment

1. Have your students complete the Section 2.1 Assessment.
2. Assign an activity from the *Student Activity Workbook*.

CLOSE

Have students write a paragraph describing how they will research and plan for their career.

SECTION 2.2

FOCUS

Motivation

Use the classified ads to find enough entry-level positions for each student in the class. Assign a different job to each student. Tell the students that the assigned job will be their summer job. Ask the students: "Do you think you would like this job? Would you rather have found your own job?" Have the students explain their answers.

Prereading

1. Have your students skim the section, looking at pictures, reading captions, and noting headings.

2. Have "What You'll Learn" listed on page 42 read aloud.
3. Write each Key Term on the board. Ask your students to define each of these terms and use them in a sentence.
4. Ask the students to state the purpose of studying this chapter.

TEACH

Guided Practice

1. Read the section with your students.
2. Assign an activity from the *Student Activity Workbook*.

Independent Practice

1. Invite a representative from a temporary job agency, such as Norrell Staffing Services, Kelly Services, or Manpower, to talk to the class about the kinds of jobs that are available through staffing agencies.
2. Have your students begin collecting advertisements for jobs and careers that interest them. The newspapers, Internet, and the school career center are good sources for locating these ads.
3. Have the students attend a local job fair. Ask them to be prepared to make a good impression by dressing appropriately and preparing their résumés. When the students return to class, have them share their experiences.

*C*areers in Finance

Cashier

1. Have the students research various types of cash registers. Ask them to find out how computerized systems differ from manual cash registers.
2. Ask your students to interview a cashier who is working at a local retail store. Find out what he or she likes the most and the least about the job. Compile the results as a class.

3. Have the students answer this question: "Why is 'likes to work with people' one of the skills necessary to be a successful cashier?"

$avvy Saver

Where to Find Money for College

Organize a "Where to Find Money for College" night. Divide your students into groups and have them prepare displays on the variety of ways to find money for college. Then invite their parents to attend the evening activity and have the students present their findings.

ASSESS

Reteaching

1. Review the key terms from the section. Make sure the students understand the terms.
2. To emphasize the importance of evaluating both the pay and benefits offered by an employer, bring in a list of benefits offered by several employers in your community. Generate a discussion about the types of benefits the students believe are important. Make sure they justify their answers.

Enrichment

1. Practice mock interviewing in the classroom. Then invite some businesspeople to your class to conduct interviews. Make sure the students dress for the interview. Ask the guests to evaluate each student after the interview.
2. Invite a lawyer to your class to discuss employee rights with the students.

Assessment

1. Have the students complete the Section 2.2 Assessment.
2. Assign the Chapter Assessment.
3. Administer the test for Chapter 2 from the Reproducible Tests in the *Teacher Resource Binder*.

CLOSE

Life-long learning is a requirement for success in the workplace of the 21st century. Ask the students to complete this statement: "I will make sure my skills remain up-to-date by…."

SECTION 2.1 ASSESSMENT
ANSWERS

CHECK YOUR UNDERSTANDING

1. Answers will vary but should include three of the following characteristics:
   (1) They work well with others.
   (2) They strive to do their best.
   (3) They don't allow conflicts with other employees or changes in their duties to affect the quality of their work.
   (4) They are creative in solving problems.
   (5) They read a variety of materials and know how to express themselves well.
   (6) They understand themselves and other people.
   People who are able to work well with others can function as part of a team. People who always want to do their best will probably be rewarded for their excellence. People who don't let conflict or change throw them off will stay calm under pressure. People who solve problems creatively can maintain progress on projects. People who are well read and know how to express their ideas can communicate more effectively. People who understand themselves and others will know what is required of them.
2. You can take special tests, such as aptitude tests or interest inventories. An aptitude test may help you find out what you do best. An interest inventory will help you identify the activities that you enjoy most. Then it will match your interests, likes, and dislikes with various kinds of work.
3. Factors include: social influences, such as demographic trends and geographic trends; economic factors, such as interest rates, prices, and the demand for certain goods

and services; and trends in industry and technology, such as increased competition from other countries and automation.

THINK CRITICALLY

4. Answers will vary but may include: Working parents do not have as much time to prepare homemade meals. They rely on schools to provide breakfasts and lunches, and they spend more money eating out. People with more leisure time can focus on their health needs.

USING COMMUNICATION SKILLS

5. Answers will vary.

SOLVING MONEY PROBLEMS

6. His annual expenses would be approximately $14,020. [ANSWER: 12 × 800 = $9,600; $4 × 5 = $20; $20 × 52 = $1,040; 52 × $65 = $3,380; $9,600 + $1,040 + $3,380 = $14,020]

SECTION 2.2 ASSESSMENT
ANSWERS

CHECK YOUR UNDERSTANDING

1. Answers will vary but should include three of the following ways: summer and part-time jobs, temporary work, volunteer work, internships, cooperative education, and class projects or after-school activities.
2. Your beginning salary will depend on your education and experience, the size of the company, and the average salary for the job you're considering. Once you've started working, your salary will increase if you receive raises and promotions. Other than salary, you should consider the types of benefits the company offers, including health care and retirement benefits.
3. Answers will vary but should include two of the following methods: improve your communication skills; develop good work habits; take action when problems arise; keep up with changes in technology; make sure your skills are up-to-date; and gain the support of a mentor.

THINK CRITICALLY

4. Answers will vary. Libraries are convenient and offer a variety of references, but materials may be outdated. Mass media are readily available, but the information may not be comprehensive. The Internet has a great deal of information, but sometimes you don't know if a source is reliable. Also, not everyone has access to a computer. School guidance offices can offer counseling by experienced professionals, but they may not always have the materials you need. Community and professional organizations offer contact with people who are in the workforce, but you might have to make a special effort to go to their meetings. Contacts can give you good advice about preparing for your career, but they may be difficult to locate.

USING MATH SKILLS

5. His employment package will be worth approximately $31,923. [ANSWER: Five personal days and five sick days are each equal to one week's vacation, or 1/52 of the base pay.]

SOLVING MONEY PROBLEMS

6. Her alternatives might include reimbursement for child-care expenses that are related to work; a child-care center on site; a flexible work schedule; working from home part-time; and extra health and life insurance for her children. She will have to consider such issues as whether she would be allowed to work from home and whether she would have to invest in new equipment or make room in her home for an office. She will have to consider whether she could fulfill her work-related duties while her children were at home. She will have to consider the cost of extra life and health insurance.

CHAPTER 2 ASSESSMENT
ANSWERS

■ **Understanding and Using Vocabulary**
Answers will vary.

■ **Review Key Concepts**
1. The more education and training you have, the greater your potential earning power.
2. You can take assessment tests such as aptitude tests and interest inventories.
3. The goal is to find a work situation that gives you the right balance of financial rewards and personal satisfaction.
4. Changes in industry and technology can decrease opportunities in some job markets while increasing opportunities in other job markets.
5. A relationship with a mentor can give you personalized training and allow you to meet other knowledgeable people. It can also provide you with emotional support during difficult times.

■ **Apply Key Concepts**
1. With only a high school education, you may not be able to make as much money as you will if you obtain a college degree. However, you may be able to earn a good salary without a college education if you have valuable skills and can market those skills to a company.
2. Answers will vary.
3. Answers will vary but should include one of the following factors: the amount of free time you have, the people you meet, how much money you make, and whether you want a career that is satisfying and expresses your values.
4. Changes in the locations of jobs could affect where you live. Differences in cost of living among regions or cities could affect your salary and financial goals. Decreased demand for goods and services could reduce job opportunities in your field.
5. Answers will vary but may note that you might need the instruction or advice of someone with more knowledge and experience; personalized training; connections with people who have the power to hire you; and emotional support during difficult times.

■ **Problem Solving Today**
(1) You will earn $7,000. (2) If you update the Web sites every six months, you will be able to achieve your goal in one year. [ANSWER: 50 × $35 = $1,750; 4 × $1,750 = $7,000; 4 × $125 = $500; 2 × $500 = $1,000; $1,000 + $7,000 = $8,000]

■ **Real-World Application**
Answers will vary.

FINANCE Online

Sites for career planning assistance:
   www.hotjobs.com
   www.careerpath.com

Sites for trends in careers and tips on preparing résumés:
   www.ajb.dni.us
   www.careerbuilder.com

Answers will vary.

Note to teacher: Web site addresses may change.

READING STRATEGIES
ANSWERS

Section 2.1
RESPOND (p. 34): Answers will vary depending on the lifestyle the student wishes to support, as well as his or her values and personal fulfillment needs.

PREDICT (p. 39): Answers might include: (1) demographic trends such as an increase in working parents, more emphasis on leisure time, an increase in the elderly population, greater demands for ongoing employment training, and populations shifts in geographical regions; (2) economic factors such as recession, inflation, or widespread prosperity; and (3) changes in industry and technology, such as automation, advances in computer technology, advances in communications technology, the use of overseas labor in the manufacturing industry and the growth of U.S. service industries.

Section 2.2

CONNECT (p. 44): Answers will vary. Students might need encouragement to translate their school projects and after-school activities into job-related experience. For example, an after-school activity, such as serving as the student manager for the basketball team, might demonstrate organizational ability, dependability, people skills, and familiarity with basic statistics.

QUESTION (p. 46): A recent high school graduate might not have a long work history or might have held several part-time jobs, such as fast food jobs, that do not necessarily show the breadth of the graduate's experience. Focusing on skills will allow the graduate to include much more detail about his or her strengths. For example, communication skills, which may be important to obtaining a job in a public relations firm, might be demonstrated by activity on the speech team, or as an officer of a school club. A cover letter is necessary to show that the job applicant knows something about the business to which he or she is applying. The letter connects the experience listed on the résumé to the company's description of the job opening. A good letter persuades managers to read the résumé carefully and enthusiastically.

STANDARD & POOR'S

CASE STUDY
ANSWERS

1. After she has worked for several years, Trina may find that she needs specialized training in her chosen field. Many companies offer "rotation" programs to college graduates that let them work for six months to a year in different departments and then choose an area to specialize in. Trina should be thinking now about companies that will offer her this type of opportunity.

2. A mentor can help Trina understand the potential opportunities that are available to her and can offer practical suggestions. A mentor can also put Trina in touch with people who might provide her with information or opportunities.

3. Informational interviews are an excellent way to learn about trends in an industry. Trina might ask her school's alumni association to refer her to past graduates who are working in the types of jobs Trina is interested in.

Chapter 3 Planning Guide

Money Management Strategy

Teacher Manual

SECT.	OBJECTIVES	NATIONAL STANDARDS FOR BUSINESS EDUCATION	FEATURES	RESOURCES
3.1	After completing this lesson, students will have learned: How to recognize the relationship between financial documents and money management strategies; How to create a system to maintain personal financial documents **Economics** I. Allocation of Resources III. Economic Institutions and Incentives	**Economics** I. Allocation of Resources III. Economic Institutions and Incentives **Personal Finance** I. Personal Decision Making VIII. Protecting Against Risk	Standard & Poor's—Q & A, p. 58 What's Your Financial ID?—Money Management Quiz, p. 60	Check Your Understanding, p. 65 Think Critically, p. 65 Using Communication Skills, p. 65 Solving Money Problems, p. 65 Student Activity Workbook
3.2	After completing this lesson, students will have learned: How to develop a personal balance sheet and cash flow statement; How to analyze their personal financial situation	**Personal Finance** I. Personal Decision Making II. Earning a Living III. Managing Finances and Budgeting	Go Figure—Net Worth, p. 68 Careers in Finance—Financial Software Designer, p. 70 Go Figure—Net Cash Flow, p. 72	Check Your Understanding, p. 74 Think Critically, p. 74 Using Math Skills, p. 74 Solving Money Problems, p. 74 Student Activity Workbook
3.3	After completing this lesson, students will have learned: How to create a budget that's practical for them; How to achieve their financial goals by increasing their savings	**Economics** VIII. International Economic Concepts IX. Aggregate Supply and Aggregate Demand **Personal Finance** I. Personal Decision Making III. Managing Finances and Budgeting	Academic Connection—Science, p. 76 Standard & Poor's—Case Study, p. 78 Savvy Saver—Have Fun for Less, p. 79 International Finance—Israel, p. 82 Common Cents—Pay or Save?, p. 83 Your Financial Portfolio—What's Your Net Worth? p. 84	Check Your Understanding, p. 85 Think Critically, p. 85 Using Communication Skills, p. 85 Solving Money Problems, p. 85 Student Activity Workbook

Unit 1 *Planning Personal Finances*

SCANS Correlation Chart

FOUNDATION SKILLS

Basic Skills	Reading	Writing	Math	Listening	Speaking
Thinking Skills	Creative Thinking	Decision Making	Problem Solving	Seeing Things in the Mind's Eye	Knowing How to Learn	Reasoning
Personal Qualities	Responsibility	Self-Esteem	Sociability	Self-Management	Integrity/Honesty

WORKPLACE COMPETENCIES

Resources	Allocating Time	Allocating Money	Allocating Material and Facility Resources	Allocating Human Resources
Information	Acquiring and Evaluating Information	Organizing and Maintaining Information	Interpreting and Communicating Information	Using Computers to Process Information
Interpersonal Skills	Participating as a Member of a Team	Teaching Others	Serving Clients/Customers	Exercising Leadership	Negotiating to Arrive at a Decision	Working with Cultural Diversity
Systems	Understanding Systems	Monitoring and Correcting Performance	Improving and Designing Systems
Technology	Selecting Technology	Applying Technology to Task	Maintaining and Troubleshooting Technology

■ INTERNET EXTENSION

Activity: Have students find online budget activities and print them out to share with the class. As a class, compare the different budget activities and determine which one would be most helpful to them now.

Keywords: financial planning

■ ENRICHMENT/APPLICATION ACTIVITY

Guest Speaker: If possible, invite to class someone with experience at a kibbutz in Israel or someone with experience as a financial software designer. Ask the speaker to share his or her experiences as they relate to chapter content.

Chapter 3 *Money Management Strategy* TM69

■ TOPIC SPOTLIGHT

⊘ **Technology:** Have students write one paragraph explaining how technology has affected the ways people record and organize their personal financial records.

⑤ **Money:** Ask students how net worth is affected by overestimating assets or underestimating liabilities?

⊙ **Marketing:** Discuss with students why a credit card company or bank might sponsor money management Web sites or offer financial planning kits to prospective customers?

additional resources

Making the Most of Your Money by Jane Bryant Quinn (©1997 Simon & Schuster). This financial reference book translates sophisticated personal finance topics into everyday language. It covers everything from checking accounts to the Roth IRA.

Basics of Saving and Investing: A Teaching Guide (© 1998 Eastern Michigan University) is free to teachers. Unit 1 is directly related to this chapter. (See Additional Resources, Chapter 1 for information about obtaining a copy of this guide.)

www.ncfe.org is the Web site for Springboard ©, a non-profit consumer credit management agency with the mission of offering education and information about using credit wisely and providing consumers with alternatives to bankruptcy.

www.financialplan.about.com/money is a Web site devoted to wise financial planning on the About.com network. This Web site covers many areas of financial planning. Especially pertinent to this chapter is a Basic Budget Worksheet, which can be accessed on the "Subjects" menu under "Budgeting."

Note to teacher: Web site addresses may change.

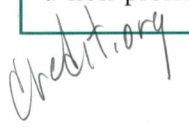

[handwritten: credit.org]

TM70 Unit 1 *Planning Personal Finances*

CHAPTER 3   Lesson Plans

SECTION 3.1

FOCUS

Motivation

Have the students share the ways they organize their schoolwork, homework, research projects, etc. Discuss whether being organized increases their ability to make good grades. Then ask if these organizational skills could transfer to other aspects of their lives including their personal finances.

Prereading

1. Have the students skim the section, looking at pictures, reading captions, and noting headings.
2. Have "What You'll Learn" listed on page 59 read aloud.
3. Write the terms *money management* and *safe deposit box* on the board. Ask the students to discuss the relationship between the two terms.
4. Ask the students to state the purpose of studying this chapter.

TEACH

Guided Practice

1. Have students read aloud the Standard & Poor's Q&A on page 58.
2. Read the section with your students.

Independent Practice

1. Have the students design a home filing system and share their ideas with the class.
2. Ask the students to research the different types of home safes. In addition, ask them to find out how much they cost. Have the students discuss whether a home safe would be a viable alternative to a safety deposit box located in a bank.

ASSESS

Reteaching

1. To reinforce the concept of opportunity cost, ask the students to think of a trade-off they have already made that day. [EXAMPLE: Chose to come to school instead of sleeping in; drank water instead of spending money on a soda; paid attention in class instead of daydreaming or sleeping.]
2. Then ask the students how this trade-off will pay off financially in the future.

Enrichment

1. Ask each student to interview a local business owner and find out how he or she organizes his or her business and financial records.
2. Have the students answer this ethical dilemma:
   You have recently begun working for a computer company. You are excited about the job because, after much research, you believe it really seems to match your skills and ability. Last week the owner of the company asked you to change some of the financial information on the reports you produce. In addition, he asked you to destroy the originals. What would you do? You really love the job.

Assessment

1. Have the students complete the Section 3.1 Assessment.
2. Assign an activity from the *Student Activity Workbook*.

CLOSE

Have students answer this question: "In order to make knowledgeable decisions about your spending, you must…." [HINT: "have organized personal financial records."]

SECTION 3.2

FOCUS

Motivation
Ask the students, "How will you know when you are meeting your financial goals?" The answers may vary, but most students will probably say when they can buy whatever they want. Explain to the students that there are many ways to determine where they are headed financially, and this section will help them better understand how to meet their financial goals.

Prereading
1. Have the students skim the section, looking at pictures, reading captions, and noting headings.
2. Have "What You'll Learn" listed on page 66 read aloud.
3. Have the students create flash cards based on the Key Terms and use their own words for the definitions rather than copying them from the text or dictionary.
4. Ask the students to state the purpose of studying this chapter.

TEACH

Guided Practice
1. Read the section with your students.
2. Assign an activity from the *Student Activity Workbook*.

Independent Practice
1. Have the students prepare a personal net worth statement. Make sure the students understand that this information is personal and you will not share it with anyone.
2. Have the students prepare a fictitious personal net worth statement for themselves in 20 years. Remind them to consider their career goals and personal goals when developing this statement.

Careers in Finance

Financial Software Designer
1. Ask the students, "Why would an accounting background be important to someone who is a financial software designer?"
2. Locate classified ads in the newspaper or on the Internet for financial software designers. Compare the required skills and education listed in the ads to those in the text. Then invite a financial software designer to speak to the class about the occupation.

ASSESS

Reteaching
1. Ask each student to pick a partner. Using the flash cards they made in this section, have them review the Key Terms with each other.
2. To reinforce the concept of discretionary income, have the students create a survey to find out what students in their school purchase with their discretionary money. Then have the students create a graph with the data they collected showing the type of items purchased.

Enrichment
1. Have the students research someone who is a millionaire. [EXAMPLE: This person could be someone famous or someone living in your community.] Ask the students to find out how this person measures the progress towards meeting his or her financial goals.
2. Invite someone from a local bank to speak to the class about how loan officers analyze someone's personal financial situation before determining whether they would loan them money or not.

Assessment

1. Have the students complete the Section 3.2 Assessment.
2. Assign an activity from the *Student Activity Workbook*.

CLOSE

Have your students explain how personal financial statements are like road maps.

SECTION 3.3

FOCUS

Motivation

Ask the students to brainstorm all the reasons why someone should create a budget and follow it. Then ask this question: "Why is budgeting only a part of money management?"

Prereading

1. Have the students skim the section, looking at pictures, reading captions, and noting headings.
2. Have "What You'll Learn" listed on page 75 read aloud.
3. Write the Key Terms *budget*, *consumer price index*, and *budget variance* on the board. As a class, write a definition for each word.
4. Ask your students to state the purpose of studying this chapter.

TEACH

Guided Practice

1. Read the section with your students.
2. Assign an activity from the *Student Activity Workbook*.

Independent Practice

1. Have the students create a workshop on personal budgeting that they might offer to other students, faculty, or senior citizens in their community.
2. Ask the students to research the amount of money people save in Japan and Germany, and compare the figures to the United States savings rate. Then have the students speculate why people in Japan and Germany save more or less than Americans.
3. Have your students research an article in a current financial publication on budgeting or saving. Ask them to write an evaluation of the information in the article.

$AVVY SAVER

Have Fun for Less

Ask the students to create a list of ways to "Have Fun for Less" in your community. Assign different students to keep the list updated each week throughout this course. Encourage students to try some of the activities.

INTERNATIONAL FINANCE
Israel

1. Have the students find out what the exchange rate is for a new shekel. Students can call a bank or use a currency exchange calculator found on the Internet.
2. Ask the students to research the amount of discretionary income a teenager in Israel has available. Compare that with the discretionary income of a U.S. teenager.
3. Divide the students into groups and have them plan an imaginary trip to Israel for two weeks. Have the students research the cost of airline tickets, hotel, tours, food, etc.

Common Cents

Pay or Save?

1. Have the students contact a local bank and find out what the interest rate is for the bank's credit card and savings accounts. What is the difference? Why is it worth

paying off the credit card balance before you begin adding to your savings account?
2. Ask your students to brainstorm a list of ways to avoid credit card balances in the first place.

ASSESS

Reteaching

1. Review the definitions the class provided for the Key Terms at the beginning of this section. Make sure the students have a clear understanding of the terms.
2. To emphasize the importance of budgeting for emergencies, ask the students to think of all crises that might occur during this school year where an emergency fund would be beneficial.

Enrichment

1. Ask the students to review their own spending and savings patterns. Have them write a paragraph on the changes they might make based on these patterns.
2. Have your students think of a plan to increase their personal savings. If they are willing, ask them to share with the class. Encourage them to implement their plans.

Assessment

1. Have the students complete the Section 3.3 Assessment.
2. Assign the Chapter Assessment.
3. Administer the test for Chapter 3 from the Reproducible Tests in the *Teacher Resource Binder*.

CLOSE

Have the students answer this question: "Why should a budget always be a written document?"

SECTION 3.1 ASSESSMENT ANSWERS

CHECK YOUR UNDERSTANDING

1. Organizing your financial documents will help you plan and measure your financial progress; handle routine money matters; determine how much money you'll have available to spend now and in the future; and make effective decisions about how to save money.
2. Sort through all your personal financial records; arrange them according to the nature and type of each document; and label all folders and boxes.
3. Safe-deposit boxes are usually kept in a locked, fireproof room, accessible only when the bank is open for business. The box can be opened only when two separate keys are used. Loss from fire and other disasters is extremely rare. The financial institution that owns the box usually has insurance to cover such losses if they do occur.

THINK CRITICALLY

4. Answers will vary but might include eating at home versus eating in a restaurant; using last year's boots (even though they may be worn out) versus buying a new pair before they go on sale; and buying a new CD versus listening to music on the radio. Explanations will vary.

USING COMMUNICATION SKILLS

5. Locations might include Maritza's home file, computer (if the agreement is available as an electronic document), or safe-deposit box.

SOLVING MONEY PROBLEMS

6. Answers will vary but may include: pay the bills; record all checks and deposits in a register; create a folder for each type of document that he has; label folders; and put paycheck stubs, receipts, and other documents into folders.

SECTION 3.2 ASSESSMENT
ANSWERS

CHECK YOUR UNDERSTANDING

1. First, determine your assets and liabilities. Then subtract your liabilities from your assets. The difference is your net worth.
2. List all your sources of income during a given month and record the amounts as your cash inflow. Make sure that you record the exact amount that is available to you to use. If you are recording income from work, you must record your take-home pay, not your gross pay. Make sure that you include your interest earnings on investments and savings.
3. If you have a deficit, you can either borrow money (increasing your liabilities) or draw from your savings (decreasing your assets).

THINK CRITICALLY

4. Answers will vary but might include automobile, musical instruments, jewelry, sports equipment, computers, or audiovisual equipment.

USING MATH SKILLS

5. Tameka had a negative net cash flow of $125. She had a deficit. [ANSWER: $2,375 − ($750 + $1,750) = −$125]

SOLVING MONEY PROBLEMS

6. Answers will vary but might include paying off part of the credit card balance; adding to the savings account; or doing some of each. If his credit card balance of $1,200 has a higher interest rate than he earns on his savings account, it would be best for him to pay off his credit card debt first.

SECTION 3.3 ASSESSMENT
ANSWERS

CHECK YOUR UNDERSTANDING

1. Make your best guesses based on your expenses from previous months. When in doubt, guess high. Compare the CPI to your actual budget to determine when you're spending too much for various items. Talk to friends and relatives about their variable expenses to see if your spending is comparable.
2. First, you have to determine where the shortfalls occur and decide whether you can make any trade-offs in those areas. Then you might take another look at your financial goals. Ask yourself which purchases fit into your overall plan for the future. Determine how quickly you are progressing toward your objectives. If your goals are changing, or if they are outdated, revise your goals to meet your needs.
3. Answers should include three of the following: setting aside a fixed amount as savings before you pay your bills; taking a payroll savings deduction; spending less each day; and beginning to save the money that you didn't spend.

THINK CRITICALLY

4. Answers will vary but might include car maintenance, food, entertainment, or telephone bills. Estimated figures will vary.

USING COMMUNICATION SKILLS

5. Answers will vary, but students should discuss problems that lie ahead if Tara does not reduce her spending, or they may suggest ways for Tara to cut expenses.

SOLVING MONEY PROBLEMS

6. Answers will vary, but students should query the cost of maintaining a car, how long Hiroko will need to work to pay off its purchase price, and whether she could reduce any existing expenses.

CHAPTER 3 ASSESSMENT
ANSWERS

■ **Understanding and Using Vocabulary**
Answers will vary.

■ Review Key Concepts
1. The amount of a fixed expense stays about the same each month; variable expenses can change from month to month.
2. Safe-deposit box, home file, and home computer.
3. Liquid assets, real estate, personal property, and investment assets.
4. (1) Set financial goals; (2) estimate income; (3) budget for unexpected expenses and savings; (4) budget fixed expenses; (5) budget variable expenses; (6) record what you spend; (7) review your spending and saving patterns.
5. A surplus is an excess of cash inflow over cash outflow; a deficit is cash outflow in excess of cash inflow.

■ Apply Key Concepts
1. Answers will vary but might include a higher than anticipated deficit or a lower than anticipated savings or surplus.
2. Answers will vary but might include obtaining an up-to-date balance of bank accounts and tracking expenses.
3. Answers will vary, but students might suggest that some people with big houses and lots of money would most likely have big mortgages and expensive lifestyles.
4. Answers will vary. Students may agree that estimating their variable expenses is the most difficult step.
5. Answers will vary. Students may cite commercials and advertisements that encourage people to spend indiscriminately; the wide availability of credit cards; and "no payment down" offers.

❓ Problem Solving Today
To save $600 in five months, the student would have to earn a surplus of $120 each month. [ANSWER: $600 ÷ 5 = $120] Working 20 hours at the computer center and 20 hours at the deli would only pay the student's fixed and variable expenses. [ANSWER: $290 + $210 = $500; 20 × $18 = $360; 20 × $7 = $140; $360 + $140 = $500] If the student worked approximately 18 extra hours each month at the deli, it would result in a monthly surplus of $126. [ANSWER: $120 ÷ $7/hr. = 17.14 hrs.] Answers will vary.

■ Real-World Application
Answers will vary.

FINANCE Online

One possible Web site is:
www.bankofamerica.com

Also, many colleges and universities offer information on financial aid packages and budgeting. Some Web sites include:
www.virtual.clemson.edu/groups /finaid/COSTS.HTM
www.aug.edu/startup/aces

Answers will vary.

Note to teacher: Web site addresses may change.

READING STRATEGIES
ANSWERS

Section 3.1
CONNECT (p. 60): Answers will vary.

PREDICT (p. 61): Keeping your records organized will help you plan your financial progress better, take care of routine transactions, such as paying bills and making deposits more efficiently, keep track of how much money you have to spend, and make good decisions about saving.

Section 3.2
RESPOND (p. 68): Answers will vary.

QUESTION (p. 71): Net worth will only tell you your general financial situation. Cash flow will tell you how much money you have to spend or save during a given time period.

Section 3.3

PREDICT (p. 76): Examples include medical costs, energy bills, car repairs, or emergency travel.

CONNECT (p. 80): Answers will vary.

STANDARD & POOR'S

CASE STUDY

ANSWERS

1. A high percentage of their income is being used to pay their credit cards. Unless they pay more than the minimum due each month, it may take them 10 to 15 years to pay off their existing balances.

2. By looking at the reasons behind their spending patterns, they can make some simple changes. For example, if they eat out during the week because they are too tired to cook, they can plan to cook meals in advance on the weekend.

3. The sooner they start to save for retirement, the more time they have to take advantage of compound earnings.

Chapter 4 Planning Guide

Consumer Purchasing Strategies and Legal Protection

Teacher Manual

SECT.	OBJECTIVES	NATIONAL STANDARDS FOR BUSINESS EDUCATION	FEATURES	RESOURCES
4.1	After completing this lesson, students will have learned: How to determine the factors that influence their buying decisions. How to use a research based approach to buying goods and services. How to apply strategies to make wise buying decisions	**Economics** I. Allocation of Resources II. Economic Systems III. Economic Institutions and Incentives **Personal Finance** I. Personal Decision Making III. Managing Finances and Budgeting V. Buying Goods and Services	**Standard & Poor's**—Q & A, p. 88 **Savvy Saver**—Shopping for Clothes, p. 95 **What's Your Financial ID?**—Are You a Smart Shopper? p. 96 **Go Figure**—Unit Pricing, p. 101 **Common Cents**—Impulse Buying, p. 102 **Standard & Poor's**—Case Study, p. 103	**Check Your Understanding,** p. 104 **Think Critically,** p. 104 **Using Math Skills,** p. 104 **Solving Money Problems,** p. 104 **Student Activity Workbook**
4.2	After completing this lesson, students will have learned: How to identify ways to solve consumer problems. How to describe the legal alternatives available to consumers	**Economics** III. Economic Institutions and Incentives VIII. International Economic Concepts **Personal Finance** V. Buying Goods and Services	**International Finance**—Canada, p. 107 **Academic Connection**—Language Arts, p. 109 **Careers in Finance**—Retail Sales Associate, p. 110 **Your Financial Portfolio**—Your Budget, p. 112	**Check Your Understanding,** p. 113 **Think Critically,** p. 113 **Using Communication Skills,** p. 113 **Solving Money Problems,** p. 113 **Student Activity Workbook**

SCANS Correlation Chart

FOUNDATION SKILLS

Basic Skills	Reading	Writing	Math	Listening	Speaking
Thinking Skills	Creative Thinking	Decision Making	Problem Solving	Seeing Things in the Mind's Eye	Knowing How to Learn	Reasoning
Personal Qualities	Responsibility	Self-Esteem	Sociability	Self-Management	Integrity/Honesty

WORKPLACE COMPETENCIES

Resources	Allocating Time	Allocating Money	Allocating Material and Facility Resources	Allocating Human Resources
Information	Acquiring and Evaluating Information	Organizing and Maintaining Information	Interpreting and Communicating Information	Using Computers to Process Information
Interpersonal Skills	Participating as a Member of a Team	Teaching Others	Serving Clients/Customers	Exercising Leadership	Negotiating to Arrive at a Decision	Working with Cultural Diversity
Systems	Understanding Systems	Monitoring and Correcting Performance	Improving and Designing Systems
Technology	Selecting Technology	Applying Technology to Task	Maintaining and Troubleshooting Technology

Chapter 4 *Consumer Purchasing Strategies and Legal Protection*

INTERNET EXTENSION

Activity: Have students access the *Consumer Reports* Web site at www.consumerreports.org and write a brief report on how they might use this Web site before making a major purchase.

ENRICHMENT/APPLICATION ACTIVITY

Guest Speaker: Take students to the public library or a full-sized bookstore to see the many financial planning books available. Have each student write the name, title, and brief description of two books that they would choose to read, and explain why.

TOPIC SPOTLIGHT

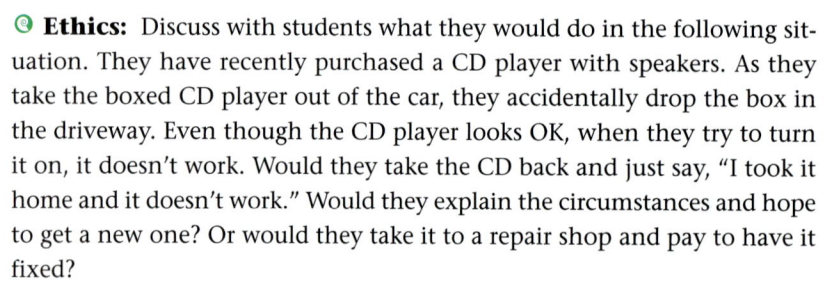

Ethics: Discuss with students what they would do in the following situation. They have recently purchased a CD player with speakers. As they take the boxed CD player out of the car, they accidentally drop the box in the driveway. Even though the CD player looks OK, when they try to turn it on, it doesn't work. Would they take the CD back and just say, "I took it home and it doesn't work." Would they explain the circumstances and hope to get a new one? Or would they take it to a repair shop and pay to have it fixed?

Marketing: Ask students to describe the kinds of advertisements that they like. Are they on the radio or television, billboards or magazines? Do they think these advertisements really get them to buy the product? Why or why not?

Money: Tell students that they are shopping for two new pair of jeans and ask which sale would be the best buy—jeans that regularly sell for $29.99 on sale for 30 percent off, or jeans priced at $29.99 that are part of a buy one/get one at half price sale? [ANSWER: $29.99 × 30% = 8.99; $29.99 − 8.99 = $21.00; $21.00 × 2 = $42.00; $29.99 × 50% = $14.99; $29.99 + $14.99 = $44.98]

additional resources

The Complete Tightwad Gazette: Promoting Thrift as a Viable Alternative Lifestyle by Amy Dacyczyn (First edition, paperback © 1999 Random House). This book is a compilation of six years of Ms. Dacyczyn's very popular newsletter of the same name, which advocates less costly living. The newsletters contain sensible advice, hints, recipes, tips, tricks, and strategies.

Consumer Action Handbook (formerly ***Consumer's Resource Handbook***) is published by the Consumer Information Center. Single copies of this handbook are available **free** by writing to CRH, Consumer Information Center, Pueblo, CO 81009, or by accessing the CIC Web site at www.pueblo.gsa.gov. Part 1 contains information on buying wisely and Part 2 is the Consumer Assistance Directory.

www.bbb.org is the Web site of the Better Business Bureau. It offers a directory of BBB offices, information on marketplace scams, and links to other BBB Web sites.

www.ftc.gov/bcp/bcp.htm is the Web site of the Bureau of Consumer Protection, an agency of the Federal Trade Commission. This agency is responsible for enforcing consumer protection laws and providing information to consumers in order to protect them from unfair or deceptive business practices. Links to the agency's five divisions are listed on the home page.

Note to teacher: Web site addresses may change.

CHAPTER 4   Lesson Plans

SECTION 4.1

FOCUS

Motivation
Tell your students to imagine they are going to buy a new outfit for school. Have them discuss the factors that will influence their buying decisions.

Prereading
1. Have your students skim the section, looking at pictures, reading captions, and noting headings.
2. Have "What You'll Learn" listed on page 89 read aloud.
3. Write the Key Terms on the board. Ask the students to guess at their meaning. Write the guesses on the board.
4. Ask the students to state the purpose of studying this chapter in their own words.

TEACH

Guided Practice
1. Have students read aloud the Standard & Poor's Q&A on page 88.
2. Read the section with your students.

Independent Practice
1. Have your students select a big-ticket item to purchase and research through the Internet, *Consumer Reports*, or a government agency.
2. Many people lease cars instead of purchasing them. Ask the students to research the pros and cons of leasing versus buying automobiles.
3. Have your students research store brands versus name brands. Ask them to find at least five examples of different products, and compare price, quality, and availability.
4. Ask students to bring in a service contract or warranty for a car, appliance, or piece of electronic equipment. In groups, have your students evaluate the service contract to see if it is worth the cost.

$avvy Saver

Shopping for Clothes
1. Ask your students to create two additional tips to add to the list "Shopping for Clothes."
2. Have the students answer this question: "Is it always a good idea to buy clothes from the sale rack? Why or why not?"

Common Cents

Impulse Buying
1. Have the students contact a local bank to determine the interest rate charged on their credit cards and the interest rate paid on their savings account.
2. Have the students contact three different retail stores in their community to determine if they offer credit cards. If so, ask them to find out the interest rate and minimum monthly payment charged.

ASSESS

Reteaching
1. Review the guesses the students made when beginning this section. Clarify any questions the students might have.
2. Divide the students into pairs. Ask each group to select two concepts and write summary sentences about the concepts.
3. To reinforce the concept that "the purchasing process is an ongoing activity," tell

the students you are planning to make a purchase of a big-ticket item. [HINT: car, computer, stereo, home] Ask the class to brainstorm the different phases you will go through before, during, and after the purchase.

Enrichment

1. Have your students form groups and create a public service announcement (PSA) that emphasizes the strategies for making wise buying decisions. They should write a script, add music, and perform the PSA for the class.
2. Divide the students into groups. Bring in several grocery store items, and have each group select one item and analyze the product label. Ask the groups to determine what additional information should be included on each label that would help consumers when making a buying decision. Then have your students redesign the label to include the additional information.
3. Ask the students to bring in a warranty for an item they purchased recently. Then have them read and interpret the warranty. Ask your students if they have ever used a warranty.
4. Invite a member of the Better Business Bureau, or some other consumer protection agency member, to discuss with students the rights of consumers in today's marketplace.

Assessment

1. Have your students complete the Section 4.1 Assessment.
2. Assign an activity from the *Student Activity Workbook*.

CLOSE

As a class, have students answer this question: "What steps do I need to take in order to get the best value for my money when making a purchase?"

SECTION 4.2

FOCUS

Motivation

Present this example to the class: Mark needed new tires for his car. Last weekend he took his car to a shop that advertised $99 for four tires. When Mark picked his car up, his bill was $199, and he noticed the tires were not very good quality. Mark did not realize that there would be an installation charge of $25 per tire, and that the tires only had a life of 10,000 miles. Mark questioned the shop owner who told Mark there was nothing he could do. Ask your students these two questions: "Is there anything Mark can do now to resolve the difference in his bill? What should Mark do to protect himself from this situation in the future?"

Prereading

1. Have the students skim the section, looking at pictures, reading captions, and noting headings.
2. Have "What You'll Learn" listed on page 105 read aloud.
3. Divide the class into five groups and assign each group one of the Key Terms from this section. Ask each group to create a definition for the term using their own words and present it to the class. Have other groups add to the definitions as necessary.
4. Ask the students to state the purpose of studying this chapter.

TEACH

Guided Practice

1. Read the section with your students.
2. Assign an activity from the *Student Activity Workbook*.

Independent Practice
1. Ask your students to research the United States Office of Consumer Affairs to find out what services they provide.
2. Have the students select another country and research how the government sets safety standards for food, drugs, chemicals, and household devices.
3. Take the class on a field trip to a small claims court. Have them watch the cases being presented. Then have your students hold a mock small claims court and role-play a variety of consumer cases. [HINT: The students can find potential cases in the newspaper or Internet as examples.]
4. Invite someone from the legal aid society to speak to the class about the services they provide.

INTERNATIONAL FINANCE
Canada
1. Have your students research the Canadian government. Then have them analyze how it is similar to and different than the government of the United States.
2. Ask the students to find out how important tourism is to the economy in Montreal. What other sites, in addition to the Underground, are popular among visitors?
3. Ask the students this question: "Do you think you would pay more for items purchased in the Underground than you would in stores located in other parts of the city? Why or why not?

Careers in Finance
Retail Sales Associate
1. Find out how many students in the class work or have worked in retail sales. Ask them what they liked and didn't like about the job.
2. Have your students conduct undercover research. Ask them to pretend to be a customer and observe retail sales associates in three different stores. Ask your students the following questions: "Was the sales associate friendly? Did he/she greet you in a timely fashion? Was the sales associate courteous, respectful, and enthusiastic even though you were not going to be making a purchase?" Then have your students write a one-page conclusion about their findings.
3. Ask your students to contact the same retail stores they visited in the above activity and find out what training is offered to new retail sales associates. Compile the results as a class. Is there a relationship between the amount of training offered and the quality of the sales associate?

ASSESS
Reteaching
1. Review the original definitions of the Key Terms provided by students at the beginning of this section. Ask your students to modify or enhance their definitions as necessary.
2. To reinforce the importance of the local, state, and federal consumer agencies, ask the students to brainstorm a list of problems that might occur if these agencies did not exist.
3. Ensure that your students understand the difference between mediation and arbitration. Write the two terms on the board and ask the students to list the characteristics of each.

Enrichment
1. Ask your students to interview local business owners to find out how they resolve consumer complaints. Compile and analyze the results.
2. Have the students research a class-action suit and write a paper on the issue, legal action taken, parties involved, and the resolution.

Assessment

1. Have the students complete the Section 4.2 Assessment.
2. Assign the Chapter Assessment.
3. Administer the test for Chapter 4 from the Reproducible Tests in the *Teacher Resource Binder*.

CLOSE

Have the students answer this question: "What strategies will you use to protect yourself from consumer fraud?"

SECTION 4.1 ASSESSMENT
ANSWERS

CHECK YOUR UNDERSTANDING

1. Answers will vary but may include: prices, interest rates, product quality, supply and demand, convenience, product safety, brand names, maintenance costs, warranties.
2. Before you shop: identify why you need or want in-line skates in particular; gather information by talking to friends who have skates and by reading reports in sports or consumer magazines; be aware of the marketplace (i.e., different kinds and features of in-line skates). Weighing the alternatives: rent skates from a sporting goods store to understand better the choices that are available and whether you really want to spend money on this product; borrow skates from a friend if possible; compare stores and prices.
3. Answers will vary but may include: timing purchases to take advantage of sales; considering the benefits and limitations of different types of stores and selecting the right type of store in which to buy an item; comparing brands; comparing prices and unit prices; reading labels carefully; evaluating warranties and service contracts.

THINK CRITICALLY

4. Answers will vary, but students' examples should demonstrate an awareness of economic, social, and personal factors as these apply to the scenarios that they have created.

USING MATH SKILLS

5. The cat food from animal hospital is $2.25/pound. The 25-pound bag is $2.38/pound, and the 50-pound bag is $1.99/pound. The 50-pound bag is the best buy in terms of price. Answers may include: it's not organic, and that may present a problem if Gilda's cat really needs organic cat food or won't eat any other kind. Also, a 50-pound bag of food may spoil before the cat can eat all of it.

SOLVING MONEY PROBLEMS

6. Answers will vary, but may include: Marta may be able to take advantage of special sales, such as Fourth of July sales, Labor Day sales, and back-to-school sales. With six months to go before the holidays, Marta can visit many stores to compare prices and brands. The time she has to shop may also help her avoid impulse buying, which she might be more likely to do during the hectic holiday season.

SECTION 4.2 ASSESSMENT
ANSWERS

CHECK YOUR UNDERSTANDING

1. Document the process. Keep a file of receipts, names of people you talk to, dates of attempted repairs, copies of letters you wrote, and any fees that you have had to pay.
2. The five methods are: return to the place of purchase; contact the company headquarters; get help from a consumer agency; use dispute resolution programs such as mediation or arbitration; take legal action.

3. Answers will vary. Advantages of small claims courts include: legal costs are low; the whole process usually takes only a few weeks; courts often rule in your favor; the process usually does not include lawyers or juries. Disadvantages include: the decision of the judge is final; you have to submit your own evidence and present your own case; awards have predetermined limits from $1,000 to $25,000, depending on the state.

THINK CRITICALLY

4. Answers will vary. Reasons for dissatisfaction might include defective or low-quality products, unexpected costs, deceptive pricing, poor repair service, or fraud.

USING COMMUNICATION SKILLS

5. Answers will vary but may include: telephone and mail scams that offer free "prizes" (including trips to popular or exotic vacation locales); low-cost travel packages; work-at-home schemes; miraculous diet products. Ways to avoid becoming a victim of fraud may include: do business with reputable companies; don't sign contracts or other documents that you don't understand; be wary of offers that seem too good to be true; don't rush into what seems to be a good deal.

SOLVING MONEY PROBLEMS

6. Answers will vary but may include that they should first try to contact the company and see if they can resolve the matter over the phone. If that doesn't work, they should write a complaint letter to the company. If the company doesn't respond or satisfy their complaint, their next step might be to see whether a consumer agency can help them. They may also check out dispute resolution programs. In the end, they may have to take the matter to small claims court to recover their money.

CHAPTER 4 ASSESSMENT
ANSWERS

■ Understanding and Using Vocabulary
Answers will vary.

■ Review Key Concepts
1. Buying decisions are based on a number of economic, social, and personal factors.
2. Answers will vary, but findings may compare hours of operation, location, reputation, policies, services, prices, and the quality and variety of merchandise.
3. Comparison shopping allows you to compare prices and other features of similar items at different stores so that you can make an informed decision about where to buy.
4. Consumer agencies can help you avoid problems by providing information about companies and the experiences other consumers have had in dealing with them. The agencies can help you resolve problems by enforcing an existing law or by alerting the public to a potential problem.
5. Consumers can go to small claims court, become involved in a class-action suit, hire a lawyer, or seek help from a legal aid society.

■ Apply Key Concepts
1. Answers will vary but may include: price, product quality, convenience, product safety, brand names, warranty, lifestyle, peer influence, advertising, income, age, and gender.
2. Answers will vary. Students may visit and investigate department stores, specialty stores, warehouse stores, discount stores, and others. Becoming more aware of the marketplace can help you make better buying decisions and have more success at finding what you need.
3. Answers will vary but may include: prices, quality, label information, brands, warranties, and service contracts.
4. Answers will vary.
5. Answers will vary.

❓ Problem Solving Today

You would save $24 a year if you bought the snowshoes instead of renting them. [ANSWER: 4 × $6 = $24] Your credit card interest for the year would total $18. [ANSWER: 12 × $1.50 = $18] Answers will vary, but students will have to decide whether having their own snowshoes is more important to them than paying off a debt and avoiding interest charges. Their decisions will also depend upon their overall financial situations.

■ Real-World Application
Answers will vary.

FINANCE Online

Possible Web sites include:
- www.expedia.msn.com
- www.priceline.com
- www.checkbook.org

Answers will vary.

Note to teacher: Web site addresses may change.

READING STRATEGIES
ANSWERS

Section 4.1
CONNECT (p. 91): Typical answers might include: price, performance, reputation for quality, and warranties or service agreements.

QUESTION (p. 102): Considerations in ranking include replacement expense and the potential for the product to break or need service. The following items are ranked in order of importance of having a good warranty:
  (1) car
  (2) CD player
  (3) baseball glove
  (4) wool blazer

Section 4.2
RESPOND (p. 107): Answers might include: frustrated, cheated, angry, inconvenienced, and impatient. Managers and salespeople will be more likely to respond positively and helpfully to a calm customer who explains his or her complaint rationally.

PREDICT (p. 110): Options include: going to small claims court, participating in a class action lawsuit, hiring a lawyer, or obtaining the services of a legal aid society.

STANDARD & POOR'S
CASE STUDY
ANSWERS

1. Commuting costs should be factored in when choosing a place to live and considering accepting a job offer. Using public transportation is generally much cheaper than the cost of driving and maintaining a car.
2. It's a good idea to check with the local Better Business Bureau before making a major purchase from an unfamiliar dealer. When purchasing a used car, it's common practice to have the car inspected by an independent garage and insist that needed repairs be completed before the sale is completed.
3. Francine may be legally responsible to the new buyer for existing problems with the car.

UNIT 1 — Planning Guide

PLANNING PERSONAL FINANCES

Chapter 1—
Personal Financial Planning

Chapter 2—
Financial Aspects of Career Planning

Chapter 3—
Money Management Strategy

Chapter 4—
Consumer Purchasing Strategies and Legal Protection

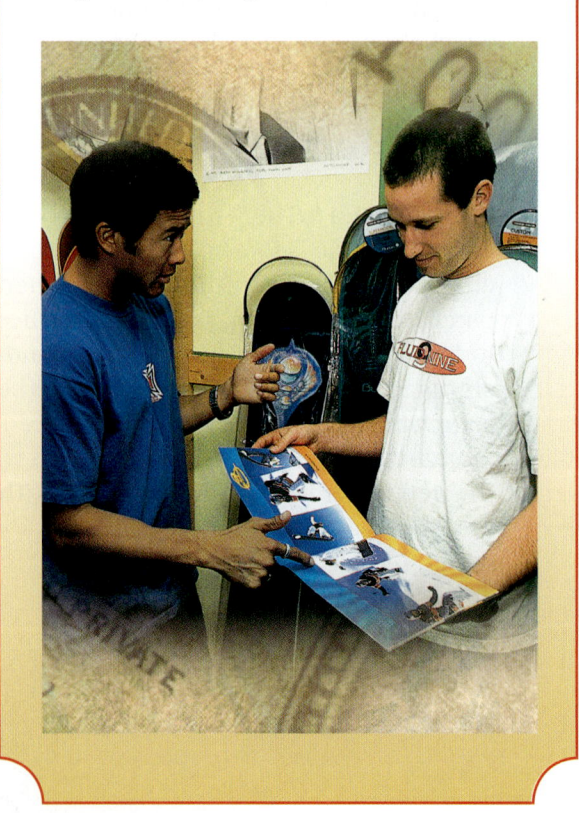

OVERVIEW

This unit introduces students to the concept of financial planning and provides the foundation for using personal financial planning techniques. In Chapter 1, students will learn how to create a financial plan using the six steps of the financial planning process. Chapter 2 discusses the relationship between work, careers, and financial planning. Students will learn how to identify the personal issues to consider when choosing a career and how to apply effective strategies to obtain employment. Chapter 3 explains the relationship between financial documents and money management strategies and how to create a budget, and Chapter 4 describes the importance of wise buying decisions.

INTRODUCTION

To introduce the concept of personal financial planning, ask students to spend 10 to 15 minutes writing a description of the life they expect for themselves as adults. Ask them to describe where they will live, what kind of work will they do, whether or not they expect to marry and have a family, if they would like to travel and where, and what kind of car they would like to own. Then ask them how they expect to achieve these goals and is it enough just to make big bucks. Finally, explain that financial planning helps us achieve our life's goals. Through careful planning, wise spending, and choosing an appropriate career, they can achieve their goals.

Get a Financial Life!

CASE STUDY 1

Teaching Guide

Step A — THE PROCESS

Make sure students have access to all necessary materials. Lead students through the process:

1. Remind them of the future life they wrote about in the unit introduction. They can use this description to help them develop their goals.
2. Help students arrange to take the aptitude test or interest inventory. Contact the school counselor so he or she is prepared for the students' requests.
3. Give students the list of Web sites from the Additional Resources section of the Chapter 2 Planning Guide. These sites can help students research careers.
4. Help students secure an opportunity to interview or job shadow someone working in their area of interest.
5. If students have questions about how to obtain college catalogs from distant schools, point out that colleges will happily mail information to prospective students. Using the Internet or reference books from the public library, students can obtain the addresses of schools of interest.
6. Explain that by creating templates for a résumé and a cover letter, students will not have to re-enter the text every time they need one of these documents, but they will be able to customize their letters and résumés.

Step B — CREATE YOUR PORTFOLIO

Review students' portfolios regularly to make sure they are working on them over time and not waiting until the last minute. Consider creating a schedule for completion of each section in the portfolio.

Step C — PRESENTATION

Evaluate the presentations based on the following criteria:

- Check that students have read their chosen book thoroughly. Allow time for questions to determine how well the students understand what they read.
- Presentations should be clear and easy to understand. They should be interesting and informative.
- Make sure students explain why they would or would not recommend the book to Karla.

UNIT CLOSURE

Have each student write a one- or two-page answer to this question: On a scale from one to ten (one being unimportant and ten being very important), how would you rate financial planning and its impact on your life?

EVALUATION

Administer the Unit 1 test from the **ExamView** Pro Testmaker CD-ROM.

Chapter 5 Planning Guide

Banking

Teacher Manual

SECT.	OBJECTIVES	NATIONAL STANDARDS FOR BUSINESS EDUCATION	FEATURES	RESOURCES
5.1	After completing this lesson, students will have learned: How to identify available financial services How to distinguish among various types of financial institutions	**Economics** I. Allocation of Resources III. Economic Institutions and Incentives VII. The Role of Government **Personal Finance** I. Personal Decision Making II. Earning a Living III. Managing Finances and Budgeting IV. Saving and Investing V. Buying Goods and Services VI. Banking VII. Using Credit VIII. Protecting Against Risk	**Standard & Poor's—**Q & A, p. 120 **What's Your Financial ID?—**Basic Banking Quiz, p. 123 **Careers in Finance—**Bank Teller, p. 124	**Check Your Understanding,** p. 132 **Think Critically,** p. 132 **Using Math Skills,** p. 132 **Solving Money Problems,** p. 132 **Student Activity Workbook**
5.2	After completing this lesson, students will have learned: How to compare the costs and benefits of different savings plans How to evaluate savings plans How to compare the costs and benefits of different types of checking accounts How to use a checking account effectively	**Economics** I. Allocation of Resources II. Economic Systems III. Economic Institutions and Incentives VIII. International Economic Concepts **Personal Finance** I. Personal Decision Making II. Earning a Living III. Managing Finances and Budgeting IV. Saving and Investing VI. Banking VIII. Protecting Against Risk	**Standard & Poor's—**Case Study, p. 136 **Go Figure—**Interest Compounded Monthly, p. 138 **Go Figure—**Rate of Return, p. 139 **International Finance—**Switzerland, p. 141 **Academic Connection—**Math, p. 142 **Savvy Saver—**Bank on It, p. 143 **Common Cents—**Money Toss, p. 147 **Your Financial Portfolio—**Comparison Shopping for Banking Services, p. 148	**Check Your Understanding,** p. 149 **Think Critically,** p. 149 **Using Communication Skills,** p. 149 **Solving Money Problems,** p. 149 **Student Activity Workbook**

SCANS Correlation Chart

FOUNDATION SKILLS

Basic Skills	Reading	Writing	Math	Listening	Speaking
Thinking Skills	Creative Thinking	Decision Making	Problem Solving	Seeing Things in the Mind's Eye	Knowing How to Learn	Reasoning
Personal Qualities	Responsibility	Self-Esteem	Sociability	Self-Management	Integrity/Honesty

WORKPLACE COMPETENCIES

Resources	Allocating Time	Allocating Money	Allocating Material and Facility Resources	Allocating Human Resources
Information	Acquiring and Evaluating Information	Organizing and Maintaining Information	Interpreting and Communicating Information	Using Computers to Process Information
Interpersonal Skills	Participating as a Member of a Team	Teaching Others	Serving Clients/Customers	Exercising Leadership	Negotiating to Arrive at a Decision	Working with Cultural Diversity
Systems	Understanding Systems	Monitoring and Correcting Performance	Improving and Designing Systems
Technology	Selecting Technology	Applying Technology to Task	Maintaining and Troubleshooting Technology

■ INTERNET EXTENSION

Activity: Have students use the Internet to locate various bank rates and compare the rates of two banks or two banking plans from one bank. Bank rates can be found at **www.bankrate.com** or **www.banx.com**. They can also enter the name of a particular bank to find out whether or not it has its own Web site.

Key Words: banking, bank rates

■ ENRICHMENT/APPLICATION ACTIVITY

Field Trip: Take students to visit a local bank. Arrange for them to talk with a loan officer, bank manager, and teller. Request information brochures that you can copy for the students to study. Have students compare the bank's services with information presented in the chapter.

Chapter 5   *Banking*   TM91

■ TOPIC SPOTLIGHT ▶

◉ **Ethics:** Have students review the personality traits for a bank teller given in the Careers in Finance feature. Ask your students, "What does *discreet* mean? Why is it an important trait for a bank teller?"

◉ **Technology:** Discuss how technology has affected *where* people do their banking.

◉ **Government:** Ask students to name two ways the government protects consumers who use banks and other financial institutions.

additional resources

The Federal Reserve System has produced many informative, attractive, and **free** publications. The ***Public Information Catalog*** is online at **http://app.ny.frb.org/cfpicnic /frame1.cfm** and lists most publications and audiovisual materials prepared by the 12 Federal Reserve Banks and the Board of Governors of the Federal Reserve System. These materials are designed to increase public understanding of the functions and operations of the Federal Reserve System, monetary policy, financial markets and institutions, consumer finance, and the economy. Publications include *Banking Basics, The Story of American Currency, In Plain English: Making Sense of the Federal Reserve, Electronic Money,* and *The Story of Checks and Electronic Payments* and may be ordered from this Web site.

Some additional Federal Reserve Web sites include:

    www.stls.frb.org (St. Louis)
    www.chicagofed.org (Chicago)
    www.bos.frb.org (Boston)
    www.frbsf.org (San Francisco)

All Federal Reserve Bank Web sites are accessible through **www.ny.frb.org**.

www.asec.org is the Web site of the American Savings Education Council, a coalition of private and public sector institutions, that undertakes initiatives to raise public awareness about what is needed to ensure long-term personal financial independence. This Web site offers savings tools and plans, and lists programs and events.

www.aba.com is the Web site of the American Bankers Association and provides information about banking services.

www.fdic.gov is the Federal Deposit Insurance Corporation Web site, which provides access to consumer information, press releases, and banking statistics.

www.publicdebt.treas.gov provides current information on U.S. savings bonds. This site includes a downloadable software program called "Savings Bond Wizard" that helps inventory your savings bonds and determine redemption values and earned interest. The "Savings Bond Calculator" offers the same features online.

Note to Teacher: Web site addresses may change.

CHAPTER 5   Lesson Plans

SECTION 5.1

FOCUS

Motivation

Have your students share information about the financial services they currently use (savings accounts, ATM cards, debit cards, checking accounts). Generate a list of them during the discussion. Then ask the students to describe the services they couldn't live without and why.

Prereading

1. Have the students skim the section, looking at pictures, reading captions, and noting headings.
2. Have "What You'll Learn" listed on page 121 read aloud.
3. List and review the Key Terms with your students. Acknowledge students' correct answers by writing a brief definition next to the terms they know. Place an asterisk by the terms they do not know.
4. Ask the students to state the purpose of studying this chapter.

TEACH

Guided Practice

1. Have students read aloud the Standard & Poor's Q&A on page 120.
2. Read the section with your students.

Independent Practice

1. More and more people are paying their bills electronically. Ask the students to find out how electronic payments are protected against theft.
2. Have your students investigate and write a paper on ATM fraud.
3. Have the students research e-cash—the electronic equivalent of cash that is used when making purchases online.
4. Ask the students to find out if the local banks in their community participate in the FDIC program.

Careers in Finance

Bank Teller

1. Have your students research the Institute of Financial Education or the American Institute of Banking to find out what courses and certifications they offer.
2. Ask the students to describe why they think many bank managers began their careers as bank tellers.
3. Generate a discussion with your students on the interpersonal skills that bank tellers need to be successful. Ask them to justify their answers.

ASSESS

Reteaching

1. Review with your students the Key Terms that you placed an asterisk next to during the Prereading section.
2. To help students understand the various deposit and non-deposit type financial institutions, ask your students to write one characteristic of each type of institution. Compile the characteristics on the board. Then have your students determine which feature(s) makes each institution unique.

Enrichment

1. Ask your students to find out if any of the local banks offer special savings accounts for students.
2. Ask the students to find out why some businesses that accept Visa debit cards require

PIN numbers and some do not. Is one safer than another?
3. Have your students select two financial institutions—one from the deposit and one from the non-deposit group. Ask them to research each one (using the library, Internet and live interviews) and write a paper that will compare and contrast the two.

Assessment
1. Have your students complete the Section 5.1 Assessment.
2. Assign an activity from the *Student Activity Workbook*.

CLOSE
Have students answer this question: "Which features of financial services and institutions will best meet your needs today? In five years? In ten years?"

SECTION 5.2

FOCUS

Motivation
Ask the students to share their plans after high school graduation. Most students will probably say they will be going to college. Have the students discuss how they are saving money for college. For those students who say they will be going directly into the workplace, ask them if they should be saving money as well.

Prereading
1. Have your students skim the section, looking at pictures, reading captions, and noting headings.
2. Have "What You'll Learn" listed on page 133 read aloud.
3. Divide the students into four groups and have each group generate definitions for the words without using the text. Limit this exercise to 15 minutes. When the time is up, have each group give its definition. When there are groups that disagree with the definitions, use this as an opportunity to clarify information.
4. Ask your students to state the purpose of studying this chapter in their own words.

TEACH

Guided Practice
1. Read the section with your students.
2. Assign an activity from the *Student Activity Workbook*.

Independent Practice
1. Have your students create a bulletin board showing the various savings options. Ask them to include checking accounts, savings accounts, money market accounts, CDs, and U.S. savings bonds. The bulletin board should include current interest rate, financial risk, and liquidity.
2. Ask the students to create a math lesson on how to figure the rate of return and compound interest. Then have them teach the lesson to other students in the class or even to a math class in the school.
3. Invite someone from a bank to your class to share with the students the process of opening a checking account.
4. Have the students research the different kinds of traveler's checks that are on the market.

INTERNATIONAL FINANCE
Switzerland
1. Ask your students, "Since total secrecy is no longer the unique feature of Swiss bank accounts, what do you think the Swiss could do to make their banks more globally competitive."
2. Have your students research a Swiss bank to find out: (1) the location of its headquarters; (2) the year it was founded;

(3) the services it provides; and (4) whether there are branches located in the United States, and if so, where.
3. Switzerland has been a leader in facilitating international trade. Have your students discuss why they think this is the case.

$avvy Saver

Bank on It—Finding the Best Savings Account
1. Ask your students to discuss whether the highest interest rate should be the deciding factor when choosing a savings account.
2. Have your students answer this question: "Why does it matter how often the bank credits interest to your account?"
3. Have the students survey local banks and determine how many offer simple interest or compound interest on their savings accounts.

Common Cents

Money Toss
1. Bring a large jar into the classroom and have the students volunteer to deposit all their pennies each day during the next month. At the end of the month, add up the total and donate it to a charity selected by the class.
2. Ask your students to volunteer to toss their change each night. Each week ask them to add up the total. Then have them graph their weekly totals and use computer software if possible.

ASSESS

Reteaching
1. Review the original definitions of the Key Terms provided by the students at the beginning of this section. Ask the students to modify or enhance them as necessary.

2. To reinforce the math concepts required to figure out the rate of return and compounding, have your students create a math problem for each. Use some of these questions on a quiz or test.

Enrichment
1. Have your students select a bank in your community and research all the charges related to checking accounts. Compile the answers as a class and find out which bank is the most cost effective.
2. Ask a bank to print "dummy" checks for your class or create them yourself. Have the students practice writing checks and endorsing them.
3. Invite a banker to the class to demonstrate how to reconcile a bank statement. If any of your students is willing to share their own statement, ask them to bring it to class and demonstrate how they reconcile their statement.

Assessment
1. Have the students complete the Section 5.2 Assessment.
2. Assign the Chapter Assessment.
3. Administer the test for Chapter 5 from the Reproducible Tests in the *Teacher Resource Binder*.

CLOSE
Have your students answer this question: "Why is it important to evaluate the different savings and checking accounts available?"

SECTION 5.1 ASSESSMENT
ANSWERS

CHECK YOUR UNDERSTANDING
1. The categories are savings, payment services, and borrowing.
2. Electronic services include direct deposit, automatic payments, ATMs, and plastic payments.

Chapter 5   *Banking*   TM95

3. Deposit-type institutions include commercial banks, savings and loan associations, mutual savings banks, and credit unions. Nondeposit-type institutions include life insurance companies, investment companies, finance companies, and mortgage companies.

THINK CRITICALLY

4. Answers will vary, but services used now may include savings accounts and checking accounts. In five years students may also need borrowing services and more sophisticated savings and payment services, such as automatic payments, direct deposit, or other services. Reasons for the changes might be that students will have more money to manage and may need to borrow for large expenses, such as a car, home, or a business.

USING MATH SKILLS

5. The annual cost of using this ATM is $234. [ANSWER: 3 × $1.50 = $4.50; 52 × $4.50 = $234]

SOLVING MONEY PROBLEMS

6. Answers will vary, but Dakota would probably best meet his needs by choosing a full-service commercial bank, a savings and loan association, or—if the company where he works has one—a credit union. He needs a savings account, a checking account, electronic banking, and borrowing services.

SECTION 5.2 ASSESSMENT
ANSWERS

CHECK YOUR UNDERSTANDING

1. Costs: You have to leave your money on deposit for a set amount of time; you will usually have to pay a penalty if you take the money out before the maturity date; and you may need to make a certain minimum investment. Benefits: A CD carries a relatively low risk, and it offers a higher interest rate than a regular savings account.
2. Your selection of a savings plan will be influenced by several factors, including the rate of return, inflation, tax considerations, liquidity, and restrictions and fees.
3. Regular checking accounts usually don't require a minimum balance. However, if they do have a minimum balance requirement and your account drops below that amount, you will have to pay a monthly fee. Some institutions will waive the service charge if you keep a certain amount in your savings account. Activity accounts don't require a minimum balance but institutions do charge you for each transaction and may also have a monthly fee. Interest-earning accounts offer interest (usually a very low rate) but often require a minimum balance; if you go below that balance, you may not earn interest and may have to pay a service charge.
4. To maintain your checking account, you need to write all transactions in your check register and fill out a bank reconciliation form when your statement arrives. You'll have to make sure that the balance in your check register and the adjusted bank balance on the reconciliation form are the same.

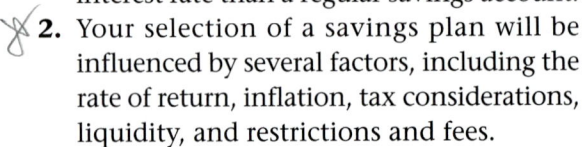

THINK CRITICALLY

5. Answers will vary but may include that with a standard method of calculating interest and of explaining terms and conditions of savings plans, consumers are able to make well-informed decisions when they compare the different rates and compounding frequencies that different financial institutions offer.

USING COMMUNICATION SKILLS

6. Posters will vary, but savings account services may include high rate of return, low fees, and few restrictions. Checking account features may include low or no fees, low or no minimum balances, interest, and overdraft protection.

SOLVING MONEY PROBLEMS

7. Matthew's alternatives are a regular checking account, an activity account, and an interest-earning account. He will probably want a regular account. He probably would not want an interest-earning account that pays low interest and requires a minimum balance. He would want an account that offers overdraft protection.

CHAPTER 5 ASSESSMENT
ANSWERS

■ **Understanding and Using Vocabulary**
Answers will vary.

■ **Review Key Concepts**
1. With your authorization, your financial institution will withdraw from your bank account the amount of your monthly payment to a utility company, lender, or other business.
2. Accept any three: high interest versus liquidity, convenience of using ATMs versus higher fees, free checking versus no interest on the minimum balance.
3. Find out where you can get the best rate. Use the Internet to find out what rates banks all over the country are offering. Buy a long-term CD if interest rates are relatively high so that your money will continue to earn the high rate even if interest rates go down because of changes in the economy.
4. Rate of return, frequency of compounding, effect of inflation and taxes, liquidity, types of restrictions and fees.
5. Steps in writing a check are: (1) write the current date; (2) write the name of the party who will receive the check; (3) write the amount of the payment in figures; (4) write the amount in words; (5) sign the check the same way you signed the bank signature card; (6) make a note of the reason for the payment.

■ **Apply Key Concepts**
1. Answers will vary. Drawbacks may include not having enough money in the account to cover the amount of the payment when the financial institution goes to withdraw it. You could then have to pay fees to the financial institution as well as a late payment to the lender or other business. You also have to take the time to make sure that your transactions are handled correctly.
2. Answers will vary but may include that money is tangible and easy to put a value on, whereas it is harder to put a price on a person's time. As a result, people tend to undervalue their time.
3. Answers will vary but should indicate that the person would have enough cash available to buy a certificate of deposit and that he or she would not need the money for a predetermined period of time.
4. The table should show that students understand the formula for calculating interest: the beginning balance ($100) is multiplied by the rate of interest (5 percent). Because the interest is compounded quarterly (four times a year), the result is divided by 4 and that amount is added to the balance. The same procedure is carried out on the new balance for the remaining quarters.

1	$(100.00 \times .05)/4 = \$1.25$
2	$(101.25 \times .05)/4 = \$1.27$
3	$(102.52 \times .05)/4 = \$1.28$
4	$(103.80 \times .05)/4 = \$1.30$

Total interest is $5.09. The $100 would grow to $105.09.

5. Answers will vary but should include: Checks offer you a way to keep track of your spending, and you may be able to stop payment if necessary. In some cases you may earn interest on the balance in your account. Some banks offer additional services to checking account customers.

❓ Problem Solving Today

You will be able to pay your parents in five years; you will pay them a total of $7,200 in monthly payments. [ANSWER: $120 × 12 = $1,440; 5 × $1,440 = $7,200] The $10,000 CD, with 8 percent interest compounded annually, will earn approximately $3,701 in interest over five years, for a total value of $13,701. That amount, with the $7,200, will repay the $20,000 loan.

■ Real-World Application
Answers will vary.

FINANCE Online

Possible Web sites include:
www.privacyrights.org
www.pirg.org/calpirg/consumer/privacy/index.htm

Answers will vary.

Note to teacher: Web site addresses may change.

READING STRATEGIES
ANSWERS

Section 5.1
CONNECT (p. 125): Answers will vary. Pros might include convenience and the ability to make transactions instantly or automatically. Cons might include ATM transaction fees and the increased likelihood of losing track of point-of sale purchases or ATM withdrawals.

PREDICT (p. 131): One would want to know the following information: interest rates on savings accounts, fees for checking accounts, availability of credit cards or loans, availability of free financial advice, availability of FDIC or SAIF-insured accounts, branch locations, availability of online or other special services.

Section 5.2
RESPOND (p. 138): Daily. The more frequently interest is compounded, the greater the rate of return.

QUESTION (p. 147): Balancing your checkbook helps you to keep track of transactions that you've made since the mailing date of your statement. It also alerts you to errors that the bank may have made when handling your transactions.

STANDARD & POOR'S

CASE STUDY

ANSWERS

1. A checkbook makes it easy to keep track of account balances and requires more effort than a cash sale. Some businesses do not accept checks.
2. The location of the bank's branches and ATM machines are important considerations. Carter will also want to choose a bank that offers low-cost or free checking and ATM services.
3. There is no "right" way to keep from overspending. Some people keep their ATM and credit cards in a block of ice in the freezer, forcing them to wait 24 hours before they can spend on unplanned purchases.

Chapter 6 Planning Guide

Consumer Credit

Teacher Manual

SECT.	OBJECTIVES	NATIONAL STANDARDS FOR BUSINESS EDUCATION	FEATURES	RESOURCES
6.1	After completing this lesson, students will have learned: How to analyze the advantages and disadvantages of consumer credit. How to distinguish among various types of consumer credit	**Economics** III. Economic Institutions and Incentives VII. The Role of Government **Personal Finance** I. Personal Decision Making III. Managing Finances and Budgeting V. Buying Goods and Services VII. Using Credit	**Standard & Poor's**—Q & A, p. 152 **What's Your Financial ID?**—Your Credit IQ, p. 156 **Careers in Finance**—Credit Counselor, p. 162	Check Your Understanding, p. 163 Think Critically, p. 163 Using Communication Skills, p. 1635 Solving Money Problems, p. 163 Student Activity Workbook
6.2	After completing this lesson, students will have learned: How to determine whether they can afford a loan How to describe what creditors look for in a credit applicant How to develop an effective strategy to build and maintain their credit rating	**Economics** I. Allocation of Resources III. Economic Institutions and Incentives **Personal Finance** I. Personal Decision Making III. Managing Finances and Budgeting V. Buying Goods and Services VII. Using Credit	**Go Figure**—Debt Payments-to-Income Ratio, p. 165 **Go Figure**—Simple Interest on a Loan, p. 169 **Standard & Poor's**—Case Study, p. 170 **Academic Connection**—History, p. 172 **International Finance**—Panama, p. 177	Check Your Understanding, p. 179 Think Critically, p. 179 Using Math Skills, p. 179 Solving Money Problems, p. 179 Student Activity Workbook

TM100 Unit 2 *Banking and Credit*

Chapter 6 Planning Guide

SECT.	OBJECTIVES	NATIONAL STANDARDS FOR BUSINESS EDUCATION	FEATURES	RESOURCES
6.3	After completing this lesson, students will have learned: How to identify ways to protect their credit	**Economics** III. Economic Institutions and Incentives **Personal Finance** III. Managing Finances and Budgeting V. Buying Goods and Services VI. Banking VII. Using Credit		Check Your Understanding, p. 186 Think Critically, p. 186 Using Communication Skills, p. 186 Solving Money Problems, p. 186 Student Activity Workbook
6.4	After completing this lesson, students will have learned: How to discuss ways to manage their debt	**Economics** I. Allocation of Resources III. Economic Institutions and Incentives VIII. International Economic Concepts **Personal Finance** I. Personal Decision Making III. Managing Finances and Budgeting VII. Using Credit	Savvy Saver—Develop a Good Credit Rating, p. 189 Common Cents—One Is Enough, p. 191 Your Financial Portfolio—Credit Cards: Getting the Best Deal, p. 192	Check Your Understanding, p. 193 Think Critically, p. 193 Using Math Skills, p. 193 Solving Money Problems, p. 193 Student Activity Workbook

SCANS Correlation Chart

FOUNDATION SKILLS

Basic Skills	Reading	Writing	Math	Listening	Speaking
Thinking Skills	Creative Thinking	Decision Making	Problem Solving	Seeing Things in the Mind's Eye	Knowing How to Learn	Reasoning
Personal Qualities	Responsibility	Self-Esteem	Sociability	Self-Management	Integrity/Honesty

WORKPLACE COMPETENCIES

Resources	Allocating Time	Allocating Money	Allocating Material and Facility Resources	Allocating Human Resources
Information	Acquiring and Evaluating Information	Organizing and Maintaining Information	Interpreting and Communicating Information	Using Computers to Process Information
Interpersonal Skills	Participating as a Member of a Team	Teaching Others	Serving Clients/Customers	Exercising Leadership	Negotiating to Arrive at a Decision	Working with Cultural Diversity
Systems	Understanding Systems	Monitoring and Correcting Performance	Improving and Designing Systems
Technology	Selecting Technology	Applying Technology to Task	Maintaining and Troubleshooting Technology

Teacher Manual

■ INTERNET EXTENSION

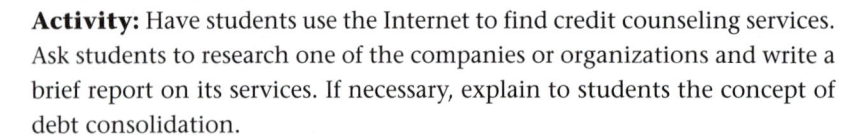

Activity: Have students use the Internet to find credit counseling services. Ask students to research one of the companies or organizations and write a brief report on its services. If necessary, explain to students the concept of debt consolidation.

Key Words: credit counseling, debt counseling

■ ENRICHMENT/APPLICATION ACTIVITY

Guest Speaker: Invite to class the credit manager of a large department store or other retail outlet. Ask him or her to bring a credit application for the class to see, and discuss the credit problems he or she has witnessed.

Unit 2 *Banking and Credit*

■ TOPIC SPOTLIGHT ■

◉ **Marketing:** Discuss with students why retail outlets encourage the use of credit cards.

◉ **Technology:** Invite students to share their ideas about smart cards. Ask them, "How will these be helpful?" How do you think they will link the physical world with the Internet? How might these be misused?"

◉ **Money:** Have students solve this word math problem using simple interest. Rebecca wants to buy a new saddle for her horse. The one she wants usually costs $500, but this week it's on sale for $400. She doesn't have $400, but she could buy it with $50 down and pay the rest in 6 months with 10 percent interest. Does Rebecca save any money buying the saddle this way? If so, how much does she save? [ANSWER: Yes, she saves $82.50. $400 − $50 = $350; $350 × 10% = $35 per year; $35 × .5 = $17.50 per 6 months; $400 + $17.50 = $417.50; $500 − 417.50 = $82.50]

additional resources

The Jump$tart Coalition for Personal Financial Literacy (see Additional Resources in Chapter 1) offers a number of **free** publications on the subject of credit, as well as other financial topics. You can access their publications at www.jumpstartcoalition.org by going to the Personal Finance Clearinghouse and clicking the link to the list of free educational materials. Publications include *Ready, Set... Credit* and *Credit Crossroads: New Credit—Is the Deck Shuffled in Your Favor?* which provide information about establishing first credit, making the right credit choices, and managing credit wisely. You can order from their Web site or call (888) 45-EDUCATE.

At **www.edgate.com** students can access Practical Money Skills for Life on the main Web page. This is a money management activity that covers making and sticking to a budget, saving and investing, the danger of irresponsible spending, and maintaining a good credit history.

Current rates for credit cards and consumer loans are at **www.bankrate.com** and **www.banx.com**.

Information on credit reports can be found at **www.equifax.com** and **www.transunion.com**.

Credit law information is available at **www.ftc.gov**, the Web site of the Federal Trade Commission, and **www.pirg.org**, the network for Public Interest Research Groups.

Note to teacher: Web site addresses may change.

CHAPTER 6   Lesson Plans

SECTION 6.1

FOCUS

Motivation
Tell your students that credit card companies have made their cards into status symbols. Companies are offering gold cards, platinum cards, and cards with favorite sports teams or colleges on them. Ask the students why they think the credit card companies offer so many different kinds of cards. Then ask the students if using credit encourages people to live beyond their means.

Prereading
1. Have your students skim the section, looking at pictures, reading captions, and noting headings.
2. Have "What You'll Learn" listed on page 153 read aloud.
3. Have students write each bold-faced term in the section, and based on its definition, generate a picture or symbol that identifies it.
4. Ask the students to state the purpose of studying this chapter.

TEACH

Guided Practice
1. Have students read aloud the Standard & Poor's Q&A on page 152.
2. Read the section with your students.

Independent Practice
1. Have your students contact a hotel or car rental business and find out whether they do business with someone who does not have a credit card. Have the students find out why some businesses set a minimum total dollar amount before allowing you to charge your purchase to a bank credit card.
2. Ask the students to research the different types of credit accounts offered at local retailers.

Careers in Finance

Credit Counselor
1. Ask your students why they think being a credit counselor might be a stressful job.
2. Divide the students into pairs. Have one student pretend to be a credit counselor and provide advice to the other student who is deeply in debt.
3. Have students research the certification requirements offered by the National Foundation for Consumer Credit.

ASSESS

Reteaching
1. Review the Key Terms with the students. Find out if the students still are unsure about a definition, and if so, clarify it for them.
2. Write this statement on the board: "Credit is like a two-edged sword." Have the students list the advantages and disadvantages of credit to reinforce this concept.

Enrichment
1. Divide the students into groups and ask each group to research the history of consumer credit in the United States. Then have the groups make a presentation to the class about what they found out.
2. Have the students create a brochure, rap song, skit or poster to emphasize the factors people should consider before financing a major purchase.

Assessment
1. Have students complete the Section 6.1 Assessment.
2. Assign an activity from the *Student Activity Workbook*.

CLOSE

Have students react to this statement: "Using credit does not increase your purchasing power nor does it mean you have more money."

SECTION 6.2

FOCUS

Motivation

Have your students respond to this statement: "If a bank or credit card company wants to loan me money, then I imagine I can afford it."

Prereading

1. Have the students skim the section, looking at pictures, reading captions, and noting headings.
2. Have "What You'll Learn" listed on page 164 read aloud.
3. Have students create flash cards based on the Key Terms and use their own words for the definitions rather than copying them from the text or dictionary.
4. Ask the students to state the purpose of studying this chapter.

TEACH

Guided Practice

1. Read the section with your students.
2. Assign an activity from the *Student Activity Workbook*.

Independent Practice

1. Have your students prepare a debt payment-to-income ratio for themselves. Ask them if they are below the 15 percent to 20 percent limit.

2. Ask the students to obtain a credit card application from a retail store or gas station. Have the students find out what the APR is for the credit card.
3. Invite a banker to your classroom to discuss the topics in this section—lender risk, variable interest rate, secured loans, and collateral.

INTERNATIONAL FINANCE

Panama

1. Panama has a strong services sector, especially in transportation, banking, and international trade. Ask the students why they think this is the case. [HINT: One reason is the country's strategic location.]
2. Have students research the Colon Free Zone and determine its financial impact on Panama.
3. Ask the students to research the history of the Panama Canal.

ASSESS

Reteaching

1. Ask each student to pick a partner. Using the flash cards they made in this section, have them review the Key Terms with each other.
2. To reinforce the concept of the cost of credit, have the students review the chart in **Figure 6-4**. Point out that credit cards usually charge between 15 percent and 21 percent interest on the unpaid balance.

Enrichment

1. Ask your students to research the age someone has to be in your state before they can sign a contract for a loan.
2. As a class, develop a list of examples that would adversely affect a person's credit rating.

3. Have the students contact one of the three major credit bureaus to find out how long it takes to verify a customer's credit history.
4. Ask your students to imagine that they have requested a copy of their credit report and found it to contain an error. Have students write a letter requesting the credit bureau to remove the incorrect item.
5. Have the students research the Fair Credit Reporting Act and write a short paper on the consumer's legal rights.

Assessment

1. Have your students complete the Section 6.2 Assessment.
2. Assign an activity from the *Student Activity Workbook*.

CLOSE

Have your students complete this sentence: "A good credit rating is very important because…." [EXAMPLE: "it will increase your chances of getting the credit you want or need."]

SECTION 6.3

FOCUS

Motivation

Discuss with your students the word "protection." Have them brainstorm a list of all the ways they have been protected by their parents, families, friends, teachers, policemen, etc. Then ask them the ways they have recently protected someone or something. Ask the students if protecting their credit is important. Make sure they justify their answers.

Prereading

1. Have the students skim the section, looking at pictures, reading captions, and noting headings.

2. Have "What You'll Learn" listed on page 180 read aloud.
3. Write the Key Term, *co-signing* on the board. As a class, write a definition for the word.
4. Ask the students to state the purpose of studying this chapter.

TEACH

Guided Practice

1. Read the section with your students.
2. Assign an activity from the *Student Activity Workbook*.

Independent Practice

1. Have your students interview a banker to find out how to protect their bank accounts, debit cards, and credit cards.
2. Ask the students to research the Consumer Credit Protection Act. In addition to finding out what it actually protects, the students should discover when and why it was enacted.
3. Ask the students to research Internet viruses that cause a security breech or allow someone to capture credit card numbers from a secure site.
4. Divide the students into groups and have them create a flyer or brochure on ways to protect their credit. As a class, vote on the best one and distribute it to the students in the school.

ASSESS

Reteaching

1. Review the definition for the term *co-signing*.
2. Remind students that protecting their credit is extremely important. Have your students review what they have learned in this section and brainstorm a list of ways to protect their credit. Post their list in the classroom as a continual reminder of the importance of this issue.

Enrichment

1. Ask your students to survey a group of adults to find out ways to protect their credit.
2. Invite a lawyer to your class to discuss what can be done if your identity is stolen.

Assessment

1. Have the students complete the Section 6.3 Assessment.
2. Assign an activity from the *Student Activity Workbook*.

CLOSE

Have your students explain this statement: "Your credit is like your reputation; it must always be protected."

SECTION 6.4

FOCUS

Motivation

Write this statement on the board: "In the first quarter of the year 2002, Americans owed their creditors $1.7 trillion, or more than $6,060 for every man, woman and child in the country. This figure doesn't even include mortgages." Ask your students to react to this statement.

Prereading

1. Have the students skim the section, looking at pictures, reading captions, and noting headings.
2. Have "What You'll Learn" listed on page 187 read aloud.
3. Have your students create flash cards based on the Key Terms and use their own words for the definitions rather than copying them from the text or dictionary.
4. Ask the students to state the purpose of studying this chapter.

TEACH

Guided Practice

1. Read the section with your students.
2. Assign an activity from the *Student Activity Workbook*.

Independent Practice

1. Have your students read an article in a newspaper or magazine on debt or debt management. Ask them to write a summary of the article.
2. Tell the students that the federal government uses credit to pay for many of the services it provides. Ask the students to find out what the national debt is at this time. Then ask them to debate whether the government should be able to purchase on credit or not.
3. Have the students research debtors' prisons and write a short paper on whether they think these prisons were an appropriate deterrent to too much debt.
4. Invite a bankruptcy attorney to your class and ask him or her to discuss the personal bankruptcy laws in your state.

$AVVY SAVER

Develop a Good Credit Rating

1. Ask students, "How does having a checking account help you establish credit?"
2. Have the students research ways that credit card companies market themselves in order to get more customers? [EXAMPLES: cash rebates, frequent flyer miles, free gas, and lower interest rates for a short period of time]

Common Cents

One Is Enough
1. Ask your students to track the number of credit card applications that come in the mail during the next month.
2. "In order to protect your credit, you should always tear up the credit card applications that come in the mail before you toss them into the trash." Ask your students to respond to this statement.

ASSESS

Reteaching
1. Ask each student to pick a partner. Using the flash cards they made in this section, have them review the Key Terms with each other.
2. Tell the students that a $5,000 credit card bill you intend to pay off over a five-year period at 20 percent interest could cost almost $3,000 in interest. Ask your students to explain how this type of credit could lead to debt problems.

Enrichment
1. Ask the students to divide into groups and debate this statement: "Managing your debt can be just as important as sound investing."
2. Have the students create a game (like *Monopoly*, *Wheel of Fortune*; students can be creative) that will teach the debt management concepts.

Assessment
1. Have the students complete the Section 6.4 Assessment.
2. Assign the Chapter Assessment.
3. Administer the test for Chapter 6 from the Reproducible Tests in the *Teacher Resource Binder*.

CLOSE
Have your students write a paragraph about what they plan to do to prevent the possibility of serious financial difficulties in the future.

SECTION 6.1 ASSESSMENT
ANSWERS

CHECK YOUR UNDERSTANDING
1. Answers will vary but may include: Advantages are immediate enjoyment of goods and services, ability to purchase goods and services when funds are low, efficiency, and the safety of carrying less cash. Disadvantages may include overspending, negative consequences of failure to repay, effect on future income, and costs.
2. Closed-end credit is a one-time loan that you will pay back over a specified period of time and in payments of equal amounts (including interest). It involves a definite amount of money. Open-end credit allows you to borrow money for a variety of goods and services. The company issuing the credit gives you a certain limit on the amount of money you can borrow. A line of credit is the maximum amount of money the creditor has made available to you. You make as many purchases as you wish, as long as you don't exceed your line of credit. You are then billed periodically for at least partial payment of the total amount you owe.
3. Answers will vary. An inexpensive loan might be one with low or no interest from a parent or other family member. A medium-priced loan, with moderate interest, might come from a commercial bank, savings and loan association, or credit union. An expensive loan, with high interest, might come from a finance company or retail store, or from a bank through a cash advance.

THINK CRITICALLY

4. Answers will vary but may note that it depends on your money management strategies. For example, if you plan to pay your balance in full every month, you will select a card that offers a low annual fee and a grace period. If you plan to carry an ongoing balance, you will look for a card with a low interest rate.

USING COMMUNICATION SKILLS

5. Answers will vary.

SOLVING MONEY PROBLEMS

6. Answers will vary.

SECTION 6.2 ASSESSMENT
ANSWERS

CHECK YOUR UNDERSTANDING

1. One way is to add up all your basic monthly expenses and then subtract the total from your take-home pay. If the difference is not enough to make the monthly loan payment and still have a little left over, you can't afford the loan. A second way is to consider what you might give up to make the monthly loan payment. Decide whether you're willing to make the necessary trade-offs. Finally, you can figure out your debt payments-to-income ratio. You should spend no more than 20 percent of your monthly net income on monthly debt payments.
2. Character, capacity, capital, collateral, and credit history.
3. Answers will vary but may include: Do not borrow more than you can afford; do not overdraw your checking account; pay bills on time; limit the number of credit cards you have; review your credit files every two years; correct mistakes in billing statements and credit reports.

THINK CRITICALLY

4. Answers will vary but may include: Accept a variable interest rate loan; accept a secured loan; make a larger down payment; accept a shorter-term loan.

USING MATH SKILLS

5. Kim's debt payments-to-income ratio with the college loan is 31.85 percent; without the college loan it is 14.07 percent. According to the 20 percent rule, she cannot afford the college loan. However, after Kim pays off her credit card debts, her debt payments-to-income ratio with the college loan will be 17.5 percent. Therefore, once she pays off her credit cards, she will be able to afford the loan. [ANSWER: $820 − $145 = $675; $95 + $120 = $215; $215 ÷ $675 = 31.39%; $120 ÷ $675 = 17.8%]

SOLVING MONEY PROBLEMS

6. Answers will vary but may include: Eleanor has the right to know why she was denied credit. If the denial is based on a credit report, she is entitled to know the specific information in the report that led to the denial. She can request a free copy of the report from the credit bureau within 60 days of notification that her application was denied. She is entitled to ask the bureau to investigate any inaccurate or incomplete information and correct its records. She can sue a credit bureau or creditor that has not followed the rules of the Fair Credit Reporting Act.

SECTION 6.3 ASSESSMENT
ANSWERS

CHECK YOUR UNDERSTANDING

1. You should notify your creditor in writing and include any information that might support your case. Then you should pay the portion of the bill that is not in question. The creditor must acknowledge your letter within 30 days. Then, within two billing periods (but not longer than 90 days), the creditor must either adjust your account or tell you why the bill is correct. If the creditor made a mistake, you

don't have to pay any finance charges on the disputed amount. If no mistake is found, the creditor must promptly send you an explanation of the situation and a statement of what you owe, including any finance charges and any minimum payments you missed while you were questioning the bill.

2. You can tear or shred any papers that contain personal information before you throw them out. Be sure that your card is returned to you after a purchase. Keep a record of your credit card number separate from your card. Notify the credit card company immediately if your card is lost or stolen.

3. The Fair Credit Reporting Act allows you to sue any credit bureau or creditor that violates the rules regarding access to your credit records or that fails to correct errors in your credit file. You're entitled to actual damages plus any punitive damages the court allows if the violation is proven to have been intentional.

THINK CRITICALLY

4. Answers will vary but may include: having your identity stolen; being billed for goods you have not received or did not order.

USING COMMUNICATION SKILLS

5. Answers will vary but may include: I've decided not to co-sign your loan because of the risk that is involved. I'll be responsible for the debt if you can't pay. I may have to pay up to the full amount of the debt as well as late fees or collection costs. The creditor can collect the debt from me without first trying to collect from you. The creditor can use the same collection methods against me that can be used against you. If the debt is not repaid, that fact appears on my credit record.

SOLVING MONEY PROBLEMS

6. Answers will vary but may include: Tear or shred any papers containing personal information before throwing them out; close bank accounts immediately upon noticing a problem; stop payment on stolen checks; cancel a stolen debit card and get another with a new PIN; contact the Privacy Rights Clearinghouse.

SECTION 6.4 ASSESSMENT
ANSWERS

CHECK YOUR UNDERSTANDING

1. Answers will vary but may include: You pay only the minimum monthly payment on credit cards; you're having trouble making even the minimum monthly payment on your credit card bills; the total balance on your credit cards increases every month; you miss loan payments or often pay late; you use savings to pay for necessities such as food and utilities; you receive second or third payment due notices from creditors; you borrow money to pay off old debts; you exceed the credit limits on your credit cards; you've been denied credit because of a bad credit bureau report.

2. The Consumer Credit Counseling Service provides (1) services that aid families with serious debt problems by helping them to manage their money better and set up a realistic budget and (2) services that help people prevent indebtedness by teaching them the necessity of budget planning, educating them regarding the pitfalls of unwise credit buying, and encouraging credit institutions to withhold credit from those who cannot afford it. In addition, universities, credit unions, military bases, and state and federal housing authorities sometimes provide similar nonprofit counseling services.

3. Answers will vary but may include: Chapter 7 bankruptcy allows you to clear most of your debts at once, but you may lose most of your property. It may also make it harder for you to obtain credit in the future. Chapter 13 bankruptcy allows you to pay back your debts over a period of time. You may be able to keep most of your

property, and it may be slightly easier for you to obtain credit in the future.

THINK CRITICALLY
4. Answers will vary.

USING MATH SKILLS
5. U.S. bankruptcies experienced a 43 percent increase between 1990 and 2000. [ANSWER: 1,250 − 875 = 375; 375 ÷ 875 = 43%] Answers will vary but may include: It depends on whether the U.S. Congress reforms the bankruptcy laws. If the laws remain unchanged and consumers continue to declare bankruptcy, the number of bankruptcy cases will probably continue to rise. If Congress makes it more difficult for individuals to declare bankruptcy, the rate might decrease. Above all, the number of credit card holders in the United States increases the likelihood that some people will not be able to repay their debts and will have to declare bankruptcy.

SOLVING MONEY PROBLEMS
6. Deanne might contact her creditors and try to work out an adjusted repayment plan, or she can contact a nonprofit financial counseling program. The last resort would be to declare personal bankruptcy.

CHAPTER 6 ASSESSMENT
ANSWERS

■ Understanding and Using Vocabulary
Answers will vary.

■ Review Key Concepts
1. Issues to consider include whether you have the cash you need for the down payment; whether you want to use your savings instead of credit; whether you can afford the item; whether you could use the credit in some better way; whether you could put off your purchase for a while; what would happen if you don't buy the item now; the costs of using credit.
2. Credit card: ability to buy goods and services now and pay later; one monthly payment. Some credit card companies may offer a grace period, a time period during which no finance charges will be added to your account. Smart card: all the services of a traditional credit card plus the ability to carry multiple forms of data on the same card. Debit card: convenience of being able to purchase goods and services without having to carry cash. Amount is automatically deducted from savings or checking account. Travel and entertainment card: ability buy goods now and pay later; one monthly payment.
3. Debt payments-to-income ratio is the percentage of debt you have in relation to your income. You can calculate this ratio by dividing your total monthly debt payments (not including your mortgage) by your monthly net income.
4. Contact credit bureaus; contact creditors; file a police report.
5. Filing for bankruptcy.

■ Apply Key Concepts
1. Answers will vary. Agree: A young adult doesn't have a family to support and therefore probably doesn't have many monthly debt payments. With a steady income, he or she should be able to take on the expense of a mortgage. Disagree: A young adult may not have the savings needed for the down payment and may not be able to make the monthly loan payments, especially if he or she has just recently entered the workforce. It might be wiser to purchase a house when he or she has established a career and built up savings.
2. Those who don't want to carry a large amount of cash and who know that they will be able to pay their debts in full at the end of each month.
3. This calculation allows you to compare the amount of money you have with the amount of money you will need to make

payments on a loan, so that you will not spend more than 20 percent of your income on debt payments.

4. Contacting credit bureaus will alert them to the fact that someone else is using your personal information and protect your credit rating from damage. Contacting creditors will prevent the thief from being able to continue using your information. Filing a police report will help the police find the thief.

5. Declaring bankruptcy might cause the young adult to experience difficulty obtaining credit in the future. This consequence would be particularly damaging for someone who was just beginning to build a credit history. Such a person would probably have to rely on his or her parents or spouse to be able to purchase goods and services on credit until the bankruptcy declaration was cleared from his or her records.

❓ Problem Solving Today
Victor's total monthly debt payment would be $510. His debt payments-to-income ratio would be 25.5 percent. [ANSWER: $250 + $270 + $5,000 + $600 = $6,120; $6,120 ÷ 12 = $510; $510 ÷ 2,000 = 25.5%]

■ **Real-World Application**
Answers will vary.

FINANCE Online
Possible Web sites include:
www.collegenet.com
www.fafsa.ed.gov

Note to teacher: Web site addresses may change.

READING STRATEGIES
ANSWERS

Section 6.1
CONNECT (p. 153): Answers will vary.

QUESTION (p. 155): Your credit history will influence your ability to obtain more credit, purchase a home, rent an apartment, and in some cases, obtain a job.

Section 6.2
PREDICT (p. 169): The bill will take much longer to pay off than if you repaid a larger portion of the debt each month. The longer it takes to pay off the debt, the more expensive the finance charges will be.

RESPOND (p. 173): Answers will vary.

Section 6.3
PREDICT (p. 181): A thief can take your personal information from papers left in the garbage can, from the Internet, or from lost or stolen credit or debit cards, and use that information to purchase items or withdraw your money.

CONNECT (p. 182): Web browsers, such as AOL Netscape or Microsoft Explorer, display small icons that indicate whether information, such as a credit card number, is transmitted securely.

Section 6.4
RESPOND (p. 188): Answers will vary but may include preparing a strict budget, working extra to pay off bills, seeking credit counseling, or filing for bankruptcy as a last resort.

QUESTION (p. 191): Filing for bankruptcy will damage one's borrowing reputation for ten years. It will make it difficult to obtain a credit card necessary for online purchases or telephone reservations. Obtaining a mortgage will be difficult and possibly more expensive.

STANDARD & POOR'S

CASE STUDY

ANSWERS

1. Credit card companies often charge an annual fee, in addition to higher interest rates. Also, credit card purchases are generally for consumer goods and services rather than investments.

2. It may be difficult to obtain financing for a car that is more than four years old. Also, automobile loans generally require a 20 percent down payment. In order to finance a car, Estella may end up buying a more expensive car than she really needs or can afford.

3. A good rule of thumb is not to borrow for things that have no lasting value. Vacations, clothes, and entertainment fall into this category. If debt is used to acquire an asset, such an automobile or home, the overall net worth of the borrower remains the same.

Chapter 7 Planning Guide

The Finances of Housing

Teacher Manual

SECT.	OBJECTIVES	NATIONAL STANDARDS FOR BUSINESS EDUCATION	FEATURES	RESOURCES
7.1	After completing this lesson, students will have learned: How to evaluate available housing alternatives	**Economics** I. Allocation of Resources **Personal Finance** I. Personal Decision Making II. Earning a Living III. Managing Finances and Budgeting V. Buying Goods and Services VIII. Protecting Against Risk	**Standard & Poor's**—Q & A, p. 196 **What's Your Financial ID?**—Where Would You Like to Live? p. 199 **Careers in Finance**—Real Estate Agent, p. 201	Check Your Understanding, p. 202 Think Critically, p. 202 Using Communication Skills, p. 202 Solving Money Problems, p. 202 Student Activity Workbook
7.2	After completing this lesson, students will have learned: How to assess the advantages, disadvantages, and costs of renting	**Economics** I. Allocation of Resources **Personal Finance** I. Personal Decision Making III. Managing Finances and Budgeting V. Buying Goods and Services		Check Your Understanding, p. 209 Think Critically, p. 209 Using Math Skills, p. 209 Solving Money Problems, p. 209 Student Activity Workbook
7.3	After completing this lesson, students will have learned: How to describe the process of buying a home How to calculate the costs associated with buying a home How to develop a plan for selling a home	**Economics** I. Allocation of Resources VII. The Role of Government VIII. International Economic Concepts **Personal Finance** I. Personal Decision Making II. Earning a Living III. Managing Finances and Budgeting V. Buying Goods and Services VII. Using Credit VIII. Protecting Against Risk	**Savvy Saver**—Furnishing Your First Apartment, p. 213 **Standard & Poor's**—Case Study, p. 215 **Academic Connection**—Art, p. 218 **International Finance**—Egypt, p. 221 **Common Cents**—On Your Own, p. 223 **Your Financial Portfolio**—Renting Versus Buying Your Place of Residence, p. 227	Check Your Understanding, p. 229 Think Critically, p. 229 Using Communication Skills, p. 229 Solving Money Problems, p. 229 Student Activity Workbook

Unit 2 *Banking and Credit*

SCANS Correlation Chart

FOUNDATION SKILLS

Basic Skills	Reading	Writing	Math	Listening	Speaking
Thinking Skills	Creative Thinking	Decision Making	Problem Solving	Seeing Things in the Mind's Eye	Knowing How to Learn	Reasoning
Personal Qualities	Responsibility	Self-Esteem	Sociability	Self-Management	Integrity/Honesty

WORKPLACE COMPETENCIES

Resources	Allocating Time	Allocating Money	Allocating Material and Facility Resources	Allocating Human Resources
Information	Acquiring and Evaluating Information	Organizing and Maintaining Information	Interpreting and Communicating Information	Using Computers to Process Information
Interpersonal Skills	Participating as a Member of a Team	Teaching Others	Serving Clients/Customers	Exercising Leadership	Negotiating to Arrive at a Decision	Working with Cultural Diversity
Systems	Understanding Systems	Monitoring and Correcting Performance	Improving and Designing Systems
Technology	Selecting Technology	Applying Technology to Task	Maintaining and Troubleshooting Technology

■ INTERNET EXTENSION

Activity: Have students use the Internet to access the classified ads of a large local or regional newspaper. Then have them access the real estate section and write a brief report explaining what information is available. They may find home buyers and sellers guides, information on local schools and neighborhoods, and virtual home tours.

Keywords: the name of the local or regional newspaper of your choice

■ ENRICHMENT/APPLICATION ACTIVITY

Guest Speaker: Invite the real estate agent who comes to class to discuss his or her career to also talk about the steps involved in buying a home. Ask him or her to discuss finding and choosing a home, negotiating prices, and financing.

Chapter 7 *The Finances of Housing* TM115

■ TOPIC SPOTLIGHT

✪ **Government:** Discuss with students why the Federal government helps people secure a home loan.

☻ **Marketing:** Bring to class advertisements for apartments in your area. (Some areas publish brochures strictly for apartments.) Circulate the ads among the students and ask if the ads are effective. Would students want to live in a particular apartment complex? Why or why not? How do the ads work?

☻ **Ethics:** Discuss with students the laws concerning discrimination in renting in your area. Can landlords choose to rent only to certain people? What would students do if a landlord refused to rent to them?

additional resources

The Jump$tart Coalition for Personal Financial Literacy (see Additional Resources in Chapters 1 and 6) offers a **free** publication entitled *How To Buy Your Own Home: Teacher's Guide and Student Workbook*. It covers topics such as budgeting, importance of credit, mortgage loans, how to establish a credit history, and monthly expenses related to your home. To receive a sample student workbook and teacher's guide call (888) 45-EDUCATE or order from their Web site at **www.jumpstartcoalition.org**.

Mortgage rate information and savings calculators are available at **www.bankrate.com**.

Fannie Mae is the largest nonbank financial services company in the world and the nation's largest source of financing for home mortgages. Their Web site is **www.homepath.com** and includes information on home buying, mortgages, refinancing, and other home ownership topics.

Other housing and mortgage information is available from the Department of Housing and Urban Development at **www.hud.gov**.

Note to teacher: Web site addresses may change.

CHAPTER 7 Lesson Plans

SECTION 7.1

FOCUS

Motivation

Ask your students to imagine that they will be renting an apartment for the first time and will need a roommate to share expenses. Have them answer these questions: "What qualities will you look for in a roommate? How might your choice of roommates affect your financial situation?"

Prereading

1. Have your students skim the section, looking at pictures, reading captions, and noting headings.
2. Have "What You'll Learn" listed on page 197 read aloud.
3. Write the three Key Terms on the board. Ask the students to define them using their own words. Write their definitions on the board.
4. Ask the students to state the purpose of studying this chapter.

TEACH

Guided Practice

1. Have students read aloud the Standard & Poor's Q&A on page 196.
2. Read the section with your students.

Independent Practice

1. Have your students interview a building contractor to find out what should be considered if they were to purchase a handyman special.
2. Ask the students to plan the furnishings they would need for their first apartment. Have them visit a furniture store to determine the cost of the furniture. Then ask them how they could save money on their furnishings. [EXAMPLES: purchase from second-hand stores, shop garage sales]
3. Invite an apartment manager to your class. Ask him or her to bring a sample lease to share with the students. Have your students prepare questions to ask before the manager comes to class.
4. Have the students research what type of information the Department of Housing provides to consumers.

Careers in Finance

Real Estate Agent

1. Ask your students to find out if, in order to sell real estate, they need a real estate license in your state. If so, then have them research the process of obtaining a license.
2. Margarett is a real estate agent who recently sold her first house for $122,000. The contract states that her commission will be 6.5 percent of the selling price. What is Margarett's commission?
3. Have your students contact the National Association of Realtors (NAR) and ask them to send materials about the real estate profession. Display the materials in the classroom.

ASSESS

Reteaching

1. Review with the students the definitions they developed for the Key Terms in this section.
2. Write "Rent vs. Buy" on the Board. Ask your students to brainstorm the pros and cons of each. Keep this list and add to it as you finish studying this chapter.

Enrichment

1. Divide the students into pairs and ask them to visit two different apartment complexes in your community. Ask them to evaluate the apartments based on their locations.

2. Have the students complete a service project for the local homeless shelter or Salvation Army. [EXAMPLES: collect clothing, blankets, children's toys, or canned goods]
3. Have your students partner with a business or church to help build a Habitat for Humanity home.
4. Ask the students to research the federal programs available for rental assistance.

Assessment

1. Have your students complete the Section 7.1 Assessment.
2. Assign an activity from the *Student Activity Workbook*.

CLOSE

Have the students complete this statement, "In order to make wise housing decisions, I….'' [EXAMPLE: "will research and evaluate all my options."]

SECTION 7.2

FOCUS

Motivation

Have your students brainstorm a list of all the options available in the rental housing market. Then ask them to share the pros and cons of each.

Prereading

1. Have your students skim the section, looking at pictures, reading captions, and noting headings.
2. Have "What You'll Learn" listed on page 203 read aloud.
3. Write the Key Terms on the board. Ask your students to write a sentence using each term.
4. Ask the students to state the purpose of studying this chapter.

TEACH

Guided Practice

1. Read the section with your students.
2. Assign an activity from the *Student Activity Workbook*.

Independent Practice

1. Divide the students into groups. Assign each group one of the following topics: (1) How to select a rental unit; (2) Advantages and disadvantages of renting; (3) Legal aspects of renting; and (4) Security deposits and renter's insurance. Ask each group to prepare a ten-minute workshop that can be presented to other students in the school.
2. Have the students find out how much money they would need to move into an apartment. Ask them to contact the utility companies to determine security deposits and installation charges.
3. Ask your students to prepare a one-year budget for their first apartment. Help them determine realistic estimates for electricity, phone, and water.

ASSESS

Reteaching

1. Review with the students the sentences they created using the Key Terms. If necessary, ask the students to modify or enhance them.
2. Remind your students that when they rent, their activities are often restricted by the landlord's rules. Ask the students to imagine they are the landlords of several large apartment complexes in a college town. Have them develop a list of rules for their tenants.

Enrichment

1. Have your students design an apartment complex they might like to own. Display their designs in the classroom.
2. Invite an attorney to the class to speak to the students about the legal issues regarding renting in your state.

Assessment

1. Have your students complete the Section 7.2 Assessment.
2. Assign an activity from the *Student Activity Workbook*.

CLOSE

Have your students write a paragraph describing the advantages and disadvantages of renting.

SECTION 7.3

FOCUS

Motivation

Tell your students the following story: Devan and his family live on a sailboat. They dock their boat at the marina during the day while they are at work and school. In the evenings they return to their boat for dinner, homework, and the usual family activities. On weekends they go sailing in the bay or up and down the coast of Florida. Ask your students if they would like a house like this. Then have the students brainstorm other housing options that might appeal to them.

Prereading

1. Have the students skim the section, looking at pictures, reading captions, and noting headings.
2. Have "What You'll Learn" listed on page 210 read aloud.
3. Dictate each of the Key Terms to the students and have them write them on a piece of paper. When they are finished, write the terms on the board. Ask the students to guess at the meaning of each term, but do not give the correct meaning. Leave the list on the board, so as students work through the section, they can see how close they were to the correct answer.
4. Ask the students to state the purpose of studying this chapter.

TEACH

Guided Practice

1. Read the section with your students.
2. Assign an activity from the *Student Activity Workbook*.

Independent Practice

1. Have your students research deed restrictions that many neighborhoods issue. Ask them to find out their purpose and how they are enforced.
2. Contact the local real estate association and find out if your students can job shadow an agent when he or she shows a house.
3. Divide the class into groups. Ask each group to imagine they have just purchased a brand new house. What other expenses will they face when they move in? [HINT: deposits and installation for utilities, window treatments, furniture, etc.]
4. Invite an attorney who handles real estate closings to speak to your students about the process of closing a mortgage sale.

$AVVY SAVER

Furnishing Your First Apartment

1. Have the students add two tips to this list.
2. Tell the students to pretend they are moving into a new apartment and have $500 to spend on furnishings. Ask them to go to garage or moving sales to see what they could buy for $500.

3. Ask the students to research the costs involved in renting furniture.

INTERNATIONAL FINANCE
Egypt
1. Teamwork is crucial in today's workplace. Have the students brainstorm a list of ways they currently have to work as a member of a team.
2. Have your students research how the pyramids were built and the teamwork it took to build them.
3. Ask the students to research the Egyptian stock market, including when it started, where it is located, and how it operates.
4. In 2000, Egypt's domestic debt rate was 54 percent of the country's gross domestic product. Although something to be concerned about, it remains lower than the 60 to 110 percent debt rate of other nations. Have students explain why growing debt can be a burden on a nation's economy.

Common Cents

On Your Own
1. Ask your students, "If you were sharing an apartment, how would you share costs, cleaning duties, and the food in the refrigerator?"
2. Ask the students what they would do if their roommate had a friend who spends weeks at a time in their apartment, but doesn't share in the expenses.

ASSESS

Reteaching
1. Review the list of Key Terms that the students were unsure about before studying this section.
2. To reinforce the different types of mortgages that are available, divide the class into groups and assign each group a different type of mortgage. Allow each group 15 minutes to prepare and present a brief presentation on their assigned mortgage type.

Enrichment
1. Have your students interview someone who conducts home appraisals. Ask the students to find out about the process used to determine the value of a home.
2. Ask the students to imagine they will be selling their house without the services of a real estate agent. Have them find out how much an ad in the newspaper will cost. Tell the students they will be running the ad for eight consecutive weekends.
3. Have your students research the housing market in another country.

Assessment
1. Have the students complete the Section 7.3 Assessment.
2. Assign the Chapter Assessment.
3. Administer the test for Chapter 7 from the Reproducible Tests in the *Teacher Resource Binder*.

CLOSE
Have your students write a paragraph describing the advantages and disadvantages of buying a home.

SECTION 7.1 ASSESSMENT
ANSWERS

CHECK YOUR UNDERSTANDING
1. Your lifestyle and your finances.
2. Buying might be a better choice for people who want a certain amount of stability in their lives and would like more space than they are able to get in an apartment; who want privacy and the freedom to do as they wish, such as owning pets and decorating in their own style; and who want the tax benefits of ownership.

3. Sources include the public library, the real estate section of a newspaper, friends and family, a real estate agent, government agencies, and the Internet.

THINK CRITICALLY

4. Answers will vary but possible housing needs include: a residence that is big enough to accommodate five people comfortably; a place that is near good schools and shopping; a neighborhood with other children. Answers will vary, but students will probably say that the family should buy their own house if they can afford it. Reasons may include: privacy; virtually no restrictions on pet ownership, activities, or noise; long-term tax and financial benefits; and stability.

USING COMMUNICATION SKILLS

5. Answers will vary.

SOLVING MONEY PROBLEMS

6. Answers will vary, but buying the house may not be a good choice because Leila is young and has few connections in the town; maintenance costs may be high; she's relying on money she doesn't yet have and may not get.

SECTION 7.2 ASSESSMENT
ANSWERS
CHECK YOUR UNDERSTANDING

1. Mobility, few responsibilities, and low initial costs.
2. Offers few financial benefits, may contribute to a more restricted lifestyle, and involves various legal concerns.
3. Rent, utilities (if not included in the rent), security deposit, and optional renters insurance.

THINK CRITICALLY

4. Answers will vary but may include: an apartment with two bedrooms or one large bedroom as well as space for recreation. The roommates will need some privacy and enough space to store their possessions.

USING MATH SKILLS

5. Raji will save about $75 a month or $900 a year if he makes the move and rents the house with Jon. [ANSWER: $900 + $300 = $1200; $1200 ÷ 2 = $600; $675 − $600 = $75; 12 × $75 = $900]

SOLVING MONEY PROBLEMS

6. Answers will vary but may include the following possibilities: trying to negotiate a change in the lease with the landlord, perhaps offering the landlord extra money; trying to sublet her apartment and find one that allows pets; letting a friend keep the cat for her until her lease is up and she can find a new apartment; breaking the lease and accepting that she may be forced to leave at any time.

SECTION 7.3 ASSESSMENT
ANSWERS
CHECK YOUR UNDERSTANDING

1. Determine your home ownership needs, find and evaluate a property to purchase, price the property, obtain financing, and close the purchase transaction.
2. Costs may include the down payment, mortgage application fee, optional home inspection, earnest money, closing costs, private mortgage insurance, points, property taxes, homeowners insurance, and mortgage payments (principal and interest).
3. To sell your house, you prepare the home for sale by fixing things where needed, obtain an appraisal if desired, set a price, and decide whether to sell it on your own or seek professional help.

THINK CRITICALLY

4. Answers will vary but may include: An evaluation will tell you what repairs the

home might need and what costs you might incur in the future; it will help you to determine the value of the home; and it will help you evaluate the price that the seller is asking for it.

USING COMMUNICATION SKILLS
5. Answers will vary.

SOLVING MONEY PROBLEMS
6. Answers will vary but may include: Renee really likes the house, but she should probably go on looking because she hasn't spent much time investigating other possibilities. She needs to determine what she can afford according to her budget and her other financial statements. She should consider how she will feel if she loses the house because she made too low an offer. She also could go ahead and make an offer for $110,000 and see if it's accepted.

CHAPTER 7 ASSESSMENT
ANSWERS

■ **Understanding and Using Vocabulary**
Answers will vary.

■ **Review Key Concepts**
1. Drawbacks include: no long-term financial gain, restricted lifestyle, certain legal concerns; benefits include low initial costs, fewer responsibilities, mobility, and more space than is available in most apartments.
2. Answers will vary but may include a lease and renters insurance for renting; mortgage, and deed for buying.
3. Determining needs, finding and evaluating a property to purchase, pricing the property, obtaining financing, closing the transaction.
4. Single-family dwelling, multiunit dwelling, condominium, cooperative housing, manufactured home, and mobile home.
5. Location, condition, market conditions, features.

■ **Apply Key Concepts**
1. Answers will vary but might stress the mobility, the lack of responsibility, and the limits on activity associated with renting.
2. Possible answers: They are both legal documents, binding the people who sign them to a financial obligation. They both require responsibility on the part of the signer. A tenant must be responsible to the landlord, and a homeowner must be responsible to the lender. They differ in the terms of the commitment, including the length of time that they cover and the amount of the financial obligation.
3. Diagrams will vary.
4. Answers will vary.
5. When the demand for homes is great in relation to the supply, buyers will compete with each other and drive prices up. This is a seller's market. When many homes are for sale but few buyers are available, sellers compete and drive prices down. This is a buyer's market.

Problem Solving Today
Answers will vary.

■ **Real-World Application**
Answers will vary.

FINANCE Online

Possible Web sites include:
http://loan.yahoo.com (Yahoo! finance mortgage rates)
www.bankrate.com

Answers will vary.

Note to teacher: Web site addresses may change.

READING STRATEGIES
ANSWERS

Section 7.1
CONNECT (p. 198): Answers will vary.

QUESTION (p. 201): Improvements to the home or neighborhood, or a shortage of good housing in the area may cause the value of a home to go up. Undesirable changes in the neighborhood, such as the construction of a nearby freeway or the closing of factories in the town, may cause the value to go down.

Section 7.2
PREDICT (p. 204): You might learn of places through friends or coworkers, through the classified section of the newspaper, through special newspapers that advertise apartments for rent, through the Internet, or through rental agencies in the area.

RESPOND (p. 208): Answers will vary.

Section 7.3
CONNECT (p. 220): Most students would need to increase monthly income, reduce any debt, and increase savings.

QUESTION (p. 229): Advantage: saving the real estate agent's commission fee. Disadvantages: potential for misjudging the market and asking price, time spent on researching the market and legal procedures for selling the home, time and money spent advertising and showing the home.

STANDARD & POOR'S

CASE STUDY
ANSWERS

1. A 10 percent down payment may be required for the loan to qualify for "conventional" financing. This type of financing carries a lower interest rate. A 20 percent down payment will eliminate the need for mortgage insurance, reducing the monthly mortgage payment. However, the couple will want to keep some of their savings intact to provide for unexpected expenses.
2. Mortgage interest and property taxes are tax deductible, so they will likely pay less in federal income taxes. Over time they will build equity in their home, increasing their net worth.
3. Home prices have risen steadily over the years. Keep in mind that the price appreciation applies to the entire value of the home. This leverage can result in a substantial return on the equity invested. As with other investments, there is a risk that the value of the home can drop. If the housing market falls substantially, the value of the home may be less than the mortgage.

UNIT 2 Planning Guide

BANKING AND CREDIT

Chapter 5—
Banking

Chapter 6—
Consumer Credit

Chapter 7—
The Finances of Housing

OVERVIEW

In Unit 2 students will learn about the wide range of services than can help them plan, manage, and save in order to achieve their financial goals. Chapter 5 discusses the selection and use of financial services, such as the different kinds of savings and checking accounts, longer-term savings (certificates of deposit and U.S. savings bonds), investment services, loans, and other credit services. In Chapter 6 students will learn about the advantages and disadvantages of consumer credit, how to calculate the cost of credit, and how to manage debt. Chapter 7 explains the finances of housing. Students will learn how to calculate the costs of buying a house and describe the process of buying a house.

INTRODUCTION

With a show of hands, find out how many students have credit cards, checking accounts, savings accounts, and car loans. Ask students how or where they obtained these financial services. Ask, "Do these financial services cost money or are they free?" If possible, bring brochures from a variety of banks or other financial institutions for students to look through. Then have students write definitions for the terms *financial services* and *financial institutions*. Point out to your students the wide variety of products and services offered by financial institutions and explain that in this unit they will learn how to shop for them.

Get a Financial Life!
CASE STUDY 2

Teaching Guide

Step A — THE PROCESS

Make sure students have access to all necessary materials.

1. $170,000. [ANSWER: $68,000 × 2.5 = $170,000]
2. Features will vary, but students should recognize that the features should be typical of a house costing $170,000 or less, and reflect the needs of a young married couple.
3. Remind students that the classified ads of larger newspapers are accessible on the Internet, and the price of the house can be input to locate only the houses in that price range.
4. Give students the names of the Web sites from the Additional Resources section of the Chapter 7 Planning Guide. These sites can help students research amortization tables.
5. If possible, provide students with the names of several insurance agents that would be willing to help.
6. Accept all reasonable costs. Ask students to explain how they determined the different costs.
7. Students should provide printed examples of their "purchases" to verify costs.
8. Budgets will vary but should include income, emergency and investment savings, mortgage, and variable expenses, such as food, clothing, and utilities.

Step B — CREATE YOUR PORTFOLIO

Evaluate students' portfolios based on whether or not all eight steps of the process are completed, the information seems reasonably well researched, and the contents are neat and in order. When presenting their summary, have students state the title, date, and author of the publication.

Step C — TECHNICAL WRITING AND READING

Evaluate students' technical papers based on completeness and accuracy. Answers for each activity will vary, however, look for the following:

Activity 1—Students should include researching various lenders and mortgage rates, determining a down payment, qualifying for a mortgage, evaluating points, and considering types of mortgages.

Activity 2—Students should include researching various cost measurements such as annual fees, finance charges, and annual percentage rates.

Activity 3—Allow students time to review each other's technical papers. Students' critiques should be fair and accurate.

UNIT CLOSURE

Have students write one page describing whether or not they were surprised by the cost of financial services, credit, and housing. If they were surprised, have them explain why. If not, why not?

EVALUATION

Administer the Unit 2 test from the **ExamView** Pro Testmaker CD-ROM.

Chapter 8 Planning Guide

The Fundamentals of Investing

Teacher Manual

SECT.	OBJECTIVES	NATIONAL STANDARDS FOR BUSINESS EDUCATION	FEATURES	RESOURCES
8.1	After completing this lesson, students will have learned: How to explain the way to prepare for and establish an investment program. How to assess the factors that affect their investment choices	**Economics** I. Allocation of Resources III. Economic Institutions and Incentives VIII. International Economic Concepts IX. Aggregate Supply and Aggregate Demand **Personal Finance** I. Personal Decision Making II. Earning a Living IV. Saving and Investing	**Standard & Poor's**—Q & A, p. 236 **What's Your Financial ID?**—Are You a Risk Taker? p. 240 **International Finance**—Liechtenstein, p. 243 **Go Figure**—Inflation Rate and Investments, p. 246 **Go Figure**—A Bond's Market Price When Interest Rates Go Up, p. 247 **Go Figure**—A Bond's Market Price When Interest Rates Go Down, p. 247	Check Your Understanding, p. 250 Think Critically, p. 250 Using Communication Skills, p. 250 Solving Money Problems, p. 250 Student Activity Workbook
8.2	After completing this lesson, students will have learned: How to identify the main types of investment alternatives. How to recognize the steps involved in developing a personal investment plan	**Economics** I. Allocation of Resources IV. Markets and Prices **Personal Finance** I. Personal Decision Making II. Earning a Living IV. Saving and Investing	**Savvy Saver**—Giving Is Fun Too, p. 253 **Careers in Finance**—Personal Property Appraiser, p. 255 **Standard & Poor's**—Case Study, p. 256	Check Your Understanding, p. 258 Think Critically, p. 258 Using Communication Skills, p. 258 Solving Money Problems, p. 258 Student Activity Workbook
8.3	After completing this lesson, students will have learned: How to identify their role and the role of a financial planner in a personal investment program. How to select sources of financial information that can reduce risk and increase investment returns	**Personal Finance** I. Personal Decision Making II. Earning a Living IV. Saving and Investing	**Academic Connection**—Language Arts, p. 262 **Common Cents**—A Dollar A Day, p. 263 **Your Financial Portfolio**—Avoiding Future Shock, p. 266	Check Your Understanding, p. 267 Think Critically, p. 267 Using Math Skills, p. 267 Solving Money Problems, p. 267 Student Activity Workbook

Unit 3 *Investing Your Financial Resources*

SCANS Correlation Chart

FOUNDATION SKILLS

Basic Skills	Reading	Writing	Math	Listening	Speaking
Thinking Skills	Creative Thinking	Decision Making	Problem Solving	Seeing Things in the Mind's Eye	Knowing How to Learn	Reasoning
Personal Qualities	Responsibility	Self-Esteem	Sociability	Self-Management	Integrity/Honesty

WORKPLACE COMPETENCIES

Resources	Allocating Time	Allocating Money	Allocating Material and Facility Resources	Allocating Human Resources	
Information	Acquiring and Evaluating Information	Organizing and Maintaining Information	Interpreting and Communicating Information	Using Computers to Process Information	
Interpersonal Skills	Participating as a Member of a Team	Teaching Others	Serving Clients/ Customers	Exercising Leadership	Negotiating to Arrive at a Decision	Working with Cultural Diversity
Systems	Understanding Systems	Monitoring and Correcting Performance	Improving and Designing Systems		
Technology	Selecting Technology	Applying Technology to Task	Maintaining and Troubleshooting Technology		

Chapter 8 *Fundamentals of Investing*

■ INTERNET EXTENSION

Activity: Have students access the Motley Fool Web site and write a one-page report explaining its purpose, describing the information available, and stating whether or not the student thinks it could be helpful to new investors and why.

Keywords: The Motley Fool

■ ENRICHMENT/APPLICATION ACTIVITY

Guest Speaker: Invite a financial planner to discuss beginning investment programs. Ask the planner to explain the different types of investments, how people choose how to invest, and why investing is important to a person's future.

■ TOPIC SPOTLIGHT

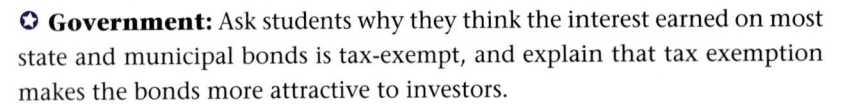

✪ **Government:** Ask students why they think the interest earned on most state and municipal bonds is tax-exempt, and explain that tax exemption makes the bonds more attractive to investors.

☉ **Marketing:** Take to class several copies of local real estate brochures and have students look through them for commercial property advertisements. Discuss how the real estate agent for the property presents the property in order to make it more saleable.

☉ **Ethics:** As a class, list on the board the personal qualities a financial planner should have. How does a financial planner's ethics affect this list?

additional resources

Basics of Saving and Investing: A Teaching Guide is **free** to teachers. Units 2, 3, and 4 are directly related to this chapter. (See Additional Resources, Chapter 1 for information about obtaining a copy of this guide.)

The Jump$tart Coalition for Personal Financial Literacy at **www.jumpstartcoalition.org** (see Additional Resources in Chapter 1) has several **free** publications that address saving and investing.

- ***High School Financial Planning Program*** includes an instructor's manual, student workbook and portfolio, activities, and tests.

- ***Saving Fitness—A Guide to Your Money and Your Financial Future*** is a free step-by-step guide to help American workers (including teens and young adults) manage money and save for financial goals.

- ***What You Should Know About Financial Planning*** describes the financial planning process, identifies types of financial advisors, and explains the consumer's role in the financial planning process.

- ***10 Questions To Ask When Choosing a Financial Planner*** is a brochure that provides a checklist of questions to ask while interviewing people before selecting your personal financial planner.

Sound Money is a radio program broadcast by Minnesota Public Radio on most public radio stations. It addresses topics, such as economics, investing, tax planning, and finding a financial planner. The host and his guests answer listener questions. Tapes of the programs may be ordered from its Web site at **www.money.mpr.org**. Also at its Web site are program listings and host Chris Farrell's list of favorite books, periodicals, and Web sites on personal finance.

Standard & Poor's has a number of different Web sites for different kinds of financial information. Investment recommendations are featured at **www.personalwealth.com**, a comprehensive Internet-based personal investment site.

Investment planning information can also be found at **www.quicken.com** and **www.moneycentral.msn.com**.

Publications such as *The Wall Street Journal*, *BusinessWeek*, *Money*, and *Kiplinger's Personal Finance* are good sources of timely economics and finance information.

The Wall Street Journal offers a classroom program including a monthly newspaper, teaching guide, and video. It is available from *The Wall Street Journal*, P.O. Box 300, Princeton, NJ 08543-0300, (800) 544-0522, or at **www.wsjclassroomedition.com/index.html**, for $99.00 per semester.

Note to teacher: Web site addresses may change.

CHAPTER 8 Lesson Plans

SECTION 8.1

FOCUS

Motivation

Write the word "sacrifice" on the board. Ask your students to discuss what this word means to them. Have them talk about the ways their parents may have sacrificed in order to raise them. Then ask the students to think back to Chapter 1 where they shared their personal financial goals and considered whether sacrifice will be necessary to achieve them.

Prereading

1. Have the students skim the section, looking at pictures, reading captions, and noting headings.
2. Have "What You'll Learn" listed on page 237 read aloud.
3. Write the Key Terms on the board. Ask the students to define them using their own words. Write their definitions on the board. Place an asterisk next to the terms the students are not sure about.
4. Ask your students to state the purpose of studying this chapter.

TEACH

Guided Practice

1. Have students read aloud the Standard & Poor's Q&A on page 236.
2. Read the section with your students.

Independent Practice

1. Have the students write a one-page paper comparing a financial checkup with a checkup at the doctor's office.
2. Ask the students to read a book about investing, and then review it. Compile the book reviews in a notebook so all the students in the class can become familiar with the variety of investment books on the market.
3. Have your students research one of the categories of investments in **Figure 8-3**.
4. Invite a stockbroker or financial planner to your classroom to speak to the students about foreign investments.

INTERNATIONAL FINANCE
Liechtenstein

1. Have the students research the Stamp Program sponsored by the U.S. Post Office.
2. Liechtenstein is a member of the European Free Trade Association. Ask your students to research this organization and its impact on the economy of the member countries.

ASSESS

Reteaching

1. Review with your students the Key Terms marked with an asterisk during the Prereading section.
2. To help students understand how to figure the inflation rate's impact on investments, ask each student to create a word problem and its answer. Then have the students partner with another student to solve each other's word problems.

Enrichment

1. Ask each student to select a long-term goal and determine how much money he or she will need to achieve the goal. Then have the students use the nine questions in this section to outline how they will achieve their goal.
2. Have the students react to this statement: "I have plenty of time to plan for retirement. I don't need to contribute to a long-term savings plan until I am much older."
3. Have the students select a stock they might want to purchase one day. Ask the students to find out about the company, its earnings,

the product(s) it sells, and whether or not the company sells its products overseas. Have the students prepare an oral presentation about the stock to the class.

Assessment

1. Have the students complete the Section 8.1 Assessment.
2. Assign an activity from the *Student Activity Workbook*.

CLOSE

Financial writer Sylvia Porter said, "It is important to forego today's luxuries to afford tomorrow's necessities." Have the students respond to Ms. Porter's statement.

SECTION 8.2

FOCUS

Motivation

Before reading this section, ask your students what they know about different types of investments. Write their responses on the board. At the end of the chapter, complete this exercise again. The students will be surprised at what they have learned.

Prereading

1. Have the students skim the section, looking at pictures, reading captions, and noting headings.
2. Have "What You'll Learn" listed on page 251 read aloud.
3. Divide the students into four groups and have each group generate definitions for the words without using the text. Limit this exercise to 15 minutes. When the time is up, have each group give its definition. When there are groups that disagree with the definitions, use this as an opportunity to clarify information.

4. Ask your students to state the purpose of studying this chapter.

TEACH

Guided Practice

1. Read the section with your students.
2. Assign an activity from the *Student Activity Workbook*.

Independent Practice

1. Have the students create a bulletin board showing the various investment alternatives. Ask them to include stocks, bonds, mutual funds, real estate, and precious metals, gems, and collectibles.
2. Have the students contact your city or municipality and find out if they have issued bonds in the past. If so, ask them what the interest rate is and when the bonds will mature.
3. Ask the students to review Ginny's personal investment plan in **Figure 8-5**. Have the students discuss how they might alter Ginny's plan to fit their own investment goals.

$AVVY SAVER

Giving is Fun Too

1. Ask the students to discuss the charities that interest them and explain why.
2. As a class, select a non-profit organization in your community and offer your assistance. [EXAMPLES: stuffing envelopes, word processing, or answering the telephones]
3. Have your students investigate Learn and Serve America, an organization that supports service learning programs in schools and community organizations. Its Web site is **http://www.cns.gov/learn/index.html**.

Note to teacher: Web site addresses may change.

Careers in Finance

Personal Property Appraiser

1. Have your students watch *The Antiques Roadshow* on public television. Ask them to observe the appraisers in action and compare their personalities to what was described in *Careers in Finance*.
2. Ask the students to contact their technical center, community college, or university to find out if there are continuing education classes that would help prepare someone to become a personal property appraiser.
3. Have your students select one of the associations or societies that offer certification for appraisers. Then ask them to research the education and experience required for that certification.

ASSESS

Reteaching

1. Review the original definitions of the Key Terms provided by the students at the beginning of this section. Ask the students to modify or enhance them as necessary.
2. To reinforce the concept of developing a personal investment plan, ask each student to create one using the eight steps on pages 255 and 257.

Enrichment

1. Have your students divide into groups. Assign each group one of the investment alternatives from this section. Ask each group to prepare a lesson for a particular investment that can be presented to middle school students. Each lesson should include a hands-on activity.
2. During the next month, have the students collect articles from the newspaper and magazines about investments. Ask the students to bring them in to class and post them on a bulletin board for all to read.

Assessment

1. Have the students complete the Section 8.2 Assessment.
2. Assign an activity from the *Student Activity Workbook*.

CLOSE

Have your students complete this statement: "If you have planned and set goals that are important to you, then you will be…." [HINT: "willing to work to obtain them."]

SECTION 8.3

FOCUS

Motivation

Ask your students to discuss their most difficult class in school. Find out why they think it is hard. Then have them share how they study for the class, how they prepare for tests, and what their teacher does to help them learn. Tell the students that studying for a difficult class is similar to the work an investor does when studying sources of financial information in preparation to making an investment. Have the students compare a teacher to a financial planner.

Prereading

1. Have the students skim the section, looking at pictures, reading captions, and noting headings.
2. Have "What You'll Learn" listed on page 259 read aloud.
3. Write the Key Terms on the board. As a class, write a definition for each word.
4. Ask the students to state the purpose of studying this chapter.

TEACH

Guided Practice

1. Read the section with your students.
2. Assign an activity from the *Student Activity Workbook*.

Independent Practice

1. Have the students review the four types of financial planners. Then have them list the pros and cons of each.
2. Have the students research the current laws regarding short-term and long-term capital gains. Then ask the students to find out what the laws were 10 years ago. How and why have they changed?
3. Ask your students to read an article about an investment they are interested in researching. Suggest that they use one of the business periodicals or government publications referred to in this section.

Common Cents

A Dollar A Day

1. Ask your students to keep a journal of all the money they spend for one week. Then for the next week, ask them to try and spend $1 a day less than they did the week before.
2. Challenge the students to begin saving and investing this extra money.
3. As a class, brainstorm ways the students can save money.

ASSESS

Reteaching

1. Review the original definitions of the Key Terms provided by the students at the beginning of this section. Ask the students to modify or enhance them as necessary.
2. Ask the students what steps they can take to make sure the source of their financial information is accurate and reliable. Help the students realize that the source of their information is critical to making successful investment decisions.

Enrichment

1. Have the students divide into groups. Ask the students to use the questions in **Figure 8.6**, and role-play an interview with a potential financial planner that they wish to hire.
2. Ask the students to find out how the Dow Jones Industrial Average is figured.

Assessment

1. Have the students complete the Section 8.3 Assessment.
2. Assign the Chapter Assessment.
3. Administer the test for Chapter 8 from the Reproducible Tests in the *Teacher Resource Binder*.

CLOSE

Have the students write a paragraph about why it is important to be an informed investor.

SECTION 8.1 ASSESSMENT
ANSWERS

CHECK YOUR UNDERSTANDING

1. You should establish investment goals, perform a financial checkup, and obtain the money you need to get started.
2. Answers may include: You should "pay yourself first"; take advantage of employer-sponsored retirement programs; participate in an elective savings program; make a special savings effort one or two months each year; and take advantage of gifts, inheritances, and windfalls.
3. One factor is the amount of risk you're willing to take. You have to examine the five components of risk in relation to your investment: inflation, interest rate, business failure, the financial market, and

global investment. You also have to consider each investment's potential for income and growth as well as its liquidity.

THINK CRITICALLY

4. Answers will vary, but students might suggest that she invest her money because even a small amount adds up over time. If she spends it on something temporary, she'll lose an opportunity to start saving for her long-term goals.

USING COMMUNICATION SKILLS

5. The five components of risk are inflation, the interest rate, business failure, the financial market, and global investment. Answers will vary but may include that inflation and interest rates will affect everyone— even those people who have very safe investments. Business failures and global investment risk may affect those who have more high-risk investments or who have more invested in individual stocks.

SOLVING MONEY PROBLEMS

6. The couple's emergency fund should have at least $7,800, the equivalent of three months' living expenses. [ANSWER: 3 × $2,600 = $7,800] However, because they are so concerned about their finances and have very little insurance, they may want to have closer to nine months' worth of living expenses, or $23,400. [ANSWER: 9 × $2,600 = $23,400] They should probably have their emergency fund money in a very liquid savings account with the highest possible interest rate. This will provide easy access and some growth.

SECTION 8.2 ASSESSMENT
ANSWERS

CHECK YOUR UNDERSTANDING

1. Stocks, bonds, mutual funds, and real estate.
2. Diversification spreads your assets among several different types of investments to lessen risk.
3. The steps are:
   (1) Establish investment goals.
   (2) Decide what amount of money you will need in order to reach those goals by a particular date.
   (3) Determine the amount of money you have to invest.
   (4) List all the investments you want to evaluate.
   (5) Evaluate the risks and potential return for each investment on your list.
   (6) Reduce the list of possible investments.
   (7) Choose at least two investments.
   (8) Recheck your investment program periodically.

THINK CRITICALLY

4. Answers will vary but may include: A pyramid has a wide base that provides a solid foundation, just as your investment program needs a good base of safe, low-risk investments. The middle level denotes moderate-risk investments. The small top reflects the idea that highly speculative investments should be the smallest piece of your investments, if you include them at all.

USING COMMUNICATION SKILLS

5. The argument against high-risk investments may include that they can lose value or become worthless. The argument for such an investment may include that some people just enjoy buying these items—for example, if they are sports fans or like antique jewelry. People who might be suited for this type of investment may include those who know about these special items, have many safe and moderate-risk investments, and have enough money to take a great risk with some of it.

SOLVING MONEY PROBLEMS

6. Answers will vary but may include: Trent has already established his investment goal, but he needs to be more specific. He should determine the amount of money that he would like to contribute to the community center and decide on a particular date by

which he would like to have gained that amount. Next he should decide on the amount of money he currently has available for investment. Then he should identify the investments he wants and evaluate and research the risks and potential return for each investment on his list. He can try to get advice from someone he knows or use free information sources, such as the Internet. After he has targeted the investments he is most likely to pursue, he should choose at least two investments for diversification. Trent will have to reevaluate his investment program as time goes on to determine whether he should make any changes.

SECTION 8.3 ASSESSMENT
ANSWERS

CHECK YOUR UNDERSTANDING

1. A financial planner should help you assess your current financial situation; offer a clearly written plan, including investment recommendations; discuss the features of the plan with you; help you keep track of your progress; and guide you to other financial experts and services as needed.
2. You should evaluate potential investments, monitor the value of your investments, keep accurate and current records, remember tax considerations, and be selective about your sources of investment information.
3. Sources of information include the Internet and online computer services, newspapers and news programs, business periodicals and government publications, corporate reports, statistical averages, and investor services and newsletters.

THINK CRITICALLY

4. Answers will vary but may include that people think that they're too busy, that they won't understand what they read, that they have a financial planner to do that, or that they don't have enough money to worry about. People should track their investments so that they can calculate their net worth.

USING MATH SKILLS

5. $30. [ANSWER: $200 × 15% = $30] Because he held the stock for less than a year, his gain, or profit, is short-term and is taxed as ordinary income.

SOLVING MONEY PROBLEMS

6. Answers will vary, but possible questions may include: Are you licensed or certified? What education and training do you have? How is your fee determined? Are you affiliated with a financial services company, or do you work alone? Am I allowed a free initial consultation? May I contact some clients as references? May I see a sample written financial plan?

CHAPTER 8 ASSESSMENT
ANSWERS

■ **Understanding and Using Vocabulary**
Answers will vary.

■ **Review Key Concepts**
1. Balance your budget and limit credit card use; have adequate insurance; set up an emergency fund; and have other sources of emergency cash, such as a line of credit.
2. Money you put aside for savings each month; employer-sponsored retirement plans; elective savings programs such as automatic payroll transfers; special savings program once a year; and gifts, inheritances, and windfalls.
3. The potential return on any investment is often directly related to the risk the investor takes.
4. Consider that a corporation does not have to repay you what you paid for the stock, so you could lose money. Also, it does not have to pay dividends.
5. Use a search engine.

■ Apply Key Concepts

1. High balances and high interest rates on credit cards mean high monthly payments, so that you will have less or no money left to use for investing.
2. Even small amounts of invested money grow in value because interest and other dividends are added to the money over a period of time.
3. Low-risk, very safe investments, such as U.S. Savings Bonds, government bonds, savings accounts, and certificates of deposit, would probably be best.
4. Stock would be a better hedge against inflation and interest risk. Stocks have a history of performing at a higher rate of return than government bonds when adjusted for inflation. Because bonds give a fixed rate of interest, they are subject to interest rate risk.
5. Answers will vary but may include that you could select government Web sites; you could do offline research to check the accuracy of information at different sites; and you could ask friends or financial professionals to recommend good sources.

Problem Solving Today

You will have $1,875 if you sell both bonds before maturity. [ANSWER: $1,125 + $750 = $1,875] You earn $90 a year on the 9 percent bond. [ANSWER: $1,000 × 9% = $90] If you sell it when rates are 8 percent, you'll get $1,125. [ANSWER: $90 ÷ 8% = $1,125] You earn $60 a year on the 6 percent bond. [$1,000 × 6% = $60] If you sell it when rates are 8 percent, you'll get $750. [ANSWER: $60 ÷ 8% = $750] You will be $125 short of the down payment for the car. You may decide to sell the bonds anyway and make up the difference from a more liquid savings account you have. You may decide to borrow more money and leave the 6 percent bond until maturity.

■ Real-World Application

Answers will vary.

Finance Online

Possible Web sites include:
- **www.personalwealth.com** (BusinessWeek Online Investing)
- **www.quicken.com** (Quicken)
- **www.financenter.com** (Financial Center, Inc.)
- **www.fool.com** (The Motley Fool)

Answers will vary.

Note to teacher: Web site addresses may change.

READING STRATEGIES
ANSWERS

Section 8.1
PREDICT (p. 244): Risks include high inflation, unfavorable changes in interest rates, business failures, drops in the stock market, and global market instabilities.

QUESTION (p. 249): Investing for growth would be better if the investor already has a good income and would like to maximize long-term gains.

Section 8.2
RESPOND (p. 252): People choose to invest in the stock market because it provides the opportunity for larger yields than more conservative investments.

CONNECT (p. 255): Answers will vary.

Section 8.3

PREDICT (p. 262): Certain government bonds are tax-exempt; some retirement accounts are tax-deferred; dividends, interest, and rental income are taxed as ordinary income; and profits from sales are taxed as capital gains. Losses from sales may be written off of one's income taxes.

RESPOND (p. 263): Answers may include considering the reputation of the source of information, the service's motives for providing the information, and the consistency with which the information matches respectable print sources.

STANDARD &POOR'S

CASE STUDY
ANSWERS

1. Stocks are subject to wide price swings in the short-term. These "paper losses" become real losses if the investor has to sell when the market is temporarily down.

2. After taxes and inflation, money invested in low-risk investments, like savings accounts, certificates of deposit, and Treasury bills, may lose purchasing power over time. For long-term goals such as retirement, it is essential to seek growth in capital over and above taxes and inflation.

3. The principle of standard deviation explains why a portfolio including bonds might outperform a portfolio consisting of stocks only. Standard deviation is a statistic that measures how much the price varies in the short term around the average long-term return. If prices of the individual investments in a portfolio do not move up and down in tandem, then the portfolio standard deviation will be less than the sum of the standard deviations of the individual investments. Typically, stock and bond investments do not move in tandem, so their price fluctuations partially offset each other. Consequently, when stock prices fall (e.g., during a recession), bonds in a portfolio will partially offset the stock losses. Therefore, a diversified portfolio consisting of stocks and bonds might at times outperform a portfolio exclusively of stocks, and at a lower level of risk.

Chapter 9 Planning Guide

Stocks

SECT.	OBJECTIVES	NATIONAL STANDARDS FOR BUSINESS EDUCATION	FEATURES	RESOURCES
9.1	**After completing this lesson, students will have learned:** How to identify the reasons for investing in common stock. How to identify the reasons for investing in preferred stock	**Personal Finance** II. Earning a Living IV. Saving and Investing	**Standard & Poor's**—Q & A, p. 270 **What's Your Financial ID?**—The Truth About Stocks, p. 272	Check Your Understanding, p. 277 Think Critically, p. 277 Using Communication Skills, p. 277 Solving Money Problems, p. 277 Student Activity Workbook
9.2	**After completing this lesson, students will have learned:** How to evaluate stock investments	**Economics** I. Allocation of Resources II. Economic Systems III. Economic Institutions and Incentives IV. Markets and Prices VIII. International Economic Concepts **Personal Finance** I. Personal Decision Making II. Earning a Living IV. Saving and Investing	**International Finance**—Mexico, p. 280 **Standard & Poor's**—Case Study, p. 283 **Go Figure**—Current Yield of a Stock Investment, p. 287 **Go Figure**—Total Return, p. 288 **Go Figure**—Earnings Per Share, p. 289 **Go Figure**—Price-Earnings Ratio, p. 289 **Careers in Finance**—Account Executive (Stockbroker), p. 290	Check Your Understanding, p. 291 Think Critically, p. 291 Using Math Skills, p. 291 Solving Money Problems, p. 291 Student Activity Workbook
9.3	**After completing this lesson, students will have learned:** How to describe how stocks are bought and sold. How to explain the trading techniques used by long-term investors and short-term speculators	**Economics** VII. The Role of Government **Personal Finance** I. Personal Decision Making II. Earning a Living IV. Saving and Investing	**Savvy Saver**—Stock Up—Research Before You Buy Stock, p. 297 **Academic Connection**—Economics, p. 298 **Common Cents**—Listen Up, p. 299 **Your Financial Portfolio**—Investing in Stock, p. 300	Check Your Understanding, p. 301 Think Critically, p. 301 Using Communication Skills, p. 301 Solving Money Problems, p. 301 Student Activity Workbook

TM138 Unit 3 *Investing Your Financial Resources*

SCANS Correlation Chart

FOUNDATION SKILLS

Basic Skills	Reading	Writing	Math	Listening	Speaking
Thinking Skills	Creative Thinking	Decision Making	Problem Solving	Seeing Things in the Mind's Eye	Knowing How to Learn	Reasoning
Personal Qualities	Responsibility	Self-Esteem	Sociability	Self-Management	Integrity/Honesty

WORKPLACE COMPETENCIES

Resources	Allocating Time	Allocating Money	Allocating Material and Facility Resources	Allocating Human Resources
Information	Acquiring and Evaluating Information	Organizing and Maintaining Information	Interpreting and Communicating Information	Using Computers to Process Information
Interpersonal Skills	Participating as a Member of a Team	Teaching Others	Serving Clients/Customers	Exercising Leadership	Negotiating to Arrive at a Decision	Working with Cultural Diversity
Systems	Understanding Systems	Monitoring and Correcting Performance	Improving and Designing Systems
Technology	Selecting Technology	Applying Technology to Task	Maintaining and Troubleshooting Technology

Chapter 9 *Stocks* TM139

■ INTERNET EXTENSION

Activity: Have students print out a copy of the quarterly or annual report of a company who publishes their financial reports on their Web site. Allow them to compare different reports and discuss the information contained in them.

Keywords: Input the name of a business, such as Timberland, Barnes & Noble, or Ford Motor Company, then click on Company, Investor Relations, or Investor Information.

■ ENRICHMENT/APPLICATION ACTIVITY

Guest Speaker: Invite the editor of the business/finance section of a local or regional newspaper to speak about businesses in the area that have recently issued stock or whose stock is traded. Ask him or her to explain where the stocks are traded (NYSE), (AMEX), or (NASDAQ), how much the stocks cost to buy, and how well the stocks have been performing.

■ TOPIC SPOTLIGHT

Ethics: Explain insider trading (the illegal use of insider information for profit in financial trading) and discuss why it is illegal.

Money: In June 2003 the exchange rate for the new peso was 1 U.S. dollar to 10.50 new pesos. Using this exchange rate, how many new pesos equal 5 U.S. dollars? [ANSWER: 5 × 10.50 = 52.50 new pesos]

Technology: Discuss with students how the Internet has changed the trading of stocks. Ask students to imagine how stocks were traded before the Internet was available to so many people.

additional resources

Basics of Saving and Investing: A Teaching Guide is *free* to teachers. Units 2 and 4 are directly related to this chapter. (See Additional Resources, Chapter 1 for information about obtaining a copy of this guide.)

The Stock Market Game, a real-world simulation that teaches about economics, finance, and the American economic system, can be found at **www.smg2000.org**. Over the course of 10 weeks, participants invest a hypothetical $100,000 in NASDAQ, AMEX, and NYSE-listed common stocks. They research stocks, study how the financial markets work, choose their portfolios, manage budgets, follow companies in the news, and make decisions on whether to buy, sell, or hold.

The SMG provides comprehensive curriculum materials for students of all ability levels and hands-on support from a nationwide network of Coordinators. The Stock Market Game is a trademarked program of the Securities Industry Foundation for Economic Education (SIFEE), an affiliate of the Securities Industry Association (SIA).

Other Web sites include **www.wsrn.com** (The Wall Street Research Net), **http://finance.yahoo.com**, and **quote.com**, which give information about investing in stocks, stock quotes, and other financial data.

Information on activities and resources and various stock exchanges can be found at **www.amex.com** (American Stock Exchange), **www.nyse.com** (New York Stock Exchange), and **www.nasdaq.com** (National Association of Securities Dealers Automated Quotation system).

Note to teacher: Web site addresses may change.

CHAPTER 9   Lesson Plans

SECTION 9.1

FOCUS

Motivation

Draw three columns on the board. The first column will be titled "What I Know About Stocks." The second column will be titled "What I Think I Know About Stocks." The third column will be titled "What I Would Like to Know About Stocks." Then, as a class, complete the three columns. When you have finished studying this chapter, go back and review the columns.

Prereading

1. Have your students skim the section, looking at pictures, reading captions, and noting headings.
2. Have "What You'll Learn" listed on page 271 read aloud.
3. Write the Key Terms on the board. Ask the students to define them using their own words. Write their definitions on the board.
4. Ask your students to state the purpose of studying this chapter.

TEACH

Guided Practice

1. Have students read aloud the Standard & Poor's Q&A on page 270.
2. Read the section with your students.

Independent Practice

1. Have the students select a well-known corporation that trades its stock publicly. Ask the students to research whether the corporation trades both common and preferred stock, how many shares of each type are currently outstanding (at the end of the last fiscal year), and what year their stock was first trading publicly.
2. Ask your students to listen to or watch radio/television shows that discuss the stock market. [EXAMPLES: CNBC, *Bloomberg's Market Watch*, CNN's *Moneyline News Hour*, *The Stock Doctor*] Have your students evaluate the experts and the type of advice they offer.
3. Have the students ask their parents or other relatives about the stocks they own. Ask them to find out why they purchased the stock they own and whether they own common or preferred stock.

ASSESS

Reteaching

1. Review with the students the Key Terms and their definitions that you wrote on the board.
2. To reinforce the concept of the dollar appreciation of the value of stock, select three or four companies with which students are familiar [EXAMPLES: Ford, McDonalds, WalMart, Microsoft], and show them how much $1,000 invested in each stock 10 years ago would be worth today.

Enrichment

1. Corporations do not have to repay the money a stockholder pays for stock. Is this ethical? Have each student work with a partner and debate this issue.
2. If possible, arrange for the class to attend a stockholders' meeting. Or invite someone to speak to the class who has attended a stockholders' meeting. Ask the students to find out what topics are discussed, how many votes were taken, and how many people attended.
3. Divide the class into three groups. Assign each group one of the following: cumulative preferred stock, convertible preferred stock, and the participation feature. Ask each group to research additional information about their assigned topic. Then ask each group to create a visual aid and present their findings to the class.

Assessment

1. Have the students complete the Section 9.1 Assessment.
2. Assign an activity from the *Student Activity Workbook*.

CLOSE

Ask the students to write a paragraph about whether or not they would like to invest in the stock market.

SECTION 9.2

FOCUS

Motivation

Ask your students to define the word "evaluation." Ask them to discuss all the different ways they are evaluated (by teachers, employers, friends, parents), and what they think goes into the evaluation process. Tell the students that before an investment is made, it should be evaluated in much the same way.

Prereading

1. Have the students skim the section, looking at pictures, reading captions, and noting headings.
2. Have "What You'll Learn" listed on page 278 read aloud.
3. Dictate each of the Key Terms to the students and have them write them on a piece of paper. When they are finished, write the terms on the board. Ask your students to guess at the meaning of each term, but do not give the correct meaning. Leave the list on the board, so that as students work through the section, they can see how close they were to the correct answer.
4. Ask the students to state the purpose of studying this chapter.

TEACH

Guided Practice

1. Read the section with your students.
2. Assign an activity from the *Student Activity Workbook*.

Independent Practice

1. Have the students create a list of Web sites that focus on personal finance and investment. In particular, ask them to note those that target teen investors. Assemble all the Web sites in a notebook so the entire class can have access to them.
2. Ask the students to read an article from one of the leading financial publications on a corporation that they are interested in researching. In their own words, summarize and review the article.

INTERNATIONAL FINANCE
Mexico

1. Have the students research how NAFTA (North American Free Trade Agreement) has impacted the Mexican economy.
2. Ask your students to find out what products the United States imports from Mexico.
3. For the next several weeks, have the students read labels on the products they own and purchase. Which ones are made in Mexico?

Careers in Finance

Account Executive (Stockbroker)

1. Have your students find out what the requirements are to take the General Securities Registered Representative Examination.
2. Ask the students to discuss why they think communication, math, computer, and interpersonal skills are important for a successful stockbroker.
3. Have the students respond to this statement: "With the Internet for researching

and online trading for purchasing, stockbrokers will no longer be needed in the very near future."

ASSESS

Reteaching

1. Review the original definitions of the Key Terms provided by the students at the beginning of this section. Clarify for the students any of the Key Terms that they still might be questioning.
2. To review the calculations investors use when evaluating their stocks, have the students create a word problem and its answer for each of the following:
   - current yield
   - total return
   - earnings per share
   - price-earnings ratio

   Use some of the students' problems on the next quiz or test.

Enrichment

1. Have the students research cyclical stocks. As a class, create a list of them and ask the students to explain why they think the stocks are cyclical.
2. Divide the class into groups of four or five. Have each group select eight different stocks—one in each category—blue-chip, income, growth, cyclical, defensive, large cap, small cap, and penny stocks—and justify their selection. Ask them to present their findings to the class.
3. Have the students create a "mock" stock advisory service. Ask the students to report on the stocks they have been researching and studying in this chapter. The students could produce a radio show, TV segment, or newsletter.

Assessment

1. Have the students complete the Section 9.2 Assessment.
2. Assign an activity from the *Student Activity Workbook*.

CLOSE

Have the students write a paragraph describing the current stock market and whether it is a bull or bear market. Ask them to make sure they explain why.

SECTION 9.3

FOCUS

Motivation

Have the students create a list of all the ways products are bought or sold. Then ask the students if they know how stocks are bought and sold. After studying this section, review their answers and clarify any points if necessary.

Prereading

1. Have the students skim the section, looking at pictures, reading captions, and noting headings.
2. Have "What You'll Learn" listed on page 292 read aloud.
3. Have the students write each bold-faced term in the section, and based on its definition, generate a picture or symbol that identifies it.
4. Ask your students to state the purpose of studying this chapter.

TEACH

Guided Practice

1. Read the section with your students.
2. Assign an activity from the *Student Activity Workbook*.

Independent Practice

1. Ask your students to find out what hours the major United States stock markets are open for trading. Have them research whether there are any stocks that can be purchased after hours. Then ask them to investigate the possibility of 24-hour-a-day trading and its implications for the economy.
2. Have the students research the procedure used to purchase stocks through the direct investment method.
3. Ask the students to write a one-page paper outlining the risks and benefits of buying stock on margin.

$avvy Saver

Stock Up—Research Before You Buy Stock

1. Ask the students to investigate reports and tools that can be used to research stocks.
2. Have your students locate two or three Web sites that can be used to research stocks.
3. Many investors and would-be investors love to give stock tips to others. Ask the students how they would know which tips to take seriously and which ones they should ignore.

Common Cents

Listen Up

1. Ask the students what other products they should try out before they make a purchase.
2. Tell the students this story: "Your friend, Dana, will always buy a CD, bring it home, burn a copy on her CD burner, and then return the CD for a refund." Ask the students what they think about this situation and whether or not Dana is stealing.
3. File-sharing software allows people to get free music over the Internet. Have the students write a paper explaining the impact of file-sharing software on the local CD stores.

ASSESS

Reteaching

1. Review the Key Terms from the section. Make sure the students understand the terms.
2. To reinforce the types of orders used to trade stock write these terms on the board: market order, limit order, stop order, and discretionary order. Have the students describe each type of order with a phrase or two. Write the phrases on the board and use them as a review for the end-of-chapter assessment.

Enrichment

1. Divide the class into six groups. Assign each group either a short-term or long-term investment strategy. Ask each group to prepare a skit explaining the strategy to the rest of the class.
2. Have the students contact brokerage firms in your community and find out what the commission charges are for buying and selling stock.
3. Ask the students to interview a stockbroker and find out why he or she chose the occupation, the best and worst part of the job, what training is required, and any recommendations for the would-be stockbrokers in the class.

Assessment

1. Have the students complete the Section 9.3 Assessment.
2. Assign the Chapter Assessment.
3. Administer the test for Chapter 9 from the Reproducible Tests in the *Teacher Resource Binder*.

CLOSE

Have the students complete this statement: "To increase your total return on your investments, you should…." [HINT: "use a variety of investment strategies."]

SECTION 9.1 ASSESSMENT ANSWERS

CHECK YOUR UNDERSTANDING

1. Corporations issue common stock to raise money to start up their business and then to help pay for its ongoing activities.
2. Investors purchase common stock as a way to make money. They may make money from dividends, from the dollar appreciation of stock value, and when the stock splits and increases in value.
3. Preferred stock gives the owner the advantage of receiving cash dividends before common stockholders receive any. If the company were having a hard time financially, then the preferred stockholder might get a dividend when the common stockholder would not. The yield is generally lower than the yield on bonds, but higher than the yield on common stock. When you buy preferred stock, you know the actual dollar amount of the dividend you will receive before you buy.

THINK CRITICALLY

4. The company can bring the stock price down to a range that it considers reasonable. A split also makes the stock affordable to a larger number of investors. In addition, a stock split could attract investors who believe that a company splits its stock when it is doing particularly well.

USING COMMUNICATIONS SKILLS

5. Answers will vary. If a stockholder wants to influence major changes in company policy or the selection of individuals to the board of directors, he or she should exercise his or her voting rights. Voting is also important if the company is poorly managed or is in financial trouble.

SOLVING MONEY PROBLEMS

6. $67.50. [ANSWER: $45 × .06 = $2.70, and $2.70 × 25 = $67.50]

SECTION 9.2 ASSESSMENT ANSWERS

CHECK YOUR UNDERSTANDING

1. A blue-chip stock is considered a safe investment that generally attracts conservative investors. An income stock pays higher-than-average dividends compared to other stock issues. It has predictable dividends. A growth stock is issued by a corporation whose earnings may be higher than the average earnings predicted for all the firms in the country. A cyclical stock has a market value that tends to reflect the state of the economy. A defensive stock is a stock that remains stable during declines in the economy. A large cap stock is the stock of a corporation that has a large amount of stock outstanding and a large amount of capitalization. A small cap stock is a stock issued by a company with a capitalization of $500 million or less. A penny stock typically sells for less than $1 a share, although it can sell for as much as $10 a share. Penny stocks are issued by new companies or companies whose sales are very unsteady.
2. Sources include the financial section of the newspaper, the Internet, stock advisory services, corporate news, and financial publications.
3. Numerical measures include current yield, total return, earnings per share, and price-earnings ratio.

THINK CRITICALLY

4. The earnings per share calculation is related to the profitability of a company, so an increase in earnings per share can be a sign that the corporation's stock would be a good

investment. A low price-earnings (PE) ratio may indicate that a stock would be a good investment. A high PE ratio may indicate that the stock would be a poor investment.

USING MATH SKILLS

5. $1,100. [ANSWER: $.50 × 100 × 2 = $100; $20 × 100 = $2,000; $30 × 100 = $3,000; $3,000 − $2,000 = $1,000; $1,000 + $100 = $1,100]

SOLVING MONEY PROBLEMS

6. The PE ratio and the price would be helpful. The PE ratio is considered a key indicator of the reasonableness of the market price of a corporation's stock. Stock analysts believe that if the PE ratio is high compared to the average PE ratio over a period of time, the stock is not a good buy or could be near its peak value. On the other hand, if it is low, the stock might be a good buy. Noting the price allows the investor to determine the stock's value over time.

SECTION 9.3 ASSESSMENT
ANSWERS

CHECK YOUR UNDERSTANDING

1. The primary market is a market in which an investor purchases securities from a corporation through an investment bank or another representative of the corporation. The investors are commercial banks, insurance companies, pension funds, mutual funds, and the general public. After stocks are sold on the primary market, they are sold in the secondary market. The secondary market is a market for existing financial securities that are currently traded, or bought and sold, among investors. They may be sold time and again to many different investors on securities exchanges or through the over-the-counter market.
2. Generally, full-service and discount brokerage firms charge higher commissions than online brokerage firms. Full-service firms usually charge the highest commissions in exchange for personalized service and free research information. Discount and online firms may charge lower rates but will also charge extra for research. The account executives for these firms generally do not discuss investing decisions. However, these firms usually have printed material or information on their Web sites to help you become a better investor.
3. Investors use the buy-and-hold technique, dollar cost averaging, and direct investment and dividend reinvestment plans. Speculators routinely buy and sell investments within short periods of time, and may also buy stock on margin and sell short.

THINK CRITICALLY

4. Answers will vary. The handout should discuss the buy-and-hold technique, dollar cost averaging, direct investment, and dividend reinvestment.

USING COMMUNICATION SKILLS

5. Answers will vary.

SOLVING MONEY PROBLEMS

6. Answers will vary but should emphasize that Bruce must take responsibility for his investments and make all final decisions. The danger of poor decisions or even dishonest behavior on the part of the account executive should be part of the argument.

CHAPTER 9 ASSESSMENT
ANSWERS

■ Understanding and Using Vocabulary
Answers will vary.

■ Review Key Concepts
1. Corporations don't have to repay the money a stockholder pays for stock.
2. Cyclical stocks have a market value that tends to reflect the state of the economy. When the economy is improving, the market value of a cyclical stock usually goes up.

During an economic decline, the market value of a cyclical stock generally decreases. In contrast, a defensive stock remains stable during declines in the economy.
3. A securities exchange is a marketplace where brokers who represent investors meet to buy and sell securities. It typically trades the stocks of large corporations that trade many shares. An over-the-counter market is a network of dealers who buy and sell stocks of mostly small corporations that are not listed on a securities exchange. However, stocks of a few large corporations may also be traded in the over-the-counter market.
4. By telephone, in person at a brokerage firm, or over the Internet.
5. Short-term trading strategies, such as selling short, depend heavily on the ability to predict accurately the movement of a stock's price.

■ Apply Key Concepts
1. Student presentations should mention that by issuing common stocks, a corporation can raise money to start up the business and then to help pay for its ongoing activities. Issuing common stocks provides a form of equity because the corporation doesn't have to repay the money a stockholder pays for stock. In addition, dividends are not mandatory.
2. Answers may include that the market value of a cyclical stock will rise when the economy is strong and fall when the economy is in a decline. A defensive stock will stay at the same level during good and bad economic periods. Many blue-chip stocks and income stocks are in this category.
3. Answers may include that the Nasdaq has a reputation for trading the stocks of forward-thinking companies. Trading in this over-the-counter market might lead investors to believe that the company is on the cutting edge in terms of technology or future trends.
4. With a stop order, you are guaranteed the stock at a specified price; there is no guarantee that a limit order will be filled before the stock price changes.
5. Students may say that if the value of the stock goes up rather than down, you would have to purchase the stock at the higher price to replace it. Also, if dividends are due, they may absorb any profits you make on the transaction.

❓ Problem Solving Today
Your total return on the penny stock is $1,800. [ANSWER: $18 \times 100 = \$1,800$] Your total return on the blue chip stock is $3,124. [ANSWER: Step 1: $\$0.52 \times 4 = \$2.08$; Step 2: $\$2.08 \times 100 \times 3 = \$624$; Step 3: $\$25 \times 100 = \$2,500$; Step 4: $\$624 + \$2,500 = \$3,124$] Check students' graphs. Answers will vary. Blue-chip stocks have a longer history of success than penny stocks, which are considered very risky.

■ Real-World Application
Answers will vary.

FINANCE Online

Possible Web sites include:
www.princetonreview.com
www.careers-in-business.com
http://about.com/money

Answers will vary.

Note to teacher: Web site addresses may change.

READING STRATEGIES
ANSWERS

Section 9.1
CONNECT (p. 271): Answers will vary.

RESPOND (p. 274): Preemptive rights might be beneficial if you disagreed with a significant portion of other stockholders about the management of the company. With preemptive rights, you could purchase more shares of the stock and gain more votes to influence the board of directors.

Section 9.2
QUESTION (p. 279): An investor who is willing to take a few more risks and able to research and predict a company's potential to be a future industry leader might prefer growth stocks to blue-chip stocks.

PREDICT (p. 286): Factors to consider are: the state of the market (bull or bear), a company's profits and investments, the current yield, total return, earnings per share, and price-earnings ratio.

Section 9.3
RESPOND (p. 295): Answers will vary.

QUESTION (p. 299): A dividend reinvestment plan might be attractive to long-term investors who don't need investment income and who believe that the price of their shares in the company will continue to grow.

STANDARD & POOR'S

CASE STUDY
ANSWERS

1. Angela will pay a higher commission to purchase stocks through a broker. However, a good broker will help her evaluate her choices and can also provide her with additional research material.

2. A mutual fund offers professional stock selection, diversification, and convenience. Mutual funds buy and sell stocks and pass dividends and capital gains on to shareholders in the form of dividend income and capital gains distributions. These distributions are taxable. Many people prefer to purchase stocks on their own in order to have greater control of the tax aspects of their investments.

3. Simulated trading can help you practice implementing the basic principles of investing. However, emotions also come into play in investing. You may find that you are less willing to take risks when real money is at stake.

Chapter 10 Planning Guide

Bonds and Mutual Funds

Teacher Manual

SECT.	OBJECTIVES	NATIONAL STANDARDS FOR BUSINESS EDUCATION	FEATURES	RESOURCES
10.1	After completing this lesson, students will have learned: How to identify the characteristics of corporate bonds. How to explain the reasons corporate bonds are bought and sold	**Economics** I. Allocation of Resources **Personal Finance** I. Personal Decision Making II. Earning a Living IV. Saving and Investing	**Standard & Poor's**—Q & A, p. 304 **Go Figure**—A Bond's Annual Interest, p. 306 **What's Your Financial ID?**—What's Your Investing IQ?, p. 309 **Common Cents**—Savings Mind-Set, p. 310 **Go Figure**—Approximate Market Value of a Bond, p. 312	**Check Your Understanding,** p. 314 **Think Critically,** p. 314 **Using Communication Skills,** p. 314 **Solving Money Problems,** p. 314 **Student Activity Workbook**
10.2	After completing this lesson, students will have learned: How to discuss the reasons governments issue bonds. How to describe the reasons investors purchase government bonds	**Economics** III. Economic Institutions and Incentives VII. The Role of Government VIII. International Economic Concepts **Personal Finance** I. Personal Decision Making II. Earning a Living IV. Saving and Investing	**Savvy Saver**—Save Gasoline—and Money, p. 316 **International Finance**—Nepal, p. 318	**Check Your Understanding,** p. 319 **Think Critically,** p. 319 **Using Math Skills,** p. 319 **Solving Money Problems,** p. 319 **Student Activity Workbook**
10.3	After completing this lesson, students will have learned: How to analyze information to select wise bond investments	**Personal Finance** I. Personal Decision Making II. Earning a Living IV. Saving and Investing	**Standard & Poor's**—Case Study, p. 324 **Go Figure**—Current Yield of a Bond Investment, p. 325	**Check Your Understanding,** p. 326 **Think Critically,** p. 326 **Using Math Skills,** p. 326 **Solving Money Problems,** p. 326 **Student Activity Workbook**

Unit 3 *Investing Your Financial Resources*

Chapter 10 Planning Guide

SECT.	OBJECTIVES	NATIONAL STANDARDS FOR BUSINESS EDUCATION	FEATURES	RESOURCES
10.4	After completing this lesson, students will have learned: How to recognize the characteristics of mutual fund investments How to distinguish among the types of mutual funds	**Personal Finance** II. Earning a Living IV. Saving and Investing	**Go Figure**—Net Asset Value, p. 329 **Careers in Finance**—Certified Financial Planner, p. 330 **Academic Connection**—Math, p. 333	**Check Your Understanding,** p. 335 **Think Critically,** p. 335 **Using Math Skills,** p. 335 **Solving Money Problems,** p. 335 **Student Activity Workbook**
10.5	After completing this lesson, students will have learned: How to evaluate mutual funds to determine which funds might be right for them How to describe the reasons investors buy and sell mutual funds and the methods they use	**Economics** I. Allocation of Resources **Personal Finance** I. Personal Decision Making II. Earning a Living IV. Saving and Investing	**Your Financial Portfolio**—Evaluating Mutual Funds, p. 345	**Check Your Understanding,** p. 347 **Think Critically,** p. 347 **Using Communication Skills,** p. 347 **Solving Money Problems,** p. 347 **Student Activity Workbook**

Teacher Manual

Chapter 10 *Bonds and Mutual Funds*   TM151

SCANS Correlation Chart

FOUNDATION SKILLS

Basic Skills	Reading	Writing	Math	Listening	Speaking
Thinking Skills	Creative Thinking	Decision Making	Problem Solving	Seeing Things in the Mind's Eye	Knowing How to Learn	Reasoning
Personal Qualities	Responsibility	Self-Esteem	Sociability	Self-Management	Integrity/Honesty

WORKPLACE COMPETENCIES

Resources	Allocating Time	Allocating Money	Allocating Material and Facility Resources	Allocating Human Resources
Information	Acquiring and Evaluating Information	Organizing and Maintaining Information	Interpreting and Communicating Information	Using Computers to Process Information
Interpersonal Skills	Participating as a Member of a Team	Teaching Others	Serving Clients/Customers	Exercising Leadership	Negotiating to Arrive at a Decision	Working with Cultural Diversity
Systems	Understanding Systems	Monitoring and Correcting Performance	Improving and Designing Systems
Technology	Selecting Technology	Applying Technology to Task	Maintaining and Troubleshooting Technology

■ INTERNET EXTENSION

Activity: Have students research investment clubs on the Internet. Ask them, "How can clubs help people with their investments?"

Keywords: investment clubs, National Association of Investors Corporation (NAIC)

■ ENRICHMENT/APPLICATION ACTIVITY

Guest Speaker: Invite a representative from an investment club to speak to the class about the club and why he or she joined. Ask the speaker to talk about researching and choosing mutual funds and corporate and government bonds, as well as stocks. NAIC Online at **www.better-investing.org** lists their chapters throughout the country.

■ TOPIC SPOTLIGHT ■

◎ **Marketing:** After looking at both corporate and mutual fund annual reports, discuss how these publications are a form of marketing.

⑤ **Money:** What is the rate of return on a Treasury bill with a face value of $1,000 and a purchase price of $875? [ANSWER: 14.29%; $1,000 − 875 = 125 ÷ 875 = 14.29%]

◎ **Technology:** Discuss how the Internet has made more investment information available to many more people. Then ask how investors know they are getting accurate information. Discuss with students the importance of using reliable sources.

additional resources

Basics of Saving and Investing: A Teaching Guide is **free** to teachers. Unit 4 is directly related to this chapter. (See Additional Resources, Chapter 1 for information about obtaining a copy of this guide.)

The Jump$tart Coalition for Personal Financial Literacy (see Additional Resources in Chapter 1) has several **free** publications that address saving and investing.

- **Invest Wisely**, **Mutual Funds** provides basic information on how to select a brokerage firm and salesperson, and how to open an account. Provides names and addresses of securities regulations and identifies signs of investment fraud.

- **Get the Facts on Saving and Investing** is an introduction to the basics of saving and investing. Includes self-assessment, investment choices, monitoring your progress, and avoiding problems.

www.bonds-online.com provides information, education, and direction in making bond investment decisions from tracking bond prices and bond market news to self-directed education, active personal advice, and bond trading.

The Vanguard Group is an investment company whose Web site, **www.vanguard.com**, provides information about investing in mutual funds.

The Federal Reserve Bank of San Francisco offers details for buying U.S. Savings Bonds and Treasury notes and bonds at **www.frbsf.org**.

The Web site of the U.S. Securities & Exchange Commission (SEC) **www.sec.gov** provides a great deal of information on the securities market, including how the SEC protects investors and the laws that govern the industry. Investor education and publications are available at **www.sec.gov/oiea1.htm**.

Note to teachers: Web site addresses may change.

CHAPTER 10 Lesson Plans

SECTION 10.1

FOCUS

Motivation
Ask the students if they have ever loaned money to a friend or acquaintance. If so, have them explain the details of the loan. Did you require an IOU? Was interest charged? Did you ask for collateral? Then tell the students that a bond is just an organization's IOU; a promise to repay a sum of money at a certain interest rate and over a certain period of time.

Prereading
1. Have your students skim the section, looking at pictures, reading captions, and noting headings.
2. Have "What You'll Learn" listed on page 305 read aloud.
3. Have the students write each bold-faced term in the section, and based on its definition, generate a picture or symbol that identifies it.
4. Ask your students to state the purpose of studying this chapter.

TEACH

Guided Practice
1. Have students read aloud the Standard & Poor's Q&A on page 304.
2. Read the section with your students.

Independent Practice
1. Have your students research the relationship between the prevailing interest rates and the interest earned from the purchase of corporate bonds.
2. Ask the students to create a brochure entitled *What to Look For When Investing in Corporate Bonds*. As a class, vote on the best one and publish it for other students in the school.

3. Have the students research the Bond Market Association. Ask your students to find out when it was started, who can join, and what the association does.

Common Cents

Savings Mind-Set
1. Ask the students who are working if they have ever received a raise. If so, have them explain what they did with it.
2. Tell your students to imagine they earn $9.05 per hour. After six months, they receive a $.50 per hour pay increase. If they work 40 hours per week, how much extra will they earn during the next 26 weeks? [ANSWER: $.50 × 40 × 26 = $520]

ASSESS

Reteaching
1. Review the Key Terms from the section. Make sure the students understand the terms.
2. To clarify the different types of corporate bonds, divide the students into groups. Assign each group a different type of bond. Ask each group to prepare a one-minute explanation of their assigned bond.

Enrichment
1. Tell your students that bearer bonds were actually made illegal in the United States in 1982. Have the students research why.
2. As a class, create a list of questions people should ask before they invest in bonds.

Assessment
1. Have your students complete the Section 10.1 Assessment.
2. Assign an activity from the *Student Activity Workbook*.

CLOSE

Have the students complete this statement, "When you buy a corporate bond, you are really...." [HINT: "loaning money to a corporation."]

SECTION 10.2

FOCUS

Motivation

Ask your students why they think so many people give savings bonds as gifts.

Prereading

1. Have your students skim the section, looking at pictures, reading captions, and noting headings.
2. Have "What You'll Learn" listed on page 315 read aloud.
3. Write the three Key Terms on the board. Ask the students to discuss the definitions and write their answers on the board.
4. Ask the students to state the purpose of studying this chapter.

TEACH

Guided Practice

1. Read the section with your students.
2. Assign an activity from the *Student Activity Workbook*.

Independent Practice

1. Have the students research the new U.S. Treasury inflation-indexed security bond. Ask them to write a paragraph on its features, how it is purchased, and the interest rate it pays.
2. Ask the students to write a step-by-step set of instructions on how to purchase savings bonds online.

3. Have your students research the Municipal Securities Rulemaking Board. Ask the students to find out what the board does and why it was created.

$AVVY SAVER

Save Gasoline—and Money
1. Have your students add two tips to this list.
2. Invite an auto mechanic to the class to discuss ways people can improve their automobile's gasoline mileage.
3. Ask the students to keep track of everywhere they drive, or are driven, for one week. Then ask them to record how many of the trips could have been made by walking or riding a bike.

INTERNATIONAL FINANCE
Nepal
1. Have the students research the business culture in Nepal. Ask them to find out about the protocol, business customs, and business etiquette.
2. Ask your students to explain the political structure of Nepal and how it has changed over the last 15 years.
3. Nepal is one of the least developed nations in the world. Have the students discuss how the economy is impacted by a lack of natural resources.

ASSESS

Reteaching

1. Review the definitions of the three Key Terms provided by the students at the beginning of this section. Ask the students to modify or enhance them as necessary.
2. Take the class on a field trip to the bank and have a bank officer show the students how easy it is to purchase Treasury bills, notes, and bonds.

Enrichment

1. Have the students create a list of resources to use when researching municipal bonds. The list could include books, newsletters, newspapers, and Web sites.
2. Ask the students to research one of the companies that insure municipal bonds. Have them find out what type of coverage is offered.

Assessment

1. Have the students complete the Section 10.2 Assessment.
2. Assign an activity from the *Student Activity Workbook*.

CLOSE

Ask the students to explain the advantages and disadvantages of purchasing government bonds and securities.

SECTION 10.3

FOCUS

Motivation

Ask your students if they have ever been assigned a school research project that they just didn't know how to begin. Tell the students that there is a lot of investment information available, but the key is being able to narrow down and analyze the information so that wise decisions can be made.

Prereading

1. Have the students skim the section, looking at pictures, reading captions, and noting headings.
2. Have "What You'll Learn" listed on page 320 read aloud.
3. Write the two Key Terms on the board. Ask your students to guess at their meaning. Write the guesses on the board.
4. Ask the students to state the purpose of studying this chapter.

TEACH

Guided Practice

1. Read the section with your students.
2. Assign an activity from the *Student Activity Workbook*.

Independent Practice

1. Have your students find out what the cost is for a yearlong subscription to *The Wall Street Journal* and *Barron's*.
2. Divide the students into groups of three. Ask each group to create two word problems and the answers for calculating the yield on a bond investment. Then have the groups exchange problems and try to solve them.

ASSESS

Reteaching

1. Review the two Key Terms and the students' guesses that you wrote on the board. Revise and clarify them as necessary.
2. Reinforce the importance of ratings for evaluating a bond as an investment. Ask the students to imagine purchasing bonds of a company that is in bankruptcy. Ask the students these questions: "Should the price of the bond be high or low? How risky is the bond? Why?"

Enrichment

1. Have your students create a lesson on how to read the bond section of the newspaper.
2. Ask the students to research the bond rating system and the factors that are considered before a bond is rated.
3. Ask local investment brokers and bankers to donate business magazines and financial newsletters. Have the students select an article about bonds from one of them, and write a summary of the article.

Assessment

1. Have the students complete the Section 10.3 Assessment.
2. Assign an activity from the *Student Activity Workbook*.

CLOSE

Have the students explain why knowing how to calculate yield on your investments is important.

SECTION 10.4

FOCUS

Motivation

Write this statement on the board: "People want to be told where to put their money. They want to invest in stocks and bonds, but don't know how and would rather someone else do it for them." Have the students respond to this quote.

Prereading

1. Have your students skim the section, looking at pictures, reading captions, and noting headings.
2. Have "What You'll Learn" listed on page 327 read aloud.
3. Write the key terms on the board. Ask the students to guess at the meaning of each term, but do not give the correct meaning. Leave the list on the board, so that as students work through the section, they can see if they were correct.
4. Ask your students to state the purpose of studying this chapter.

TEACH

Guided Practice

1. Read the section with your students.
2. Assign an activity from the *Student Activity Workbook*.

Independent Practice

1. Have the students select a mutual fund that invests in stocks. Ask the students to research the types of stocks that are in the investment portfolio. Then evaluate the portfolio for its diversity.
2. Bring in copies of *The Wall Street Journal* for the students to use. Have them find an example of one closed-end fund and one open-end fund.

Careers in Finance

Certified Financial Planner

1. Have the students research the requirements for becoming a certified financial planner (CFP).
2. Ask your students to prepare a list of questions they would ask a financial planner before they hired one.

ASSESS

Reteaching

1. Review the list of Key Terms that the students were unsure about before studying the chapter.
2. To help the students remember and understand the 12 categories of stock mutual funds, divide the class into 12 groups. Assign each group a different category and ask the groups to prepare a short presentation of their assigned category.

Enrichment

1. Ask the students to discuss the advantages and disadvantages of purchasing international funds.
2. Have your students choose two categories of bond mutual funds. Ask them to compare and contrast them with each other.

Assessment

1. Have the students complete the Section 10.4 Assessment.
2. Assign an activity from the *Student Activity Workbook*.

CLOSE

Have your students explain why investors might want to switch among the mutual funds in a family.

SECTION 10.5

FOCUS

Motivation

Discuss with the students how they would decide which mutual funds would be the best for them. Write their ideas on the board and add to them as you study this section.

Prereading

1. Have your students skim the section, looking at pictures, reading captions, and noting headings.
2. Have "What You'll Learn" listed on page 336 read aloud.
3. Write the three Key Terms on the board. Ask the students to define them using their own words.
4. Write their definitions on the board.

TEACH

Guided Practice

1. Read the section with your students.
2. Assign an activity from the *Student Activity Workbook*.

Independent Practice

1. Bring in copies of the newspaper or *The Wall Street Journal* and have the students practice reading the mutual fund section.

2. Ask the students to use a mutual fund's prospectus or annual report and research the fund manager's background. Have the students find out how long the manager has been in the job, his or her success rate, and any personal information, i.e., education.

ASSESS

Reteaching

1. Review the three Key Terms and the definitions the students created. Revise them if necessary.
2. Clarify for the students the four ways to withdraw money from a mutual fund. If possible, invite a certified financial planner to your class to discuss both purchase options and withdrawal options.

Enrichment

1. Have your students write a one-page paper discussing their financial objectives and how mutual funds can or cannot help them meet their goals.
2. Ask the students to select a mutual fund and look it up on the Internet. The students should report on the current market value, a price history and a profile.
3. Interview a tax accountant or attorney and have him or her explain the tax laws as they relate to mutual funds.

Assessment

1. Have your students complete the Section 10.5 Assessment.
2. Assign the Chapter 10 Assessment.
3. Administer the Chapter 10 Reproducible Test from the *Teacher Resource Binder*.

CLOSE

Tell the students to imagine that their best friend just inherited $5,000 and wants to invest the money but doesn't know where to begin. Have the students write a letter to their friend offering advice.

SECTION 10.1 ASSESSMENT
ANSWERS

CHECK YOUR UNDERSTANDING

1. Interest rate, maturity date, and face value.
2. A company might issue corporate bonds in order to finance regular business activities; raise money at a time when it is difficult or impossible to sell stock; reduce the taxes it must pay (interest paid to bondholders is tax-deductible).
3. Investors buy corporate bonds because many are safe investments; bonds may help diversify an investment portfolio; most bonds provide interest income; bonds may increase in value; the face value of a bond is repaid when it reaches maturity.

THINK CRITICALLY

4. Bonds guarantee investors repayment at a future date. Companies are required to pay interest on bonds. If a corporation files for bankruptcy, bondholders' claims to assets are paid before the claims of stockholders.

USING COMMUNICATION SKILLS

5. Answers will vary but may include: Many corporate bonds are safer investments than stocks. You can use corporate bonds to diversify your investment portfolio. Bonds provide interest income. Bonds may increase in value. The face value of bonds is repaid when they reach maturity. Convertible bonds allow an investor to trade the bonds for shares of the company's stock. Convertible bonds gain value when the company's stock value increases, while also offering the safety and interest income of a bond.

SOLVING MONEY PROBLEMS

6. Answers will vary, but the best choice for Mr. Blackhorse may be a subordinated debenture. This unsecured bond has less risk than a debenture bond but more risk than a mortgage bond. Because of the increased risk, investors who buy subordinated debentures usually receive higher interest rates than other bondholders.

SECTION 10.2 ASSESSMENT
ANSWERS

CHECK YOUR UNDERSTANDING

1. The federal government sells bonds and other securities to help fund its regular activities and to reduce the national debt.
2. State and local governments sell bonds to help pay for ongoing activities and to finance major projects.
3. Answers will vary but might include: They are thought to be almost risk-free; they have a low risk of default; state and local governments do not tax income on U.S. government securities; some states offer to guarantee payments on selected securities.

THINK CRITICALLY

4. Like corporate bonds, municipal bonds pay for ongoing activities and special projects. They pay interest to the bondholder. They are redeemed at the maturity date. They may be callable. You can hold them until the maturity date or sell them to another investor.

USING MATH SKILLS

5. Joshua will earn $60 from his T-bill. [ANSWER: $1,000 − $940 = $60] The annual rate of return on his investment is 6.38 percent. [ANSWER: 60 ÷ $940 = 6.38%] Sharon will receive $30 from her T-bill. [ANSWER: $1,000 − $970 = $30] The annual rate of return on her investment is 6.18 percent. [ANSWER: $30 ÷ $970 = 0.0309; 0.0309 × 2 = 6.18%]
6. Answers will vary but should show an understanding that there can be conflict between short-term personal satisfaction and long-term financial goals.

SECTION 10.3 ASSESSMENT
ANSWERS

CHECK YOUR UNDERSTANDING

1. Accept any three of the following answers: name of the issuing company; annual

interest rate; maturity date; the bond's current yield, or return; the number of bonds traded on a particular day; the price given as a percentage of the face value; the net change in the price of the bond from one day to the next.

2. Answers will vary but should reflect the understanding that any information that could indicate the financial strength and stability of the company and its prospects for the future is important to a potential bond investor. Students may list any of the following: detailed financial information about the company; descriptions of its products, services, and activities; information about the company's goals and future plans; news about the company's position in its industry and what major trends are affecting the company and the industry.

3. You could use the Internet to research bonds and the companies that issue them, to track your bond investments, and to buy or sell bonds.

THINK CRITICALLY

4. Moody's Investors Services, Inc. (*Moody's Bond Survey*) and Standard & Poor's Corporation (*Standard & Poor's Stock and Bond Guide*) are two sources of bond ratings. A bond rating will give you a good idea of the quality of a particular bond and the risk associated with it.

USING MATH SKILLS

5. The actual market price of the bond is $980. [ANSWER: $1,000 × 98% = $980]

SOLVING MONEY PROBLEMS

6. The current yield on each of the AT&T bonds is approximately 7.7 percent. [ANSWER: $1,000 × 7% = $70; $70 ÷ $910 = 7.69%] The current yield on the Coca-Cola bond is 8.3 percent. [ANSWER: $1,000 × 8.5% = $85; $85 ÷ $1,020 = 8.3%]

SECTION 10.4 ASSESSMENT
ANSWERS
CHECK YOUR UNDERSTANDING

1. A closed-end fund is a mutual fund with a fixed number of shares that are issued by an investment company when the fund is first organized. After all the original shares have been sold, an investor can buy shares only from another investor. Shares of closed-end funds are traded (bought and sold) on the floors of stock exchanges or in the over-the-counter market.

2. An open-end mutual fund features an unlimited number of shares that are issued and redeemed by an investment company at the investors' request. Shares of open-end funds are traded on the floors of stock exchanges or in the over-the-counter market and through investment companies or brokerage firms.

3. Stock mutual funds, bond mutual funds, and mixed mutual funds.

THINK CRITICALLY

4. Answers will vary but should reflect an understanding of the categories of stock mutual funds and bond mutual funds. Stock mutual funds may include aggressive growth funds, equity income funds, global stock funds, growth funds, growth and income funds, index funds, international funds, mid cap funds, regional funds, sector funds, small cap funds, and utility funds. Bond mutual funds may include high-yield (junk) bond funds, insured municipal bond funds, intermediate corporate bond funds, intermediate U.S. bond funds, long-term corporate bond funds, long-term U.S. bond funds, municipal bond funds, short-term corporate bond funds, and short-term U.S. bond funds.

USING MATH SKILLS

5. The load that Noah must pay to invest in this mutual fund is $85. [ANSWER: $1,000 × 8.5% = $85] Students should advise

Noah to look for a no-load fund because no-load funds have the same advantages as load funds. Also, with a no-load fund, Noah would be able to invest all of his $1,000 because he wouldn't have to pay an $85 load before investing.

SOLVING MONEY PROBLEMS

6. Ana's advice best addresses Hilda's concerns. Utility funds and money-market funds are considered safe and secure investments. The aggressive growth funds and high-yield (junk) bond funds that Jack recommends are risky investments.

SECTION 10.5 ASSESSMENT
ANSWERS

CHECK YOUR UNDERSTANDING

1. A newspaper mutual fund quotation provides information about a fund's net asset value, objective, performance, and cost.
2. Income dividends, capital gain distributions, and capital gains.
3. If you have at least $5,000 worth of shares in a mutual fund, most funds will offer you four ways of withdrawing money. First, you may withdraw a certain amount each investment period until your fund has been exhausted. A second option is to liquidate a certain number of shares each investment period. A third choice lets you withdraw a prearranged percentage of your investment's asset growth. A final option allows you to withdraw all income that results from income dividends and capital gains distributions earned during an investment period.

THINK CRITICALLY

4. Answers will vary but will discuss one of three sources: newspaper mutual fund quotations, financial magazines, or the Internet. Students' answers should reflect a clear understanding of the type of information provided by the source selected and how that information would be helpful in finding a mutual fund that matches the students' financial objectives. Answers may also reflect personal preferences. For example, a student might choose to begin searching over the Internet because she enjoys surfing the Internet and finds it more convenient than buying a newspaper or reading a magazine at the library.

USING COMMUNICATION SKILLS

5. Flyers will vary. Investors may ask: What is the fund's past performance? What are the objectives of the fund? What has been the professional manager's past performance? How is the fund diversified?

SOLVING MONEY PROBLEMS

6. Students may recommend that Malia choose the voluntary savings plan or the reinvestment plan. The voluntary savings plan might offer the convenience of a payroll deduction plan. The reinvestment plan is also convenient because income dividends and capital gain distributions are automatically reinvested to buy additional shares of the fund. Also, this plan would most likely allow Malia to reinvest without paying additional sales charges or commissions. Students should advise Malia to avoid the contractual savings plan because she will pay penalty fees if she does not make the required purchases. Financial experts and government agencies disapprove of contractual savings plans because many investors lose money with these plans.

CHAPTER 10 ASSESSMENT
ANSWERS

■ **Understanding and Using Vocabulary**
Answers will vary.

■ **Review Key Concepts**
1. The call feature allows the corporation to buy back bonds from bondholders before the maturity date. This feature allows the

corporation to take advantage of changes in overall interest rates.
2. Treasury bills, Treasury notes, and U.S. Savings Bonds.
3. Calculating a yield on a bond investment will help you determine how much profit a particular bond may produce.
4. Answers will vary. Students should identify the primary characteristics of two of the following: aggressive growth funds, equity income funds, global stock funds, growth funds, growth and income funds, index funds, international funds, mid cap funds, regional funds, sector funds, small cap funds, or utility funds.
5. Answers will vary but may include a summary of the fund's objective; a fee table that lists the fees charged by the fund; a description of the risk factor associated with the fund; a description of the fund's past performance; a description of the types of investments contained in the fund's portfolio; information about dividends, distributions, and taxes; information about the fund's management; information on limitations or requirements the fund must honor when choosing investments; the process that investors can use to buy or sell shares in the fund; a description of services provided to investors and any related fees; and information about how often the fund's investment portfolio changes (sometimes referred to as its turnover ratio).

■ **Apply Key Concepts**

1. Usually companies agree not to call their bonds for the first five to ten years. When they do call their bonds, they may have to pay bondholders an additional amount of money above the face value of the bond.
2. Similarities: Treasury bills and notes are issued in units of $1,000. They can be held until maturity or cashed in before maturity. You must pay federal income tax on the interest you receive from these investments. Differences: Treasury bills are discounted securities. They may reach maturity in 13 weeks, 26 weeks, or 52 weeks. Treasury notes have a maturity of between 1 and 10 years. Interest rates for Treasury notes are slightly higher than those for Treasury bills.
3. One way to measure a bond's yield is to calculate its current yield. To find the current yield of a bond, you would divide the dollar amount of annual interest income by its current market value. This calculation lets you compare the yield on a bond investment with the yields of other investment alternatives. If the current market value is higher than the bond's face value, the current yield decreases. If the current market value is less than the bond's face value, the current yield increases. The higher the current yield, the better.
4. Equity income funds, growth and income funds, and utility funds might appeal to conservative or retired investors. They provide steady income to shareholders, and they are considered stable and safe investments.
5. Answers will vary.

❓ Problem Solving Today

One share in the mutual fund is worth $28. [ANSWER: $500 million − $24 million = $476 million; $476 million ÷ 17 million = $28] You will receive $4,200 if you sell all of your shares in the fund. [ANSWER: $28 × 150 = $4,200]

■ **Real-World Application**

Answers will vary. Remind students that in real life, you can't decide whether a bond or mutual fund is a good investment merely by tracking its performance for a week.

Possible Web sites include:
   www.moneycentral.msn.com
   www.fundz.com
   www.bwnt.businessweek.com
      /mutual_fund/

Note to teacher: Web site addresses may change.

READING STRATEGIES
ANSWERS

Section 10.1
QUESTION (p. 310) Diversification means purchasing a variety of investments. It protects investors from losing too much of their money if one of the investments loses value.

PREDICT (p. 311) Interest rates, the perceived financial condition of the company or municipality issuing the bond, and the law of supply and demand will affect a bond's value.

RESPOND (p. 312) Pros: Corporate bonds are generally low-risk and can help diversify a portfolio. They provide interest income, and the face value is repaid when it reaches maturity. Cons: Historically, corporate bonds offer lower returns than stocks. The company that issued the bonds may not be able to make the interest payments or repay the bonds at maturity.

Section 10.2
CONNECT (p. 317) Answers will vary.

Section 10.3
RESPOND (p. 322) The bid price is what a buyer wants to pay to purchase the bond. The ask price is what the seller wants to receive for the bond.

QUESTION (p. 325) An experienced investor who already has a sound portfolio of more secure investments may choose to speculate on a riskier bond because it offers the potential for a high yield. The investor also runs a greater risk of losing money on the bond.

Section 10.4
PREDICT (p. 328) Advantages include the greater possibility for diversification and professional management of the fund.

CONNECT (p. 331) Answers will vary.

Section 10.5
QUESTION (p. 342) The law of supply and demand, the track record of the fund's manager, anticipated future profits, and the general state of the stock and bond markets will influence mutual fund share prices.

RESPOND (p. 346) Answers will vary. The voluntary savings plans and reinvestment plans would help a young person invest for the long-term future. A contractual plan is probably too inflexible for a beginning investor.

STANDARD & POOR'S

CASE STUDY
ANSWERS

1. People who are retired often invest for income and to preserve their capital rather than to generate growth. In general, individual bonds that can be held to maturity pose less risk than do shares of bond mutual funds.
2. If Rafael is investing for goals that are three to five years away, bonds are appropriate. For longer time horizons, he should consider investing a portion of his portfolio in stocks or stock mutual funds.
3. Bond prices generally fall when interest rates rise. If Rafael needs to sell his bonds before they mature, he may get less than their face value if interest rates are above the rates paid on his bonds.

Chapter 11 Planning Guide

Real Estate and Other Investment Alternatives

Teacher Manual

SECT.	OBJECTIVES	NATIONAL STANDARDS FOR BUSINESS EDUCATION	FEATURES	RESOURCES
11.1	After completing this lesson, students will have learned: How to identify different types of real estate investments How to assess the advantages and disadvantages of real estate investments	**Economics** I. Allocation of Resources II. Economic Systems III. Economic Institutions and Incentives IV. Markets and Prices VII. The Role of Government **Personal Finance** I. Personal Decision Making II. Earning a Living IV. Saving and Investing V. Buying Goods and Services	**Standard & Poor's—**Q & A, p. 350 **What's Your Financial ID?—**All that Glitters, p. 354 **Savvy Saver—**Wedding Bells with Smaller Bills, p. 355 **Standard & Poor's—**Case Study, p. 356 **Careers in Finance—**Commercial Property Manager, p. 359 **Common Cents—**Gift Giving, p. 360	Check Your Understanding, p. 361 Think Critically, p. 361 Using Communication Skills, p. 361 Solving Money Problems, p. 361 Student Activity Workbook
11.2	After completing this lesson, students will have learned: How to analyze the risks and rewards of investing in precious metals, gems, and collectibles	**Economics** I. Allocation of Resources II. Economic Systems III. Economic Institutions and Incentives IV. Markets and Prices VIII. International Economic Concepts **Personal Finance** I. Personal Decision Making II. Earning a Living IV. Saving and Investing V. Buying Goods and Services VI. Banking	**Academic Connection—**Science, p. 365 **International Finance—**South Africa, p. 367 **Your Financial Portfolio—**Collecting Treasures, p. 370	Check Your Understanding, p. 371 Think Critically, p. 371 Using Math Skills, p. 371 Solving Money Problems, p. 371 Student Activity Workbook

SCANS Correlation Chart

FOUNDATION SKILLS

Basic Skills	Reading	Writing	Math	Listening	Speaking
Thinking Skills	Creative Thinking	Decision Making	Problem Solving	Seeing Things in the Mind's Eye	Knowing How to Learn	Reasoning
Personal Qualities	Responsibility	Self-Esteem	Sociability	Self-Management	Integrity/Honesty

WORKPLACE COMPETENCIES

Resources	Allocating Time	Allocating Money	Allocating Material and Facility Resources	Allocating Human Resources
Information	Acquiring and Evaluating Information	Organizing and Maintaining Information	Interpreting and Communicating Information	Using Computers to Process Information
Interpersonal Skills	Participating as a Member of a Team	Teaching Others	Serving Clients/Customers	Exercising Leadership	Negotiating to Arrive at a Decision	Working with Cultural Diversity
Systems	Understanding Systems	Monitoring and Correcting Performance	Improving and Designing Systems
Technology	Selecting Technology	Applying Technology to Task	Maintaining and Troubleshooting Technology

■ INTERNET EXTENSION

Activity: Have students use the Internet to research the price of a home in your area. Allow them to present the price of the home and its features to the class.

Keywords: Searches can be conducted through a local newspaper with on-line classifieds, by using the name of a real estate agency that sells property in your area, or by using Web sites such as **www.buyowner.com** or **www.realtor.com**.

■ ENRICHMENT/APPLICATION ACTIVITY

Guest Speaker: Invite an auctioneer to class to talk about the antiques, collectibles, and property he or she has sold during his or her career. Ask the auctioneer to discuss what makes things valuable and how auctions work.

Chapter 11 *Real Estate and Other Investment Alternatives*

■ TOPIC SPOTLIGHT

✪ **Government:** Discuss why interest charges on mortgages and property taxes are deductions on income taxes. Explain that the federal government uses deductions on income tax as incentives to buy homes.

✪ **Ethics:** Ask students how collectors know they are buying from reputable dealers. How can new collectors find out who's reputable or not?

✪ **Money:** Have students calculate the following. Josephine owns a rental house. She is making mortgage payments of $600 per month, which include insurance, and pays $1,800 per year in property taxes and maintenance. All utilities are paid by the renter. How much should Josephine charge for monthly rent to cover her costs? To earn $1,000 profit in one year? [ANSWER: $750 per month ($1,800 ÷ 12 = $150; $600 + $150 = $750); $833.33 per month ($1,000 ÷ 12 = $83.33; $750 + $83.33 = $833.33)]

additional resources

The CCIM Institute Web site **www.ccim.com** offers commercial real estate owners an array of services including news, market trends, conferences, and a library. It also lists upcoming events.

www.creonline.com is the Web site for Creative Real Estate Online and is targeted at those interested in creative real estate investments. Categories at the Web site include How-To Articles, Money-Making Ideas, Legal Corner, and Cash Flow Corner.

The Web site for the National Association of Real Estate Investment Trusts is located at **www.nareit.com**. Topics covered include how to invest in REITs, Government Relations, Research and Statistics, and tax-reporting information.

Several auction Web sites are both interesting and informative. **www.ebay.com** is the Internet's most successful auction Web site, selling many items to many people. **www.icollector.com** is home to more than 200 auction houses, dealers, and galleries, and **www.sothebys.com** is the Web site for Sotheby's, the world's oldest and most venerable auction house.

For more information on gems, Gemological Institute of America has a Web site at **www.gia.org**. Topics include GIA Education, Gem Trade Laboratory, Gems & Gemology, and How to Buy a Diamond.

Note to Teacher: Web site addresses may change.

CHAPTER 11   Lesson Plans

SECTION 11.1

FOCUS

Motivation
Tell the students that instead of rent, a homeowner has to pay a mortgage, real estate taxes, and homeowner's insurance. In addition, a homeowner usually has a lawn to take care of as well as a variety of maintenance and repair expenses. Ask the students to discuss the advantages of homeownership and why they think so many Americans desire to own a home.

Prereading
1. Have the students skim the section, looking at pictures, reading captions, and noting headings.
2. Have "What You'll Learn" listed on page 351 read aloud.
3. Dictate the Key Terms to the students. Ask each student to write definitions for the terms. Have the students revise their definitions as necessary.
4. Ask the students to state the purpose of studying this chapter.

TEACH

Guided Practice
1. Have students read aloud the Standard & Poor's Q&A on page 350.
2. Read the section with your students.

Independent Practice
1. Have the students choose two countries and research the concept of owning real estate in those countries. In particular, ask them to compare the concepts to the American cultural beliefs of owning property.
2. Ask the students to research the median price of a home in the United States in 1950, 1960, 1970, 1980, 1990, and 2000. Then, have them create a graph that will show whether or not owning a home is a good investment.
3. Have the students research the Tax Reform Act of 1986 to find out why it was written into law.

$avvy Saver

Wedding Bells with Smaller Bills
1. As a class, have the students add to this list.
2. Divide the class into groups and assign each group one of the following: invitations, dress, flowers, reception, favors, and photographs. Then ask each group to determine an estimated cost of their particular assignment. Total all the estimates to determine the cost of a wedding.

Careers in Finance

Commercial Property Manager
1. Have the students discuss which skill is the most important for a commercial property manager to possess and why.
2. Ask the students to brainstorm a list of all the problems that the manager of a high-rise apartment complex might face.
3. Invite a commercial property manager to your classroom. Have the students prepare questions to ask the guest. In particular, find out what he or she likes and dislikes about the job and why.

Common Cents

Gift Giving
1. Have the students share their ideas for making gifts for family and friends.
2. Using craft, family, woodworking, and other magazines, ask students to bring in one idea for a homemade gift. Compile the ideas in a notebook for the students.

ASSESS

Reteaching

1. Have your students review the Key Terms and their definitions. If necessary, clarify any terms the students still might not understand.
2. Ask students to brainstorm a list of advantages and disadvantages without using their textbooks. As a class, compile all the lists. Then, have the students use their books to clarify and add to the compiled lists.

Enrichment

1. Invite a financial expert who specializes in real estate investments to the class. Ask him or her to discuss direct and indirect investments.
2. Ask your students to interview someone who owns rental property and manages it. Have the students find out the advantages and disadvantages of doing so.
3. Divide the class into four groups. Assign each group one of the federal agencies. [EXAMPLES: Ginnie Mae, Freddie Mac, Fannie Mae, or Sallie Mae] Ask each group to research purchasing participation certificates.

Assessment

1. Have the students complete the Section 11.1 Assessment.
2. Assign an activity from the *Student Activity Workbook*.

CLOSE

Have the students write a paragraph describing why real estate is a good investment.

SECTION 11.2

FOCUS

Motivation

Ask your students to discuss collections they have (i.e., baseball cards, beanie babies, coins, etc.) that might be valuable one day.

Prereading

1. Have the students skim the section, looking at pictures, reading captions, and noting headings.
2. Have "What You'll Learn" listed on page 362 read aloud.
3. Write the three key terms *precious metals*, *precious gems*, and *collectibles*—on the board. Ask your students to brainstorm examples of each.
4. Ask your students to state the purpose of studying this chapter.

TEACH

Guided Practice

1. Read the section with your students.
2. Assign an activity from the *Student Activity Workbook*.

Independent Practice

1. Have the students research the history of gold and why it is so valuable.
2. Queen Elizabeth owns a variety of precious gems that are worn or used in political ceremonies. Ask your students to research another country and the precious gems that are used in its ceremonies.
3. Ask the students to select a collectible. Then, using the Internet, find out how much the collectible is selling for online.

INTERNATIONAL FINANCE
South Africa

1. Have the students research apartheid in South Africa.
2. Coal is South Africa's second most valuable mineral product. Ask the students to find out how it is used, which countries import it from South Africa, and how it is mined.
3. Ask the students to discuss the impact of having 11 official languages on the economy, the culture, and education in South Africa.

ASSESS

Reteaching

1. Review the original lists the students developed for the three Key Terms. Ask the students to modify or enhance them as necessary.
2. To emphasize the importance of "Let the Collector Beware," have your students discuss the problems associated with buying and selling collectibles online.

Enrichment

1. Invite a jeweler to your class to discuss with the students how gems are graded, cut, and priced.
2. Have the students research the tradition of diamonds being used as engagement and/or wedding rings.
3. Have the students create a list of online auctions and exchange sites. Then, ask the students how they know which ones are reputable.

Assessment

1. Have your students complete the Section 11.2 Assessment.
2. Assign the Chapter Assessment.
3. Administer the test for Chapter 11 from the Reproducible Tests in the *Teacher Resource Binder*.

CLOSE

Ask the students to write a paragraph explaining why it is important to understand both the risks and rewards when investing in precious metals, gems, and collectibles.

SECTION 11.1 ASSESSMENT
ANSWERS

CHECK YOUR UNDERSTANDING

1. Direct real estate investments may include single-family houses, vacation homes, duplexes, apartments, land, and commercial property. Indirect real estate investments include real estate syndicates or limited partnerships, real estate investment trusts (REITs), high-risk mortgages, and participation certificates.
2. Advantages include a hedge against inflation, easy entry, possible profit, limited financial liability, and possible financial leverage.
3. Disadvantages include real estate's illiquidity, declining property values, lack of diversification, lack of a tax shelter, and management problems.

THINK CRITICALLY

4. Similarity: Groups of people combine their money to make real estate investments. Differences: In a limited partnership, a general partner forms the partnership and sells shares to other investors, whose liability is limited to the amount they invest. Shares in REITs are traded on stock exchanges or the over-the-counter market. The federal government regulates REITs, unlike limited partnerships. Investors can purchase participation certificates from government agencies. PCs are risk-free because they are guaranteed by agencies with close ties to the federal government and some state governments.

USING COMMUNICATION SKILLS

5. Advertisements will vary but should stress the limited financial commitment and the guaranteed nature of the investment.

SOLVING MONEY PROBLEMS

6. Advice will vary, but students may suggest indirect investments, such as syndicates, REITs, and participation certificates.

SECTION 11.2 ASSESSMENT
ANSWERS

CHECK YOUR UNDERSTANDING

1. Precious metals can lose value when the political situation, international relations, and the economy are stable. They do not

earn interest or dividends but depend upon your making the correct predictions of market behavior.
2. Small size, ease of storage, great durability, and potential as protection against inflation.
3. Buying an item on the Internet does not allow you to deal with a person face-to-face, nor does it give you the opportunity to easily examine the item for flaws or trademarks. Also, the possibility of fraud is a danger.

THINK CRITICALLY
4. Answers will vary, but the value of diamonds will generally rise during periods of inflation and political unrest, especially within diamond-producing countries. Prices will fall during times of economic prosperity and political stability. Also, actions taken by the De Beers company can cause prices to rise or fall.

USING MATH SKILLS
5. Raul sold 25 ounces of gold at $300 an ounce in 1980; his profit was $6,625. [ANSWER: $7,500 − $875 = $6,625] He sold 25 ounces in 1982; his profit was $9,125. [ANSWER: $10,000 − $875 = $9,125] If he had sold all his gold in 1980, his profit would have been $13,250. [ANSWER: $15,000 − $1,750 = $13,250]

SOLVING MONEY PROBLEMS
6. Answers will vary but may include: Samantha should have the stones evaluated by an independent geological laboratory to determine their worth. If the stones are of high quality and very valuable, she might sell them and invest the money in a financial instrument that pays interest or dividends or one that is guaranteed. If the stones have some historical value, Samantha would be wise to hold on to them and perhaps use them as collateral for borrowing money for other investments. Finally, if the stones are of minimal financial value but have sentimental value, Samantha could have them reset and enjoy wearing her new necklace.

CHAPTER 11 ASSESSMENT
ANSWERS

■ **Understanding and Using Vocabulary**
Answers will vary.

■ **Review Key Concepts**
1. In a direct real estate investment, the investor holds legal title to the property and assumes all risk and liability. In an indirect real estate investment, investors combine their money, own varying percentages of the total investment, and assume varying degrees of risk and liability.
2. Real estate often maintains or increases its value, even during inflation, when the purchasing power of money declines.
3. The least risky real estate investment is a participation certificate because its value is guaranteed by the government.
4. Precious metals and gems can fluctuate greatly in value and can be difficult to convert into cash on short notice. These investments can be difficult to store and often need to be insured at the investor's expense.
5. The Internet has brought collectors together from around the world in a virtual marketplace. Collectors can use the Internet to research their collections or sell pieces. Collectors must be aware of Internet fraud.

■ **Apply Key Concepts**
1. The cost of investing in a limited partnership is much less than that of buying property outright. The limited partners' liability cannot be more than the amount of their investments. The partnership provides professional management for the purchased property. All of these factors make the investment attractive to beginning investors.
2. During periods of inflation, the purchasing power of money declines. Real estate, however, usually maintains its value or increases in value. Thus, the money in the savings account would decline in value while the money in the home would likely retain its value.

3. Investments in participation certificates are guaranteed by agencies with ties to the federal government, making the investment risk-free.
4. When the economy is strong, precious metals and gems usually lose value. During periods of economic instability, the value of precious metals and gems rises.
5. Collectors who have done research by using a resource such as the Internet may get better prices for their collectibles and will be able to spot bargains as they seek to increase their collections.

❓ Problem Solving Today
Answers will vary.

■ Real–World Application
Answers will vary.

FINANCE Online
Possible Web sites include:
- www.nareit.com
- www.reitnet.com
- www.chipreit.com
- www.preit.com

Note to teacher: Web site addresses may change.

READING STRATEGIES
ANSWERS

Section 11.1
PREDICT (p. 352) Real estate investments generally increase in their value even when inflation reduces the buying power of other sources of income. Certain real estate investments, such as family and vacation homes, provide tax benefits to the owners.

QUESTION (p. 358) These regulations make sure that REIT profits are not appropriated or misused by corrupt trust managers, that the trust is run responsibly and professionally, and that one or two primary shareholders don't use the trust to gamble on risky investments.

Section 11.2
RESPOND (p. 364) Since precious metals tend to increase in value during times of political or economic instability, they might provide a safety-net that could counter losses your other investments might incur during such hard times.

CONNECT (p. 367) Answers will vary.

STANDARD & POOR'S

CASE STUDY
ANSWERS

1. A REIT is a stock representing a diversified pool of many different properties. These are generally commercial properties, such as office buildings and apartment buildings.
2. REITs are affected by the health of the economy and interest rates. If the economy is growing and businesses are expanding, REITs may provide good growth potential. During recessions REITs may underperform other types of investments.
3. Another type of investment that is missing from their portfolio is international investments. They might buy shares of a mutual fund that invests abroad or buy individual stocks of foreign companies traded on the NYSE.

UNIT 3 Planning Guide

INVESTING YOUR FINANCIAL RESOURCES

Chapter 8—
The Fundamentals of Investing

Chapter 9—
Stocks

Chapter 10—
Bonds and Mutual Funds

Chapter 11—
Real Estate and Investment Alternatives

OVERVIEW

Unit 3 describes how to put financial plans into action through investing. The unit discusses how investing can increase your resources, which is an important part of achieving your financial goals. In Chapter 8 students learn how to prepare for an investment program, identify investment alternatives, and obtain investment information. Chapter 9 explains the difference between common and preferred stocks, how to evaluate stocks, and how to buy and sell stocks. Chapter 10 describes corporate bonds, government bonds, and mutual funds. Chapter 11 explores the advantages and disadvantages of real estate investments, as well as alternative investments, such as precious metals, gems, and collectibles.

INTRODUCTION

Ask students to write a brief definition of the word *invest*. Then explain that to invest is to put your money to use by purchase or expenditure in something offering profitable returns, especially interest or income. Tell students that *invest* is derived from the Latin *investire*, which means to clothe or surround, and that the garment called a *vest* is also derived from *investire*. Ask your students for ideas about how *investire* came to mean *invest* as we use it today. One idea is that many years ago, when clothing was very expensive for the average person, the word came to mean purchasing something expensive that offered the profitable return of staying warm.

Get a Financial Life!

CASE STUDY 3

Teaching Guide

Step A — THE PROCESS

Make sure students have access to all necessary materials.

1. Remind students that the Career in Finance feature in Chapter 10 describes a certified financial planner. Students can use this description as a model for their résumé.
2. Accept all reasonable options that fall within the categories of stocks, bonds, mutual funds, and real estate.
3. Give students names of some of the Web sites from the Additional Resources section of the chapter planning guides from this unit. They might include the Sound Money Web site at **www.soundmoney.org**, *BusinessWeek* at **www.businessweek.com/investor**, The Wall Street Research Net at **www.wsrn.com**, **www.bonds-online.com**, the Commercial Real Estate Network at **www.ccim.com**, and auction Web sites, such as **www.ebay.com** and **www.icollector.com**. Publications include *The Wall Street Journal*, *BusinessWeek*, *Money*, and *Kiplinger's Personal Finance*.
4. If you invite a financial planner to class as a guest speaker (see the Chapter 8 Planning Guide), allow students time to ask their interview questions after his or her presentation.

Step B — CREATE YOUR PORTFOLIO

Evaluate students' portfolios based on whether or not the four steps are competed, the information seems reasonably well researched, and the contents are neat and in order.

Step C — TEAMWORK

If necessary, organize the teams for the class. Evaluate the teams' seminars based on the following:

1. Participation from all team members is evident.
2. The information presented should be informative, interesting, and reasonably well researched.
3. The written outline should be presented at the time of the seminar.
4. Information in the handouts should reinforce the information given in the oral presentation.
5. Graphs should indicate the audience's understanding of the subject before and after the seminar.

UNIT CLOSURE

Have students create crossword puzzles using Key Terms from all the chapters of the unit. Allow students to complete one another's puzzles.

EVALUATION

Administer the Unit 3 test from the **ExamView** Pro Testmaker CD-ROM.

Chapter 12 Planning Guide

Planning Your Tax Strategy

SECT.	OBJECTIVES	NATIONAL STANDARDS FOR BUSINESS EDUCATION	FEATURES	RESOURCES
12.1	After completing this lesson, students will have learned: How to describe the importance of taxes in financial planning; How to identify taxable income; How to complete a W-4 form	**Economics** I. Allocation of Resources II. Economic Systems III. Economic Institutions and Incentives VII. The Role of Government **Personal Finance** I. Personal Decision Making II. Earning a Living	**Standard & Poor's**—Q & A, p. 378 **What's Your Financial ID?**—Test Your Tax Facts, p. 380 **Academic Connection**—Law, p. 382 **International Finance**—France, p. 383 **Careers in Finance**—Tax Preparer, p. 388	Check Your Understanding, p. 389 Think Critically, p. 389 Using Communication Skills, p. 389 Solving Money Problems, p. 389 Student Activity Workbook
12.2	After completing this lesson, students will have learned: How to prepare a federal tax return	**Economics** VII. The Role of Government **Personal Finance** II. Earning a Living V. Buying Goods and Services	**Standard & Poor's**—Case Study, p. 392 **Savvy Saver**—Reasons to Join Your Company's 401(k) Plan, p. 393	Check Your Understanding, p. 402 Think Critically, p. 402 Using Math Skills, p. 402 Solving Money Problems, p. 402 Student Activity Workbook
12.3	After completing this lesson, students will have learned: How to identify sources of tax assistance; How to select the best tax strategies for financial and personal needs	**Economics** I. Allocation of Resources II. Economic Systems III. Economic Institutions and Incentives VII. The Role of Government VIII. International Economic Concepts **Personal Finance** I. Personal Decision Making II. Earning a Living IV. Saving and Investing V. Buying Goods and Services	**Common Cents**—Layaway Works, p. 405 **Your Financial Portfolio**—Take It EZ, p. 406	Check Your Understanding, p. 407 Think Critically, p. 407 Using Communication Skills, p. 407 Solving Money Problems, p. 407 Student Activity Workbook

SCANS Correlation Chart

FOUNDATION SKILLS

Basic Skills	Reading	Writing	Math	Listening	Speaking
Thinking Skills	Creative Thinking	Decision Making	Problem Solving	Seeing Things in the Mind's Eye	Knowing How to Learn	Reasoning
Personal Qualities	Responsibility	Self-Esteem	Sociability	Self-Management	Integrity/Honesty

WORKPLACE COMPETENCIES

Resources	Allocating Time	Allocating Money	Allocating Material and Facility Resources	Allocating Human Resources
Information	Acquiring and Evaluating Information	Organizing and Maintaining Information	Interpreting and Communicating Information	Using Computers to Process Information
Interpersonal Skills	Participating as a Member of a Team	Teaching Others	Serving Clients/Customers	Exercising Leadership	Negotiating to Arrive at a Decision	Working with Cultural Diversity
Systems	Understanding Systems	Monitoring and Correcting Performance	Improving and Designing Systems
Technology	Selecting Technology	Applying Technology to Task	Maintaining and Troubleshooting Technology

■ INTERNET EXTENSION

Activity: Have students access the Internal Revenue Service Web site and their online 'zine called TAXi (TAXinteractive) for understanding taxes at **www.irs.ustreas.gov/taxi**. While accessing TAXi, have students work through one of the two options offered at *It's Payday! Money in Your Pocket?* This segment of the IRS Web site allows students to learn about the taxes taken from paychecks.

Keyword: Internal Revenue Service

■ ENRICHMENT/APPLICATION ACTIVITY

Guest Speaker: Contact your local IRS Taxpayer Assistance Center to arrange for a speaker and tax forms for students to view or fill out. Your local Center can be found at the Teachers' Toolkit at TAXi on the IRS Web site.

TOPIC SPOTLIGHT

Marketing: Ask students to describe how they would look for someone who could give tax assistance. How and where do these professionals advertise their businesses?

Government: Tell students that some U.S. legislators and citizens would like to have income taxes banned and would like to collect taxes solely through sales tax. Discuss whether this form of tax collection would be more or less fair to the majority of the population.

Money: Explain to students that in some states, sales tax is not collected on used cars sold by private owners but is collected by used car dealers. If the sales tax in such a state were 7 percent and the price of the car is $12,000, how much is saved by purchasing the car from the private owner? [ANSWER: $12,000 × 7% = $840]

additional resources

The IRS offers free curriculum kits for high school educators. The program is called ***Understanding Taxes*** and includes units on Your Role as a Taxpayer, Tax Forms, Fairness Issues, and the Impact of Taxes. To order, call your IRS Taxpayer Education Coordinator (TPEC). You can find a state-by-state list of local IRS offices with addresses and phone numbers at **www.irs.gov**.

Tax planning suggestions and guides from Ernst & Young can be found at **www.ey.com** and from H & R Block at **www.hrblock.com**.

Federal tax forms and tax tips can be found at **www.1040.com** and **www.irs.gov**.

State tax information and forms are available at **www.taxadmin.org**.

Note to teacher: Web site addresses may change.

CHAPTER 12 Lesson Plans

SECTION 12.1

FOCUS

Motivation
Tell the students that the first income tax in the United States was imposed on the public in 1864 in order to help finance the Civil War. Ask the students to discuss how our federal government currently uses the income tax money it collects.

Prereading
1. Have the students skim the section, looking at pictures, reading captions, and noting headings.
2. Have "What You'll Learn" listed on page 379 read aloud.
3. Have your students write each bold-faced term in the section, and based on its definition, generate a picture or symbol that identifies it.
4. Ask the students to state the purpose of studying this chapter.

TEACH

Guided Practice
1. Have students read aloud the Standard & Poor's Q&A on page 378.
2. Read the section with your students.

Independent Practice
1. Have the students find out which goods and services are taxed in your state. Then ask them to choose another state and do the same. Compare the results.
2. Ask your students to compile a list of goods that have an excise tax. Then have them write a paragraph explaining why they think these particular products were selected for taxation.
3. Have the students log onto the Internal Revenue Services Web site for young people. The address is **http://www.irs.gov/taxi**. Ask them to review the site by answering these questions: "Is the site easy to use? Does it contain information that young people are looking for? What other information could be added?"

INTERNATIONAL FINANCE
France
1. Have the students choose one of the winners of the Tour de France and write a one-page biography on that person.
2. Write this statement on the board: "France has been described as one of the most culturally significant nations in the world." Ask your students to react to this statement and explain why they think it is or isn't true.
3. Ask the students to research taxes in France. In particular, have them find out the answers to these questions: What goods and services are taxed? Is there an income tax? Is there social security for the elderly and disabled?

*C*areers in Finance

Tax Preparer
1. Have your students compile a resource list of Web sites that a tax preparer would find helpful.
2. Using the newspaper and/or the Internet, ask your students to locate a company looking for a tax preparer. Have the students read the ad and see if the skills requested are similar to those listed in this feature. If not, offer suggestions as to why.
3. Ask your students what criteria they would use when hiring a tax preparer.

ASSESS

Reteaching
1. Review the Key Terms with the students. Find out if the students are still unsure

about a definition and, if so, clarify it for them.
2. Divide the students into groups of three or four. Ask each group to prepare and present a two-minute presentation [EXAMPLES: song, skit, or role-play] on one of the topics in this section.

Enrichment

1. Have your students explain how sales taxes, excise taxes, and inheritance taxes are affected by the economy.
2. Taxes seem to always be in the political limelight. Ask the students to research the most recent presidential election to find out how the candidates addressed the various taxes in the United States.

Assessment

1. Have the students complete the Section 12.1 Assessment.
2. Assign an activity from the *Student Activity Workbook*.

CLOSE

Have your students complete this statement: "In order to prepare a financial plan that will reduce the amount of taxes owed, you should…." [ANSWER: "learn as much as possible about local, state, and federal taxes."]

SECTION 12.2

FOCUS

Motivation

Obtain enough copies of the 1040EZ tax form for each student in the class. Pass them out with no explanation. Ask the students for their reactions. Do they know what this form is used for? Could they fill it out without any instructions? Is it easy to understand? As you study this section, clarify this form for the students as necessary.

Prereading

1. Have the students skim the section, looking at pictures, reading captions, and noting headings.
2. Have "What You'll Learn" listed on page 390 read aloud.
3. Ask the students to state the purpose of studying this chapter.

TEACH

Guided Practice

1. Read the section with your students.
2. Assign an activity from the *Student Activity Workbook*.

Independent Practice

1. Have the students find out what interest rate is charged by the IRS if you file your taxes late. In addition, ask them to find out what interest rate the IRS would pay you if you were owed additional money.
2. Ask your students to write a paragraph describing the process a person should use when filing a tax return electronically.
3. By studying this section, students will realize that the process of paying federal income taxes can be complicated. Divide the students into groups and ask each group to develop an easier way to collect taxes from United States citizens.

$AVVY SAVER

Reasons to Join Your Company's 401(k) Plan

1. Ask your students to explain why it is an advantage not to pay taxes on the 401(k) money until it is withdrawn, usually, years later.
2. Using *Money* magazine, the Internet, or other sources, find out what is the 401(k) match on the employer contribution for three national or local companies.

TM178　Unit 4　*Protecting Your Finances*

3. Ask the students to discuss other benefits that they would like to receive from their employers or future employers.

ASSESS

Reteaching
1. Write the names of the three basic tax forms on the board: 1040EZ, 1040A, and 1040. Ask the students to create a chart explaining the requirements for completing each form.

Enrichment
1. Ask each student to prepare a mini-lesson on either "How to complete the 1040EZ Form" or "How to complete the 1040A Form." Have students volunteer to present their lessons to other classes in the school.
2. Have your students write a paragraph describing how they will file, store, and keep track of the information they will need to file their income tax returns.

Assessment
1. Have the students complete the Section 12.2 Assessment.
2. Assign an activity from the *Student Activity Workbook*.

CLOSE
Ask the students to write a paragraph explaining why it is important to complete their income tax returns correctly.

SECTION 12.3

FOCUS

Motivation
Ask your students to define "tax assistance." Then have them brainstorm a list of job titles that they think provide tax assistance. As you study this section, add to or clarify this list.

Prereading
1. Have your students skim the section, looking at pictures, reading captions, and noting headings.
2. Have "What You'll Learn" listed on page 403 read aloud.
3. Write the Key Term on the board. Ask the students to write a definition for it.
4. Ask the students to state the purpose of studying this chapter.

TEACH

Guided Practice
1. Read the section with your students.
2. Assign an activity from the *Student Activity Workbook*.

Independent Practice
1. Ask your students to explain why interest on municipal bonds is not usually taxed.
2. Have the students write a paragraph describing their tax strategy now. Then write another paragraph describing what their tax strategy might be at age 40.

Common Cents

Layaway Works
1. Ask the students to explain why stores offer layaway options for their customers.
2. Ask the students if they have ever used a layaway plan. If so, have them share their experiences.

ASSESS

Reteaching
1. Review the Key Term and the definitions the students wrote. Revise and clarify their definitions if necessary.
2. Tell the students that tax laws are constantly changing. In addition, their personal financial situations are always changing. Ask the students to write a paragraph explaining how they will keep abreast of these changes in order to plan their tax strategy.

Enrichment
1. Have your students research job opportunities and career paths with the Internal Revenue Service.
2. Ask the students to describe the structure of the IRS, as a branch of the Department of the Treasury down to the district offices.

Assessment
1. Have the students complete the Section 12.3 Assessment.
2. Assign Chapter Assessment.
3. Administer the test for Chapter 12 from the Reproducible Tests in the *Teacher Resource Binder*.

CLOSE

Have the students write a paragraph describing what they would do if their tax return were audited.

SECTION 12.1 ASSESSMENT
ANSWERS

CHECK YOUR UNDERSTANDING
1. Taxes are an everyday part of life. To avoid becoming one of those people who have no money left after paying taxes and living expenses, you have to practice effective tax planning. If you plan wisely, you'll pay your fair share of taxes while taking advantage of various tax benefits.
2. To figure out your taxable income, first you would determine your adjusted gross income (AGI). Then you would subtract allowable tax deductions and exemptions from your AGI.
3. To complete a W-4: Fill in your name and address, fill in your Social Security number, indicate whether you are single or married, check the box if your last name differs from the name on your Social Security card, write the number of allowances you are claiming, indicate how much additional money (if any) you wish to have withheld from each paycheck, indicate whether you're exempt from paying income tax, and sign and date the form.

THINK CRITICALLY
4. A tax deduction is an expense that you are allowed to subtract from your adjusted gross income to arrive at your taxable income. A tax credit is an amount subtracted directly from the amount of taxes you owe.

USING COMMUNICATION SKILLS
5. Answers will vary.

SOLVING MONEY PROBLEMS
6. Because Eric will claim fewer allowances, he will have the greater amount of money withheld from his paycheck.

SECTION 12.2 ASSESSMENT
ANSWERS

CHECK YOUR UNDERSTANDING
1. You are required to file an income tax return if you are a citizen or resident of the United States or a United States citizen who resides in Puerto Rico and if your income is above a certain amount. That amount is based on your filing status and other factors, such as your age.
2. Form 1040EZ is the simplest tax form. You may use the form if you meet the following

qualifications: You are single or married (filing a joint tax return), under age 65, and claiming no dependents; your income consisted of only wages, salaries, tips, and not more than $400 of taxable interest; your taxable income is less than $50,000; and you don't itemize deductions, claim any adjustments to income, or claim any tax credits. Form 1040A is an option if you meet the following criteria: You have less than $50,000 in taxable income from wages, salaries, tips, unemployment compensation, interest, or dividends; you claim the standard deduction; you claim deductions for IRA contributions; you claim a tax credit for child-care and dependent care expenses. Form 1040 is an expanded version of Form 1040A. You are required to use this form if your taxable income exceeds $50,000 or you can be claimed as a dependent on your parents' income tax return and you had interest or dividends over a set limit. Form 1040 also allows you to itemize your deductions using Schedule A.

3. You need the most current tax forms and instructions, copies of your tax returns from previous years, your W-2 form, and (if applicable) Form 1099-INT and Form 1099-DIV.

THINK CRITICALLY

4. It would be advantageous to use Form 1040A if you are able to claim tax deductions and tax credits.

USING MATH SKILLS

5. Shirley will receive a refund of $469.

SOLVING MONEY PROBLEMS

6. Answers will vary, but students should suggest that Fred needs to make sure that he has the most current tax forms and instructions; copies of his tax returns from previous years (unless he is filing for the first time); his W-2 form; and, if applicable, his Form 1099-INT and 1099-DIV. If he needs any additional forms, he can find them at many post offices, libraries, banks, and the local IRS office. He can also download forms and instructions from the Internal Revenue Service's Web site. If Fred lives in a state that has its own income tax, he will need to obtain the appropriate forms to file a state income tax return.

SECTION 12.3 ASSESSMENT
ANSWERS
CHECK YOUR UNDERSTANDING

1. The IRS Web site and local IRS offices, books and personal finance magazines, tax preparation software, and tax professionals.
2. If you purchase a house, both the interest you pay on your mortgage and the real estate property taxes you pay are deductible. You can also deduct the interest on a home equity loan. Some job-related expenses may also be deductible. These include union dues, some travel and education expenses, business tools, and certain job search expenses.
3. A house, municipal bonds, and investments that are tax-deferred.

THINK CRITICALLY

4. Answers will vary. Taxpayers should check their math for accuracy and fill out all forms completely. In addition, they should make sure that they are taking the appropriate type and amount of deductions. If they have a particularly complicated tax situation, they might consult a tax professional or speak to someone at their local IRS office.

USING COMMUNICATION SKILLS

5. Students playing the role of the tax professional should suggest deducting mortgage interest, interest on home equity loans, and job-related expenses. They should also mention the impact of investment and retirement planning decisions on tax liability.

Chapter 12 *Planning Your Tax Strategy*

SOLVING MONEY PROBLEMS

6. Action plans will vary but might include the following: (1) Locate and organize all paperwork related to the tax year that will be audited. These include copies of tax returns, W-2 forms, 1099 forms, receipts, and so on. (2) If a professional prepared her taxes, Felicia should try to make sure that he or she will accompany her to the audit. If she completed her taxes herself, she should consult a tax professional who may be able to pinpoint the reason for the audit and suggest solutions. (3) At the audit, Felicia should remain calm and composed. She should answer all questions directly and truthfully, but she shouldn't offer any unsolicited information.

CHAPTER 12 ASSESSMENT
ANSWERS

■ Understanding and Using Vocabulary
Answers will vary.

■ Review Key Concepts
1. Taxes on purchases, property, wealth, and earnings.
2. Gross income is your total income. Adjusted gross income is your gross income after certain reductions have been made, but before exemptions and deductions have been taken. Taxable income is your adjusted gross income less allowable tax deductions and exemptions. It is the amount on which your income tax is computed.
3. The W-4 form tells your employer the number of allowances you wish to claim. The W-2 form reports your earnings and taxes withheld.
4. Form 1040EZ, Form 1040A, and Form 1040.
5. To determine whether taxpayers are paying all of their required taxes.

■ Apply Key Concepts
1. If you lived in a state that has an inheritance tax, you would be prohibited from collecting your inheritance until you pay the tax.

2. Subtract allowable exemptions and tax deductions from your adjusted gross income to arrive at your taxable income.
3. The more allowances you claim, the less tax will be withheld from your paycheck. The fewer allowances you claim, the more tax will be withheld.
4. Similarities may include the following: They are both easy forms to complete; neither form allows itemized deductions; they are both suitable for people whose income is less than $50,000. Differences may include the following: Form 1040EZ may be used only by taxpayers with no dependents; Form 1040EZ puts a limit of $1,500 on taxable interest; Form 1040A allows taxpayers to claim deductions and tax credits, whereas Form 1040EZ does not.
5. Answers will vary but may include claiming unusually large deductions; claiming deductions that are not allowed for someone with your filing status; falsifying information, such as the number of dependents you have; claiming tax credits to which you are not entitled.

❓ Problem Solving Today
Students should state that 1040A is the appropriate form to use. Your adjusted gross income would be $21,881. To calculate the adjusted gross income, you would add wages and taxable interest and subtract student loan interest. [ANSWER: ($22,500 + $21) − $640 = $21,881]

■ Real-World Application
Reports will vary.

FINANCE Online

Possible Web sites include:
www.quicken.com
www.intuit.com

Note to teacher: Web site addresses may change.

READING STRATEGIES
ANSWERS

Section 12.1
CONNECT (p. 381) Answers will vary according to state and local sales tax rates.

RESPOND (p. 386) When the tax deadline comes, you won't want to search around in cluttered boxes and drawers for scraps of information needed to file your return accurately. You may have to pay unnecessary taxes or penalties if your disorganization causes you to make a mistake on your return.

Section 12.2
QUESTION (p. 394) If you have large deductions, such as costly medical bills, mortgage interest payments, or property taxes, you may save money by itemizing these deductions on Form 1040.

PREDICT (p. 398) You can mail the traditional paper forms to the IRS, authorize a tax professional to transmit tax information to the IRS electronically, use tax-preparation software to transmit tax information to the IRS via computer, or use the IRS TeleFile option to file Form 1040EZ over the telephone.

Section 12.3
CONNECT (p. 405) Answers will vary, but people would most likely describe the experience as anxiety producing, annoying, or tedious.

QUESTION (p. 405) If people plan and save wisely for their retirement, they will be less likely to suffer economic hardship when they grow older. The government will also be less burdened with the responsibility of providing services for low income and impoverished retired persons.

STANDARD & POOR'S
CASE STUDY
ANSWERS

1. If Mira can be claimed as a dependent on her parent's tax return, she may not need to report her income if it is below a certain amount. However, because Mira earned income that was not subject to Social Security taxes, she must file an income tax return regardless of the amount earned.
2. Mira's employer is expected to pay a portion of the Social Security taxes due on her wages. By not reporting this income, her employer may be seeking to avoid this responsibility.
3. Mira should file her income tax return and ask for an installment agreement allowing her to pay her taxes, interest, and penalties on a monthly basis.

Chapter 13 Planning Guide
Home and Motor Vehicle Insurance

SECT.	OBJECTIVES	NATIONAL STANDARDS FOR BUSINESS EDUCATION	FEATURES	RESOURCES
13.1	After completing this lesson, students will have learned: How to identify the main types of risks and risk management methods. How to develop an insurance program as a way to manage risks. How to recognize the importance of property and liability insurance	**Personal Finance** I. Personal Decision Making VIII. Protecting Against Risk	Standard & Poor's—Q & A, p. 410 What's Your Financial ID—Motor Vehicle Insurance Quiz, p. 412 Savvy Saver—Motor Vehicle Insurance Tips, p. 417	Check Your Understanding, p. 419 Think Critically, p. 419 Using Communication Skills, p. 419 Solving Money Problems, p. 419 Student Activity Workbook
13.2	After completing this lesson, students will have learned: How to describe the insurance coverages and policy types available to homeowners and renters. How to analyze the factors that influence the amount of coverage and cost of home insurance	**Economics** I. Allocation of Resources **Personal Finance** VIII. Protecting Against Risk	International Finance—Vietnam, p. 424 Common Cents—Student Discount, p. 425 Academic Connection—Language Arts, p. 426 Careers in Finance—Insurance Claims Adjuster, p. 429	Check Your Understanding, p. 430 Think Critically, p. 430 Using Math Skills, p. 430 Solving Money Problems, p. 430 Student Activity Workbook
13.3	After completing this lesson, students will have learned: How to identify the important types of motor vehicle insurance coverage. How to evaluate factors that affect the cost of motor vehicle insurance	**Economics** III. Economic Institutions and Incentives VIII. International Economic Concepts **Personal Finance** I. Personal Decision Making VIII. Protecting Against Risk	Standard & Poor's—Case Study, p. 436 Your Financial Portfolio—Motor Vehicle Insurance—How Much Will It Cost? p. 438	Check Your Understanding, p. 439 Think Critically, p. 439 Using Communication Skills, p. 439 Solving Money Problems, p. 439 Student Activity Workbook

SCANS Correlation Chart

FOUNDATION SKILLS

Basic Skills	Reading	Writing	Math	Listening	Speaking
Thinking Skills	Creative Thinking	Decision Making	Problem Solving	Seeing Things in the Mind's Eye	Knowing How to Learn	Reasoning
Personal Qualities	Responsibility	Self-Esteem	Sociability	Self-Management	Integrity/Honesty

WORKPLACE COMPETENCIES

Resources	Allocating Time	Allocating Money	Allocating Material and Facility Resources	Allocating Human Resources
Information	Acquiring and Evaluating Information	Organizing and Maintaining Information	Interpreting and Communicating Information	Using Computers to Process Information
Interpersonal Skills	Participating as a Member of a Team	Teaching Others	Serving Clients/Customers	Exercising Leadership	Negotiating to Arrive at a Decision	Working with Cultural Diversity
Systems	Understanding Systems	Monitoring and Correcting Performance	Improving and Designing Systems
Technology	Selecting Technology	Applying Technology to Task	Maintaining and Troubleshooting Technology

Chapter 13 *Home and Motor Vehicle Insurance*

■ INTERNET EXTENSION

Activity: Have students research the car insurance rates for a specific car. Give them an automobile make and model, a rating territory or residence area, and driver classification, and see who can find the lowest rate.

Keywords: automobile insurance rates

■ ENRICHMENT/APPLICATION ACTIVITY

Guest Speaker: Invite a fire fighter from your community to talk to the class about fire safety in the home and how it can reduce the cost of homeowner's insurance.

■ TOPIC SPOTLIGHT

○ **Technology:** Have students explain how technology can have an impact on the cost of homeowner's insurance.

○ **Government:** Discuss the laws in your state regarding uninsured drivers and no-fault insurance.

○ **Marketing:** Have students bring to class copies of printed advertisements or written descriptions of a radio or television commercial for motor vehicle insurance. Discuss the differences in marketing techniques among different insurance companies.

additional resources

The Jump$tart Coalition for Personal Financial Literacy (see Additional Resources in Chapter 1) lists the following **free** publication: *InVEST Automobile Insurance Manual for Teachers*. This manual accompanies the student workbook and provides tools to teach basic business management skills with a focus on automobile insurance.

The Web site for the Insurance Research Council offers current information on various insurance research studies, public policy issues, and IRC publications, as well as links to related Web sites at **www.ircweb.org**.

At **www.insure.com** you'll find answers to questions regarding basic information and current developments in auto and home insurance.

Insurance rate information and quotes for a variety of insurance needs can be found at **www.insweb.com**, the Quicken insurance Web site. Links to over 20 major insurance companies are also provided at this site.

Note to Teacher: Web site addresses may change.

TM186 Unit 4 *Protecting Your Finances*

CHAPTER 13 Lesson Plans

SECTION 13.1

FOCUS

Motivation

Ask the students if they have taken any risks in their lives. Have them discuss their experiences and then ask them if they think there was something they could have done to reduce the risks they took. Ask the students if they think there is a type of insurance to cover those risks.

Prereading

1. Have your students skim the section, looking at pictures, reading captions, and noting headings.
2. Have "What You'll Learn" listed on page 411 read aloud.
3. Dictate the Key Terms to the students. Ask the students to write a definition of each term. As they study this section, have the students revise their definitions as necessary.
4. Ask your students to state the purpose of studying this chapter.

TEACH

Guided Practice

1. Have students read aloud the Standard & Poor's Q&A on page 410.
2. Read the section with your students.

Independent Practice

1. Invite someone from the risk management department of your school system or city government to speak to the students in the class. Have the students ask the guest to share how he/she developed the plan for protecting the organization represented. Then ask them to compare how the development of this plan is similar to one that might be developed for an individual.
2. Ask your students to interview their parents or other family members about the insurance coverage they carry. Have them find out how their parents decided which type of insurance to purchase.
3. Have the students research the variety of careers in the insurance industry. Some examples might include: sales agents, underwriters, customer service representatives, actuaries, and marketing specialists.

$AVVY SAVER

Vehicle Insurance Tips
1. Have your students add two tips to this list.
2. Some motor vehicle insurance companies offer a discounted rate for students who make good grades. Ask the students why they think this is so.
3. Ask the students to use the Internet to see if they can obtain a quote for motor vehicle insurance.

ASSESS

Reteaching

1. Have your students review the Key Terms and their definitions. Clarify any terms the students still might not understand.
2. To clarify the terms *risk avoidance*, *risk reduction*, *risk assumption*, and *risk shifting*, divide the students into groups of four. Ask each group to develop an example of all four terms. Then have each group partner with another group and share their examples.

Enrichment

1. The Independent Insurance Agents Association (IIAA) offers a program for students called InVEST. InVEST is a national program administered by IIAA that teaches insurance-related business skills to high school and community college students in order to increase awareness of careers in the

insurance industry, as well as educate and train students for entry-level careers in the field. Have your students research this program and determine whether they might like to participate. Their Web site can be found at **http://www.investprogram.org/**.
2. Divide the class into groups. Have each group design a bulletin board that explains insurance to a novice. As a class, vote on the best one and have that group actually create and display it.
3. The National Highway Traffic Safety Administration conducts crash tests on vehicles in order to determine to safety of particular makes of vehicles. Have the students research how much of an impact the NHTSA has on motor vehicle insurance rates.
4. Have the students review the telephone yellow pages book to categorize the various types of insurance available.

Assessment

1. Have your students complete the Section 13.1 Assessment.
2. Assign an activity from the *Student Activity Workbook*.

CLOSE

Have the students complete this statement: "To help reduce the risks of unexpected personal and financial loss, you should... ." [EXAMPLE: "plan and develop an insurance program."]

SECTION 13.2

FOCUS

Motivation

Write this statement on the board: "Insurance is a necessary evil." Ask the students to explain what this means and whether or not they agree.

Prereading

1. Have your students skim the section, looking at pictures, reading captions, and noting headings.
2. Have "What You'll Learn" listed on page 420 read aloud.
3. Dictate each of the Key Terms to the students and have them write them on a piece of paper. When they are finished, write the terms on the board. Ask the students to guess at the meaning of each term, but do not give the correct meaning. Leave the list on the board, so that as students work through the section, they can see how close they were to the correct answer.
4. Ask your students to state the purpose of studying this chapter.

TEACH

Guided Practice

1. Read the section with your students.
2. Assign an activity from the *Student Activity Workbook*.

Independent Practice

1. Have the students create a list of the problems that could cause damage to a home. Then ask your students to categorize those that they think would be covered by a homeowner's policy and those that would not be covered. Consult an insurance agent for clarification if necessary.
2. Obtain an inventory form from an insurance agent. Have the students use it to take inventory of their personal household goods.
3. Invite an appraiser to your class. Have the students ask him or her to explain how appraisals are done. Encourage the students to ask questions about specific items, such as silver, jewelry, and antique furniture.

INTERNATIONAL FINANCE
Vietnam
1. Have the students research the recreational and sports activities enjoyed by the youth of Vietnam.
2. Ask your students to find out how the economy of Vietnam was impacted by the Vietnam War.
3. The United States imposed a trade embargo on North Vietnam in 1964 and all of Vietnam in 1976; this embargo was lifted in 1994. Have the students find out how lifting this trade embargo has changed Vietnam.

Common Cents

Student Discounts
1. Have the students find out which stores and merchants in your town offer student discounts. Compile the list for all to use. Add to the list whenever possible.
2. Ask your students who are working in food service or retail if they get a discount on the products they sell. If so, ask the students if they take advantage of the discounts offered by their employers.

Careers in Finance

Insurance Claims Adjuster
1. Have the students interview a claims adjuster or invite one to the class. Find out what he or she likes or doesn't like about the job.
2. Ask your students to conduct research on insurance fraud. Find out what the claims adjuster's role is in protecting the insurance company from fraud.
3. A digital camera is becoming a valuable part of a claims adjuster's equipment. Have the students research the cost and features of two different brands of digital cameras. Ask the students which camera they would recommend to a claims adjuster and why.

ASSESS
Reteaching
1. Review the original definitions of the Key Terms provided by the students at the beginning of this section. Ask the students to modify or enhance them as necessary.
2. To emphasize the importance of homeowners and/or renters insurance, ask the students to discuss what would happen if their home or apartment were completely destroyed by fire and they had no insurance. Specifically, have the students answer these questions: "Where would you live? What would you do for clothing? How long do you think it would take to replace your possessions?"

Enrichment
1. Have your students research the Federal Emergency Management Agency (FEMA) to determine what services and financial assistance they provide in the event of a natural disaster.
2. Obtain copies of the home insurance policies forms HO-1 through HO-6. Divide the class into six groups and assign each group one of the forms. Ask each group to review the form and be able to explain its purpose to the rest of the class.
3. Ask your students to investigate the features and cost of at least two different brands of each of the following: smoke detectors, fire extinguishers, dead-bolt locks, and burglar alarm systems.

Assessment
1. Have the students complete the Section 13.2 Assessment.
2. Assign an activity from the *Student Activity Workbook*.

CLOSE
Ask your students to write a letter explaining the importance of home and property

insurance to a friend who doesn't believe it is worth the expense.

SECTION 13.3

FOCUS

Motivation

Bring in automotive magazines, newspaper ads, and brochures from dealerships. Have the students find a picture of their dream vehicle. Then ask the students to estimate the cost of insurance for this vehicle. If possible, invite an insurance agent to the class to verify the students' estimates.

Prereading

1. Have the students skim the section, looking at pictures, reading captions, and noting headings.
2. Have "What You'll Learn" listed on page 431 read aloud.
3. Write the Key Terms on the board. Ask the students to guess at their meaning. Write the guesses on the board.
4. Ask your students to state the purpose of studying this chapter.

TEACH

Guided Practice

1. Read the section with your students.
2. Assign an activity from the *Student Activity Workbook*.

Independent Practice

1. Have your students research the financial responsibility law in your state.
2. Ask the students to visit an auto body repair shop to find out the actual cost of repairing a vehicle that was damaged in an accident.

ASSESS

Reteaching

1. Review the Key Terms and the definitions you wrote on the board. Revise and clarify guesses if necessary.
2. Help the students understand the different types of motor vehicle coverage. Ask them to create a chart with two columns labeled "Bodily Injury Coverages" and "Property Damage Coverages." Then ask the students to list the types of coverage in each category. Have them save this chart to use as a study guide for the chapter assessment.

Enrichment

1. Have the students clip articles from the newspaper about traffic accidents. Ask your students to read the articles and answer these questions: "What was the cause of the accident? What was the damage? Were people injured? How could the accident have been prevented?" Post the articles and the students' answers around the classroom.
2. If your school offers driver's education classes, invite the instructor to speak to your class about developing defensive driving skills.
3. Invite an attorney to your class to talk to the students about their legal liability if they are involved in a vehicle accident.

Assessment

1. Have your students complete the Section 13.3 Assessment.
2. Assign the Chapter 13 Assessment.
3. Administer the test for Chapter 13 from the Reproducible Tests in the *Teacher Resource Binder*.

CLOSE

Have your students write a paragraph explaining why insurance is a necessary cost of being a responsible vehicle owner.

SECTION 13.1 ASSESSMENT
ANSWERS

CHECK YOUR UNDERSTANDING

1. Personal risks, property risks, and liability risks.
2. When you buy an insurance policy, you shift your risk to the insurance company. In return for the fees paid by policyholders, the company agrees to pay for their losses.
3. Property and liability insurance can protect a homeowner by covering damage to or loss of the homeowner's property or the property of others as well as expenses related to injuries to other people.

THINK CRITICALLY

4. Answers will vary. Students who argue in favor of insurance may say that it enables you to know that the money will be available if disaster strikes. They may say that insurance is a safe way to deal with risk and that the cost of insurance is worthwhile as protection from financial loss. Students who argue against insurance may say that the cost is too high, that they can protect themselves against many forms of risk, and that they shouldn't have to pay for protection from events that may never happen to them.

USING COMMUNICATION SKILLS

5. Answers will vary, but students should demonstrate an understanding that having insurance will lessen the consequences of loss or damage to property.

SOLVING MONEY PROBLEMS

6. Answers will vary, but most students should agree that it is worth the price of the insurance to protect the valuable car.

SECTION 13.2 ASSESSMENT
ANSWERS

CHECK YOUR UNDERSTANDING

1. The basic form (HO-1), the broad form (HO-2), the special form (HO-3), the tenants' form (HO-4), the comprehensive form (HO-5), and condominium owner's insurance (HO-6).
2. A personal property floater is additional insurance that covers the loss or damage of a specific item of high value, such as jewelry, electronic equipment, or expensive musical instruments.
3. Insurance companies charge lower rates to insure homes that are near a fire hydrant or other water supply or located in an area that has a good fire department. They charge higher rates for homes in high-crime areas or regions that experience severe weather.

THINK CRITICALLY

4. Answers will vary. Examples may include: A neighbor or guest slips on your driveway and is seriously injured, or a member of your family accidentally breaks an expensive glass statue while at another person's house.

USING MATH SKILLS

5. Students should find the amount of coverage provided for personal belongings by multiplying the insured value of the house ($80,000) by the percentage of coverage (55%). [ANSWER: $80,000 \times 55\% = \$44,000$] Because the value of the lost items was $25,000, Carolina will receive payment for all of them.

SOLVING MONEY PROBLEMS

6. A house located in an area where flooding occurs will cost more to insure. In addition, an older house may be more difficult to restore to its original condition, which means that it will cost more to insure. The more economical choice, therefore, is the newer house that is located farther from the river.

SECTION 13.3 ASSESSMENT
ANSWERS

CHECK YOUR UNDERSTANDING
1. The three main types are bodily injury liability, medical payments coverage, and uninsured motorist's protection. Bodily injury liability pays for injuries caused by a vehicle accident for which you were responsible. Medical payments coverage pays for the medical expenses of anyone injured in your vehicle, including you. This type of coverage also provides additional medical benefits for you and members of your family. Uninsured motorist's protection covers you and your family members if you are involved in an accident with an uninsured or hit-and-run driver.
2. Collision insurance covers damage to your vehicle when it is involved in an accident. Comprehensive physical damage coverage protects you if your vehicle is damaged in a non-accident situation.
3. Insurance companies offer discounts for vehicles with security devices because the devices reduce the risk of theft.

THINK CRITICALLY
4. Answers will vary. Students may give any of the following answers: Maintain a good driving record; get good grades in school; comparison shop; take advantage of discounts; increase your deductible; don't smoke.

USING COMMUNICATION SKILLS
5. Answers will vary.

SOLVING MONEY PROBLEMS
6. Depending on the insurance company that he chooses, Malcolm will probably pay more for insurance because he wants a vehicle that will be costly to repair, and he has recently received a traffic ticket. Ishiro's good driving record and the type of vehicle that he wants to insure will probably make his rate lower than Malcolm's.

CHAPTER 13 ASSESSMENT
ANSWERS

■ **Understanding and Using Vocabulary**
Answers will vary.

■ **Review Key Concepts**
1. Risk avoidance, risk reduction, risk assumption, and risk shifting.
2. Set insurance goals, develop a plan to reach your goals, put your plan into action, and review your results.
3. Homeowners insurance covers the building and other structures; renters insurance does not.
4. Location of home, type of structure, coverage amount, policy type, discounts, and differences among insurance companies.
5. Amount of coverage; vehicle type; rating territory; driver classification; differences among insurance companies; the availability of discounts; increasing deductibles.

■ **Apply Key Concepts**
1. Answers will vary.
2. Setting insurance goals allows you to know what you're trying to achieve; developing a plan helps you reach your goals; putting the plan into action allows the plan to become reality; reviewing results lets you see if your plan works for your current circumstances or if changes are needed.
3. A homeowner needs insurance for the building in which he or she lives. A renter does not need insurance for the building because it belongs to someone else. Both need coverage for personal property, additional living expenses, and personal liability.
4. Answers will vary, but students should show an understanding of the different types of insurance coverage that are available.
5. If you decide not to buy comprehensive and collision coverages, your premium will be reduced. If you buy a vehicle that has reasonable costs for repairs and replacement, your premium will probably be lower. Vehicles in a good rating territory stand less risk of theft or vandalism. Maintaining a good driving record will keep your

premiums low. Comparison shopping among insurance companies will help you get the best buy. Taking advantage of discounts reduces the amount you pay for the coverage you purchase. Increasing your deductible lowers the amount the insurance company will have to pay.

❓ Problem Solving Today
Answers will vary.

■ Real-World Application
Answers will vary.

FINANCE Online

Possible Web sites may include:
   www.fema.gov (Federal Emergency
      Management Agency)
   www.nhtsa.dot.gov (National Highway
      Traffic Safety Administration)

Answers will vary.

Note to teacher: Web site addresses may change.

READING STRATEGIES
ANSWERS

Section 13.1
QUESTION (p. 413): Answers will vary but might include to protect themselves against serious financial loss or to protect others who may be injured while in their vehicle or home.

RESPOND (p. 417): Answers will vary but might include that they might require more insurance if they have children, move to a more expensive home, move to an area with high fire, flood, or earthquake risk, or purchase more expensive vehicles. They may need less insurance if and when their children become adults or if they move to a smaller home when they retire.

Section 13.2
PREDICT (p. 422): Risks covered include injuries to one's guests or visitors and damage to others' property caused by you or your family members.

QUESTION (p. 428): A policy with replacement value coverage would probably pay more.

Section 13.3
CONNECT (p. 433): Answers will vary according to state.

PREDICT (p. 435): The kind of vehicle you own, the risks associated with where you live, your age, gender, driving record, and grades will influence the cost of your insurance.

STANDARD & POOR'S

CASE STUDY
ANSWERS

1. It may not be worth carrying insurance to replace an inexpensive car if the annual premiums cost more than the car is worth. However, liability insurance that will pay for the repair or replacement of other vehicles involved in an accident is essential and usually required.
2. Your insurance may cover a lower dollar amount than the value of the car you are renting. In addition, if you file a claim against your personal insurance there is a good chance that your rates will rise.
3. If you are found liable for damage or injury to others and have insufficient insurance, the court may order you to sell your assets and can also make a claim on your future income to satisfy your obligations.

Chapter 14 Planning Guide

Health, Disability, and Life Insurance

Teacher Manual

SECT.	OBJECTIVES	NATIONAL STANDARDS FOR BUSINESS EDUCATION	FEATURES	RESOURCES
14.1	**After completing this lesson, students will have learned:** How to explain the importance of health insurance in financial planning. How to analyze the costs and benefits of various types of health insurance coverage. How to assess the trade-offs of different health insurance policies	**Economics** I. Allocation of Resources II. Economic Systems **Personal Finance** I. Personal Decision Making II. Earning a Living VIII. Protecting Against Risk	**Standard & Poor's**—Q & A, p. 442 **What's Your Financial ID?**—Insurance Facts and Fiction, p. 444 **International Finance**—Pitcairn Island, p. 448 **Common Cents**—Fitness Fun, p. 449 **Academic Connection**—Speech, p. 450	**Check Your Understanding,** p. 453 **Think Critically,** p. 453 **Using Communication Skills,** p. 453 **Solving Money Problems,** p. 453 **Student Activity Workbook**
14.2	**After completing this lesson, students will have learned:** How to evaluate the differences among health care plans offered by private companies and by the government	**Economics** VII. The Role of Government **Personal Finance** I. Personal Decision Making V. Buying Goods and Services VIII. Protecting Against Risk	**Savvy Saver**—Kick the Smoking Habit—and Save, p. 456 **Careers in Finance**—Insurance Agent, p. 458	**Check Your Understanding,** p. 460 **Think Critically,** p. 460 **Using Math Skills,** p. 460 **Solving Money Problems,** p. 460 **Student Activity Workbook**

TM194 Unit 4 *Protecting Your Finances*

Chapter 14 Planning Guide

SECT.	OBJECTIVES	NATIONAL STANDARDS FOR BUSINESS EDUCATION	FEATURES	RESOURCES
14.3	After completing this lesson, students will have learned: How to explain the importance of disability insurance How to identify sources of disability income How to determine the trade-offs of different private disability income insurance policies	**Economics** VII. The Role of Government **Personal Finance** VIII. Protecting Against Risk		Check Your Understanding, p. 464 Think Critically, p. 464 Using Communication Skills, p. 464 Solving Money Problems, p. 464 Student Activity Workbook
14.4	After completing this lesson, students will have learned: How to describe the purpose of life insurance How to analyze various types of life insurance coverage How to identify the key provisions in a life insurance policy	**Economics** III. Economic Institutions and Incentives VIII. International Economic Concepts **Personal Finance** I. Personal Decision Making III. Managing Finances and Budgeting IV. Saving and Investing VIII. Protecting Against Risk	**Standard & Poor's—**Case Study, p. 470 **Your Financial Portfolio—**Comparing Life Insurance, p. 472	Check Your Understanding, p. 473 Think Critically, p. 473 Using Math Skills, p. 473 Solving Money Problems, p. 473 Student Activity Workbook

Teacher Manual

Chapter 14 *Health, Disability, and Life Insurance*

SCANS Correlation Chart

FOUNDATION SKILLS

Basic Skills	Reading	Writing	Math	Listening	Speaking

Thinking Skills	Creative Thinking	Decision Making	Problem Solving	Seeing Things in the Mind's Eye	Knowing How to Learn	Reasoning

Personal Qualities	Responsibility	Self-Esteem	Sociability	Self-Management	Integrity/Honesty

WORKPLACE COMPETENCIES

Resources	Allocating Time	Allocating Money	Allocating Material and Facility Resources	Allocating Human Resources

Information	Acquiring and Evaluating Information	Organizing and Maintaining Information	Interpreting and Communicating Information	Using Computers to Process Information

Interpersonal Skills	Participating as a Member of a Team	Teaching Others	Serving Clients/Customers	Exercising Leadership	Negotiating to Arrive at a Decision	Working with Cultural Diversity

Systems	Understanding Systems	Monitoring and Correcting Performance	Improving and Designing Systems

Technology	Selecting Technology	Applying Technology to Task	Maintaining and Troubleshooting Technology

■ INTERNET EXTENSION

Activity: Have each student choose a health topic to research on the Internet using at least one of the Web sites given in the text.

Keywords: Healthfinder; Medline; and National Institute of Health

■ ENRICHMENT/APPLICATION ACTIVITY

Guest Speaker: Invite a physical or occupational therapist to class to explain how physical therapy helps people who have had disabling accidents.

TM196   Unit 4   *Protecting Your Finances*

■ TOPIC SPOTLIGHT

⊙ **Ethics:** Ask students how they would respond to a doctor who charges more for services to someone with physician's insurance than to someone without physician's insurance.

⊙ **Marketing:** Discuss how hospitals in your region market their services. Ask, "Do your families prefer a certain hospital? If so, why?"

⊙ **Technology:** With the class, create a list of the new technologies used in health care today, such as CT scans and laser surgery. Discuss how these might affect health care costs.

additional resources

LIFE, the Life and Health Insurance Foundation for Education, offers a *free* educational program designed to teach young people about life, health, and disability income insurance.

The Life and Health Insurance Foundation for Education Web site, **www.life-line.org**, provides information, such as types of insurance, choosing an agent, and needs analysis, for life, health, and disability insurance.

Next Generation: Insuring Your Future is a multimedia insurance education program that consists of a 21-minute video, teacher's guide, student magazine, and classroom-size poster. The program is distributed by Video Placement Worldwide and can be ordered online from its Web site at **www.vpw.com**.

Links to various health Web sites may be accessed at **www.healthseek.com**

The Web site **www.insweb.com** acts as a virtual, personal insurance agent and provides cost information on many kinds of insurance. It also has a number of estimator, analyzer, and calculator tools for figuring the cost of auto, life, home, renters, and health insurance.

Information on Medicare can be found at the Social Security Administration Web site, **www.ssa.gov/mediinfo.htm**.

Note to Teacher: Web site addresses may change.

Chapter 14 *Health, Disability, and Life Insurance*

CHAPTER 14   Lesson Plans

SECTION 14.1

FOCUS

Motivation

Tell your students that health insurance is important for financial planning. Ask them to explain why they think this is so. Write their responses on the board and add to them as you study this section and chapter.

Prereading

1. Have the students skim the section, looking at pictures, reading captions and headings.
2. Have "What You'll Learn" listed on page 443 read aloud.
3. Write the Key Terms on the board. As a class, write a definition for the words.
4. Ask your students to state the purpose of studying this chapter.

TEACH

Guided Practice

1. Have students read aloud the Standard & Poor's Q&A on page 442.
2. Read the section with your students.

Independent Practice

1. Have the students research two different individual health insurance plans and compare them for benefits, co-payments and/or deductibles, and cost.
2. Take the students on a tour of a hospital. Ask them to note all the different departments and services that a patient might use.
3. Ask your students to research whether traditional insurance plans cover alternative procedures, such as herb therapy, music therapy, and experimental treatments.

INTERNATIONAL FINANCE
Pitcairn Island

1. Have the students draw a picture of the Pitcairn Island's flag, and provide an explanation of how it was designed and when it first was flown.
2. As a class, read *Mutiny on the Bounty*. Then ask each student to illustrate one chapter from the book.

Common Cents

Fitness Fun

1. Ask the students to discuss the ways they exercise. Are they on sports teams at school? Have they joined a health club? Do they go to the YMCA?
2. Have your students research the cost of joining a health club in your community.

ASSESS

Reteaching

1. Review the original definitions of the Key Terms provided by the students at the beginning of this section. Ask the students to modify or enhance them as necessary.
2. To reinforce the importance of health insurance, research the costs associated with a serious disease or injury. Share these costs with the students and remind them that insurance is a form of protection.

Enrichment

1. Have your students research the cost of nursing home care for an elderly person.
2. Ask the students to research the controversy surrounding the national health care issue in the United States.
3. Have the students discuss the factors that should be considered when choosing health insurance.

Assessment

1. Have the students complete the Section 14.1 Assessment.
2. Assign an activity from the *Student Activity Workbook*.

CLOSE

Ask your students to write a paragraph explaining how adequate health insurance will help them meet their financial goals.

SECTION 14.2

FOCUS

Motivation

Brainstorm with the students a list of services offered by the government that are also offered by private companies. (EXAMPLES: education, housing, health care plans). Tell them that there are often advantages and disadvantages of government sponsored services. When you have finished studying this section, ask the students to list the advantages and disadvantages of the health care plans offered by the government.

Prereading

1. Have the students skim the section, looking at pictures, reading captions, and noting headings.
2. Have "What You'll Learn" listed on page 454 read aloud.
3. Have your students write each bold-faced term in the section, and based on its definition, generate a picture or symbol that identifies it.
4. Ask the students to state the purpose of studying this chapter.

TEACH

Guided Practice

1. Read the section with your students.
2. Assign an activity from the *Student Activity Workbook*.

Independent Practice

1. Have the students research the features of Blue Cross and Blue Shield plans that are offered in your state.
2. Ask your students to research the National Committee for Quality Assurance (NCQA). This organization reports on the quality of managed care programs. Have the students find out how the NCQA can help consumers make informed decisions about their managed care provider.
3. Have the students research hospices in your community or state to find out what services are provided for the terminally ill.

$avvy SAVER

Kick the Smoking Habit—and Save

1. Have your students create a list of smoke-free restaurants in your community.
2. Ask students to research a disease caused by smoking—lung cancer, emphysema, or others. Have your students share their findings with the class.
3. Have the students research the smoking habits of European teens. How do their habits differ from U.S. teens?

Careers in Finance

Insurance Agent

1. Have your students create a list of questions they would ask when selecting an insurance agent.
2. Ask the students to research the licensing and certification required by insurance agents.
3. Have your students contact an insurance company or independent agency in your town and find out what the requirements are for an entry-level position at the firm. Then ask how likely it would be to move into an insurance agent's position.

Chapter 14 *Health, Disability, and Life Insurance*

ASSESS

Reteaching

1. Review the Key Terms with the students. Find out if the students are still unsure about a definition, and if so, clarify it for them.
2. Tell your students that there is a wealth of information available to help them evaluate various health care plans. Divide the class into groups of three and ask each group to find a Web site or other resource that can provide health insurance information. As a class, compile the findings.

Enrichment

1. Ask your students to write a paragraph summarizing the pros and cons of employer self-funded health plans.
2. Have the students write an imaginary letter to their grandmother explaining Medicare and how it works.
3. Have the students download one of the publications from the Medicare Web site (**www.medicare.gov**). Ask them to read it and see if it is easy to understand and use.

Assessment

1. Have the students complete the Section 14.2 Assessment.
2. Assign an activity from the *Student Activity Workbook*.

CLOSE

Have the students explain why Medicare has been in constant financial trouble.

SECTION 14.3

FOCUS

Motivation

Have the students discuss their dreams for the future. Ask them how money will impact their dreams. Then ask them how different their dreams might be if they were unable to work and earn a living.

Prereading

1. Have the students skim the section, looking at pictures, reading captions and headings.
2. Have "What You'll Learn" listed on page 461 read aloud.
3. Write the Key Term, *disability income insurance,* on the board. As a class, write a definition for the word.
4. Ask the students to state the purpose of studying this chapter.

TEACH

Guided Practice

1. Read the section with your students.
2. Assign an activity from the *Student Activity Workbook*.

Independent Practice

1. Have your students choose a company that offers disability insurance and find out what it covers and how much it costs.
2. Ask the students to research the disability benefits provided by Social Security.

ASSESS

Reteaching

1. Review the definition for the term *disability income insurance*.
2. Generate a discussion with the students about who should have disability insurance. Guide the discussion so that the students realize how important it is.

Enrichment

1. Divide the students into groups, and ask each group to select a disability that might occur through a work-related accident. Have the groups write a paragraph about the problems a person with this disability would encounter.

2. Tell the students that disability benefits take from one to six months before they begin. Ask them to write a plan for covering their expenses during this time.

Assessment

1. Have the students complete the Section 14.3 Assessment.
2. Assign an activity from the *Student Activity Workbook*.

CLOSE

Ask the students to complete this statement: "Because you're young, you may overlook…" (EXAMPLE: "the very real need for disability income insurance.")

SECTION 14.4

FOCUS

Motivation

Ask the students if they think it is possible to avoid all financial risks by carrying enough insurance. Have them explain their answers.

Prereading

1. Have the students skim the section, looking at pictures, reading captions and headings.
2. Have "What You'll Learn" listed on page 465 read aloud.
3. Write the Key Terms on the board. Ask the students to define them using their own words. Write their definitions on the board.
4. Ask the students to state the purpose of studying this chapter.

TEACH

Guided Practice

1. Read the section with your students.
2. Assign an activity from the *Student Activity Workbook*.

Independent Practice

1. Have the students select a life insurance company that is a stock company. Ask the students to track the stock for one week.
2. Ask the students to write a paragraph explaining the advantages and disadvantages of having life insurance.
3. Ask the students to use the Internet to get a term-life insurance quote for themselves.

ASSESS

Reteaching

1. Review with the students the definitions they developed for the Key Terms in this section.
2. Clarify the variety of whole life policies that are discussed in this section. Have your students list one or two characteristics of each one. Remind them to use this information as a study guide for the Chapter Assessment.

Enrichment

1. Tell the students that many financial planners recommend that people purchase life insurance equal to six times their annual salary. Ask your students this question: "If you earn $24,000 per year, how much life insurance should you purchase?" [$144,000]
2. Invite someone from an insurance company to your class to explain to the students the variety of policies available and the riders that are offered.

Assessment

1. Have the students complete the Section 14.4 Assessment.
2. Assign the Chapter 14 Assessment.
3. Administer the Chapter 14 Reproducible Test from the *Teacher Resource Binder*.

CLOSE

Ask your students to react to this statement: "Life insurance protects the standard of living of a policyholder's survivors."

SECTION 14.1 ASSESSMENT
ANSWERS

CHECK YOUR UNDERSTANDING

1. Health insurance eases the financial burden people might experience as a result of illness or injury. A health insurance plan may reimburse you for hospital stays, doctors' visits, medications, and sometimes vision and dental care.
2. Hospital expense coverage pays for some or all of the daily costs of room and board during a hospital stay. Routine nursing care, minor medical supplies, and the use of other hospital facilities are covered as well. Surgical expense coverage pays all or part of the surgeon's fees for an operation. Physician expense coverage meets some or all of the costs of physician care that do not involve surgery.
3. Trade-offs include reimbursement versus indemnity, internal limits versus aggregate limits, deductibles and coinsurance, out-of-pocket limits, and benefits based on reasonable and customary charges.

THINK CRITICALLY

4. Answers will vary, but students may state that limits are necessary to ensure that hospitals and doctors charge reasonable rates. The limits may discourage some individuals from seeking medical tests or treatments that they don't need.

USING COMMUNICATION SKILLS

5. Answers will vary but may include the fact that a healthy lifestyle is no guarantee against illness, or the chance that she could experience extreme financial loss if she suffered a serious accident.

SOLVING MONEY PROBLEMS

6. Answers will vary, but students may argue that Richard should choose the third plan with the $250 deductible. It has no additional monthly premium, a reasonable lifetime limit, and a low deductible.

SECTION 14.2 ASSESSMENT
ANSWERS

CHECK YOUR UNDERSTANDING

1. Blue Cross provides hospital care benefits. Blue Shield provides benefits for surgical and medical services performed by physicians.
2. The premiums for PPOs are slightly higher than the premiums for HMOs. HMOs require members to receive care from HMO providers only, while PPOs allow members greater flexibility. Members can either visit a preferred provider (a physician whom you select from a list, as in an HMO) or go to their own physicians. Patients who decide to use their own doctors do not lose coverage as they would with an HMO. Instead they must pay deductibles and larger copayments.
3. Medicare is a federally funded health insurance program available to people over 65 and to people with certain disabilities. Medicaid is a state and federally funded medical program offered to certain low-income individuals and families.

THINK CRITICALLY

4. Benefits: HMOs typically cover routine immunizations and checkups, screening programs, and diagnostic tests. They also provide customers with coverage for surgery, hospitalization, and emergency care. If you have an HMO, you will usually pay a small copayment for each covered service. Drawbacks: You must receive care through your plan physician; if you don't, you are responsible for the cost of the service. The only exception to this rule is in the case of a medical emergency. Many HMO customers complain that their HMOs deny them necessary care.

USING MATH SKILLS

5. Rose had to pay a total of $410. [ANSWER: $850 − $300 = $550; $550 × 20% = $110; $300 + $110 = $410]. The PPO had to pay $440. [ANSWER: $550 × 80% = $440]

SOLVING MONEY PROBLEMS

6. Answers will vary. Students may advise her to drop the HMO or switch to another because she doesn't like the plan. Others may point out that Medicare is not designed to cover all medical expenses, and therefore she should keep the HMO coverage. She could also consider Medigap and Medicare+Choice and compare the costs and benefits of these plans with the HMO.

SECTION 14.3 ASSESSMENT
ANSWERS

CHECK YOUR UNDERSTANDING

1. Disability can cause great financial problems. Disabled persons lose their earning power but still have to meet their living expenses. They often face huge costs for medical treatment and special care that their disabilities require.
2. Worker's compensation, a group insurance plan through your employer, Social Security, and private income insurance programs.
3. Answers will vary but should include two of the following: You'll have to weigh the length of the elimination period against the amount of the premium; you'll have to consider the duration of benefits as compared to your needs; you have to make a trade-off between the benefit amount and the cost of the insurance; you'll have to determine whether a policy that pays for accidents only is acceptable or whether you need a policy that also pays for sickness; you'll have to weigh guaranteed coverage against the higher premiums that you would pay for this coverage.

THINK CRITICALLY

4. Answers will vary. Situations may include suffering a repetitive stress injury. This could apply to people who work on an assembly line in a manufacturing plant or those who work with computers in almost any setting. Other situations might include contracting a sudden disease that forces a person to stay in the hospital or at home, and becoming pregnant.

USING COMMUNICATION SKILLS

5. Students should mention the possibility of an entertainer being unable to perform because of a disability, and the financial dangers of becoming disabled without insurance.

SOLVING MONEY PROBLEMS

6. Answers will vary but may include: He should have a policy that pays benefits for at least seven years; he shouldn't rely on Social Security; he can probably choose a plan with a long elimination period because he has enough saved to get him through that period.

SECTION 14.4 ASSESSMENT
ANSWERS

CHECK YOUR UNDERSTANDING

1. Most people buy life insurance to protect the people who depend upon them from financial losses caused by their death. Life insurance benefits may be used to pay off a home mortgage or other debts at time of death; provide lump-sum payments through an endowment for children when they reach a certain age; provide an education or income for children; make charitable donations after death; provide a retirement income; accumulate savings; establish a regular income for survivors; set up an estate plan; or make estate and death tax payments.
2. Term insurance provides protection against loss of life for only a specified term, or period of time. If you stop paying the premiums, your coverage stops. If you have a renewable term policy, the premium will increase each time you renew your insurance. Whole life policies have higher annual premiums. You will pay a specified premium each year for the rest of your life. The insurance company pays your

beneficiary a stated sum when you die, regardless of your age at the time. Whole life insurance can serve as an investment.
3. Naming your beneficiary, the incontestability clause, and the suicide clause.

THINK CRITICALLY
4. Answers will vary. Students who agree may say that it provides flexibility, allowing you to buy insurance coverage for the time when you most need it. Students who disagree may say that it is restrictive because it pays a benefit only if you die during the period covered by the policy. Also, you accept the possibility that your premium will increase over time, depending on the type of term insurance that you buy.

USING MATH SKILLS
5. Students' graphs should show a line that gradually rises.

SOLVING MONEY PROBLEMS
6. Answers will vary. Issues may include whether his sister will need help (whether his parents have provided for her through their insurance or wills); how wealthy his parents are; and how soon he can pay off the loans. He may need only a short-term policy, a decreasing term policy, or none at all.

CHAPTER 14 ASSESSMENT
ANSWERS

■ **Understanding and Using Vocabulary**
Answers will vary.

■ **Review Key Concepts**
1. Major medical insurance is a plan that pays the large costs involved in long hospital stays and multiple surgeries.
2. POSs use a network of participating physicians and medical professionals who have contracted to provide services for certain fees. As with an HMO, you choose a plan physician who manages your care and controls referrals to specialists. As long as you receive care from a plan provider, you pay little or nothing, just as with an HMO. However, you're allowed to seek care outside the network at a higher charge, as with a PPO.
3. Answers may include whether you would receive disability income through your employer or another source and if so, whether you would need to supplement the income from that source.
4. People who are single and childless, or those who don't have major financial responsibilities, might not need life insurance.
5. A waiver of premium disability benefit would allow you to stop paying premiums if you were totally and permanently disabled before you reached a certain age, usually 60. An accidental death benefit would pay twice the value of the policy if you were killed in an accident before you reached a certain age, usually 60 or 65. A guaranteed insurability option would allow you to buy a specified additional amount of life insurance at certain intervals without undergoing medical exams.

■ **Apply Key Concepts**
1. Answers will vary but may include: if you have a chronic or terminal illness and know that you will have to undergo multiple surgeries; if you have a dependent who has a long-term illness.
2. Answers will vary.
3. Answers might include the state of your overall health, your financial obligations, and the number of people who depend on your income.
4. Answers will vary. In general, the best candidates for life insurance are those who have many dependents.
5. Answers will vary. If you had a history of serious disease in your family, especially when family members reached a certain age, you might decide to add this rider before you reached that age.

❓ Problem Solving Today
At 5 percent, the annual premium would be $1,954.67. At 4 percent, the annual premium would be $1,776.29.

■ **Real-World Application**
Answers will vary.

Finance Online

Possible Web sites include:
  www.quickquote.com
  www.quotesmith.com

Note to teacher: Web site addresses may change.

READING STRATEGIES
ANSWERS

Section 14.1
Respond (p. 445): Answers will vary, but may include unexpected illnesses or injuries.

Predict (p. 446): Major medical expense insurance covers long hospital stays and multiple surgeries. It pays for procedures that your normal health insurance might not cover.

Section 14.2
Question (p. 456): Insurance buyers might want to combine the low cost of routine health care through the HMO with the freedom to choose their own specialists for more complicated medical problems.

Connect (p. 458): Answers will vary, but most likely will include retirement savings plans such as IRAs.

Section 14.3
Predict (p. 461): Disability insurance protects you against loss of income should you be unable to work due to serious injury or illness.

Respond (p. 462): Answers will vary. Since Social Security benefits are limited, a person may want to supplement Social Security with insurance that pays higher benefits sooner.

Section 14.4
Connect (p. 467): Answers will vary. The need for life insurance may increase in 10 or 15 years if a person has children or aging parents.

Question (p. 468): Benefits include fixed payments so that your insurance costs don't increase as you age and the possibility of increasing your cash value through the stock, bond, or money markets. Risks include a drop in your cash value if the stock, bond, or money markets crash.

STANDARD & POOR'S

CASE STUDY
ANSWERS

1. Term insurance provides coverage for a specified period of time. The chance that you will die during that period is less than 100 percent. With permanent insurance, it is assumed that you will claim on the policy.
2. It's a good idea to have whole life insurance in place as you get older if you do not have sufficient savings to provide for funeral costs and estate settlement costs. Older couples may need a "surviving spouse" policy to ensure that one spouse will have funds to live on if the first to die incurs uninsured medical expenses.
3. The value of these policies will vary over time depending on the performance of the variable investment portfolios.

Chapter 15 Planning Guide

Retirement and Estate Planning

Teacher Manual

SECT.	OBJECTIVES	NATIONAL STANDARDS FOR BUSINESS EDUCATION	FEATURES	RESOURCES
15.1	After completing this lesson, students will have learned: How to recognize the importance of retirement planning How to estimate retirement living costs How to identify retirement housing needs	**Economics** III. Economic Institutions and Incentives VII. The Role of Government **Personal Finance** I. Personal Decision Making III. Managing Finances and Budgeting IV. Saving and Investing	Standard & Poor's—Q & A, p. 476 What's Your Financial ID?—What's Your Personality? p. 478 Careers in Finance—Estate Planning Attorney, p. 483	Check Your Understanding, p. 485 Think Critically, p. 485 Using Communication Skills, p. 485 Solving Money Problems, p. 485 Student Activity Workbook
15.2	After completing this lesson, students will have learned: How to describe the role of Social Security in planning for retirement How to discuss the retirement benefits offered under employer pension plans How to distinguish among various personal retirement plans How to plan the best use of retirement income	**Economics** III. Economic Institutions and Incentives VII. The Role of Government **Personal Finance** I. Personal Decision Making II. Earning a Living III. Managing Finances and Budgeting IV. Saving and Investing	Academic Connection—Technololgy, p. 489 International Finance—Brazil, p. 491 Standard & Poor's—Case Study, p. 494 Savvy Saver—Making the Most of Your Company's 401(k) Plan, p. 495	Check Your Understanding, p. 498 Think Critically, p. 498 Using Math Skills, p. 498 Solving Money Problems, p. 498 Student Activity Workbook

Unit 4 *Protecting Your Finances*

Chapter 15 Planning Guide

SECT.	OBJECTIVES	NATIONAL STANDARDS FOR BUSINESS EDUCATION	FEATURES	RESOURCES
15.3	After completing this lesson, students will have learned: How to distinguish among various types of formats of wills; How to discuss several types of trusts; How to describe common characteristics of estates	**Economics** III. Economic Institutions and Incentives; VII. The Role of Government; VIII. International Economic Concepts **Personal Finance** I. Personal Decision Making; II. Earning a Living; III. Managing Finances and Budgeting	Common Cents—Be a Volunteer, p. 507	Check Your Understanding, p. 511; Think Critically, p. 511; Using Communication Skills, p. 511; Solving Money Problems, p. 511; Student Activity Workbook
15.4	After completing this lesson, students will have learned: How to identify the types of taxes that affect estates; How to assess strategies for paying taxes	**Economics** I. Allocation of Resources; III. Economic Institutions and Incentives; VII. The Role of Government **Personal Finance** I. Personal Decision Making; II. Earning a Living	Your Financial Portfolio—Saving for Retirement, p. 514	Check Your Understanding, p. 515; Think Critically, p. 515; Using Math Skills, p. 515; Solving Money Problems, p. 515; Student Activity Workbook

Teacher Manual

Chapter 15 *Retirement and Estate Planning*

SCANS Correlation Chart

FOUNDATION SKILLS

Basic Skills	Reading	Writing	Math	Listening	Speaking
Thinking Skills	Creative Thinking	Decision Making	Problem Solving	Seeing Things in the Mind's Eye	Knowing How to Learn	Reasoning
Personal Qualities	Responsibility	Self-Esteem	Sociability	Self-Management	Integrity/Honesty

WORKPLACE COMPETENCIES

Resources	Allocating Time	Allocating Money	Allocating Material and Facility Resources	Allocating Human Resources
Information	Acquiring and Evaluating Information	Organizing and Maintaining Information	Interpreting and Communicating Information	Using Computers to Process Information
Interpersonal Skills	Participating as a Member of a Team	Teaching Others	Serving Clients/Customers	Exercising Leadership	Negotiating to Arrive at a Decision	Working with Cultural Diversity
Systems	Understanding Systems	Monitoring and Correcting Performance	Improving and Designing Systems
Technology	Selecting Technology	Applying Technology to Task	Maintaining and Troubleshooting Technology

■ INTERNET EXTENSION

Activity: Have students access the Web site for Aging With Dignity and report on the organization's mission statement. (**www.agingwithdignity.org**)

Keywords: Aging With Dignity

■ ENRICHMENT/APPLICATION ACTIVITY

Field Trip: Arrange for the class to visit a seniors' community center or an assisted living facility. Arrange for students to talk with several retired people about their retirement lifestyle.

Teacher Manual

TM208 Unit 4 *Protecting Your Finances*

■ TOPIC SPOTLIGHT

⊙ **Ethics:** Tell your students, "Greg and Beth, both college students, lost their mother in a car accident. She had left no letter of last instructions. Greg wants to have a big funeral, but Beth believes their mother wouldn't have wanted it." Ask, "How should they deal with this situation? Is there a 'right' or 'wrong' thing to do?"

⊙ **Money:** How much would a retired couple spend in dollars on medical care if medical care took 11.3 percent of their income and their annual income was $24,000? [ANSWER: 11.3% × $24,000 = $2,712]

⊙ **Government:** Review with students why there are taxes—to pay for services such as police and fire protection; public schools; road maintenance; parks; libraries; and safety inspection of foods, drugs, and other products.

additional resources

The Social Security Administration has a **free** teaching kit for high school students called **Social Security and You**. It consists of five lessons plus an overview and includes factsheets, handouts, and quizzes. A 25-minute videotape is also available. You can download the text from the Social Security Administration Web site **www.ssa.gov** or you can receive the kit, including the video, by sending a blank 60 minute VHS videotape with your mailing information to: Social Security, 4-J-8 WHR, Baltimore, MD 21235. Be sure to mention that you would like the tape duplicated.

The Social Security Administration Web site also has a directory of their other publications and a site called Youthlink, which provides educational information for kids, teens, and teachers.

At **www.investorguide.com** there is an estate-planning guide. It is a basic primer on financial planning and includes the topics 401(k), IRAs, Social Security, After Retirement, Estate Planning, Calculators, Discussion Groups, and Organization.

The Motley Fool Web site, **www.fool.com**, includes retirement planning information.

The public radio program, **Sound Money**, frequently features financial planning for retirement. For a list of programs, broadcast schedule, resources, and audio archives, visit their Web site at **www.soundmoney.org**.

Note to Teacher: Web site addresses may change.

CHAPTER 15 Lesson Plans

SECTION 15.1

FOCUS

Motivation
Ask your students to brainstorm a list of all the activities in which a retired person might participate. Help the students realize that retirement can be a time to relax and enjoy life, but it takes financial planning in order to achieve this kind of lifestyle.

Prereading
1. Have the students skim the section, looking at pictures, reading captions, and headings.
2. Have "What You'll Learn" listed on page 477 read aloud.
3. Write the Key Term *assisted-living facility* (ALF) on the board. Ask your students to define the word.
4. Ask the students to state the purpose of studying this chapter.

TEACH

Guided Practice
1. Have students read aloud the Standard & Poor's Q&A on page 476.
2. Read the section with your students.

Independent Practice
1. One of the common mistakes people make about retirement is believing "that you will spend less money when you retire." Ask the students to explain why this might be a mistaken way of thinking.
2. Ask the students to research retirement housing in your community.

Careers in Finance
Estate Planning Attorney
1. Have your students investigate the requirements for gaining admission to law school.
2. Attorneys are sometimes called counselors. Ask the students to explain why this is especially true for estate planning attorneys.

ASSESS

Reteaching
1. Have the students review the Key Term and its definition.
2. Ask the students to brainstorm a list of reasons it is so important for people to begin saving for retirement as early as possible. During the rest of this chapter, have the students add to the list.

Enrichment
1. Ask the students to interview someone who has retired. Have them find out how that person prepared for retirement and what advice he or she would offer to a young person about retirement planning.
2. Divide the students into groups of two or three. Ask each group to choose one or two of the outdated beliefs listed in this section and explain why they are not accurate.

Assessment
1. Have the students complete the Section 15.1 Assessment.
2. Assign an activity from the *Student Activity Workbook*.

CLOSE
Have the students complete this statement: "Retirement planning is important because...."

SECTION 15.2

FOCUS

Motivation
Ask the students to explain what retirement means to them. Then have them describe how they will plan for their own retirement.

Prereading

1. Have the students skim the section, looking at pictures, reading captions and noting headings.
2. Have "What You'll Learn" listed on page 486 read aloud.
3. Write the Key Terms on the board. Ask the students to guess at their meaning. Write the guesses on the board.
4. Ask the students to state the purpose of studying this chapter.

TEACH

Guided Practice

1. Read the section with your students.
2. Assign an activity from the *Student Activity Workbook*.

Independent Practice

1. Have the students research the reasons Social Security was first established.
2. Ask your students to research the retirement plans offered through the Veteran's Administration.
3. Invite a certified financial planner to your class to discuss the various types of individual retirement accounts (IRAs). Have the students prepare questions to ask.

INTERNATIONAL FINANCE
Brazil

1. Draw a map of South America, the Amazon River, and its tributaries. Write a one-page paper describing the Amazon River and its economic impact on the land around it.
2. Inflation has been very high in Brazil. Have the students research the causes of this high inflation and the effect it has had on the economy of Brazil.
3. Ask the students to research a form of popular music of Brazil and its cultural significance. Then have them make an oral presentation about the music.

$AVVY SAVER

Making the Most of Your Company's 401(k) Plan

1. Have the students research why the "401(k) Plan" is so named.
2. Ask the students to discuss why it is important to begin contributing to their company's 401(k) plan as soon as possible.
3. Ask the students: "If your 401(k) is managed by a professional, why is it necessary to review your investments periodically?"

ASSESS

Reteaching

1. Review the Key Terms and the students' guesses that you wrote on the board. Revise and clarify as necessary.
2. Have the students research the free and low-cost recreation opportunities for retirees in your community. Then have the class create a "Retirement Fun Guide" and, as a service, print and distribute copies to the retirees in your town.

Enrichment

1. Ask students to debate whether or not the government should be responsible for providing all of a person's retirement income.
2. Have the students research the current amount employees are allowed to contribute annually to a 401(k) or 403(b) plan.

Assessment

1. Have the students complete the Section 15.2 Assessment.
2. Assign an activity from the *Student Activity Workbook*.

CLOSE

Ask the students to imagine they are 75 years old and retired. Have them write a letter to their heirs describing how they saved for their retirement years.

SECTION 15.3

FOCUS

Motivation

Tell the students that their class will be leaving their high school next week and will be attending a new one. Ask each student to write a last will and testament to those students who will be staying behind.

Prereading

1. Have the students skim the section, looking at pictures, reading captions, and noting headings.
2. Have "What You'll Learn" listed on page 499 read aloud.
3. Write the key terms on the board. Ask the students to guess the meaning of each term, but don't give the correct meaning. Leave the list on the board, so that as students work through the section, they can see how close they were to the correct answer.
4. Ask the students to state the purpose of studying this chapter.

TEACH

Guided Practice

1. Read the section with your students.
2. Assign an activity from the *Student Activity Workbook*.

Independent Practice

1. Ask the students to take an inventory of their own legal documents.
2. Have the students research the steps in the probate process and the ways to avoid probate.
3. Invite an attorney or financial planner to speak to the class about trusts. Ask the students to prepare specific questions to ask.

Common Cents

Be a Volunteer

1. Have the students investigate volunteer opportunities in a career field of their preference. Compile the opportunities so the class will be able to take advantage of them.
2. As a class, discuss the skills and knowledge that can be obtained through volunteer work.

ASSESS

Reteaching

1. Review the list of Key Terms that the students were unsure about before studying the chapter.

Enrichment

1. Have the students research a nonprofit group such as Aging with Dignity to obtain information about living wills.
2. Ask the students to find out whether or not your state is a community property state.

Assessment

1. Read the section with your students.
2. Assign an activity from the *Student Activity Workbook*.

CLOSE

Have the students write a paragraph describing why it is important to create an estate plan.

SECTION 15.4

FOCUS

Motivation

Tell the students that there are various types of taxes that affect estates. Without proper planning, a loved one's death can cause financial hardship. Ask the students to discuss how people must feel when they are grieving over a loved one's death and yet must settle the estate, pay off debts, and pay taxes.

Prereading

1. Have the students skim the section, looking at pictures, reading captions, and noting headings.
2. Have "What You'll Learn" listed on page 512 read aloud.
3. Ask the students to state the purpose of studying this chapter.

TEACH

Guided Practice

1. Read the section with your students.
2. Assign an activity from the *Student Activity Workbook*.

Independent Practice

1. Have the students obtain copies of the IRS forms for estates and trusts. Ask the students to review the forms for ease of use.
2. Ask the students to debate whether or not they think inheritance taxes are fair.

ASSESS

Reteaching

1. Divide the class into four groups and assign each group one of the major types of taxes. Ask each group to present a skit, song, or role-play about their tax.

Enrichment

1. Have the students research the gift tax laws in your state. Then have them select another state and research the gift tax there. Ask them to compare the results.

Assessment

1. Have the students complete the Section 15.4 Assessment.
2. Assign the Chapter Assessment.
3. Administer the test for Chapter 15 from the Reproducible Tests in the *Teacher Resource Binder*.

CLOSE

Ask the students to complete this statement "Assessing strategies for paying estate taxes can…." [ANSWER: "help limit financial hardship for your heirs."]

SECTION 15.1 ASSESSMENT
ANSWERS

CHECK YOUR UNDERSTANDING

1. It may help you cope with any unforeseen changes that occur in your life. It can give you a sense of control over your future. It will help you make your retirement a happy and comfortable time in your life.
2. You'll probably spend more money on recreation, health insurance, and medical care and less on transportation and clothing. Your taxes will probably be lower. You'll need to put money into an emergency fund and plan for inflation.
3. Housing options include houses, condominiums, apartments, living with other family members, and assisted-living facilities. Assisted-living facilities (ALFs) offer personal and medical services for elderly retirees who might not be able to live alone and care for themselves. Some ALFs provide full and continuous nursing care.

THINK CRITICALLY

4. The advantage of investing in an expensive home 20 years before retirement is that the house would become a valuable financial asset when you prepare to retire. At that point you could sell it or plan to leave it to your heirs. The disadvantage is that

the money you spend on the house is not invested in your retirement savings plans.

USING COMMUNICATION SKILLS

5. Answers will vary.

SOLVING MONEY PROBLEMS

6. Answers will vary, but options include: move to a less expensive home to reduce living expenses; move closer to family in California to reduce travel expenses.

SECTION 15.2 ASSESSMENT
ANSWERS

CHECK YOUR UNDERSTANDING

1. You must have earned a certain number of credits. These are based on the length of time you've paid into the system. People born after 1928 need 40 quarters of credit. Also, your dependents may receive benefits if you die or are disabled.
2. They are both employer pension plans. Defined-contribution plans determine how much money your employer will contribute annually, but they do not guarantee any particular benefit. Defined-benefit plans specify the benefits you'll receive at retirement but not how much the employer must contribute each year.
3. A regular IRA lets you contribute an annual amount up to $3,000 ($4,000 in 2005–2007 and $5,000 in 2008 and after) until age $70 1/2$. You must begin to withdraw minimum distributions by age $70 1/2$ or pay a penalty. A Roth IRA lets you contribute the same amount as a regular IRA, provided your adjusted gross income (AGI) is less than a certain amount. Your annual contributions are not tax-deductible, but earnings are tax-free. You can continue making annual contributions to a Roth IRA even after age $70 1/2$. There is no penalty for non-withdrawal.
4. Your financial circumstances, your age, and how much you want to leave to your heirs. You also have to consider how long your savings will last if you make regular withdrawals.

THINK CRITICALLY

5. You might consider selling some of your assets or other valuables instead of saving them to pass on to your heirs. You might think about how you could use your skills and time instead of your money. Maybe you would take care of your own cleaning and gardening. You might decide not to take an expensive vacation and to take advantage of free or low-cost activities instead. You might decide to go back to work part-time or start a new part-time career to cover your expenses.

USING MATH SKILLS

6. The answer is $2,839.44 as shown below.

Year 1	$1,110.00	Year 6	$1,870.42
Year 2	$1,232.10	Year 7	$2,076.17
Year 3	$1,367.63	Year 8	$2,304.55
Year 4	$1,518.07	Year 9	$2,558.05
Year 5	$1,685.06	Year 10	$2,839.44

SOLVING MONEY PROBLEMS

7. Answers will vary but may include the use of a rollover IRA or an annuity. A rollover IRA would allow Mike to continue to earn tax-deferred income from his money. An annuity would also produce tax-deferred interest, and Mike could arrange to receive payments from the annuity to supplement his retirement income.

SECTION 15.3 ASSESSMENT
ANSWERS

CHECK YOUR UNDERSTANDING

1. The four basic types of wills are the simple will, the traditional marital share will, the exemption trust will, and the stated dollar amount will.
2. A credit-shelter trust is one that enables the spouse of a deceased person to avoid paying federal taxes on a certain amount of assets

left to him or her as part of an estate. A disclaimer trust is for couples who do not yet have enough assets to need a credit-shelter trust but who may in the future. With a disclaimer trust, the surviving spouse receives everything, but he or she has the right to disclaim, or deny, some portion of the estate. Anything that is disclaimed goes into a credit-shelter trust. A living trust, also known as an inter vivos trust, allows you as trustor to receive benefits during your lifetime and avoids fees and delays in settling your estate when you die.

3. Owning property as joint tenants with the right of survivorship means that the property is considered to be owned 50-50 for estate tax purposes and will automatically pass to one spouse at the other's death. No estate tax is paid at the first death. Owning property as tenants in common means that each individual is considered to own a certain share of property for tax purposes, and only your share is included in your estate. That share does not go to the other tenant in common at your death. Instead, it's included in your probate estate, and you decide who gets it.

THINK CRITICALLY

4. A formal will is best from a legal point of view because some states do not recognize holographic, or handwritten, wills. If you prepare a holographic will and the state does not recognize its validity, your survivors could suffer financial losses.

USING COMMUNICATION SKILLS

5. Answers will vary but should make these general connections: An estate is everything you own. Your estate may be held in trust as a way of protecting yourself and your heirs. Your will gives instructions on how the estate held in trust is to be distributed at the time of your death.

SOLVING MONEY PROBLEMS

6. A simple will leaves everything to your spouse. Such a will is generally sufficient for people with small estates. However, if you have a large or complex estate, it may not meet your objectives. It may also result in higher overall taxation, since everything you leave to your spouse will be taxed as part of his or her estate. A traditional marital share will leaves one-half of the estate to the spouse; the other half may go to children, other heirs, or a trust. In this type of will, half the estate will be taxed at your death and half at your spouse's death (unless that amount is put in trust). This results in the lowest federal taxes on estates above a certain size; but state taxes may be higher. An exemption trust will passes everything to the surviving spouse except for an amount equal to the marital exemption, which goes into a trust. The tax benefits of this arrangement may be considerable. With a stated dollar amount will, you can pass on to a spouse any amount that satisfies your objectives. Tax benefits may be significant, but this type of will is not good for estates in which the assets may decrease in value. Based on these considerations, Irving and Irma would probably be best off with either a traditional marital share will or an exemption trust will.

SECTION 15.4 ASSESSMENT
ANSWERS

CHECK YOUR UNDERSTANDING

1. An estate tax is a federal tax on the value of a person's property at the time of his or her death. An inheritance tax is a state tax on the property left by a person in his or her will. This tax is paid by the heirs for the right to acquire the inherited property. The amount of the tax due depends on the value of the property and insurance received. It also depends on the relationship of the heir to the deceased.

2. The law allows you to give gifts to your spouse, children, or anyone else at any

time. You may give $11,000 per person per year free of any gift tax. A married couple, acting together, may give up to $22,000 per person per year.
3. Options for paying the taxes include: Use life insurance to pay taxes; set aside enough cash ahead of time to pay taxes and expenses when they're due; sell assets to pay taxes; borrow money to pay taxes; make deferred or installment payments to the IRS. Using life insurance is the best option because it allows beneficiaries to receive tax-free cash to pay taxes and debts without having to sell assets or borrow money.

THINK CRITICALLY
4. Answers will vary but may include: If older, wealthy citizens live in a particular state, that state will benefit from any taxes it may be able to impose on the residents while they are alive, as well as on their estates when they die; the state's economy will benefit from the large amount of money that wealthy people often spend on goods and services; the state would be able to finance its ongoing activities with the investments that these citizens might make by purchasing municipal bonds.

USING MATH SKILLS
5. The surviving spouse will have to pay $192,000 in taxes.

SOLVING MONEY PROBLEMS
6. Answers will vary, but students should consider the fact that Roland will need money for his living expenses and any uncovered medical expenses and that any gifts that he gives to his children within three years of his death may be subject to gift taxes.

CHAPTER 15 ASSESSMENT
ANSWERS

■ **Understanding and Using Vocabulary**
Answers will vary.

■ **Review Key Concepts**
1. Retirees usually spend more money on recreation, health and life insurance, and medical care during retirement than they do now. However, they tend to spend less on transportation and clothing. Their federal income taxes may be lower. They will still need to plan for emergencies.
2. When people retire, or by age $70^1/_2$ at the latest, they must begin to receive "minimum lifetime distributions" from most tax-deferred retirement plans, except the Roth IRA. If they don't withdraw the minimum distributions, the IRS will charge a penalty.
3. Reasons may include moving to a new state that has different laws; selling property that is mentioned in the will; changes in the size and composition of the estate; marriage, divorce, or remarriage; and the death of potential heirs or the birth of new ones.
4. They can write a living will and assign someone power of attorney.
5. In community-property states each spouse owns 50 percent of the property. Thus, half of the couple's assets is included in each spouse's estate. In noncommunity-property states, property is included in the estate of the spouse who owns it.

■ **Apply Key Concepts**
1. Answers will vary.
2. One way: You could invest in a Roth IRA. You may continue making contributions even after age $70^1/_2$. A second way: Invest in a rollover IRA. This plan will let you roll over all or a portion of your taxable distribution from a retirement plan or other IRA.
3. You may have to alter or rewrite your will if you move to a state that has different laws.
4. Answers will vary. Students may say that a living will might not have been important to someone who was retiring 100 years ago because medicine was not as advanced at that time as it is now. Therefore, the option of keeping someone alive by artificial means would not have been available.
5. The car would be considered community property owned equally by both.

❓ Problem Solving Today
Answers will vary. (Note to teacher: Students may be able to find information by calling the local chamber of commerce, contacting the state's tax department, reading the Sunday edition of a local newspaper, calling a local CPA to find out about taxes, and checking with local utility companies about costs.)

■ Real-World Application
Answers will vary.

Finance Online
Possible Web sites include:
- www.lifenet.com
- www.nolo.com
- www.webtrust.com

Answers will vary.

Note to teacher: Web site addresses may change.

READING STRATEGIES
ANSWERS

Section 15.1
RESPOND (p. 478): Answers will vary. It is better to start saving for retirement early so that investments can grow. Costs will rise because of inflation. On average, people are living longer. Insurance may not cover higher medical expenses and pension plans may not keep up with the cost of living.

QUESTION (p. 481): You might want to invest more conservatively (income stocks or secure bonds) as you get closer to retiring.

Section 15.2
CONNECT (p. 487): Answers will vary.

PREDICT (p. 488): Other options include employer pension plans, defined contribution plans, defined benefit plans, 401(k) plans, IRAs, and Keogh plans.

Section 15.3
PREDICT (p. 504): Major life changes might motivate you to change your will.

RESPOND (p. 509): Trusts can save your beneficiaries taxes, prevent disputes among heirs, avoid probate, help you manage your assets, ensure that your wishes are heeded if you become seriously ill or incapacitated, and provide income for your survivors.

Section 15.4
QUESTION (p. 513): You might consult reference sources at your local library, contact the tax collecting agency of your state government, search your state government's Web pages, or contact a local estate attorney.

CONNECT (p. 515): Answers will vary. Some possibilities are anger, confusion, or sadness.

STANDARD & POOR'S

CASE STUDY
ANSWERS

1. This income is taxable and may exceed the deductible moving expenses. If Josephine will have difficulty paying tax on this income, she could invest the leftover relocation money in a tax-deductible traditional IRA up to the contribution limit.
2. Josephine might decide to invest in a Roth IRA, and the rest in the 401(k) plan. A Roth IRA is not tax deductible but the investment earnings can be withdrawn tax-free.
3. Up to 90 percent might be allocated to stock funds, which carry greater risk of loss in the short-term but also offer higher long-term returns.

UNIT 4 Planning Guide

PROTECTING YOUR FINANCES

Chapter 12—
Planning Your Tax Strategy

Chapter 13—
Home and Motor Vehicle Insurance

Chapter 14—
Health, Disability, and Life Insurance

Chapter 15—
Retirement and Estate Planning

OVERVIEW

This unit introduces students to basic information about protecting their financial resources. In Chapter 12, they will learn how to prepare a federal income tax return and how to select the best tax strategies for their financial and personal needs. Chapter 13 explains and discusses home and motor vehicle insurance, and Chapter 14 describes health, disability, and life insurance. Finally, Chapter 15 discusses protecting financial resources for retirement and explains the importance of estate planning.

INTRODUCTION

Divide the class into small groups and have each group brainstorm a list of their most valuable possessions. Then have each group write a commercial for a product or service that protects some or all of the valuables on their list. As a class, create a master list of valuable possessions on the board and discuss the list. Does it include one's health or a loved one's security? Are all the possessions material?

Explain that this unit describes how planning and insurance products can help a person protect his or her valuable possessions. Have students consider how the products and services advertised in their commercials are similar to or different from those presented in this unit.

TM218

Get a Financial Life!

CASE STUDY 4

Teaching Guide

Step A — THE PROCESS

Make sure students have access to all the necessary materials. Explain that this case study will lead them to better understand how it feels to get older.

1. Suggest students think about an older person whom they admire and use that person's life as an example for thinking about their own life when they get older. Ask them to consider why they admire this person. In what ways would they like their life to be similar and different?
2. Give students the names of the Web sites listed in the Chapter 14 Planning Guide, such as the Life and Health Insurance Foundation for Education Web site, **www.life-line.org** and **www.insweb.com**.
3. If time permits, show the 1985 movie *Cocoon*, directed by Ron Howard and starring Don Ameche. Allow students to discuss the issues of the retirees.
4. Invite the recreation director of a seniors' community center or assisted living facility to discuss student activities for seniors.

Step B — CREATE YOUR PORTFOLIO

Evaluate students' portfolios based on whether or not all four steps of the process are completed, the information seems reasonably well researched, and the contents are neat and in order. Make sure the short story covers a person's basic needs, and references are cited for the long-term care insurance research. Find out if students were able to implement their activities.

Step C — MATHEMATICS

If necessary, organize the class into groups of three. Evaluate the students' word problems using the following criteria:

1. Participation from all team members is evident. Each member should contribute about ten problems.
2. Each member has the opportunity to solve another member's set of problems.
3. Word problems should be understandable by the majority of students, even if they are difficult to solve.

UNIT CLOSURE

Have students outline the steps they would now take to protect their most valuable possessions. Have them describe what insurance they would buy and when and how they would plan for taxes, retirement, and death.

EVALUATION

Administer the Unit 4 test from the **Exam***View* Pro Test Generator CD-ROM.

Chapter 16 Planning Guide

Introduction to Financial Management for Business

Teacher Manual

SECT.	OBJECTIVES	NATIONAL STANDARDS FOR BUSINESS EDUCATION	FEATURES	RESOURCES
16.1	After completing this lesson, students will have learned: How to identify the three parts of a business plan; How to explain the importance of financial management for business; How to describe the aspects of a financial plan	**Economics** III. Economic Institutions and Incentives **A. Personal Finance** I. Personal Decision Making II. Earning a Living VII. Using Credit	**Standard & Poor's**—Q & A, p. 522 **What's Your Financial ID?**—What's Your Business Personality? p. 524 **International Finance**—Greece, p. 529 **Academic Connection**—Language Arts, p. 533	Check Your Understanding, p. 534; Think Critically, p. 534; Using Communication Skills, p. 534; Solving Money Problems, p. 534; Student Activity Workbook
16.2	After completing this lesson, students will have learned: How to recognize the importance of accounting in financial management; How to discuss the primary functions of accounting	**Economics** III. Economic Institutions and Incentives VI. Productivity VIII. International Economic Concepts **Personal Finance** I. Personal Decision Making II. Earning a Living IV. Saving and Investing	**Standard & Poor's**—Case Study, p. 536 **Common Cents**—Bag It, p. 537 **Savvy Saver**—Avoid Unnecessary Fees, p. 538 **Careers in Finance**—Accounting Teacher, p. 541 **Your Financial Portfolio**—Planning for Success, p. 542	Check Your Understanding, p. 543; Think Critically, p. 543; Using Math Skills, p. 543; Solving Money Problems, p. 543; Student Activity Workbook

SCANS Correlation Chart

FOUNDATION SKILLS

Basic Skills	Reading	**Writing**	**Math**	Listening	Speaking
Thinking Skills	Creative Thinking	Decision Making	Problem Solving	Seeing Things in the Mind's Eye	Knowing How to Learn	Reasoning
Personal Qualities	Responsibility	Self-Esteem	Sociability	Self-Management	Integrity/Honesty

WORKPLACE COMPETENCIES

Resources	Allocating Time	Allocating Money	Allocating Material and Facility Resources	Allocating Human Resources
Information	Acquiring and Evaluating Information	Organizing and Maintaining Information	Interpreting and Communicating Information	Using Computers to Process Information
Interpersonal Skills	Participating as a Member of a Team	Teaching Others	Serving Clients/Customers	Exercising Leadership	Negotiating to Arrive at a Decision	Working with Cultural Diversity
Systems	Understanding Systems	Monitoring and Correcting Performance	Improving and Designing Systems
Technology	Selecting Technology	Applying Technology to Task	Maintaining and Troubleshooting Technology

Teacher Manual

Chapter 16 *Introduction to Financial Management for Business*

■ INTERNET EXTENSION

Activity: Have students access the Small Business Administration Web site. Ask them how the information presented on the Web site can help new business owners.

Key Word: Small Business Administration

■ ENRICHMENT/APPLICATION ACTIVITY

Guest Speaker: Contact your local SBA office and invite a representative to talk about starting a new business. Also ask for a copy of their *Small Business Resource Guide* or a district office Start-Up Kit for the class to review. To contact your local SBA office, access the SBA Web site at **www.sba.gov** and click on Local SBA Resources.

■ TOPIC SPOTLIGHT

✪ **Government:** Further define free enterprise as freedom of private business to organize and operate for profit in a competitive system without interference by government beyond regulation necessary to protect public interest and keep the national economy in balance. Ask students for examples of government regulation of business.

✪ **Marketing:** Choose a local business with which the students are familiar and ask them to describe its services offered, current area pricing, potential customers, and advertising and promotions. Allow students to discuss whether or not that business's marketing choices are helping the business grow.

✪ **Money:** Give students the following math word problem: The costs to promote the opening of your retail business were $5,000 for advertising and giveaways the first week of operation. Operating expenses for the week, including payroll, inventory, and utilities, were $10,000. If you brought in $3,000 a day for your first week of business, how many days would it be before you recovered your first week's costs? [ANSWER: 5 days; $15,000 ÷ 3,000 = 5]

TM222 Unit 5 *Introduction to Business Finance*

additional resources

The Small Business Administration offers a great deal of information at its Web site, **www.sba.gov**. This site includes a list of publications at the Online Library at **www.sba.gov/lib/library.html**. A business plan outline, a tutorial, as well as a Small Business Startup Kit are available at Starting Your Business at **www.sba.gov/starting_business/**.

At **www.sba.gov/young/indexyoung.html** students can find the Discover Business! Web site and learn about starting their own businesses. Teachers can find curriculum guides designed to augment a semester course in entrepreneurship or small business ownership. Each lesson has a different goal and includes a teaching guide/topic outline, black-line print masters for overheads, activities, answer keys, and work sheets.

www.bplans.com provides information about real business plans for small businesses and includes actual sample plans.

Young Money, Todd Romer, publisher. This magazine has a regular feature called "Enterprising Youth" that reports on young entrepreneurs and their businesses and gives entrepreneurial advice. Its Web site is **www.youngmoney.com**.

Note to Teacher: Web site addresses may change.

CHAPTER 16 Lesson Plans

SECTION 16.1

FOCUS

Motivation

Ask your students, "What skills and knowledge do you think are needed to run a business?"

Prereading

1. Have the students skim the section, looking at pictures, reading captions, and noting headings.
2. Have "What You'll Learn" listed on page 523 read aloud.
3. Write the Key Terms on the board. Ask your students to write a sentence using each term. Allow them to skim the text for clues if they are unsure of the meaning of the word.
4. Ask the students to state the purpose of studying this chapter.

TEACH

Guided Practice

1. Have students read aloud the Standard & Poor's Q&A on page 522.
2. Read the section with your students.

Independent Practice

1. Have the students choose a country and research its economic system. Then write a one- or two-page paper comparing and contrasting the particular economic system to America's free enterprise system.
2. Ask the students to interview a business owner in your community. Have the students find out what goal-setting process the owner used when starting business and what goals have been set to sustain the business.
3. Tell your students that they have been asked by Mike and Erin to help select and purchase a computer for their business. Mike and Erin need a system that can handle word processing and spreadsheet applications. In addition, they will use it to produce brochures and flyers to advertise their business. Next year Mike wants to develop a Web site for the business. Have the students research the features and price of a computer system they could recommend to Mike and Erin.

INTERNATIONAL FINANCE
Greece

1. Have the students research why Greece is considered to be the first democracy.
2. Ask your students to find out what types of investments are most common among the Greek people.
3. Greece became part of the European Economic Community (now the European Union or EU) in 1981. Have the students investigate how belonging to the EU has helped improve the economy of Greece.

ASSESS

Reteaching

1. Have your students review the Key Terms and the sentences they wrote. Clarify any terms that the students still might not understand.
2. To stress the importance of sound financial management to a business, reinforce the three aspects of a financial plan: (1) identifying the assets you'll need; (2) the method you'll take to acquire these assets; and (3) the recording, summarizing, reporting, and analyzing of your business's finances. Invite an accountant who specializes in small business operations to speak to the students about financial management.

Enrichment

1. Divide the class into groups. Have each group think of a business they would like

to start. Ask the students to create the following:
- Name of their business
- Product or service they will sell
- Two short-term and two long-term goals for the business
- How they plan to advertise/market their business
- Assets they will need to start the business

2. Have the students read a magazine article on an aspect of starting or running a business. Magazines like *Young Entrepreneur*, *Fast Company*, *Fortune*, and *Forbes* would be good resources for finding an appropriate article. Then, have the students create a poster or other visual depicting the important points of the article.

Assessment

1. Have the students complete the Section 16.1 Assessment.
2. Assign an activity from the *Student Activity Workbook*.

CLOSE

Have the students complete this statement, "When you own a business, most of your decisions are based on…." [HINT: "financial information."]

SECTION 16.2

FOCUS

Motivation

Generate a discussion with the students about the ways they keep track of their money. Write their comments on the board. Then ask how many of these methods could be used by a business.

Prereading

1. Have the students skim the section, looking at pictures, reading captions, and noting headings.
2. Have "What You'll Learn" listed on page 535 read aloud.
3. Dictate each of the Key Terms to the students and have them write them on a piece of paper. When they are finished, write the terms on the board. Ask the students to guess at the meaning of each term, but do not give the correct meaning. Leave the list on the board, so that as students work through the section, they can see how close they were to the correct answer.
4. Ask your students to state the purpose of studying this chapter.

TEACH

Guided Practice

1. Read the section with your students.
2. Assign an activity from the *Student Activity Workbook*.

Independent Practice

1. Have the students request a copy of the budget from their school system or city government. Ask them to find out what the total payroll costs are. Then have them determine what percentage payroll costs are in relation to the total budget.
2. Ask your students to job shadow someone who is taking inventory. Have them find out what skills are necessary for the job and what part of the job is the most difficult.

Bag It

1. Ask the students, "What would be your idea of a great brown bag lunch?"

Chapter 16 *Introduction to Financial Management for Business* TM225

2. Have your students conduct a survey of the students who bring their lunch to school and find out why they do so.
3. Ask the students to complete this math problem: "If your school year has 180 days, how much would you save by brown bagging it all year? Every other day?"

$avvy Saver

Avoid Unnecessary Fees
1. Have the students add two tips to this list.
2. Ask your students to survey students in their school to find out how much money students spend on various fees. Have the students graph their results.
3. Have the students research the cost of cell phones and pagers to find out if there are fees or other charges that could be avoided.

Careers in Finance

Accounting Teacher
1. Have the students job shadow an accounting teacher for a day to preview this career.
2. Have the students ask their accounting teacher (or another teacher) if they could prepare and teach a lesson one period. Encourage the students to work with the teacher on the creation of their lesson and the instructional strategies they will use.
3. Ask your students this question: "Why is time management an important skill for a teacher to possess?"

ASSESS

Reteaching
1. Review the original definitions of the Key Terms provided by the students at the beginning of this section. Ask the students to modify or enhance them as necessary.

2. Divide the class into five groups. Assign each group one of the essential functions of accounting that they learned about in this section: budgeting, inventory, payroll, cash flow, and investments. Ask each group to write a description, draw a picture, and list three characteristics of their assigned function.

Enrichment
1. For one week, ask the students to record all the transactions they conduct with a business. Then, have the students write a paragraph explaining why it's important for a business to keep a record of their transactions.
2. Ask the students if they have ever been to a store where they were out of the product they wanted to purchase. With a partner, have the students role-play a similar situation and depict how the store might handle the problem.

Assessment
1. Have the students complete the Section 16.2 Assessment.
2. Assign the Chapter Assessment.
3. Administer the test for Chapter 16 from the Reproducible Tests in the *Teacher Resource Binder*.

CLOSE
Ask the students to explain how financial management is the glue that holds a business together as well as the oil that keeps a business running smoothly.

SECTION 16.1 ASSESSMENT
ANSWERS
CHECK YOUR UNDERSTANDING
1. The basic parts of a business plan are a strategic plan, which outlines your business goals and the steps you'll take to achieve them; a marketing plan, which

outlines how you'll promote your business to increase customers and sales in order to make a profit; and a financial plan, which outlines how you'll get money to create and operate your business as well as how you'll maintain your financial operations and business records.
2. The strategic and marketing components of a business plan depend on the efficient management of money. Also, sound financial decisions provide the opportunity for sales to rise, expenses to fall, profits to increase, assets to be acquired, liabilities to be paid, credit to expand, customers to increase, and new products to be developed.
3. Aspects include identifying needed assets, determining the method to purchase needed assets, and recording and reporting business finances.

THINK CRITICALLY

4. Answers will vary. Sample answer: The business owner or operator might make a decision to purchase assets without realizing the extent of outstanding debts of the business. As a result, the business might not be able to pay its debts on time, jeopardizing its ability to obtain funding for its operations.

USING COMMUNICATION SKILLS

5. Flyers will vary.

SOLVING MONEY PROBLEMS

6. Santiago's list should include the merchandise he will be selling—doughnuts and hot chocolate mix—as well as materials for advertising, a table, an urn, cups, napkins, plastic spoons, paper plates, and so on. Students may point out that he may be able to borrow a table and an urn from the school, but he will need to purchase the merchandise and the supplies.

SECTION 16.2 ASSESSMENT
ANSWERS

CHECK YOUR UNDERSTANDING

1. Accounting is a systematic process of recording and reporting the financial position of a business. It plays a role in the daily activities of every business in two ways. First, it keeps track of the financial transactions that occur in the daily operation of the business. Second, businesses use the language of accounting in financial statements. These statements are a way of communicating the financial position of the business.
2. Five of the most essential functions of accounting are budgeting, inventory, payroll, cash flow, and investments.
3. By tracking inventory, businesses can determine how much merchandise is being sold, what merchandise is selling well, when they need to reorder merchandise, and what merchandise should be reordered. The wrong level of inventory can cause a business to lose sales or lack the money it needs to make purchases.

THINK CRITICALLY

4. Without enough cash reserves, a business may not be able to pay for emergencies or other unexpected costs that might arise.

USING MATH SKILLS

5. The toy store had a positive cash flow of $21,500.

SOLVING MONEY PROBLEMS

6. Answers will vary. Groups may suggest that Kim examine the budget to determine where their spending has increased and why. Kim should also evaluate the business's inventory. Vince and Kim might have inadequate inventory of some products, causing customers to go elsewhere.

CHAPTER 16 ASSESSMENT
ANSWERS

■ Understanding and Using Vocabulary
Answers will vary.

■ Review Key Concepts
1. Profit is the amount of money earned over and above the amount spent to keep a business operating. It is important because the continued operation and success of a business requires profit.
2. A marketing plan outlines how you will promote your business and increase sales in order to make a profit. A financial plan outlines how you'll get money to start and run a business and how you'll maintain financial operations and business records.
3. You'll have to perform a careful analysis of your existing finances, determining how much cash is available, how much cash is needed for future expenses, and the amount of debt you can handle. Then investigate the sources of credit available to you. You may have to wait to purchase some of the assets that you want.
4. Using GAAP allows investors, banks, suppliers, and government agencies to make comparisons of the financial condition of various companies. It also allows owners and managers to determine their company's financial position.
5. Determining whether you have the proper number of employees working at the proper times and ensuring that generally accepted accounting principles (GAAP) are used in preparing payrolls.

■ Apply Key Concepts
1. Answers will vary but should demonstrate that students understand that goal setting helps them focus on a particular result and work toward achieving that result.
2. Answers will vary. Students should demonstrate an understanding that business owners and operators will not be able to make intelligent financial decisions regarding the direction and future of their businesses without a financial plan.
3. Answers will vary. Sample scenario: Business owner wants to buy a building for the distribution of items from a mail-order catalog. Because the business is new, the owner does not have the cash to be able to buy the building, and he cannot obtain the necessary credit. Other options would be to rent a building or rent general warehouse space.
4. Answers will vary. Investors, bankers, suppliers, and government agencies will not know whether the business is strong or in trouble. They might not be willing to lend money to the business or provide the goods and services that the business needs to operate. Businesses may be unaware of their financial trouble and may not be profitable enough to stay in business.
5. Answers will vary. Some responses might be: Understaffed—poor customer service, business might not open on time, inventory not on shelves, bookkeeping not completed. Overstaffed—too much money spent on payroll, employees might become unproductive.

❓ Problem Solving Today
129 mouse pads must be sold to pay for the vendor cart. Long-term goals will vary. Some examples might be to have a sales goal of 5,000 mouse pads per month, add different merchandise, hire a staff, and so on. Marketing suggestions will vary.

■ Real-World Application
Answers will vary but may include: Charlotte needs to devise a marketing plan for her business. She needs to research the competition and find out whether her competitors advertise and if so, where and how often. She should also investigate advertising possibilities and prices in her town, such as the local newspaper.

FINANCE Online

Answers will vary. Students might locate local flower shop sites on the Internet or use industry Web sites, such as www.1800flowers.com and www.ftd.com.

Note to teacher: Web site addresses may change.

READING STRATEGIES
ANSWERS

Section 16.1
CONNECT (p. 527): Answers will vary.

RESPOND (p. 533): Mike and Erin will want to consider the customers they might lose as well as the extra labor costs they might have to pay if they do not have a computer system to help them advertise, track orders and inventory, create designs, print out business documents, and manage finances.

Section 16.2
PREDICT (p. 537): Businesses need realistic predictions of the amount of money they will earn and spend for a specified period of time so that managers can make good financial decisions.

QUESTION (p. 539): Since payroll is often the most costly expense for a business, it is important to know how the payroll money is being distributed. Workers also have a right to consistency and accuracy in their pay.

STANDARD & POOR'S

CASE STUDY
ANSWERS

1. Key financial statements are a balance sheet, completed at least once a year, and an income statement, completed monthly. In addition, they need to keep a daily journal of income and expenses, and manage their cash flow by tracking their accounts receivable.
2. A rise in interest rates may result in less demand for new housing, which could mean less work for Phil and Chris.
3. Borrowing to finance their business may be an excellent idea. First, however, they need to project the potential increase in their current market and other markets they intend to pursue. They may be able to finance equipment purchases and accounts receivable balances with little risk of default.

Chapter 17 Planning Guide

Sources of Funding

Teacher Manual

SECT.	OBJECTIVES	NATIONAL STANDARDS FOR BUSINESS EDUCATION	FEATURES	RESOURCES
17.1	**After completing this lesson, students will have learned:** How to distinguish among start-up costs, operating costs, and reserve funds / How to identify sources of personal and private financing / How to discuss the options available through bank funding / How to explain the criteria used in approving commercial loans	**Economics** II. Economic Systems / III. Economic Institutions and Incentives / **Personal Finance** I. Personal Decision Making / II. Earning a Living / IV. Saving and Investing / VII. Using Credit / VIII. Protecting Against Risk	**Standard & Poor's**—Q & A, p. 546 / **What's Your Financial ID?**—Are You a Go-Getter?, p. 549 / **Careers in Finance**—Commercial Loan Officer, p. 550 / **Common Cents**—Paid in Full, p. 551 / **Academic Connection**—Language Arts, p. 552 / **Standard & Poor's**—Case Study, p. 553 / **Savvy Saver**—Credit Cards—Paying with Plastic, p. 555 / **International Finance**—Japan, p. 556 / **Go Figure**—A Home Equity Loan, p. 557	**Check Your Understanding,** p. 562 / **Think Critically,** p. 562 / **Using Math Skills,** p. 562 / **Solving Money Problems,** p. 562 / **Student Activity Workbook**
17.2	**After completing this lesson, students will have learned:** How to describe the function of the Small Business Administration / How to identify alternative sources of funding for a business	**Economics** III. Economic Institutions and Incentives / VIII. International Economic Concepts / **Personal Finance** II. Earning a Living / VII. Using Credit	**Your Financial Portfolio**—Tanya's Toys, p. 568	**Check Your Understanding,** p. 569 / **Think Critically,** p. 569 / **Using Communication Skills,** p. 569 / **Solving Money Problems,** p. 569 / **Student Activity Workbook**

Unit 5 *Introduction to Business Finance*

SCANS Correlation Chart

FOUNDATION SKILLS

Basic Skills	Reading	Writing	Math	Listening	Speaking
Thinking Skills	Creative Thinking	Decision Making	Problem Solving	Seeing Things in the Mind's Eye	Knowing How to Learn	Reasoning
Personal Qualities	Responsibility	Self-Esteem	Sociability	Self-Management	Integrity/Honesty

WORKPLACE COMPETENCIES

Resources	Allocating Time	Allocating Money	Allocating Material and Facility Resources	Allocating Human Resources
Information	Acquiring and Evaluating Information	Organizing and Maintaining Information	Interpreting and Communicating Information	Using Computers to Process Information
Interpersonal Skills	Participating as a Member of a Team	Teaching Others	Serving Clients/Customers	Exercising Leadership	Negotiating to Arrive at a Decision	Working with Cultural Diversity
Systems	Understanding Systems	Monitoring and Correcting Performance	Improving and Designing Systems
Technology	Selecting Technology	Applying Technology to Task	Maintaining and Troubleshooting Technology

Teacher Manual

Chapter 17 *Sources of Funding* TM231

■ INTERNET EXTENSION

Activity: Have students access ACE-*Net* and print out the Welcome Page. Ask, "What university publishes the ACE-*Net* Web site?" [ANSWER: University of New Hampshire]

Keywords: ACE-*Net*

■ ENRICHMENT/APPLICATION ACTIVITY

Guest Speaker: Invite a commercial loan officer to class to describe his or her job. Ask the speaker to explain his or her career path—the education and experience that led to this position, what the speaker likes about the job, and any difficulties associated with it. Have each student write a question to ask the guest speaker.

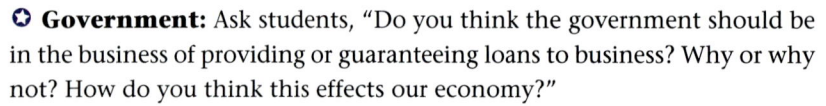

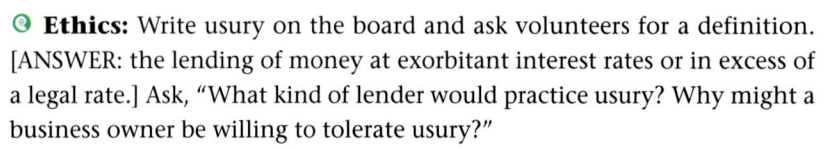

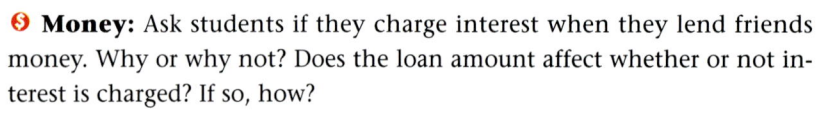

■ TOPIC SPOTLIGHT

✪ **Government:** Ask students, "Do you think the government should be in the business of providing or guaranteeing loans to business? Why or why not? How do you think this effects our economy?"

☯ **Ethics:** Write usury on the board and ask volunteers for a definition. [ANSWER: the lending of money at exorbitant interest rates or in excess of a legal rate.] Ask, "What kind of lender would practice usury? Why might a business owner be willing to tolerate usury?"

💲 **Money:** Ask students if they charge interest when they lend friends money. Why or why not? Does the loan amount affect whether or not interest is charged? If so, how?

TM232   Unit 5   *Introduction to Business Finance*

additional resources

The young Entrepreneurs Organization (YEO) has a Web site at **www.yeo.org** that aims to serve business owners under age 40. The YEO is a global, non-profit educational organization that aims to help its members achieve success through an array of learning and networking opportunities.

The venture capital firm Accel has a Web site for entrepreneurs. At **www.accel.com**, Accel posts articles that its partners have presented over the years, such as "Advice for the First-Time Entrepreneur" and "How to Win a Venture Capitalist."

www.morebusiness.com is the Web site for the Business Resource Center. This site has many, many articles on starting and running your own business.

The Venture Capital Resource Library Web site is **www.vfinance.com**. It has links to many venture capital firms plus news from and about them.

To find out about the lending programs available from the Small Business Administration, log on to **www.sba.gov** and click on Financing Your Business. There you will find links to Financing Eligibility Topics, SBA Loan Topics, Surety Bond Topics, and other useful information.

Note to Teacher: Web site addresses may change.

CHAPTER 17   Lesson Plans

SECTION 17.1

FOCUS

Motivation
Ask your students to imagine they will be opening an on-campus school store. Have them brainstorm where the store would be located, how the interior would be decorated, a list of products they would sell, and how they would advertise the store to other students in the school. Then ask the students where they would get the funding for this store.

Prereading
1. Have the students skim the section, looking at pictures, reading captions, and noting headings.
2. Have "What You'll Learn" listed on page 547 read aloud.
3. Write the Key Terms on the board. Ask the students to define them using their own words. Write their definitions on the board. Place an asterisk next to the terms the students are not sure about.
4. Ask your students to state the purpose of studying this chapter.

TEACH

Guided Practice
1. Have students read aloud the Standard & Poor's Q&A on page 546.
2. Read the section with your students.

Independent Practice
1. Have your students write a story about a small business they had or might have had when they were younger. [EXAMPLES: lemonade stand, lawn mowing business, pet sitting, and babysitting] If they didn't run a business, have them write an imaginary story.
2. Ask the students to select a business located in your community. Have the students create a list of startup costs they think the business might have incurred before they opened their doors.
3. Ask the students to scan the newspapers for ads from banks and other financial institutions that offer home equity loans. Have the students bring the ads into class and compare interest rates, terms, and the process it takes to secure the loan.

Careers in Finance

Commercial Loan Officer
1. Ask the students this question: "What are the advantages of paying the commercial loan officer a commission instead of a salary?"
2. Have your students explain why they think a degree in finance, economics, business, or accounting is important for a commercial loan officer.
3. Invite a commercial loan officer to your class to discuss the skills and knowledge needed for a career in this field.

Common Cents

Paid in Full
1. Have the students suggest ways to keep track of their monthly credit card expenditures.
2. Have the students research the advantages of using a credit card for big-ticket items, such as electronic equipment.
3. Have each student find out the interest rate for three different credit cards. Then as a class, compile the data and determine the average interest rate of the three cards.

$avvy Saver

Credit Cards—Paying with Plastic

1. Ask the students why it is important to pay for small items in cash when it is so convenient to use a credit card.
2. Have your students research why some credit card companies charge an annual fee. If possible, ask the students to find out what the fees are used for.
3. Discuss with the students why credit card companies spend so much money on advertising trying to get new customers.

INTERNATIONAL FINANCE

Japan

1. Manufacturing and construction employ one-third of the Japanese workforce. Have students make a list of all the products in their homes and schools that have been manufactured in Japan. Compile the list as a class.
2. Ask your students to research the educational system in Japan and compare it to the United States' system.
3. Many Americans go to Japan to teach English. Research the process someone must go through in order to teach in Japan.

ASSESS

Reteaching

1. Review with students the Key Terms that you placed an asterisk next to during the prereading section.
2. To help the students remember the five Cs of Credit, divide the students into groups. Have each group create a jingle using the five Cs. Allow each group to perform their jingle and have the students vote on the best one. Award a prize, and then have the winning group teach the jingle to the rest of the class.

Enrichment

1. Take the students on a tour of a bank. Arrange for the students to see all the different departments. Organize an opportunity for the students to meet with a commercial loan officer so they can ask questions about business financing.
2. Obtain a copy of a commercial loan application. Make copies for each student and have them review the application for the information that is requested. Then ask the students to correlate the information on the application with the five Cs they learned about in this section.

Assessment

1. Have the students complete the Section 17.1 Assessment.
2. Assign an activity from the *Student Activity Workbook*.

CLOSE

Have the students write a paragraph explaining the best way to accurately estimate the amount of funding needed by a business to open.

SECTION 17.2

FOCUS

Motivation

Tell the students that the federal government has a variety of programs to help small businesses get started, grow, and expand. Ask the students to discuss why they think the federal government is so interested in small business development.

Prereading

1. Have the students skim the section, looking at pictures, reading captions, and noting headings.

2. Have "What You'll Learn" listed on page 563 read aloud.
3. Write each one of the Key Terms on the board. Ask each student to write a definition for every term. Then divide the students into groups of three. Ask each group develop a group definition of the Key Terms.
4. Ask the students to state the purpose of studying this chapter.

TEACH

Guided Practice

1. Read the section with your students.
2. Assign an activity from the *Student Activity Workbook*.

Independent Practice

1. The Small Business Administration provides more than 15 different guaranteed loan programs. Ask the students to research one and write a summary of the program.
2. Have the students locate the SBA office closest to their school.
3. Ask the students to create a list of five FAQs (Frequently Asked Questions) and their answers that people might ask when seeking alternative sources of funding for their businesses.

ASSESS

Reteaching

1. Review the original definitions of the Key Terms provided by each group at the beginning of this section. Ask the groups to modify or enhance them as necessary.
2. To help differentiate between "angels" and "venture capitalists," write the words on the board. Have the students list the characteristics of each.

Enrichment

1. Ask the students to interview small business owners. Have them ask two questions:
   (1) What is an ideal source of funding for a new business?
   (2) What is the most realistic way to obtain money?
2. Have your students take on the role of a venture capitalist who is reviewing a business plan in anticipation of lending money to a new business. What questions would you ask the business owner who would be using the money?

Assessment

1. Have the students complete the Section 17.2 Assessment.
2. Assign the Chapter Assessment.
3. Administer the test for Chapter 17 from the Reproducible Tests in the *Teacher Resource Binder*.

CLOSE

Many entrepreneurs fail but try over and over again until they are successful. Ask your students to explain why some entrepreneurs are so persistent.

SECTION 17.1 ASSESSMENT
ANSWERS

CHECK YOUR UNDERSTANDING

1. Start-up costs are the costs or expenses of setting up your business. Operating costs are the expenses you anticipate for the first 90–120 days of operation.
2. You can use your own personal savings or investments, such as stocks or bonds. Other options include a consumer or home equity loan.
3. A small business might use a line of credit for unexpected costs or routine expenses that it cannot handle in the short term.

4. Banks use the 5 Cs of credit: character, capacity, capital, collateral, and credit history. They also examine the business plan.

THINK CRITICALLY

5. Answers will vary, but students should recognize that a home equity loan may be risky. Students may suggest that private financing may be the best idea because friends and family are more likely to provide funds to an unproven business, may not charge interest, and may be more forgiving about the time needed to repay the money.

USING MATH SKILLS

6. Mario will need to borrow $5,200. [ANSWER: start-up costs + operating costs + reserve = $8,900 + $6,300 + $10,000 = $25,200; $25,200 − $20,000 in savings = $5,200] He will borrow 20.6 percent of his total costs. [ANSWER: $5,200 ÷ $25,200 = 0.206 or 20.6%]

SOLVING MONEY PROBLEMS

7. Answers will vary, but students should identify all the primary sources of funding and present logical reasoning to explain their choices.

SECTION 17.2 ASSESSMENT
ANSWERS

CHECK YOUR UNDERSTANDING

1. The SBA offers assistance to people who are starting small businesses and to those who want to expand existing businesses. It offers a wide variety of services, including management training, organizational guidance, and most important, assistance in obtaining financing.
2. A business credit card, private investors, commercial finance companies, venture capital firms, and state and local governments.
3. One way you can get venture capital is through SBICs that are listed with the SBA.

THINK CRITICALLY

4. Answers will vary, but students should recognize that a business credit card charges high interest rates and probably should not be used for daily expenses unless the charges can be paid off every month. They are best used for emergencies.

USING COMMUNICATION SKILLS

5. Answers will vary, but students should recognize that the SBA is an agency of the federal government that can help Ashley receive a loan under the Guaranteed Loan Program.

SOLVING MONEY PROBLEMS

6. Answers will vary, but the best choices for Kimo would be a bank loan guaranteed by the SBA (note that Kimo cannot receive a loan from the SBA; they only guarantee loans) or a loan from a business "angel" in his community. Kimo probably could not get a loan from a venture capital firm because these firms usually only make investments of more than $500,000.

CHAPTER 17 ASSESSMENT
ANSWERS

■ Understanding and Using Vocabulary
Answers will vary.

■ Review Key Concepts
1. Make a realistic estimate that includes start-up costs, operating costs, and a reserve fund.
2. Disadvantages of personal financing include possibly not having enough cash available to get the business going; the risk of losing the personal assets that you have pledged as collateral if you cannot repay a consumer loan; and losing your home if you get a home equity loan and your business fails. Disadvantages of private financing include the possibility of personal conflicts if your business is not successful.

3. A small, local bank can relate better to a small business. It understands your needs, offers advice, and assists you with other services. It also offers a wide variety of loan plans. Small local banks are community-oriented and interested in seeing local businesses succeed.
4. Management training, organizational guidance, and assistance in obtaining financing.
5. Private investors invest in your business because they believe that it will help the neighborhood or town. They usually leave the management of the business to the owner. Venture capital firms expect to have a voice in major decisions that affect the business. They will examine your financial position carefully throughout the year.

■ Apply Key Concepts

1. Answers will vary but should include start-up costs such as inventory, equipment, security deposits, advertising prior to opening, insurance, legal permits, and supplies; and operating costs such as utility bills, rent, office expenses, payroll, and delivery charges. Ideas about reserve funds will vary but should reflect an understanding that these funds are usually used for expansion of the business.
2. Answers will vary.
3. Disadvantages may include: They are regulated by the government and are not allowed to take major risks; they require extensive paperwork, investigation, and documentation; they are conservative by nature and may reject your loan if your business appears to be too risky.
4. SBA loan programs were created to provide assistance to many businesses because the federal government realized the importance of small business operations in the American economy.
5. Answers will vary but should reflect the student's understanding that venture capital firms expect a large return on their investment and a voice in the decisions of the business.

❓ Problem Solving Today
Answers will vary. Students should prepare a detailed financial plan that shows realistic consideration of all costs involved in starting such a business.

■ Real-World Application
1. Cost of short-term loan: $10,000 × 10% × 0.247 year (90 days) = approximately $247 interest
2. Cost of long-term loan: $10,000 × 7% × 2 years 5 $1,400 interest
3. Cost of line of credit: $10,000 × 9.5% × 0.5 year (6 months) = $475 interest
4. The least costly alternative would be the short-term loan.

FINANCE Online

Possible Web sites include:
www.sba.gov
www.inc.com
www.youngbiz.com

Answers will vary.

Note to teacher: Web site addresses may change.

READING STRATEGIES
ANSWERS

Section 17.1
CONNECT (p. 549): Answers will vary but may include hard work, a sound business plan, and funding to provide startup capital and operating expenses.

PREDICT (p. 556): If you have equity in your home, the advantage is that a home equity loan would be fairly easy to obtain. The disadvantage is that you could lose your home if your business fails.

Section 17.2

RESPOND (p. 565): Small businesses make up the majority of businesses in the nation, so helping them thrive helps the economy.

QUESTION (p. 566): If you can obtain a bank loan, you will most likely maintain more control over your management decisions, and keep more of your profits for yourself.

STANDARD & POOR'S

CASE STUDY

ANSWERS

1. For a catering business, variable costs, such as food and labor, can be purchased after receiving a customer's order. A restaurant requires that food and labor is on hand before customers actually come into the restaurant. It is much more difficult to manage the costs of operating a restaurant.

2. A financially sound business plan is essential. Lenders are usually more willing to lend money that will be used for acquiring equipment or inventory that can be resold, if needed. Lenders also look for owners who have a personal investment in the business and who have an experienced management team.

3. They can look for a partner who is willing to invest in their business and share in a portion of their profits. A "silent" partner does not participate in the daily operations of the business. For many start-up businesses, family members and friends help provide the initial funding.

Chapter 18 Planning Guide

Financial Accounting

SECT.	OBJECTIVES	NATIONAL STANDARDS FOR BUSINESS EDUCATION	FEATURES	RESOURCES
18.1	After completing this lesson, students will have learned: How to analyze business transactions How to identify the first five steps of the accounting cycle How to describe the role of the general journal How to explain the purpose of posting How to recognize the purpose of a trial balance	**Economics** VII. The Role of Government **Personal Finance** II. Earning a Living IV. Saving and Investing	**Standard & Poor's**—Q & A, p. 572 **What's Your Financial ID?**—Do You Think Logically or Intuitively? p. 574 **Careers in Finance**—Bookkeeper, p. 576 **Academic Connection**—History, p. 577 **Common Cents**—Quantity Counts, p. 579 **Standard & Poor's**—Case Study, p. 580	**Check Your Understanding**, p. 588 **Think Critically**, p. 588 **Using Communication Skills**, p. 588 **Solving Money Problems**, p. 588 **Student Activity Workbook**
18.2	After completing this lesson, students will have learned: How to identify items included on an income statement How to explain the purpose of a balance sheet How to recognize the importance of a statement of cash flows	**Economics** VIII. International Economic Concepts **Personal Finance** II. Earning a Living VIII. Protecting Against Risk	**International Finance**—Falkland Islands, p. 594 **Savvy Saver**—Accounting for Your Money, p. 597 **Your Financial Portfolio**—Income Statements, p. 598	**Check Your Understanding**, p. 599 **Think Critically**, p. 599 **Using Math Skills**, p. 599 **Solving Money Problems**, p. 599 **Student Workbook**

Teacher Manual

TM240 Unit 5 *Introduction to Business Finance*

SCANS Correlation Chart

FOUNDATION SKILLS

Basic Skills	Reading	Writing	Math	Listening	Speaking
Thinking Skills	Creative Thinking	Decision Making	Problem Solving	Seeing Things in the Mind's Eye	Knowing How to Learn	Reasoning
Personal Qualities	Responsibility	Self-Esteem	Sociability	Self-Management	Integrity/Honesty

WORKPLACE COMPETENCIES

Resources	Allocating Time	Allocating Money	Allocating Material and Facility Resources	Allocating Human Resources
Information	Acquiring and Evaluating Information	Organizing and Maintaining Information	Interpreting and Communicating Information	Using Computers to Process Information
Interpersonal Skills	Participating as a Member of a Team	Teaching Others	Serving Clients/Customers	Exercising Leadership	Negotiating to Arrive at a Decision	Working with Cultural Diversity
Systems	Understanding Systems	Monitoring and Correcting Performance	Improving and Designing Systems
Technology	Selecting Technology	Applying Technology to Task	Maintaining and Troubleshooting Technology

Chapter 18 *Financial Accounting*

■ INTERNET EXTENSION

Activity: Have students use the Internet to find out what accounting services are available to small business owners.

Keywords: small business + accounting

■ ENRICHMENT/APPLICATION ACTIVITY

Field Trip: Arrange for students to visit a book store and computer software store to review a variety of accounting software products and books about accounting and record keeping. Have students write a review about either software or a book that tells the title, what is covered (book), what it does (software), and who wrote it or produced it.

■ TOPIC SPOTLIGHT

Technology: Discuss with students whether they'd prefer to use a computer or accounting paper to keep accounting records for a very small service business, if they had one.

Money: What is the price of one can of soda when a 12-pack of 12 oz. cans sells 2 for $5? [ANSWER: 21 cents. $5.00 ÷ 2 = $2.50; $2.50 ÷ 12 = 21 cents] If one can of soda sells for $1.00 in a vending machine, how much money can you save by bringing a can from home 5 days a week for a year? [ANSWER: $205.40. $1.00 − .21 = .79; 5 days × 52 weeks = 260 days; .79 × 260 days = $205.40]

Marketing: Have students create an advertisement for a bookkeeping or accounting firm placed in a financial magazine.

additional resources

10 Minute Guide to Accounting for Non-Accountants by Wayne A. Label (© 1998 by Hungry Minds, Inc.). This book defines accounting concepts using common terminology that is easy to understand.

Accounting for the New Business: The Strategies and Practices You Need to Account for Your Success by Christopher R. Malburg (© 1996 Adams Media Corporation). This book covers all the accounting basics a new business needs to succeed.

Accounting the Easy Way by Peter J. Eisen (© 1995 Barrons Educational Series). This book explains financial statements and has a section on the differences in partnership and corporate accounting.

www.quicken.com/small_business/ This Web site provides valuable information for small businesses on all topics including accounting.

Note to Teacher: Web site addresses may change.

CHAPTER 18   Lesson Plans

SECTION 18.1

FOCUS

Motivation

Ask your students what kind of financial record keeping they do for themselves. [EXAMPLES: maintaining a check register, developing a budget, and filing income tax returns] Tell the students that these experiences will help them in life and particularly if they go into business.

Prereading

1. Have your students skim the section, looking at pictures, reading captions, and noting headings.
2. Have "What You'll Learn" listed on page 573 read aloud.
3. Divide the class into five groups and assign each group four of the Key Terms from this section. Ask each group to create definitions for the terms using their own words and present them to the class. Have other groups add to the definitions as necessary.
4. Ask your students to state the purpose of studying this chapter.

TEACH

Guided Practice

1. Have students read aloud the Standard & Poor's Q&A on page 572.
2. Read the section with your students.

Independent Practice

1. Ask the students to create a crossword puzzle using the Key Terms from this section.
2. Have your students visit the school store or other school-based enterprise on campus to learn about the accounting system used. Ask them to report their findings to the class.
3. Ask the students to research the American Accounting Association to find out what educational opportunities are available through this organization.

Careers in Finance

Bookkeeper

1. Ask your students to use the newspaper to write down all the advertised positions for bookkeepers. In addition, have them list the skills that are requested in the ads. Then ask the students to write the "ideal ad" for a bookkeeper.
2. Have the students contact someone who runs a bookkeeping service from their home to find out the advantages and disadvantages of doing this job from home.
3. Ask the students this question: "What skills would a bookkeeper need in order to advance to a controller position?"

Common Cents

Quantity Counts

1. Have the students research the cost of soda by the case versus the cost of 24 cans of soda purchased in the school vending machine. How much will actually be saved by purchasing soda this way?
2. Ask your students to find five other products that you can save money by purchasing in quantity.
3. Ask the students this question: "Is there ever a time when items should not be purchased in quantity? Explain why."

ASSESS

Reteaching

1. Review the original definitions of the Key Terms provided by the students at the

beginning of this section. Ask the students to modify or enhance them as necessary.
2. To reinforce learning the five steps in the accounting cycle, have the students create a poster that illustrates the cycle. Display their posters in the classroom.

Enrichment

1. Have your students compare the accounting equation to another equation they use in algebra class.
2. Divide the students into groups. Have each group create another transaction for Archer Delivery Service and an analysis of that transaction. Use some of the students' transactions on a quiz or test.
3. Ask the students to prepare a list of books, magazines, and Internet sites that would be helpful to a business owner with very little experience in financial accounting.

Assessment

1. Have the students complete the Section 18.1 Assessment.
2. Assign an activity from the *Student Activity Workbook*.

CLOSE

Have the students explain why all business owners must record and summarize their transactions in the same way.

SECTION 18.2

FOCUS

Motivation

Ask your students when the last time was that they had their picture taken. Ask if they liked the way the picture turned out. Tell the students that a financial statement is like a financial snapshot of the business at a particular time—sometimes the picture is good and sometimes it is not!

Prereading

1. Have the students skim the section, looking at pictures, reading captions, and noting headings.
2. Have "What You'll Learn" listed on page 589 read aloud.
3. List and review the Key Terms with the students. Acknowledge students' correct answers by writing a brief definition next to the terms they know. Place an asterisk by the terms they do not know.
4. Ask your students to state the purpose of studying this chapter.

TEACH

Guided Practice

1. Read the section with your students.
2. Assign an activity from the *Student Activity Workbook*.

Independent Practice

1. Have your students construct an income statement for themselves. Model it after **Figure 18.8**. (Remind them that they will have revenue but no cost of goods sold.)
2. Arrange for the students to job shadow or take a field trip to an accounting department of a local business. Have the students find out how the records are kept, what statements are produced, and which technology is used.

INTERNATIONAL FINANCE
Falkland Islands

1. Have the students write a 500-word paper on the economy of the Falkland Islands.
2. Ask the students to discuss whether or not they would like to live in a country with a population of only 2,967.

$avvy Saver

Accounting for Your Money

1. Ask the students how many of the five tips they follow regularly. Then ask each student to select one and try to implement it during the next week. At the end of the week, survey the class again and see how many students were successful.
2. Have your students explain why it is so important to balance your checkbook each month.
3. Ask the students to research various financial software programs and to make a recommendation for the one they would like to use.

ASSESS

Reteaching

1. Review with the students the Key Terms that you placed an asterisk next to during the prereading section.
2. To help clarify the financial statements used in a business, ask the students to write two characteristics each of an income statement, a balance sheet, and a statement of cash flows.

Enrichment

1. Have the students discuss the Happy House's balance sheets for this year and last year. Ask the students to speculate on the financial picture of the business.
2. Have the students volunteer to create financial statements for the school store or other school-based enterprise.

Assessment

1. Have the students complete the Section 18.2 Assessment.
2. Assign the Chapter Assessment.
3. Administer the test for Chapter 18 from the Reproducible Tests in the *Teacher Resource Binder*.

CLOSE

Have your students complete this sentence: "To make sound financial decisions about your business, you need…" [HINT: "current financial statements that analyze your financial position."]

SECTION 18.1 ASSESSMENT
ANSWERS

CHECK YOUR UNDERSTANDING

1. T accounts are used in double-entry accounting to analyze business transactions.
2. The first five steps of the accounting cycle are: (1) collect and verify source documents, (2) analyze each transaction, (3) journalize each transaction, (4) post to the general ledger, and (5) prepare a trial balance.
3. All of the transactions of the business are recorded in a general journal.
4. A general ledger contains a page for each account your business uses. The accounts are grouped, and this organization allows for easy access to the information you might need.
5. A trial balance will help you determine whether your account balances are correct.

THINK CRITICALLY

6. Answers will vary. You may have made a mistake in the addition of either the debit column or the credit column. You may have reversed two digits within an amount. For example, if the figure was $352, you may have recorded it as $325. You may have omitted an account balance from the general ledger. You may have put a number in the wrong column.

USING COMMUNICATION SKILLS

7. Paragraphs will vary but should correctly explain the first five steps in the accounting cycle.

SOLVING MONEY PROBLEMS

8. Account names will vary. Some examples might include: Cash in Bank, Merchandise,

Store Equipment, Accounts Payable, Rent, Utilities, Telephone, and Payroll.

SECTION 18.2 ASSESSMENT
ANSWERS

CHECK YOUR UNDERSTANDING

1. An income statement for a merchandising business has five sections: revenue, cost of merchandise sold, gross profit on sales, operating expenses, and net income (or loss).
2. A balance sheet shows the current financial position of the business by reporting the assets of a business and the claims against those assets (creditor's claims and owner's claims).
3. Answers may vary but should include the following: A statement of cash flows can help you determine whether you have enough cash available to pay bills, buy new merchandise, or pay for emergencies. It can be a major consideration when you want to borrow money because lenders and investors want to see a positive cash flow.

THINK CRITICALLY

4. Answers will vary. A business may have made a profit during the most recent accounting period, but it may still have more cash outflows than inflows during a particular time period. If this were the case, it is possible that the business wouldn't have enough money available to pay its employees during a particular week.

USING MATH SKILLS

5. Fall semester: $5,420 − 3,500 = $1,920 gross profit on sales. Percentage of gross profit to sales: $1,920 ÷ 5,420 = 0.3542 = 35%.

   Spring semester: $4,890 − 3,060 = $1,830 gross profit on sales. Percentage of gross profit to sales: $1,830 ÷ 4,890 = 0.3742 = 37%. Profits improved.

SOLVING MONEY PROBLEMS

6. Answers will vary, but students should show an understanding of the various financial statements and what information they would provide to a potential business partner.

CHAPTER 18 ASSESSMENT
ANSWERS

■ **Understanding and Using Vocabulary**
Answers will vary.

■ **Review Key Concepts**
1. Answers will vary but might include Cash in Bank, Accounts Receivable, and Office Equipment.
2. An asset account increases on the debit side and decreases on the credit side. Liability accounts and owner's equity accounts increase on the credit side and decrease on the debit side.
3. Source documents include check stubs, invoices, memorandums, and receipts.
4. Financial statements provide up-to-date financial information so that you can make decisions and determine whether your business in on course, experiencing some difficulty, or headed for trouble.
5. Cash inflows are cash entering the business. Examples may include sales and interest earned from investments. Cash outflows are cash exiting the business. Examples may include operating expenses, merchandise purchased, supplies, and interest and taxes paid.

■ **Apply Key Concepts**
1. Assets might include motorcycles, a delivery truck, shop tools, and leather goods. The motorcycles, delivery truck, shop tools, and leather goods are items of value or property that the business owns.
2. The accounts that should be credited are Cash on Hand and Accounts Payable.
3. Answers will vary, but students should understand that source documents are proof that a business transaction took place.

4. You could use the comparison of statements to see how well your business is doing and to evaluate whether you are pricing your merchandise appropriately.
5. Examples will vary, but students should show an understanding of cash inflows and outflows.

❓ Problem Solving Today
The Cash in Bank T account should show an opening debit (+) of $150,000 and a credit (−) of $25,000. The Transportation Equipment T account should show a debit (+) of $25,000.

■ Real-World Application
Answers will vary. Students should summarize the types of financial information that should be recorded, categorize appropriate accounts, and list possible source documents.

FINANCE Online
Possible Web sites include:
    http://www.peachtree.com
    http://www.quickbooks.com
    http://www.microsoft.com/money

Answers will vary.

Note to teacher: Web site addresses may change.

READING STRATEGIES
ANSWERS

Section 18.1
PREDICT (p. 575): The basic assumptions are: a) the business is a separate entity (business and personal finances will never be mixed); and b) reports will be generated for specific accounting periods (usually monthly, quarterly, or yearly).

CONNECT (p. 582): Answers will vary. Business records must be much more exact than personal records and recorded in a uniform manner using generally accepted accounting principles. Personal records don't always keep track of purchased assets (such as the value of clothing), while business records use the double entry system to keep stricter records of both assets and liabilities.

Section 18.2
RESPOND (p. 592): Answers will vary. Happy House might want to raise prices to increase its percentage of profit. However, Happy House's increased sales may have been directly related to keeping its prices stable despite the increase in wholesale costs. Raising prices might cause a drop in sales for the next year.

QUESTION (p. 599): You will need to know the basics of accounting in order to make sure the right information is being collected and entered into the software program, and you still will need a basic understanding of accounting in order to analyze the information presented on the computer-generated reports.

STANDARD & POOR'S
CASE STUDY
ANSWERS

1. The IRS requires companies to maintain adequate records of sales, expenses, and net profit. Many of Jesse's expenditures, such as supplies, salaries, and insurance costs, may be tax deductible. Jesse can also depreciate the cost of vehicles over their "useful life" if he maintains adequate records documenting the business use of these vehicles.
2. A careful analysis of the dynamics that are affecting his business is in order. If his business is primarily a service, any additional growth in revenue will likely be accompa-

nied by an increase in labor costs. If these costs are rising, Jesse may need to increase the price of his services in order to remain profitable. He can also work towards adjusting the "mix" of products and services that he offers by putting more effort towards developing and marketing services that offer a higher level of profits. Finally, he can look for ways to reduce the cost of equipment and materials that he buys.

3. What worked for Jesse in high school may not be his dream of a lifelong vocation. Jesse can still realize substantial value from the efforts he has invested in growing his business. If he were to eventually sell the business, its market value would be based on several components including the fair market value of business equipment and property, the net value of accounts receivable minus accounts payable, and the estimated value of prospective revenues. Jesse can work to increase the eventual sale value by establishing service contracts with his clients and building the reputation and visibility of the company, assuring a prospective buyer of higher future revenues.

Chapter 19 Planning Guide

Managing Payroll and Inventory

Teacher Manual

SECT.	OBJECTIVES	NATIONAL STANDARDS FOR BUSINESS EDUCATION	FEATURES	RESOURCES
19.1	After completing this lesson, students will have learned: How to identify the steps required in managing a payroll system; How to describe the most common methods of paying employees; How to distinguish between required and voluntary payroll deductions; How to identify the accounts used in recording payroll	**Economics** I. Allocation of Resources; III. Economic Institutions and Incentives **Personal Finance** VI. Banking	**Standard & Poor's**—Q & A, p. 602; **What's Your Financial ID?**—Stocking Up on Knowledge, p. 604; **Academic Connection**—Math, p. 605; **Careers in Finance**—Purchasing Agent, p. 606; **Go Figure**—Gross Earnings and Overtime, p. 607; **Go Figure**—FICA Deduction, p. 610; **International Finance**—Australia, p. 615; **Go Figure**—Unemployment Taxes, p. 617	Check Your Understanding, p. 618; Think Critically, p. 618; Using Math Skills, p. 618; Solving Money Problems, p. 618; Student Activity Workbook
19.2	After completing this lesson, students will have learned: How to describe the methods of determining inventory quantity; How to calculate inventory using various costing methods; How to analyze inventory turnover	**Economics** VI. Productivity; VIII. International Economic Concepts **Personal Finance** II. Earning a Living	**Standard & Poor's**—Case Study, p. 624; **Common Cents**—Check It Out, p. 625; **Savvy Saver**—Eating Out on a Budget, p. 627; **Go Figure**—Average Inventory, p. 628; **Go Figure**—Inventory Turnover, p. 628; **Go Figure**—Number of Days in Stock, p. 629; **Your Financial Portfolio**—Keeping Track of Inventory, p. 630	Check Your Understanding, p. 631; Think Critically, p. 631; Using Communication Skills, p. 631; Solving Money Problems, p. 631; Student Activity Workbook

TM250 Unit 5 *Introduction to Business Finance*

SCANS Correlation Chart

FOUNDATION SKILLS

Basic Skills	Reading	Writing	Math	Listening	Speaking

Thinking Skills	Creative Thinking	Decision Making	Problem Solving	Seeing Things in the Mind's Eye	Knowing How to Learn	Reasoning

Personal Qualities	Responsibility	Self-Esteem	Sociability	Self-Management	Integrity/Honesty

WORKPLACE COMPETENCIES

Resources	Allocating Time	Allocating Money	Allocating Material and Facility Resources	Allocating Human Resources

Information	Acquiring and Evaluating Information	Organizing and Maintaining Information	Interpreting and Communicating Information	Using Computers to Process Information

Interpersonal Skills	Participating as a Member of a Team	Teaching Others	Serving Clients/ Customers	Exercising Leadership	Negotiating to Arrive at a Decision	Working with Cultural Diversity

Systems	Understanding Systems	Monitoring and Correcting Performance	Improving and Designing Systems

Technology	Selecting Technology	Applying Technology to Task	Maintaining and Troubleshooting Technology

■ INTERNET EXTENSION

Activity: Have students use the Internet to find out about job opportunities in payroll accounting. Suggest they access the online classified ads of a local newspaper. As a class make a list of the different job titles in this field.

Keywords: accounting, payroll

■ ENRICHMENT/APPLICATION ACTIVITY

Cooperative Activity: As a class, develop a small business and assign each student a job in this business. Have each student research his or her job title to find out the average pay rate for people in those jobs. To get an idea of the cost of payroll, estimate on the board your business's total gross earnings to employees for one pay period.

■ TOPIC SPOTLIGHT

Ethics: Ask students what kind of personal information is necessary to calculate an employee's earnings and deductions? [EXAMPLES: marital status, dependents, amount earned] Discuss who should have access to this information, who should not, and why.

Government: Ask students to research the income taxes in other countries. How do they compare with U.S. income taxes?

Money: Give students the following math word problem. Jamie earns a salary of $3,700 per month. Last month he worked 235 hours. The month before, he worked 212 hours. On average, how much does Jamie earn per hour? [ANSWER: $16.56. 235 + 212 = 447 hours; $3,700 × 2 = $7,400; $7,400 ÷ 447 = $16.56]

additional resources

The National Association of Purchasing Management, whose mission is to advance the purchasing and supply management profession through education and development, has a Web site at **www.napm.org**. Articles from their magazine, ***Purchasing Today***, are available at the Web site, as well as featured books and reports.

APICS (which in 1957 stood for American Production and Inventory Control Society) is now known as the Educational Society for Resources Management. At their Web site, **www.apics.org**, you can find out about workshops and access publications dedicated to the education and professional certification of managers in areas such as materials management, information services, and purchasing.

Purchasing in the 21st Century: A Guide to State-of-the-Art Techniques and Strategies by John E. Schorr (© 1995 & 1998 John Wiley & Sons). This book provides information on current purchasing trends.

Profitable Purchasing Strategies: A Manager's Guide for Improving Organizational Competitiveness Through the Skills of Purchasing by Paul T. Steele, Brian Court (Contributor) (© 1996 McGraw-Hill). This book provides a thorough view and explanation of purchasing strategies.

Note to Teacher: Web site addresses may change.

CHAPTER 19   Lesson Plans

SECTION 19.1

FOCUS

Motivation
Ask the students to brainstorm a list of tools a business owner might use to manage the payroll of the organization. [EXAMPLES: time clocks, computer, software, and calculator] Then ask them if they know what laws impact payroll and make a list of them. As you study this section, add to both lists.

Prereading
1. Have your students skim the section, looking at pictures, reading captions, and noting headings.
2. Have "What You'll Learn" listed on page 603 read aloud.
3. Ask the students to read through the list of Key Terms and note any that are familiar. Have the students orally define those terms and the context in which they were used.
4. Ask the students to state the purpose of studying this chapter.

TEACH

Guided Practice
1. Have students read aloud the Standard & Poor's Q&A on page 602.
2. Read the section with your students.

Independent Practice
1. Have the students conduct a survey of the students who are working in the class. Find out what their pay period is and compile the results. What is the most common pay period in the class?
2. Ask your students to contact the Social Security Administration to find out what FICA forms a new business owner would need to complete. If possible, obtain copies to review.
3. Have the students find out what services the American Payroll Association (APA) provides to its members.

Careers in Finance

Purchasing Agent
1. Tell the students to imagine they are purchasing agents. Have them write a paragraph about the company they are working for and the products they purchase.
2. Ask the students to write a paper on business-to-business purchasing over the Internet. Have them report on the process used, the types of businesses involved, and future trends.
3. Have your students discuss why purchasing agents have to be able to cope with stress on the job.

INTERNATIONAL FINANCE
Australia
1. The Summer Olympics were held in Australia in 2000. Have the students research the economic impact of this event on Australia.
2. Ask your students to research the banking system in Australia and compare it to the banking system in the United States.
3. Australia is part of the Asia-Pacific Economic Cooperation (APEC), an organization of 20 nations. Have the students find out which countries are part of the Cooperation and why it exists.

ASSESS

Reteaching
1. Review the list of Key Terms that the students were unsure about before studying the chapter.
2. Many young people who are new to the workforce have a difficult time understanding why so much money is deducted from their paycheck for taxes. Ask the

TM254   Unit 5   *Introduction to Business Finance*

students to describe each tax and how the money is used.

Enrichment

1. Ask your students to contact an employer who offers direct deposit to its employees. Have them research the process used to prepare payroll in this manner.
2. Many businesses outsource their payroll. Have the students research a payroll company to find out what services are provided and, if possible, the cost of those services.

Assessment

1. Have the students complete the Section 19.1 Assessment.
2. Assign an activity from the *Student Activity Workbook*.

CLOSE

Have your students list and explain the steps required in managing a payroll system.

SECTION 19.2

FOCUS

Motivation

Ask the students to think about their favorite clothing store. Have them create two lists—one of all the items that the store sells (the inventory) and one of all the products the store purchases but does not sell (supplies and equipment). Help students understand that, in this section, inventory refers to merchandise that will be sold.

Prereading

1. Have your students skim the section, looking at pictures, reading captions, and noting headings.
2. Have "What You'll Learn" listed on page 619 read aloud.
3. Write each Key Term on the board. Ask students to define each of these terms and use it in a sentence. If necessary, the students may use the chapter as a resource.
4. Ask your students to state the purpose of studying this chapter.

TEACH

Guided Practice

1. Read the section with your students.
2. Assign an activity from the *Student Activity Workbook*.

Independent Practice

1. Have the students research current business publications and find an article that describes an inventory problem. Ask the students to write a one-page paper discussing the causes of the problem, how it impacted the organization, and any solutions that were implemented.
2. Ask your students to interview a local business owner regarding the procedures he or she uses for managing inventory, any related problems, and prevention strategies for the problems. Have the students share their findings with the class.
3. Have your students recommend an inventory system for each of the following types of businesses:
   - video rental store
   - fast food hamburger restaurant
   - small boutique that sells hand-painted scarves, purses, and hats
4. Ask the students to explain their answers.

Common Cents

Check It Out

1. Have the students compare their school library collection with that of the local public library.
2. Ask your students to create a list of other items or services offered through their public library.

$avvy SAVER

Eating Out on a Budget

1. Have the students save coupons for restaurants and bring in the ones they don't use to give to others in the class.
2. Ask your students to create a list of the restaurants that offer early-bird specials, student discounts, or other money saving offers.
3. Have the students research the price of desserts at several restaurants in your community. How much do they cost? Are they worth the money?

ASSESS

Reteaching

1. Review the Key Terms from the section. Make sure the students understand the terms.
2. There are several mathematical formulas in this section. Reinforce them with the students by dividing the class into four teams. Each team will write one math problem for each of the following: (1) average inventory, (2) inventory turnover, and (3) number of days in stock. Then have the students exchange problems with another group and solve the problems.

Enrichment

1. Have your students research commercial inventory systems and write a paragraph on its features. They should find a system that would be appropriate for a retailer.
2. Take interested students on a field trip to a company that warehouses its inventory in order to ensure products are available when needed to sell. [EXAMPLES: auto parts store, furniture store]
3. Have the students create a bulletin board explaining the various inventory systems.

Assessment

1. Have the students complete the Section 19.2 Assessment.
2. Assign the Chapter Assessment.
3. Administer the test for Chapter 19 from the Reproducible Tests in the *Teacher Resource Binder*.

CLOSE

Have your students react to this statement: "The ability to maintain ideal inventory levels is only a good guess."

SECTION 19.1 ASSESSMENT
ANSWERS

CHECK YOUR UNDERSTANDING

1. Calculating gross earnings, calculating payroll deductions, preparing payroll records, preparing paychecks, recording payroll information in accounting records, and reporting payroll information to the government.
2. Salary, hourly wage, and salary plus commission.
3. Required deductions include federal income tax, FICA taxes, and state and local income tax (depending on where you work or live). Voluntary deductions include health and/or life insurance, union dues, charitable contributions, retirement plans such as 401(k) plans, and credit union deposits.
4. Salaries Expense, Liabilities, and Cash in Bank.

THINK CRITICALLY

5. Answers will vary but may include: Possible advantages—Employee may work extra hours to complete task, but the employer doesn't have to pay him or her more money for the extra time. Paying all employees a salary eases the process of calculating total gross earnings. Possible disadvantages—Even if the business is in a slow period, and you don't have enough work to keep an employee busy during the entire work week, you still have to pay him or her a

full salary. Over the long term, employees who receive a salary may earn more money than those who are paid an hourly wage.

USING MATH SKILLS

6. Shari: $6.75 \times 40 = \$270$ regular pay
   $$\$6.75 \times 1.5 \times 4 = \$40.50 \text{ overtime pay}$$
   $$\$270 + \$40.50 = \$310.50 \text{ gross earnings}$$

   Rolf: $\$7.35 \times 40 = \$294$ gross earnings

   Litisha: $185 weekly salary
   $$\$1,150 \times 4\% = \$46 \text{ commission}$$
   $$\$185 + \$46 = \$231 \text{ gross earnings}$$

   Shari earned the most money this week.

SOLVING MONEY PROBLEMS

7. Answers may vary but may include: Although overtime is expensive, it might be less expensive than hiring more employees and paying additional FICA, federal and state unemployment taxes, and possibly other employee benefits.

SECTION 19.2 ASSESSMENT
ANSWERS

CHECK YOUR UNDERSTANDING

1. The perpetual inventory system keeps a constant, up-to-date record of merchandise on hand. Every time a sale is made, the item is taken out of inventory. Computers and point-of-sale terminals have made this system easy. In a periodic inventory system, inventory records are updated only after someone makes a physical count of the merchandise on hand.
2. Specific identification method; first-in, first-out method (FIFO); and last-in, first-out method (LIFO).
3. A high inventory turnover rate is better because it means that your business has money tied up in inventory for shorter periods of time. As a result, the financing, storage, and insurance costs for the business are reduced.

THINK CRITICALLY

4. Even if a business uses a perpetual inventory system, it should conduct a physical inventory at least once a year to verify the accuracy of inventory records. Errors can be made entering inventory data when you purchase merchandise. Errors can also be made at point-of-sale terminals when you sell merchandise. Items can be lost, stolen, or identified incorrectly. A physical inventory ensures that accounting records are accurate and agree with what your business actually has in stock.

USING COMMUNICATION SKILLS

5. Answers will vary, but students may identify the following causes: stocking the wrong auto parts or slower sales for this year than last year. Suggestions might include: Analyze the current inventory based on last year's inventory and change purchasing practices; do additional advertising to increase sales.

SOLVING MONEY PROBLEMS

6. Because it's a small gallery and she can easily identify each item, Aurora should use a perpetual inventory system. She should use the specific identification costing method. She can identify the cost per item because she has so few items to sell.

CHAPTER 19 ASSESSMENT
ANSWERS

■ **Understanding and Using Vocabulary**
Answers will vary.

■ **Review Key Concepts**
1. Employees who receive an hourly wage are paid a specific amount of money per hour. Employers use time cards or a time sheet to keep track of when these employees begin and end work each day. At the end of each period, the employer checks the information on time cards or time sheets for accuracy. To calculate gross earnings you

would multiply the number of regular hours worked by the hourly rate. If the employee worked overtime, you would also multiply the overtime rate by the number of overtime hours. Then you would add the amount to be paid for regular hours worked to the amount to be paid for overtime hours worked.
2. FICA taxes are Social Security and Medicare taxes.
3. These deductions are owed to the appropriate government agency or other organization on behalf of the employees. It is money earned by employees and owed by the company. It does not belong to the employer.
4. An inventory control system tracks the quantity and cost of merchandise purchased, merchandise in stock, and merchandise sold to customers. Properly tracking the flow of merchandise provides the up-to-date information needed to make appropriate management decisions about purchases and sales.
5. In the specific identification method, the exact cost of each item is determined and assigned to that item. The actual cost of each item is obtained from the invoice. This is the most accurate costing method. It is commonly used by businesses that sell a small number of items at high prices. The first-in, first-out method (FIFO) assumes that the first items purchased (first in) are the first items sold (first out). It also assumes that the items the business purchased most recently are the ones on hand at the end of the period. The inventory cost is determined by the cost of ending inventory, or the cost of the last items purchased. The last-in, first-out method (LIFO) assumes that the last items purchased are the first items sold. It also assumes that the items purchased first are still on hand at the end of the accounting period. The earliest costs are used to assign a cost to the inventory.

■ Apply Key Concepts
1. Answers will vary. Students may point out the possibility of not paying required and voluntary deductions accurately or on time and making inappropriate financial decisions for the business based on inaccurate payroll information.
2. Answers will vary. Students may say that it is unacceptable because the business and employees could get into trouble with the government. Also, the employer and the employees would not be paying their fair share of taxes.
3. Answers will vary. One possible answer is that the employee's health insurance or life insurance would be canceled because the employer did not pay the premium on time.
4. Answers will vary but should show that the students understand the consequences of a business having excess inventory or having an inventory that is too low.
5. Businesses that are still using a manual system may find the perpetual inventory system too time-consuming. This is especially true of businesses that buy and sell many different pieces of merchandise each day.

❓ Problem Solving Today
Memos and payroll systems will vary. However, students should show that they understand that payroll is a system and involves many steps or tasks.

■ Real-World Application
Questions will vary. Students should list five questions such as: Will the business need to purchase a new computer? What other equipment will be necessary? Can a handheld input device (or bar code scanner) be used with the system? Will the system recognize different sizes or colors of items? Can the system be expanded or upgraded later? Is the system easy to use? Can the system create inventory reports?

FINANCE Online

Possible Web sites include:
- www.mecsw.com
- www.register5.com
- www.rwsinfo.com

Answers will vary.

Note to teacher: Web site addresses may change.

READING STRATEGIES
ANSWERS

Section 19.1
CONNECT (p. 605): Answers will vary, but most likely will include money deducted to pay for FICA, state, and federal income taxes.

RESPOND (p. 617): Answers will vary. Some strategies might include: scheduling shifts so that several employees are on hand to cover lunch rushes, but only one employee is on hand to cover slow times; or setting the deli's hours to take advantage of peak times and closing the deli during slow times.

Section 19.2
PREDICT (p. 620) It is important to carry enough inventory to satisfy customer needs. If items are routinely out of stock, customers will shop elsewhere. It is also important not to have too much inventory in stock, because it ties up cash flow and costs money to store.

QUESTION (p. 627): Low inventory turnover rates can indicate that you are ordering too much of a particular item, or that sales are low for that accounting period. A high rate can tell you that your sales are doing well, or that your ordering practices are on target.

STANDARD & POOR'S
CASE STUDY
ANSWERS

1. Federal income tax, FICA taxes, and state and local income taxes.
2. A salary is a fixed amount of money paid to an employee for each pay period, regardless of the number of hours worked. Many of her employees work overtime, yet she still only pays them their fixed salary.
3. Alison will have to deal with language and cultural differences, and changes in time zones. She must learn the government regulations and legal systems of the countries she does business in. She will also need to establish prices in a foreign currency. Alison may have to hire local experts to support sales and assist customers, and she may lose the day-to-day control over business relationships abroad.

UNIT 5 — Planning Guide

INTRODUCTION TO BUSINESS FINANCE

Chapter 16—
Introduction to Financial Management for Business

Chapter 17—
Sources of Funding

Chapter 18—
Financial Accounting

Chapter 19—
Managing Payroll and Inventory

OVERVIEW

In previous chapters students learned about planning for personal finances. In this and the last unit, students will be reading about business finances. Unit 5 focuses on how businesses manage their finances. Chapter 16 introduces the concept of a business plan and the financial management of a business. Chapter 17 defines different business costs and identifies different sources of funding. In Chapter 18, students will learn about accounting, including analyzing business transactions and describing the accounting cycle. Chapter 19 discusses a business's two greatest expenses—payroll and inventory.

INTRODUCTION

Write this definition for *entrepreneur* on the board: *one who organizes, manages, and assumes the risks of a business or enterprise* (from the Old French *entreprendre* to undertake). Then ask if any of your students have ever thought about opening their own business one day. What kind of business would it be? Where would they get the money to start it? How would they know how much money would be needed? Allow students time to write the answers to these questions, and encourage them to use their imaginations. Then explain that these are some of the questions addressed in a business plan, and that a business plan is the first step in managing the finances of a business.

Get a Financial Life!

CASE STUDY 5

Teaching Guide

Step A — THE PROCESS

Make sure students have access to all necessary materials.

1. Remind students that the Careers in Finance feature in Chapter 18 describes a bookkeeper. Students can use the information in this feature to help them write their newspaper ad.
2. Recordkeeping systems will vary. Accounting periods could be one month, one quarter, or one year. Accounts for Party Town should include those listed in Chapter 18. However, while students have been introduced to inventories, they won't necessarily know which accounts to use. Accept all reasonably named accounts, including Inventories or Purchases. Also, students are not introduced to the partnership type of business ownership until Unit 6 but should recognize that each partner should have a capital account.
3. Accept all reasonable recommendations for a method of pay.
4. Students should recommend either a perpetual or a periodic inventory system. While a perpetual inventory system might be convenient, it could also be too expensive for a new, small retail business. Also, because the business is new and small, tracking inventory with a periodic, physical count should be enough.
5. Resources will vary. Give students the names of the Additional Resources listed in all four chapter planning guides of this unit.

Step B — CREATE YOUR PORTFOLIO

Evaluate students' portfolios based on whether or not all four steps of the process have been completed, the information seems reasonably well researched, and the contents are neat and in order.

Step C — APPLYING TECHNOLOGY

Evaluate students' research and paper based on the following criteria:

- Research should be thorough but need not be exhaustive
- If vendors for a particular technology are not readily available, accept material from catalogs or the Internet.
- Visual aids should be attractive and informative.
- Papers should cite references found through research.

UNIT CLOSURE

Have students write a one-page paper defending why they would or would not like to start and run their own business. Make sure they address the responsibilities of writing a business plan, finding funds, understanding the accounting system, hiring employees, and maintaining inventories.

EVALUATION

Administer the Unit 5 test from the **Exam*View*** Pro Test Generator CD-ROM.

Chapter 20 Planning Guide

Types of Business Ownership

Teacher Manual

SECT.	OBJECTIVES	NATIONAL STANDARDS FOR BUSINESS EDUCATION	FEATURES	RESOURCES
20.1	**After completing this lesson, students will have learned:** How to identify the advantages and disadvantages of a sole proprietorship How to explain the differences between general and limited partners How to identify the advantages and disadvantages of a partnership	**Personal Finance** I. Personal Decision Making II. Earning a Living VI. Banking	**Standard & Poor's—** Q & A, p. 638 **What's Your Financial ID?—**What Kind of Business Would You Start? p. 640 **Careers in Finance—** General Contractor, p. 642 **Common Cents—**Shop by Phone, p. 643 **Savvy Saver—**What to Ask Your Bank When Opening a Checking Account, p. 644 **Academic Connection—** Marketing, p. 646 **Standard & Poor's—** Case Study, p. 648	**Check Your Understanding,** p. 650 **Think Critically,** p. 650 **Using Communication Skills,** p. 650 **Solving Money Problems,** p. 650 **Student Activity Workbook**
20.2	**After completing this lesson, students will have learned:** How to summarize the process of forming a corporation How to describe two types of corporations How to discuss the advantages and disadvantages of a corporation	**Economics** VII. The Role of Government VIII. International Economic Concepts **Personal Finance** I. Personal Decision Making II. Earning a Living IV. Saving and Investing	**International Finance—** Iceland, p. 656 **Your Financial Portfolio—** Setting Up a Partnership, p. 659	**Check Your Understanding,** p. 661 **Think Critically,** p. 661 **Using Math Skills,** p. 661 **Solving Money Problems,** p. 661 **Student Activity Workbook**

Unit 6 *Organization and Financial Planning*

SCANS Correlation Chart

FOUNDATION SKILLS

Basic Skills	Reading	Writing	Math	Listening	Speaking
Thinking Skills	Creative Thinking	Decision Making	Problem Solving	Seeing Things in the Mind's Eye	Knowing How to Learn	Reasoning
Personal Qualities	Responsibility	Self-Esteem	Sociability	Self-Management	Integrity/Honesty

WORKPLACE COMPETENCIES

Resources	Allocating Time	Allocating Money	Allocating Material and Facility Resources	Allocating Human Resources
Information	Acquiring and Evaluating Information	Organizing and Maintaining Information	Interpreting and Communicating Information	Using Computers to Process Information
Interpersonal Skills	Participating as a Member of a Team	Teaching Others	Serving Clients/ Customers	Exercising Leadership	Negotiating to Arrive at a Decision	Working with Cultural Diversity
Systems	Understanding Systems	Monitoring and Correcting Performance	Improving and Designing Systems
Technology	Selecting Technology	Applying Technology to Task	Maintaining and Troubleshooting Technology

■ INTERNET EXTENSION

Activity: Have students use the Internet to research businesses for sale over the Internet. Students should find out what good or service the business offers, the business's form of ownership, and the cost of the business.

Keywords: businesses for sale; business opportunities

■ ENRICHMENT/APPLICATION ACTIVITY

Cooperative Activity: Remind students about the business that the class chose to develop for the Enrichment/Application Activity in Chapter 19. Divide the class into three groups and have each group research one of the following forms of ownership: corporation, partnership, and cooperative. Then have the three groups present their findings and have the class vote on which form of ownership is best for their business.

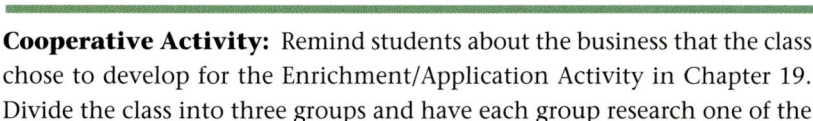

Chapter 20 *Types of Business Ownership*

■ TOPIC SPOTLIGHT

Technology: Discuss the impact technology has on a sole proprietorship. Have students consider the cost of equipment versus the need a sole proprietor has for help on the job.

Ethics: Ask students whether or not trust is an important element in a successful partnership. Have them explain why or why not.

Marketing: Explain that assistance with advertising is one of the advantages of owning a franchise. Have students brainstorm other ways a franchise is assisted with marketing.

additional resources

The Small Business Start-Up Guide, 3rd Edition by Robert Sullivan (© 1996, 2000 Information International). This guide not only offers practical advice on starting a small business but also extensive information about the different forms of business ownership.

The Small Business Administration (**www.sba.gov**) has several publications on business ownership. Some of the publications listed under the Management and Planning Series are:

- *Planning and Goal Setting for Small Business* (MP-6)
- *Checklist for Going into Business* (MP-12)
- *Developing a Strategic Business Plan* (MP-21)

Note to Teacher: Web site addresses may change.

CHAPTER 20 Lesson Plans

SECTION 20.1

FOCUS

Motivation

Ask your students if they have worked on a school project as a team or in a group. If so, have them explain the advantages and disadvantages of doing so. Then explain to the students that a sole proprietorship is like working on a project alone and a partnership is like working on a team.

Prereading

1. Have your students skim the section, looking at pictures, reading captions, and noting headings.
2. Have "What You'll Learn" listed on page 639 read aloud.
3. Write the Key Terms on the board. Ask the students to define them using their own words. Write their definitions on the board.
4. Ask the students to state the purpose of studying this chapter.

TEACH

Guided Practice

1. Have students read aloud the Standard & Poor's Q&A on page 638.
2. Read the section with your students.

Independent Practice

1. Have your students research current trends in the workforce and find out in which areas the employment growth is predicted to be the largest. Ask the students to relate their findings to the different forms of business ownership.
2. Have the students research the local requirements for starting a sole proprietorship in the community. Have them find out what kinds of business licenses are required.

Careers in Finance

General Contractor

1. Ask your students to research a school that offers an associate degree in building construction. Have them find out the cost of the program and the courses they would take.
2. Have the students explain why time management is an important skill for general contractors to possess.
3. Ask the students to find out the requirements for obtaining a general contractor's license.

Common Cents

Shop by Phone

Have the students use the "shop by phone" idea when making their next purchase of a product. Ask them to share their experiences with the class.

$avvy Saver

What to Ask Your Bank When Opening a Checking Account

1. Have your students contact different banks in the community to find out the answers to the questions in this activity.
2. Ask the students to discuss when a person should open a checking account.

ASSESS

Reteaching

1. Review the original definitions of the Key Terms provided by the students at the beginning of this section. Ask the students to modify or enhance them as necessary.
2. To reteach the concept of unlimited liability, invite someone from a credit-counseling agency to talk to the students about how debts incurred by their businesses will affect future borrowing ability and credit ratings.

Enrichment

1. Have your students research a business in the United States that started as a sole proprietorship. The students should find out when it began, problems encountered along the way, a history of the business, and its current status. Ask them to create a presentation to share with the class.
2. Have the students brainstorm a list of Web sites that potential small business owners can use to obtain information about getting started in a business.

Assessment

1. Have the students complete the Section 20.1 Assessment.
2. Assign an activity from the *Student Activity Workbook*.

CLOSE

Have the students explain why it is important to know the financial position of each partner in a business.

SECTION 20.2

FOCUS

Motivation

Have your students brainstorm the characteristics of a corporation. Leave their list on the board while you study this section and revise and update as necessary.

Prereading

1. Have the students skim the section, looking at pictures, reading captions, and noting headings.
2. Have "What You'll Learn" listed on page 651 read aloud.
3. Write the key terms on the board. Ask students to guess at the meaning of each term, but do not give the correct meaning. Leave the list on the board so that as students work through the section, they can see how close they were to the correct answer.
4. Ask the students to state the purpose of studying this chapter.

TEACH

Guided Practice

1. Read the section with your students.
2. Assign an activity from the *Student Activity Workbook*.

Independent Practice

1. Have the students select a large corporation and write a biography on the CEO.
2. Ask your students to select a franchised business they might like to own and research how much it will cost and the process needed to get started.
3. Have the students interview a business owner who has formed a corporation and find out how much it costs to do so.

INTERNATIONAL FINANCE
Iceland

1. Have the students research the products that the United States exports to and imports from Iceland.
2. Tourism in Iceland is becoming an important part of the economy. Have the students plan a trip to Iceland and include the cost as well as the sites they would like to visit.

ASSESS

Reteaching

1. Review the original definitions of the Key Terms provided by the students at the beginning of this section. Ask the students to modify or enhance them as necessary.
2. Remind the students that decisions often take a long time to make in a large corporation. Have the students brainstorm the problems that might occur when decisions cannot be made quickly.

Enrichment

1. Invite a lawyer to your class to discuss the paperwork and other documents that have to be prepared when starting a corporation.
2. Have the students create a bulletin board showing the advantages and disadvantages of the various forms of business ownership.

Assessment

1. Have the students complete the Section 20.2 Assessment.
2. Assign the Chapter Assessment.
3. Administer the test for Chapter 20 from the Reproducible Tests in the *Teacher Resource Binder*.

CLOSE

Have your students write a paragraph explaining why the corporation is a driving force in the American economy.

SECTION 20.1 ASSESSMENT
ANSWERS

CHECK YOUR UNDERSTANDING

1. You don't have to convince partners that your decisions are sound. You choose what merchandise to sell, what prices to charge, and what hours you'll work.
2. General partners take an active role in the operation of the business. They also have unlimited liability for the losses or debts of the partnership. A limited partner does not take an active role in running the business, and the partner's liability is limited to the amount of his or her investment.
3. The disadvantages include: unlimited liability for the general partners, possible disagreements, the requirement to share profits, and limited life of the partnership.

THINK CRITICALLY

4. Answers will vary. Students may state that the most important element is the description of the duties, rights, and responsibilities of each partner. This description is especially important to prevent one person from taking more control than he or she should have. Other students may point to procedures for sharing profits and losses as the most important component of the agreement because this element affects the financial situation of the co-owners.

USING COMMUNICATION SKILLS

5. Answers will vary. In looking for ways to resolve the conflict, students might consider such issues as the potential market for new items, the cost of the items, and the space available in the kiosk.

SOLVING MONEY PROBLEMS

6. Answers will vary, but students should demonstrate an understanding of the advantages and disadvantages of sole proprietorships and partnerships.

SECTION 20.2 ASSESSMENT
ANSWERS

CHECK YOUR UNDERSTANDING

1. The articles of incorporation is the application you file with the state in order to operate as a corporation. It includes your corporate name and the type of business in which the corporation will be involved. A corporate charter is the license to operate the business. It states the purpose of your business and spells out the laws and guidelines under which your business will operate. It also officially allows you to do business under your corporate name. The corporate bylaws are the rules by which your corporation will operate. Items in the bylaws include how you'll elect directors and when stockholders will meet.
2. A closely held corporation is one whose shares are owned by a small group of people and are not traded openly in stock markets. A publicly held corporation is one that sells its shares openly in stock markets, where anyone can buy them.

3. Advantages: easy to raise capital, limited liability, continued life if an owner dies or leaves, separation of ownership and management. Disadvantages: complicated and expensive to establish, slow decision making, and a tax structure in which profits are taxed twice—once as corporate profits and a second time as stockholder dividends.

THINK CRITICALLY

4. Answers will vary. Students may state that the corporation would have a greater amount of money available for growth and other purposes. However, an increase in the number of stockholders might also increase the corporation's administrative costs.

USING MATH SKILLS

5. About 33,898 shares. [ANSWER: $1,000,000 ÷ $29.50 = 33,898.3]

SOLVING MONEY PROBLEMS

6. The sole proprietorship poses the greater financial risk to Beverly because if the business fails, she could lose not only the savings she invested but also any assets she pledged as collateral in order to obtain credit. If the corporation fails, her loss will be limited to her $33,000 investment.

CHAPTER 20 ASSESSMENT
ANSWERS

■ **Understanding and Using Vocabulary**
Answers will vary.

■ **Review Key Concepts**
1. Advantages: A sole proprietorship is easy to set up. The owner has total control and keeps all the profits. There are fewer government regulations to follow, and the profits are taxed only once, as part of the owner's personal taxable income. Disadvantages: Because there's only one owner, capital is limited to the personal finances of the owner and any loans she or he has taken out. The owner is personally responsible for the debts of the business. The sole proprietorship has limited human resources, and when the owner leaves or dies, the business ceases to exist.
2. More than half of all businesses fail within five years of being established.
3. Because a partnership has more than one owner, the business benefits from a greater variety of skills, knowledge, and experience as well as more human resources. The partners can share the responsibility of decision making. In addition, several individuals can usually bring more money to the business venture than one person acting alone with his or her personal assets.
4. A closely held, or private, corporation is one whose shares are owned by a relatively small group of people and are not traded openly in stock markets. A publicly held, or public, corporation is one that sells its shares openly in stock markets so that individuals can buy them.
5. The board oversees the running of the business.

■ **Apply Key Concepts**
1. Answers will vary.
2. Answers will vary. Students may suggest such factors as a lack of knowledge and skill; not enough capital to start up, operate, or expand; or poor decision making by the owner or owners.
3. Answers will vary. Students should recognize the advantages of taking on a partner (more people, ideas, money, skills) versus the additional problems (disagreements, sharing of profits).
4. Answers will vary but should reflect an understanding of the differences between closely held and publicly held corporations.
5. Answers will vary. Some of the problems might be poor hiring decisions; weak overall management; bad business decisions.

❓ Problem Solving Today
Answers will vary. Steps may include:
(1) Find partners with appropriate skills.
(2) Draw up a partnership agreement.

(3) Choose a name for the business.
(4) Determine the amount of initial investment for each partner.
(5) Determine duties and responsibilities of each partner.
(6) Develop procedures for sharing profits and losses.
(7) Determine how assets will be divided if the partnership is dissolved.

The skills, talents, and experience desired in partners will vary. Some examples might include carpentry, door hanging, painting, roofing, tiling, wallpapering, purchasing, marketing, and recordkeeping.

■ **Real-World Application**
Answers will vary.

FINANCE Online

Students might research specific corporations, such as Subway, Burger King, and so on, to locate specific franchise information.

Two sites that will provide students with general information about franchising are:
www.aafd.org/
www.ftc.gov/bcp/franchise/
netfran.htm

Answers will vary.

Note to teacher: Web site addresses may change.

READING STRATEGIES
ANSWERS

Section 20.1
PREDICT (p. 640): Advantages include: it is easy to set-up, the owner has total control over decisions and gets to keep all of the profits. The disadvantages include limited capital, unlimited liability, and limited human resources.

CONNECT (p. 649): Answers will vary. For example, some students might have math and accounting skills to complement others with creative ideas and/or the charisma to boost sales.

Section 20.2
RESPOND (p. 655): Ownership could contribute to the financial backing without being experts on car maintenance, retail sales, or marketing. Management could then be people who are experts in these areas, regardless of their ability to invest money in the company.

QUESTION (p. 657): A franchise might benefit from the organizational structure, marketing, and brand name appeal of the parent corporation. The increased profits might then make the franchise fee worth the investment.

STANDARD & POOR'S

CASE STUDY
ANSWERS

1. Ads that sound too good to be true usually are. Although most companies are honest and reputable businesses, there are some that may lead you to invest money in a company that does not even exist. You end up losing your investment. High-earning jobs promised in some ads often end up being low paying and tedious.
2. Because Julia will be working on her own, she should start her business as a sole proprietorship. It is easy for her to set up and she can keep all the profits.
3. Julia could start by contacting the publishing company she worked for previously and ask if they have any work she could do. She could also advertise in her local newspaper.

Chapter 21 Planning Guide

Developing a Financial Plan

SECT.	OBJECTIVES	NATIONAL STANDARDS FOR BUSINESS EDUCATION	FEATURES	RESOURCES
21.1	After completing this lesson, students will have learned: How to identify start-up capital How to estimate operating capital How to analyze projected financial statements How to explain the need for reserve capital	**Economics** II. Economic Systems VI. Productivity **Personal Finance** VI. Banking VIII. Protecting Against Risk	**Standard & Poor's—** Q & A, p. 664 **What's Your Financial ID?—**Are You a Persuader? p. 666 **Common Cents—**Save, Don't Charge, p. 668 **International Finance—** Qatar, p. 679 **Standard & Poor's—** Case Study, p. 680	**Check Your Understanding,** p. 681 **Think Critically,** p. 681 **Using Communication Skills,** p. 681 **Solving Money Problems,** p. 681 **Student Activity Workbook**
21.2	After completing this lesson, students will have learned: How to prepare a financial plan How to analyze a financial plan	**Economics** VIII. International Economic Concepts **Personal Finance** II. Earning a Living VII. Using Credit	**Academic Connection—**Math, p. 684 **Savvy Saver—**Shopping for a Used Car, p. 691 **Careers in Finance—** Controller, p. 691 **Your Financial Portfolio—**Start with a Plan, p. 692	**Check Your Understanding,** p. 693 **Think Critically,** p. 693 **Using Math Skills,** p. 693 **Solving Money Problems,** p. 693 **Student Activity Workbook**

Teacher Manual

Unit 6 *Organization and Financial Planning*

SCANS Correlation Chart

FOUNDATION SKILLS

Basic Skills	Reading	Writing	Math	Listening	Speaking
Thinking Skills	Creative Thinking	Decision Making	Problem Solving	Seeing Things in the Mind's Eye	Knowing How to Learn	Reasoning
Personal Qualities	Responsibility	Self-Esteem	Sociability	Self-Management	Integrity/Honesty

WORKPLACE COMPETENCIES

Resources	Allocating Time	Allocating Money	Allocating Material and Facility Resources	Allocating Human Resources
Information	Acquiring and Evaluating Information	Organizing and Maintaining Information	Interpreting and Communicating Information	Using Computers to Process Information
Interpersonal Skills	Participating as a Member of a Team	Teaching Others	Serving Clients/ Customers	Exercising Leadership	Negotiating to Arrive at a Decision	Working with Cultural Diversity
Systems	Understanding Systems	Monitoring and Correcting Performance	Improving and Designing Systems
Technology	Selecting Technology	Applying Technology to Task	Maintaining and Troubleshooting Technology

■ INTERNET EXTENSION

Activity: Have students use the Internet to research financial plans for business start-ups.

Keywords: financial plan and start-ups

■ ENRICHMENT/APPLICATION ACTIVITY

Cooperative Activity: Using the business developed in the last two Enrichment/Application activities, make a list of the start-up capital on the board. Assign each student one item from the list to research. Have students report their findings and, as a class, develop a statement of required start-up capital.

Chapter 21 *Developing a Financial Plan*   TM271

■ TOPIC SPOTLIGHT

$ Money: Have students research the prices of different assets commonly needed by businesses. Where do students think they can get the best buys?

⚡ Technology: Have students research the latest trends in business technology. Allow them to share their findings with the class and discuss whether or not new businesses necessarily need the newest or best.

➲ Marketing: Ask volunteers to describe a new business they would like to start, and ask what marketing strategies they would use to promote their new businesses.

additional resources

Bplans.com is a Web site that offers information and advice on starting a business and writing business plans. The Web site at **www.bplans.com** offers sample business plans, articles, and a starting costs calculator.

The Small Business Administration (**www.sba.gov**) has several publications on financial and business plans, which include:

- *Financial Management for Growing Businesses* (EB-7)

- *Understanding Cash Flow* (FM-4)
- *Business Plan for Small Manufacturers* (MP-4)
- *Business Plan for Retailers* (MP-9)
- *Business Plan for Small Service Firms* (MP-11)

Note to Teacher: Web site addresses may change.

TM272 Unit 6 *Organization and Financial Planning*

CHAPTER 21 Lesson Plans

SECTION 21.1

FOCUS

Motivation
Tell your students that a financial plan is like a financial picture of a business. Ask them to imagine a business they would like to start and then draw a financial picture of that business.

Prereading
1. Have the students skim the section, looking at pictures, reading captions, and noting headings.
2. Have "What You'll Learn" listed on page 665 read aloud.
3. Write the Key Terms on the board. Ask the students to define them using their own words. Write their definitions on the board.
4. Ask the students to state the purpose of studying this chapter.

TEACH

Guided Practice
1. Have students read aloud the Standard & Poor's Q&A on page 664.
2. Read the section with your students.

Independent Practice
1. Have the students conduct surveys of local small businessmen and women. Have the students ask how they were able to identify the required start-up capital that was needed. Ask the students to share their findings with the class.

Common Cents

Save, Don't Charge
1. Have the students discuss strategies they use when saving for something they want.
2. As a class, create a list of reasons not to use a credit card to make a purchase.

INTERNATIONAL FINANCE
Qatar
1. Have your students research Qatar's major trading partners and the products, other than oil, that Qatar imports and exports.
2. Ask the students to research the history of Qatar and its government.
3. The temperature in Qatar averages 104 degrees in the summer and 50–68 degrees in winter. Have the students discuss the impact of the weather on Qatar's economy.

ASSESS

Reteaching
1. Have your students review the Key Terms and their definitions that you wrote on the board. Clarify any that the students are still unsure about.
2. To help the students understand why a financial plan is critical to a new business, tell them that a financial plan has three roles. Write these roles on the board: *Determining Required Capital*; *Sources of Funding Available*; and *How to Record, Summarize and Report Finances*. Then have the students create a list of words and phrases that represent each of the three roles.

Enrichment
1. Ask each student to select a local business and brainstorm a list of emergencies and business opportunities that might create a need for reserve capital.

Assessment
1. Have the students complete the Section 21.1 Assessment.
2. Assign an activity from the *Student Activity Workbook*.

CLOSE

Have your students complete this statement: "A good financial plan will not guarantee a successful business, but a... ." [HINT: "poorly devised financial plan will usually result in a failed business."]

SECTION 21.2

FOCUS

Motivation

Tell your students that in this section they will be serving as financial consultants to Molly Singer. Explain to the class that Molly is about to open her own business called Cricket Lane Flowers and has hired them to help with her financial plan. Set the stage by reading the section about Molly's plan.

Prereading

1. Have the students skim the section, looking at pictures, reading captions, and noting headings.
2. Have "What You'll Learn" listed on page 682 read aloud.
3. Write the Key Term on the board. Ask the students to write a definition for the term.
4. Ask your students to state the purpose of studying this chapter.

TEACH

Guided Practice

1. Read the section with your students.
2. Assign an activity from the *Student Activity Workbook*.

Independent Practice

1. As a class, discuss the short-term and long-term goals Molly has set for her business. Help Molly define each goal thoroughly.

2. Divide the class into groups of three or four. Ask each group to read and analyze Molly's projected financial statements in **Figures 21.7** through **21.12**. Have the groups explain in their own words how Molly expects her business to grow and develop over the next few years.

$AVVY SAVER

Shopping for a Used Car

1. Have the students add at least two tips to this list.
2. Ask the students to compile a list of Internet Web sites that are available for someone who wants to purchase a used car.
3. As a class, brainstorm a list of possible problems a used car might have and how they could be detected.

Careers in Finance

Controller

1. Ask your students to discuss the types of technology a controller would need to use in his or her job.
2. Have the students research the Web site for the AICPA (American Institute of Certified Public Accountants at **www.aicpa.org**) to find out what resources and conferences are available to controllers.

ASSESS

Reteaching

1. Review the Key Term and the students' definitions for that term. Clarify as necessary.

Enrichment

1. Invite an accountant or other financial advisor to your class and have the students explain Molly's projected financial plan to him or her. Then ask the professional for his or her thoughts about Molly's plan.

2. Have the students create a list of emergencies and business opportunities that could impact Cricket Lane Flowers.

Assessment

1. Have the students complete the Section 21.2 Assessment.
2. Assign the Chapter Assessment.
3. Administer the test for Chapter 21 from the Reproducible Tests in the *Teacher Resource Binder*.

CLOSE

Have your students write a letter to Molly, thanking her for hiring them as financial consultants and wishing her success in the future.

SECTION 21.1 ASSESSMENT
ANSWERS

CHECK YOUR UNDERSTANDING

1. The first category of start-up capital is the capital required to purchase the assets needed to start a business (such as equipment, display racks, and inventory). The second category is start-up costs, which include the costs or fees involved in starting a business (such as permits, legal and accounting fees, and security deposits).
2. You can estimate operating capital through financial forecasting, which involves preparing projected income statements, balance sheets, and statements of cash flows.
3. You can analyze all the available information regarding revenue and expenses for your type of business. Some of this information can be obtained from trade associations, business organizations, and government agencies such as the Small Business Administration and the Bureau of the Census.
4. Reserve capital is necessary to deal with emergencies and unexpected expenses, to take advantage of business opportunities, and for the expansion and growth of a business.

THINK CRITICALLY

5. Answers will vary but should reflect the idea that a financial plan allows a potential business owner to determine the amount of capital that will be needed to start and operate the business. Without a sound financial plan and adequate funding, a business is unlikely to succeed.

USING COMMUNICATION SKILLS

6. Answers will vary. Students should show that they understand the importance of creating a financial plan. Students should explain that making projections of revenue, expenses, future worth, and cash flows is important because it will help indicate the potential success of the business to Theo and Cole and to any potential lenders.

SOLVING MONEY PROBLEMS

7. Assets and start-up costs for Jana's business will vary. Some examples of assets might include office furniture and supplies, a computer system, a telephone and fax machine, a photocopier, basketballs, and awards or trophies. Some examples of start-up costs might include insurance, gym rental deposits, professional association fees, business permits, and advertising.

SECTION 21.2 ASSESSMENT
ANSWERS

CHECK YOUR UNDERSTANDING

1. Statement of Required Start-Up Capital, Projected 12-Month Income Statement, Projected 3-Year Income Statement, Projected 12-Month Statement of Cash Flows, Projected 3-Year Statement of Cash Flows, and Projected 3-Year Balance Sheet.
2. During the ninth month of business.
3. Molly estimated her cash receipts (cash sales to customers and accounts receivable) and her cash payments (purchase of merchandise, operating expenses, interest expense, taxes, and accounts payable) for her first 12 months in business. Her total

estimated cash payments were greater than her total estimated cash receipts, resulting in a negative cash flow.

THINK CRITICALLY

4. Answers will vary. Sample answer: She has taken several business courses and attended seminars on running a small business. She has researched locations and potential markets for a shop and decided on a store that will fit her needs. She has written a strategic plan and a marketing plan. She has saved money and asked her family to help. She has established a good credit history to ensure that she will find other sources of funding. She has consulted with an attorney and an accountant for general guidance.

USING MATH SKILLS

5. Year 1: $199,900
   Year 2: $199,900 × 35% = $69,965
   $199,900 + $69,965 = $269,865
   Year 3: $269,865 × 35% = $94,452.75
   $269,865 + $94,452.75 = $364,317.75

   Answers will vary regarding the impact on projected expenses of a 35 percent increase in sales. Some possible answers: Molly might need to hire more employees or extend store hours, thus increasing her spending on wages or utilities. She would probably spend more money on supplies.

SOLVING MONEY PROBLEMS

6. Answers will vary. Students may suggest that Molly postpone the purchase of office furniture and a photocopier until she can afford them. She might also consider using her own vehicle to deliver orders and cut back on the volume of merchandise that she wants to purchase.

CHAPTER 21 ASSESSMENT
ANSWERS

■ **Understanding and Using Vocabulary**
Answers will vary.

■ **Review Key Concepts**
1. The three aspects of a good financial plan are:
   (1) identifying the purchases you'll need to make and the other costs involved in the establishment or continued operation of a business;
   (2) addressing the various sources of funding you'll use to acquire the needed items and pay other costs; and
   (3) outlining how you will record, summarize, and report your business's finances.
2. Start-up capital, operating capital, and reserve capital.
3. If money is not available to purchase needed merchandise or pay current bills, the business will not survive.
4. Fixed expenses are expenses that remain the same regardless of business activity. Variable expenses are expenses that may vary or that can be adjusted, depending on sales or other business situations.
5. A projected income statement estimates how the income of your business will change over the next few months or years. A projected balance sheet estimates the future worth of your business one year, three years, or five years from now.

APPLY KEY CONCEPTS
1. Yes. Molly created a Statement of Required Start-Up Capital to identify the assets and other costs needed to start and continue operating Cricket Lane Flowers. She also developed projected income statements, statements of cash flows, and a projected balance sheet. All of Molly's accounting procedures will be carried out on the computer. She has prepared a chart of accounts and will prepare a trial balance and financial statements at the end of every month during the first year of operation.
2. Molly will set aside $15,000. If she needs more capital, she might borrow additional money, increase sales, or reduce the advertising budget for her business.
3. Answers may vary but should reflect that the students have analyzed Molly's assets

and start-up costs on the Statement of Required Start-Up Capital (**Figure 21-7**).
4. Fixed expenses include rent, insurance, and interest. Variable expenses include any of the following: electricity, heat/AC, telephone, maintenance/repair, miscellaneous, wages, taxes, supplies, advertising.
5. Assets will be higher, and liabilities will be higher. Answers may vary but should reflect students' understanding of the balance sheet and other financial statements for the business.

Problem Solving Today
Answers will vary.

Real-World Application
Answers will vary but some examples may include:
- inflation with fewer people willing to purchase flowers, leading to decreased sales;
- a tight labor market with fewer qualified employees to work at Cricket Lane Flowers, so Molly will have to pay higher wages or work extra hours;
- worldwide drought with poor or limited selection of flowers, resulting in higher prices and decreased sales.

Finance Online
Possible Web sites include:
Trade associations:
www.ftd.com/350/corporate/affiliates.epl
www.rosesinc.org/

Online vendors:
www.flowersale.com/
www.officedepot.com/

Business organizations: Answers will vary.
Government agencies:
www.sba.gov
www.census.gov

Answers will vary.

Note to teacher: Web site addresses may change.

READING STRATEGIES
ANSWERS

Section 21.1
PREDICT (p. 668): An estimate that is too low can cause a company to run out of cash and go out of business.

RESPOND (p. 674): Answers will include: A new business has expensive start-up costs; a new business has to build a customer base; a new business may have to spend a lot of money on advertising; a new business may be less efficient because employees need to be trained.

Section 21.2
QUESTION (p. 684): Molly could set up her business as a partnership or corporation.

CONNECT (p. 690): Answers will vary but may include: savings, loans from relatives, business loans from banks or the Small Business Administration, home equity loans, and venture capital from investors.

STANDARD & POOR'S

CASE STUDY
ANSWERS

1. Working with a local supplier, he may be able to establish a credit line. If Angelo's truck is less than five years old, he may be able to borrow up to 80 percent of its value.
2. He will need to have enough money in savings to maintain his business while he is building his customer base. Also, Angelo is offering a 24-hour service, and it may be difficult to always be available. He may need to hire employees to provide consistent service.
3. Examples include repairs for his truck, the need for insurance or security bonding in order to obtain commercial clients, accidental damages that he may cause, and uncollectible customer accounts.

Chapter 22 Planning Guide

Pricing, Costing, and Growth

Teacher Manual

SECT.	OBJECTIVES	NATIONAL STANDARDS FOR BUSINESS EDUCATION	FEATURES	RESOURCES
22.1	After completing this lesson, students will have learned: How to calculate selling price How to identify variable and fixed costs How to determine effective pricing	**Economics** IV. Markets and Prices VI. Productivity **Personal Finance** II. Earning a Living	**Standard & Poor's**—Q & A, p. 696 **What's Your Financial ID?**—Creative Thinking, p. 698 **Careers in Finance**—Chief Financial Officer, p. 701 **Common Cents**—Wash 'n Wear, p. 702 **Standard & Poor's**—Case Study, p. 703 **International Finance**—India, p. 704 **Academic Connection**—Language Arts, p. 705 **Go Figure**—Break-Even Point, p. 707	**Check Your Understanding,** p. 709 **Think Critically,** p. 709 **Using Math Skills,** p. 709 **Solving Money Problems,** p. 709 **Student Activity Workbook**
22.2	After completing this lesson, students will have learned: How to describe common forms of business growth How to discuss profit planning How to calculate target sales How to calculate margin of safety	**Economics** III. Economic Institutions and Incentives VIII. International Economic Concepts **Personal Finance** I. Personal Decision Making II. Earning a Living	**Savvy Saver**—Book Bargains, p. 711 **Go Figure**—Target Profit, p. 713 **Your Financial Portfolio**—Business Expansion Is More Than Magic, p. 716	**Check Your Understanding,** p. 717 **Think Critically,** p. 717 **Using Communication Skills,** p. 717 **Solving Money Problems,** p. 717 **Student Activity Workbook**

Unit 6 *Organization and Financial Planning*

SCANS Correlation Chart

FOUNDATION SKILLS

Basic Skills	Reading	Writing	Math	Listening	Speaking
Thinking Skills	Creative Thinking	Decision Making	Problem Solving	Seeing Things in the Mind's Eye	Knowing How to Learn	Reasoning
Personal Qualities	Responsibility	Self-Esteem	Sociability	Self-Management	Integrity/Honesty

WORKPLACE COMPETENCIES

Resources	Allocating Time	Allocating Money	Allocating Material and Facility Resources	Allocating Human Resources
Information	Acquiring and Evaluating Information	Organizing and Maintaining Information	Interpreting and Communicating Information	Using Computers to Process Information
Interpersonal Skills	Participating as a Member of a Team	Teaching Others	Serving Clients/Customers	Exercising Leadership	Negotiating to Arrive at a Decision	Working with Cultural Diversity
Systems	Understanding Systems	Monitoring and Correcting Performance	Improving and Designing Systems
Technology	Selecting Technology	Applying Technology to Task	Maintaining and Troubleshooting Technology

■ INTERNET EXTENSION

Activity: Have students use the Internet to research articles and information on growing a business

Keywords: Inc. Magazine; BusinessWeek; Wall Street Journal

■ ENRICHMENT/APPLICATION ACTIVITY

Guest Speaker: Invite a store manager or a manufacturing company manager to speak to the class about pricing strategies used in his or her store or company.

Chapter 22 *Pricing, Costing, and Growth*

■ TOPIC SPOTLIGHT

Money: Ask students if they have ever witnessed price wars between or among competitors in a given industry. Explain that they are common among gasoline stations, for example, when a new station opens and is trying to attract customers.

Marketing: Explain that the largest retailers can pay much less for their merchandise than smaller stores because the larger stores buy much greater quantities. Discuss how smaller, locally owned stores could compete against larger, national chains.

Technology: Discuss how technology affects a business's ability to stay competitive.

additional resources

Business Math for the Numerically Challenged by Inc Staff Career Press (© 1997). This book helps the reader learn the math needed for everyday business.

The Small Business Administration (**www.sba.gov**) has several publications in their Emerging Business Series dedicated to growing a business. There is also a publication on pricing, ***Pricing Your Products and Services Profitably*** (FM-13), in the SBA's Financial Management Series.

Note to teacher: Web site addresses may change.

CHAPTER 22 Lesson Plans

SECTION 22.1

FOCUS

Motivation

Write the word "price" on the board. Ask the students if the price of an item is the most important consideration when they purchase the item. If not, ask them what other factors they might consider. Then ask the students to consider pricing from a business's point of view. Find out what the students think a business must consider when setting prices for its products.

Prereading

1. Have your students skim the section, looking at pictures, reading captions, and noting headings.
2. Have "What You'll Learn" listed on page 697 read aloud.
3. Write the Key Terms on the board. Ask the students to define them using their own words. Write their definitions on the board. Place an asterisk next to the terms the students are not sure about.
4. Ask the students to state the purpose of studying this chapter.

TEACH

Guided Practice

1. Have students read aloud the Standard & Poor's Q&A on page 696.
2. Read the section with your students.

Independent Practice

1. Imagine you make chocolate chip cookies in your home. You sell them to several local grocery stores that sell them to the general public. Create a list of the direct materials that you might use in the production of the cookies.
2. Divide the students into groups. Ask each group to select a local business. Have the groups brainstorm a list of changes in the market that could impact the pricing goals of that particular business.

Careers in Finance

Chief Financial Officer

1. Ask the students to research the life of a CFO and write a one-page paper about his or her career path that led to becoming a CFO.
2. Have your students discuss why it is important for the CFO of a company to understand federal and state laws as well as international trade.
3. Ask the students to debate which business skills they think are the most important for a CFO to have. Have the students justify their answers.

Common Cents

Wash'n Wear

1. Ask the students to take an inventory of their own clothes, based on how many must be dry-cleaned and how many are wash and wear.
2. Have your students evaluate the products on the market that allow "dry-clean only" clothing to be cleaned in a regular dryer. [EXAMPLE: Dryel by Proctor & Gamble]
3. Ask the students to research the fabrics that must be dry-cleaned and why.

INTERNATIONAL FINANCE
India

1. Have the students find out how much India's GDP increased after the introduction of IT to the economy.
2. India has a large population. Ask your students to discuss how such a large population might impact the economy of a country.

3. Ask students to research the role of the Indian government in bringing IT to the nation's poor, which comprises 29% of the population.

ASSESS

Reteaching

1. Review with the students the Key Terms that you placed an asterisk next to during the prereading section.
2. To further clarify the concept of markup, ask the students to define "markup" and "profit." Then have them explain the difference between the two terms.

Enrichment

1. Have the students research the price of a product that is new on the market. Ask them to also research the prices of competing products to see if they are higher, lower, or the same as the new product. Then ask them to guess what pricing goals the businesses might have established when setting their products' prices.
2. To reinforce the differences in pricing for a retail business versus a manufacturing business, have your students create two word problems: one for "product cost-plus pricing" and one for "product costing." Then divide the students into pairs, and have them exchange problems and solve them.

Assessment

1. Have the students complete the Section 22.1 Assessment.
2. Assign an activity from the *Student Activity Workbook*.

CLOSE

Have the students complete this statement: "Effective pricing and costing are…." [HINT: "essential for a business's financial success."]

SECTION 22.2

FOCUS

Motivation

Ask your students to define "business growth." Have them create a list of all the ways businesses can grow.

Prereading

1. Have the students skim the section, looking at pictures, reading captions, and noting headings.
2. Have "What You'll Learn" listed on page 710 read aloud.
3. Write the three Key Terms on the board. As a class, write a definition for each word.
4. Ask the students to state the purpose of studying this chapter.

TEACH

Guided Practice

1. Read the section with your students.
2. Assign an activity from the *Student Activity Workbook*.

Independent Practice

1. Have the students suggest ways Molly could grow her business, Cricket Lane Flowers. Use the forms of business growth described in this section as a springboard for the suggestions.
2. Ask your students to select a local business and evaluate the customer satisfaction of the business. This can be done through surveys and interviews. Have the students report their findings to the class.

$avvy Saver

Book Bargains
1. Ask the students to compile a list of Internet Web sites that are available for someone who wants to purchase a book online.
2. Have your students compare prices on a particular book found in a large bookstore, such as Barnes & Noble or Borders, an independent bookstore, or on an Internet site.
3. As a class, set up a book exchange. Ask your students to bring in books they no longer want, and allow other students to borrow them to read.

ASSESS

Reteaching
1. Review the Key Terms and the students' definitions for the terms. Clarify as necessary.
2. Reinforce the formulas in this section by having the students create a word problem for either "target sales" or "margin of safety." Allow the students to exchange problems and solve them.

Enrichment
1. Write this statement on the board: "For a business, bigger does not always mean better." Ask the students to react to this statement.
2. Invite a business manager or owner to your class. Ask him or her to discuss ways to grow a business successfully.

Assessment
1. Have the students complete the Section 22.2 Assessment.
2. Assign the Chapter Assessment.
3. Administer the test for Chapter 22 from the Reproducible Tests in the *Teacher Resource Binder*.

CLOSE
Ask the students to answer this question: "How will I know when my business is ready to grow?"

SECTION 22.1 ASSESSMENT
ANSWERS

CHECK YOUR UNDERSTANDING
1. To obtain a given share of the market, to generate sales that produce a specific profit, and to meet competitors' prices.
2. Variable costs are costs that vary in direct proportion to the activity level of production. If the business operation increases, the variable costs will increase. If the business operation decreases, the variable costs will decrease. Fixed costs are costs that remain constant even if the activity or production level changes. The total fixed cost remains the same regardless of the number of units produced.
3. Calculating the break-even point allows a business owner to determine the sales the business must achieve to break even, or cover all costs. It helps predict how changes in costs and sales will affect the profit earned by the business. The owner could also use the break-even analysis to determine how many units of a product must be made and sold to cover expenses.

THINK CRITICALLY
4. Answers will vary. Students may say that a business would lose money because there would be nothing left to pay fixed and variable expenses.

USING MATH SKILLS
5. Unit Sales Price × n = (Unit Variable Costs × n) + Fixed Costs
$\$75n = \$25n + \$1,000$
$\$75n - \$25n = \$1,000$
$\$50n = \$1,000$
$n = 1000 \div 50$
$n = 20$ mirrors

SOLVING MONEY PROBLEMS

6. $72 \times 65\% = $46.80 (markup)
   $72 + 46.80 = $118.80 (selling price)

SECTION 22.2 ASSESSMENT
ANSWERS

CHECK YOUR UNDERSTANDING

1. Increases in the number of customers, sales, share of the market, employees, lines of merchandise, and profit.
2. An important part of the planning process is setting goals. One common goal is to increase the amount of net income, or profit. The amount of net income that a business sets as a goal is called the target profit. If you want to expand to a new line of merchandise or open another outlet or store, you'll need to generate a certain amount of profit.
3. Using the equation, *Target Sales = Variable Costs + Fixed Costs + Target Profit*, you can calculate how many units a business must sell to reach its target profit. Represent the number of units needed to achieve the target profit by a variable such as n. On the left side of the equation, multiply unit sales price by n. On the right side of the equation, multiply the unit variable costs by n. Then add fixed costs and the required profit. Solve for n.
4. Subtract break-even sales from target sales.

THINK CRITICALLY

5. Answers will vary. However, students should show that they understand that growth must be analyzed, planned, and controlled. If a business grows too rapidly or in the wrong area, serious financial problems can result.

USING COMMUNICATION SKILLS

6. Answers will vary. Students might suggest that Lil carefully consider the new areas of merchandise or services that she plans to offer. She should make sure that a market for the new items exists.

SOLVING MONEY PROBLEMS

7. Unit Sales Price $\times n$ = (Unit Variable Costs $\times n$) + Fixed Costs + Target Profit
   $13n = $7.65n + $280 + $600
   $13n - $7.65n = $880
   $5.35n = $880
   $n = $880 \div $5.35
   $n = 164.48$, or 165 bracelets

CHAPTER 22 ASSESSMENT
ANSWERS

■ Understanding and Using Vocabulary
Answers will vary.

■ Review Key Concepts

1. In product cost-plus pricing, you add the invoice cost of the item (how much the business paid for the item) to a certain percentage of this cost (known as the markup). This method is commonly used in retail businesses. In product costing, you must consider all the costs involved in creating the item. This method is commonly used in manufacturing businesses.
2. Direct materials are the raw materials used to make a finished product. Direct labor is the work required to convert raw materials into a finished product, determined by multiplying the amount of time spent to produce an item by the employee's hourly wage.
3. Total sales minus total variable costs.
4. Target sales minus the break-even sales.
5. Make sound financial decisions when setting short-term and long-term goals; set realistic financial targets; control expenditures and costs; analyze financial statements frequently; analyze your competition; evaluate current economic conditions; maintain a reserve fund for unexpected expenses.

■ Apply Key Concepts

1. $25.20. [ANSWER: $18 × 40% = $7.20 and $18 + $7.20 = $25.20]
2. Answers will vary. Examples may include leather, buckles, rivets, and zippers.
3. $21,500. [ANSWER: $36,000 − $14,500 = $21,500]

4. $1,370. [ANSWER: $3,479 − $2,109 = $1,370] Yes, it would be a safe venture because the margin of safety is high. The risk that sales will fall below the break-even point is minimal.
5. Answers will vary.

Problem Solving Today
Explanations will vary. However, students should include the fact that all costs involved in creating the item must be considered in determining price. Variable costs, including direct labor and direct materials, and fixed costs, such as rent and utilities, must be covered. Students should also mention the contribution margin and break-even point and explain why they are important when setting prices. Letters will vary as well.

Real-World Application
The variable costs for one pair of jeans equal $22. [ANSWER: Direct Materials $8 + Direct Labor $11 + Supplies $3 = $22]
  $1,100 for 50 pairs. [ANSWER: 50 × $22 = $1,100]
  $2,200 for 100 pairs. [ANSWER: 100 × $22 = $2,200]
  $5,500 for 250 pairs. [ANSWER: 250 × $22 = $5,500]

Finance Online
Answers will vary. Possible Web sites include:
  www.worldpetstore.com
  www.all-the-best.com
  www.pets.com

Note to teacher: Web site addresses may change.

READING STRATEGIES
ANSWERS

Section 22.1
PREDICT (p. 700): Manufacturing businesses have to consider the cost of raw materials and the cost of labor needed to make products. Those costs may change according to shortages and other economic conditions.

RESPOND (p. 708): Wayne and Naomi might consider discontinuing production of the sunset bracelet, using cheaper materials to produce it, paying employees less, or reducing the time needed to assemble the bracelet.

Section 22.2
CONNECT (p. 710): Answers will vary.

QUESTION (p. 711): Consider whether or not there is enough customer demand for your products to justify adding more labor costs. You also would want to explore the possibilities for increasing productivity through other means, such as purchasing newer manufacturing equipment, upgrading computers, or restructuring operations.

STANDARD & POOR'S

CASE STUDY
ANSWERS

1. Jim will need to compare his competitor's prices, quality, variety, service, and facilities with Britt's Bagels.
2. Jim should evaluate whether he can reduce his operating costs without sacrificing quality or service. He may be able to raise his prices. Jim should also look for other popular products that offer a higher profit margin.
3. Jim may need to expand his bagel product line, offer better service, and increase his advertising. Jim can also look at how other businesses are changing and the types of customers that they attract.

UNIT 6 — Planning Guide

ORGANIZATION AND FINANCIAL PLANNING

Chapter 20—
Types of Business Ownership

Chapter 21—
Developing a Financial Plan

Chapter 22—
Pricing, Costing, and Growth

OVERVIEW

In Unit 5 students learned that good financial management is necessary to successfully start a new business. In Unit 6 students will learn how good financial management is necessary to keep a business operating. Chapter 20 explains three types of business ownership—sole proprietorships, partnerships, and corporations—and how choice of ownership affects a business financially. Chapter 21 describes in detail how to develop a financial plan, and gives step-by-step guidelines. Chapter 22 discusses financial decisions that relate to pricing and growth.

INTRODUCTION

Discuss with students the similarities between a person and a business being financially successful. Have students review the money management strategies from Chapter 3 and ask how these same strategies could be used by businesses. Point out how calculating a personal net cash flow is like calculating a business's net income. Show students that the equation for a personal balance sheet is the same one used for a business's balance sheet; it is just written differently. Both net worth and owner's equity measure the difference between what is owned (assets) and what is owed (liabilities). Finally, have students predict how planning for a business's financial success is like planning for personal financial success.

TM286

Get a Financial Life!

CASE STUDY 6

Teaching Guide

Step A — THE PROCESS

Make sure students have access to all necessary materials.

1. Have students explain how their recommended new product or line will increase Party Time's market share.
2. If possible, arrange for a field trip to a local mall or shopping center that has several businesses which students could research.
3. The selling price per bouquet is $21.78. [ANSWER: $5.25 + $6 + $0.85 = $12.10; $12.10 \times 80\% = $9.68; $12.10 + $9.68 = $21.78] The break-even point is 31 (30.99) bouquets. [ANSWER: $21.78n = $12.10n + $300; $9.68n = $300]
4. Answers will vary depending on the target profit students choose. To calculate the number of bouquets that must be sold to achieve the target profit, students must use the following formula:

$$\$21.78n = \$12.10n + \$300 + \text{target profit}$$

n = number of bouquets they must sell to reach the target profit. To calculate the margin of safety, students must use this formula:

$$\frac{\text{Target}}{\text{sales}} - \frac{\text{break-even}}{\text{sales}} = \frac{\text{margin}}{\text{of safety}}$$

5. If a business owner from your community is scheduled as a guest speaker, allow students time to ask him or her questions about running a successful business and expansion strategies.

Step B — CREATE YOUR PORTFOLIO

Evaluate students' portfolios based on whether or not all steps of the process are completed, the calculations are accurate, the information seems well researched, and the contents are in order.

Step C — THE INTERNET

Evaluate students' research and policy based on the following criteria:

1. The definition for ethics is accurate. Have students cite the dictionary they used to define the word "ethics."
2. Students should explain how they arrived at their policies.
3. Research should be thorough but need not be exhaustive.
4. If possible, cite examples of information accessed that was not accurate.

UNIT CLOSURE

Have students complete this sentence: "A financial plan is often considered the most important part of an overall business plan because…." [HINT: "businesses need adequate amounts of cash to survive and grow."]

EVALUATION

Administer the Unit 6 test from the **ExamView** Pro Testmaker CD-ROM.